ULTIMATE SPIDER-MAN

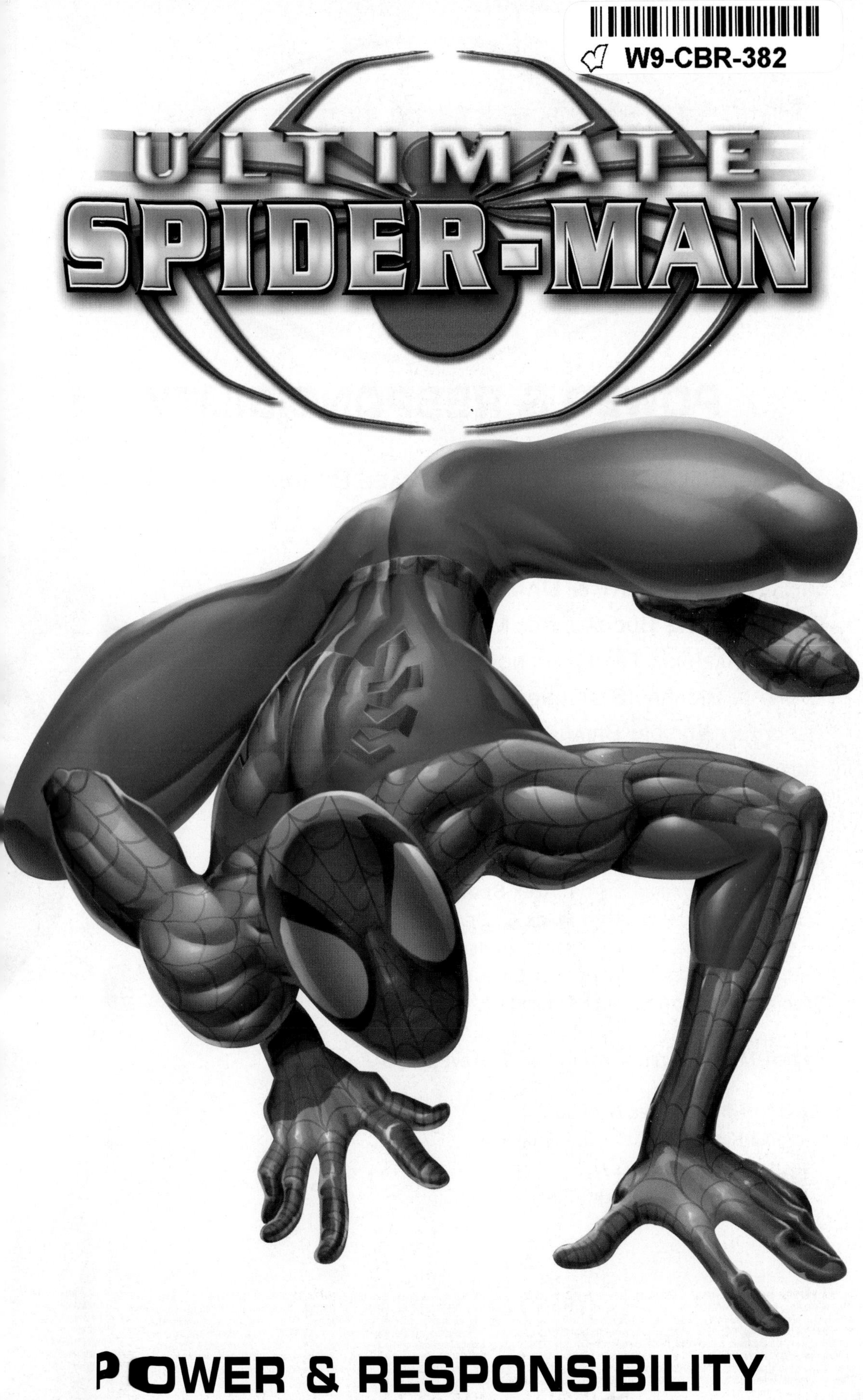

POWER & RESPONSIBILITY

ULTIMATE SPIDER-MAN

POWER & RESPONSIBILITY

STORY: BILL JEMAS & BRIAN MICHAEL BENDIS

WRITER: BRIAN MICHAEL BENDIS

PENCILS: MARK BAGLEY

INKS: ART THIBERT & DAN PANOSIAN

COLORS: STEVE BUCCELLATO, MARIE JAVINS,

COLORGRAPHIX & TRANSPARENCY DIGITAL

LETTERS: RICHARD STARKINGS & COMICRAFT

ASSISTANT EDITOR: BRIAN SMITH

EDITOR: RALPH MACCHIO

COLLECTION EDITOR: JENNIFER GRÜNWALD

ASSOCIATE EDITOR: SARAH BRUNSTAD

ASSOCIATE MANAGING EDITOR: ALEX STARBUCK

EDITOR, SPECIAL PROJECTS: MARK D. BEAZLEY

VP, PRODUTION & SPECIAL PROJECTS: JEFF YOUNGQUIST

SVP PRINT, SALES & MARKETING: DAVID GABRIEL

SPECIAL THANKS TO SPRING HOTELING & CARRIE BEADLE

SPIDER-MAN CREATED BY STAN LEE & STEVE DITKO

EDITOR IN CHIEF: AXEL ALONSO

CHIEF CREATIVE OFFICER: JOE QUESADA

PUBLISHER: DAN BUCKLEY

EXECUTIVE PRODUCER: ALAN FINE

ULTIMATE SPIDER-MAN VOL. 1: POWER & RESPONSIBILITY. Contains material originally published in magazine form as ULTIMATE SPIDER-MAN #1-7. Second edition. Fourth printing 2016. ISBN# 978-0-7851-3940-9. Published by MARVEL WORLDWIDE, INC., a subsidiary of MARVEL ENTERTAINMENT, LLC. OFFICE OF PUBLICATION: 135 West 50th Street, New York, NY 10020. Copyright © 2009 MARVEL No similarity between any of the names, characters, persons, and/or institutions in this magazine with those of any living or dead person or institution is intended, and any such similarity which may exist is purely coincidental. Printed in the U.S.A. ALAN FINE, President, Marvel Entertainment; DAN BUCKLEY, President, TV, Publishing & Brand Management; JOE QUESADA, Chief Creative Officer; TOM BREVOORT, SVP of Publishing; DAVID BOGART, SVP of Business Affairs & Operations, Publishing & Partnership; C.B. CEBULSKI, VP of Brand Management & Development, Asia; DAVID GABRIEL, SVP of Sales & Marketing, Publishing; JEFF YOUNGQUIST, VP of Production & Special Projects; DAN CARR, Executive Director of Publishing Technology; ALEX MORALES, Director of Publishing Operations; SUSAN CRESPI, Production Manager; STAN LEE, Chairman Emeritus. For information regarding advertising in Marvel Comics or on Marvel.com, please contact Vit DeBellis, Integrated Sales Manager, at vdebellis@marvel.com. For Marvel subscription inquiries, please call 888-511-5480. **Manufactured between 3/23/2016 and 4/25/2016 by R.R. DONNELLEY, INC., SALEM, VA, USA.**

10 9 8 7 6 5 4

CHAPTER 1: POWERLESS
CHAPTER 2: GROWING PAINS
CHAPTER 3: WANNABE
CHAPTER 4: WITH GREAT POWER
CHAPTER 5: LIFE LESSONS
CHAPTER 6: BIG TIME SUPER HERO
CHAPTER 7: REVELATIONS

1

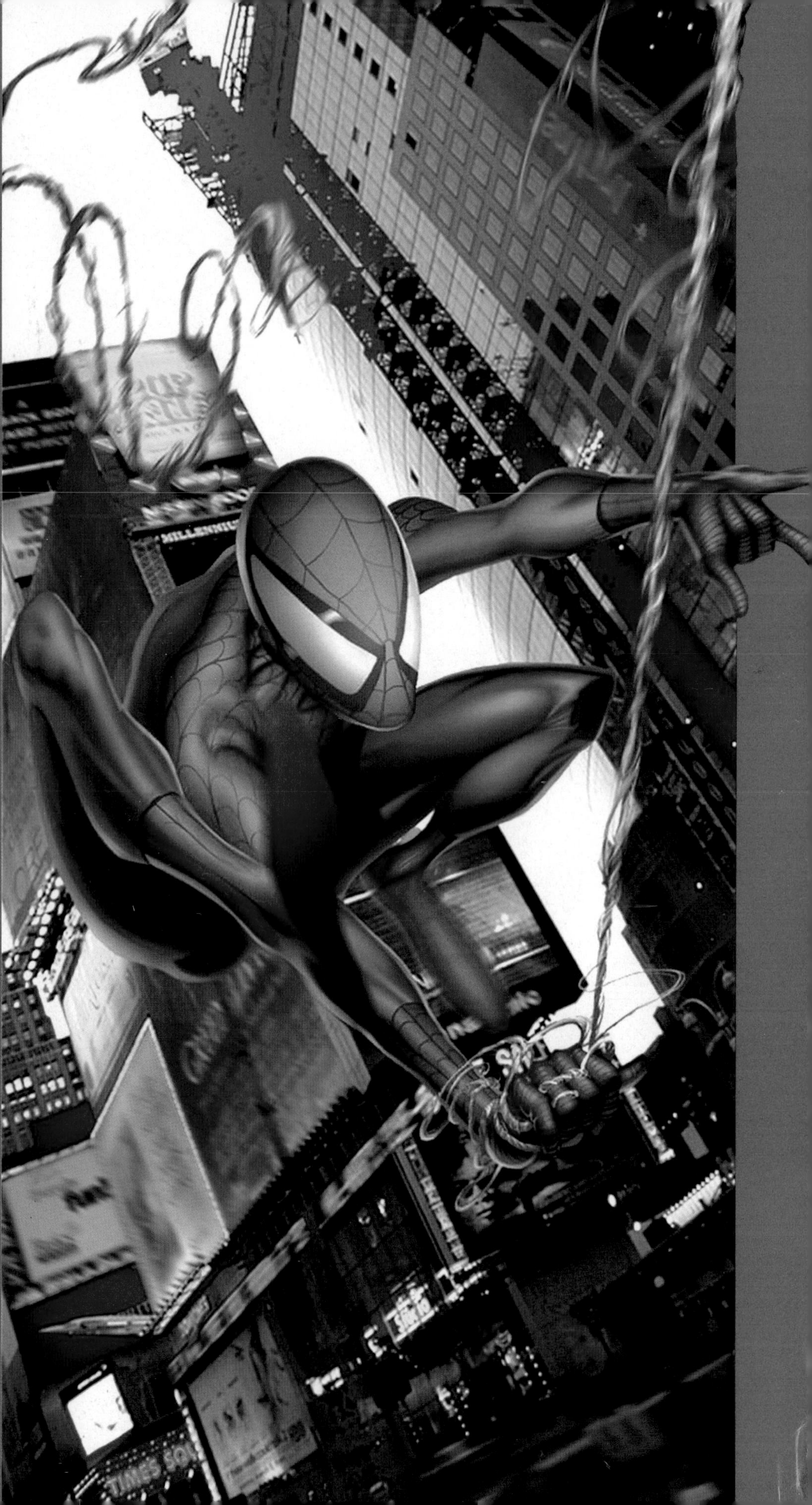

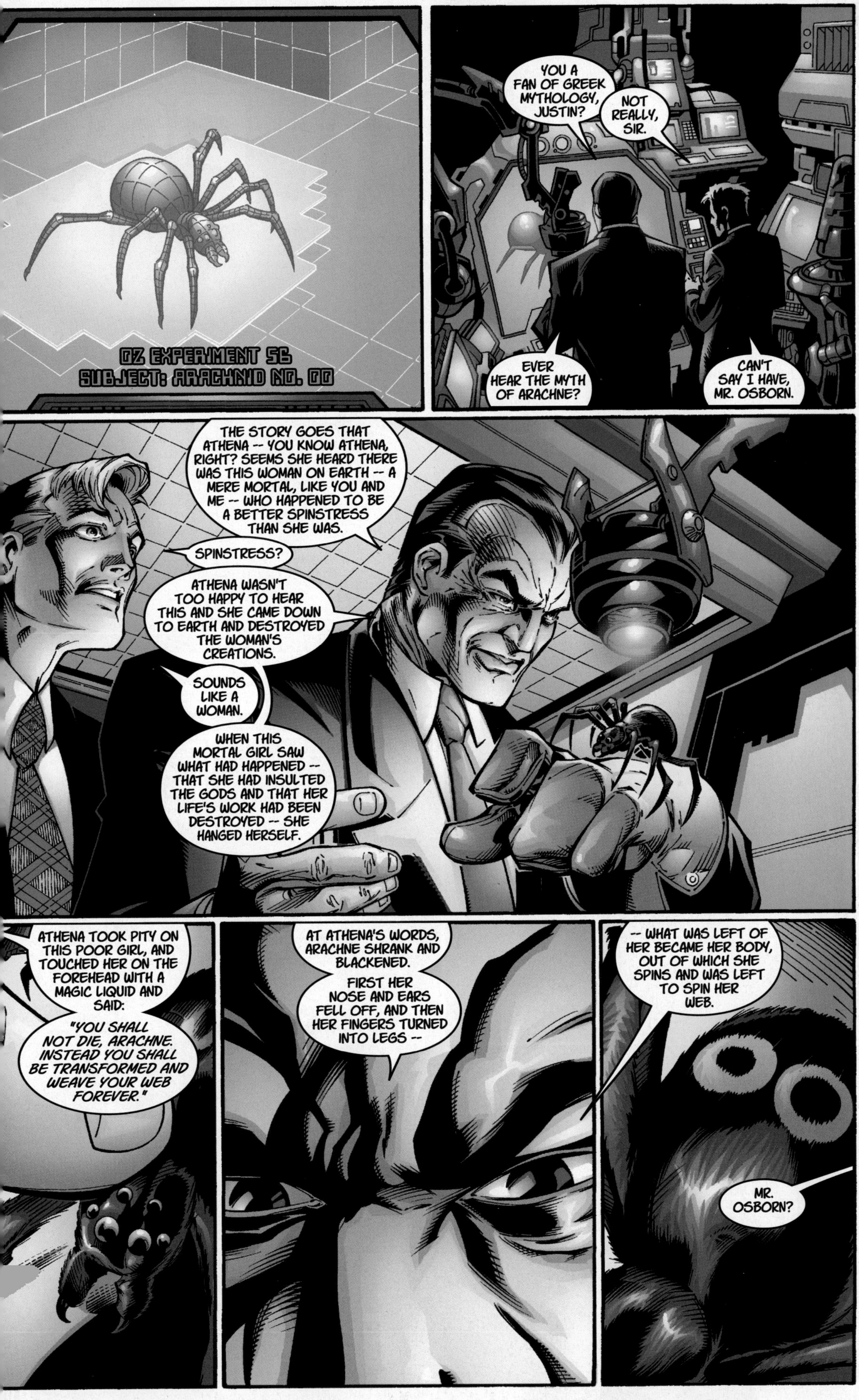
OZ EXPERIMENT 56
SUBJECT: ARACHNID NO. 00
YOU A FAN OF GREEK MYTHOLOGY, JUSTIN?
NOT REALLY, SIR.
EVER HEAR THE MYTH OF ARACHNE?
CAN'T SAY I HAVE, MR. OSBORN.
THE STORY GOES THAT ATHENA -- YOU KNOW ATHENA, RIGHT? SEEMS SHE HEARD THERE WAS THIS WOMAN ON EARTH -- A MERE MORTAL, LIKE YOU AND ME -- WHO HAPPENED TO BE A BETTER SPINSTRESS THAN SHE WAS.
SPINSTRESS?
ATHENA WASN'T TOO HAPPY TO HEAR THIS AND SHE CAME DOWN TO EARTH AND DESTROYED THE WOMAN'S CREATIONS.
SOUNDS LIKE A WOMAN.
WHEN THIS MORTAL GIRL SAW WHAT HAD HAPPENED -- THAT SHE HAD INSULTED THE GODS AND THAT HER LIFE'S WORK HAD BEEN DESTROYED -- SHE HANGED HERSELF.
ATHENA TOOK PITY ON THIS POOR GIRL, AND TOUCHED HER ON THE FOREHEAD WITH A MAGIC LIQUID AND SAID:
"YOU SHALL NOT DIE, ARACHNE. INSTEAD YOU SHALL BE TRANSFORMED AND WEAVE YOUR WEB FOREVER."
AT ATHENA'S WORDS, ARACHNE SHRANK AND BLACKENED.
FIRST HER NOSE AND EARS FELL OFF, AND THEN HER FINGERS TURNED INTO LEGS --
-- WHAT WAS LEFT OF HER BECAME HER BODY, OUT OF WHICH SHE SPINS AND WAS LEFT TO SPIN HER WEB.
MR. OSBORN?

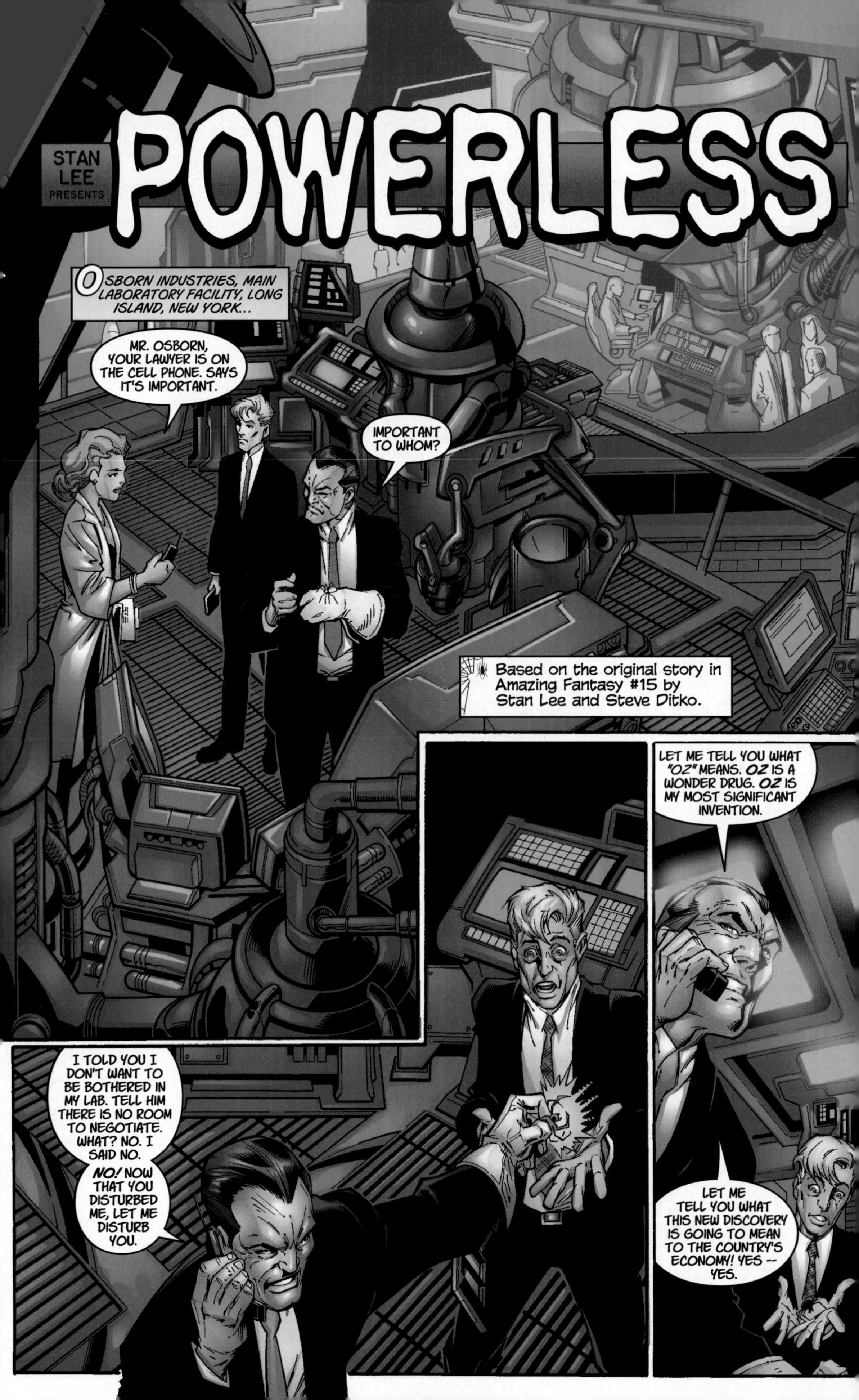
STAN LEE PRESENTS
POWERLESS
OSBORN INDUSTRIES, MAIN LABORATORY FACILITY, LONG ISLAND, NEW YORK...
MR. OSBORN, YOUR LAWYER IS ON THE CELL PHONE. SAYS IT'S IMPORTANT.
IMPORTANT TO WHOM?
Based on the original story in Amazing Fantasy #15 by Stan Lee and Steve Ditko.
LET ME TELL YOU WHAT "OZ" MEANS. OZ IS A WONDER DRUG. OZ IS MY MOST SIGNIFICANT INVENTION.
I TOLD YOU I DON'T WANT TO BE BOTHERED IN MY LAB. TELL HIM THERE IS NO ROOM TO NEGOTIATE. WHAT? NO. I SAID NO.
NO! NOW THAT YOU DISTURBED ME, LET ME DISTURB YOU.
LET ME TELL YOU WHAT THIS NEW DISCOVERY IS GOING TO MEAN TO THE COUNTRY'S ECONOMY! YES -- YES.

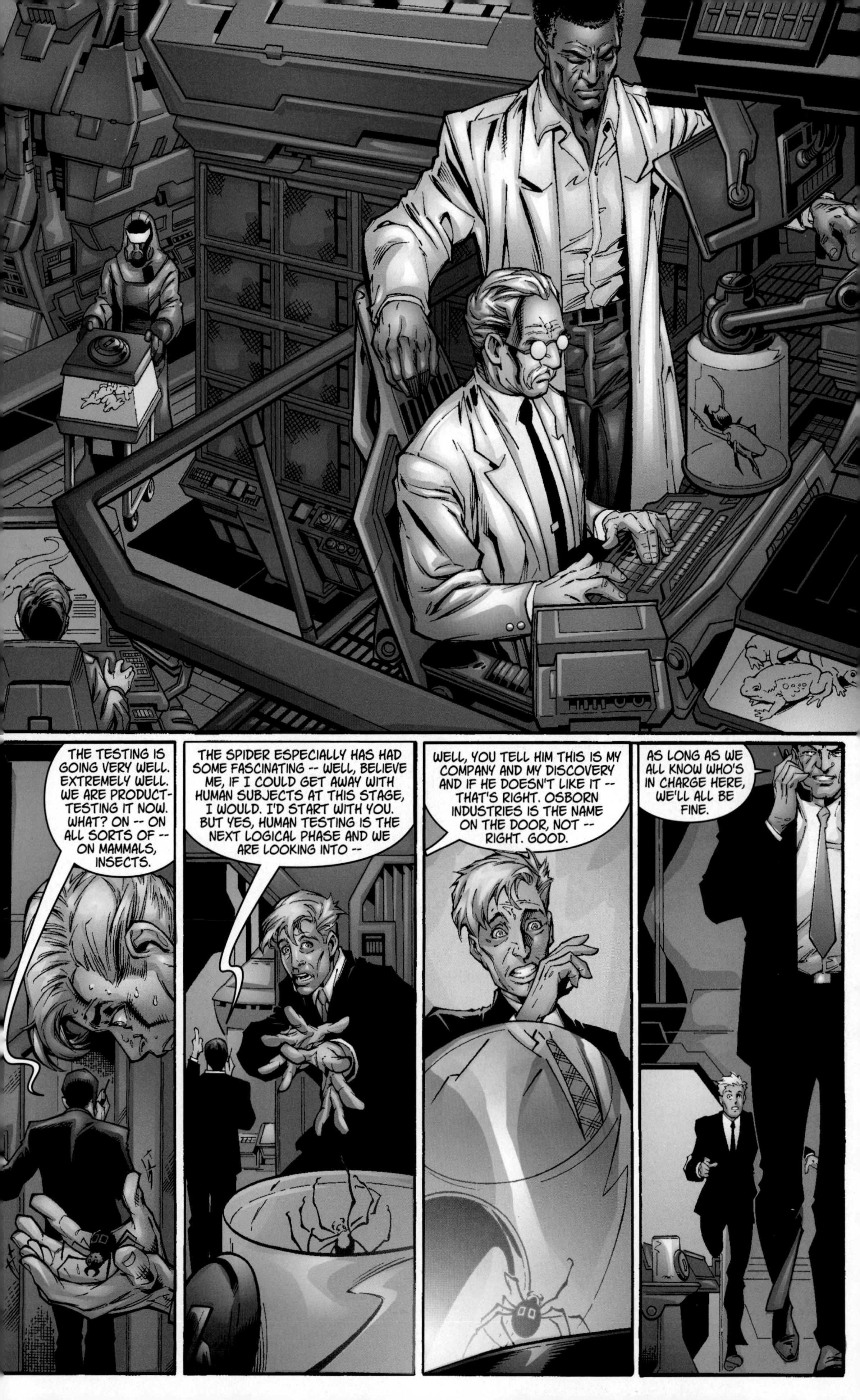
THE TESTING IS GOING VERY WELL. EXTREMELY WELL. WE ARE PRODUCT-TESTING IT NOW. WHAT? ON -- ON ALL SORTS OF -- ON MAMMALS, INSECTS.
THE SPIDER ESPECIALLY HAS HAD SOME FASCINATING -- WELL, BELIEVE ME, IF I COULD GET AWAY WITH HUMAN SUBJECTS AT THIS STAGE, I WOULD. I'D START WITH YOU. BUT YES, HUMAN TESTING IS THE NEXT LOGICAL PHASE AND WE ARE LOOKING INTO --
WELL, YOU TELL HIM THIS IS MY COMPANY AND MY DISCOVERY AND IF HE DOESN'T LIKE IT -- THAT'S RIGHT. OSBORN INDUSTRIES IS THE NAME ON THE DOOR, NOT -- RIGHT. GOOD.
AS LONG AS WE ALL KNOW WHO'S IN CHARGE HERE, WE'LL ALL BE FINE.

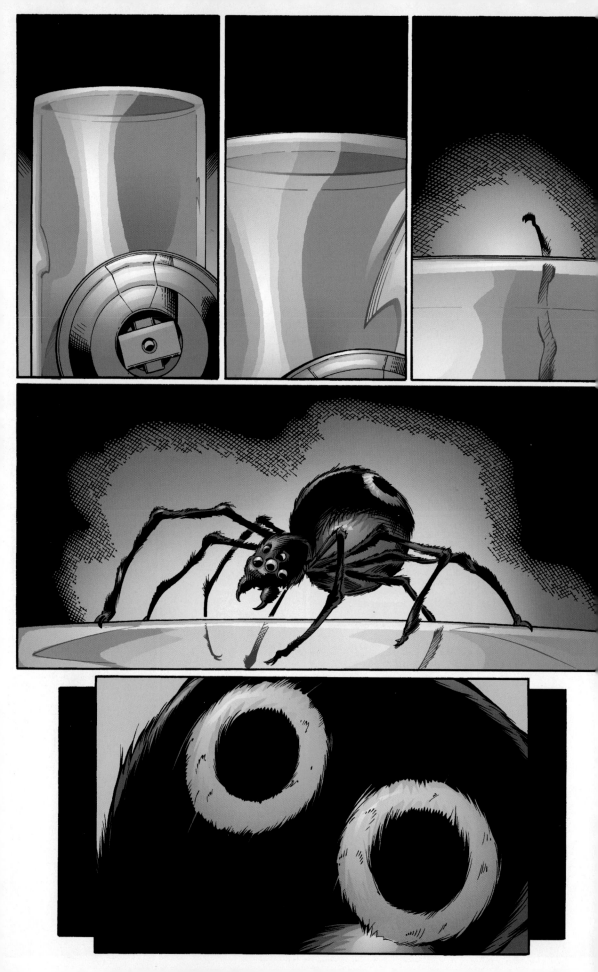

SODIUM CARBONIDE... THAT IS SUCH AN *ODD* CHOICE. I WONDER IF --

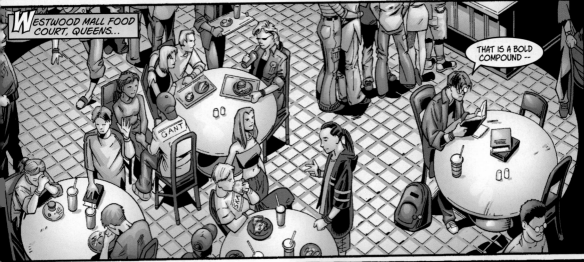

WESTWOOD MALL FOOD COURT, QUEENS...

GANT

THAT IS A BOLD COMPOUND --

AHH!

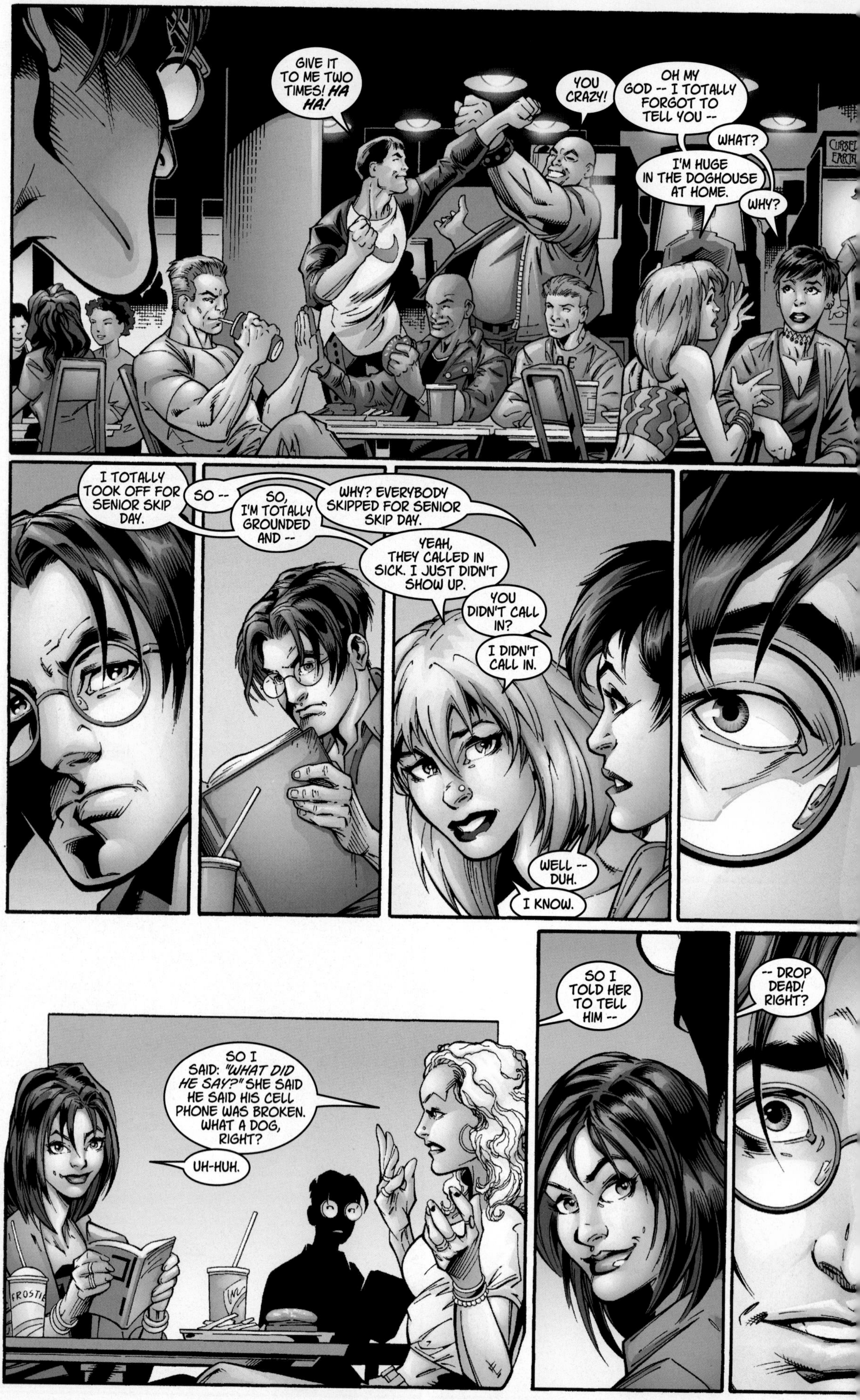
GIVE IT TO ME TWO TIMES! HA HA!
YOU CRAZY!
OH MY GOD -- I TOTALLY FORGOT TO TELL YOU --
WHAT?
I'M HUGE IN THE DOGHOUSE AT HOME.
WHY?
I TOTALLY TOOK OFF FOR SENIOR SKIP DAY.
SO --
SO, I'M TOTALLY GROUNDED AND --
WHY? EVERYBODY SKIPPED FOR SENIOR SKIP DAY.
YEAH, THEY CALLED IN SICK. I JUST DIDN'T SHOW UP.
YOU DIDN'T CALL IN?
I DIDN'T CALL IN.
WELL -- DUH.
I KNOW.
SO I SAID: "WHAT DID HE SAY?" SHE SAID HE SAID HIS CELL PHONE WAS BROKEN. WHAT A DOG, RIGHT?
UH-HUH.
SO I TOLD HER TO TELL HIM --
-- DROP DEAD! RIGHT?

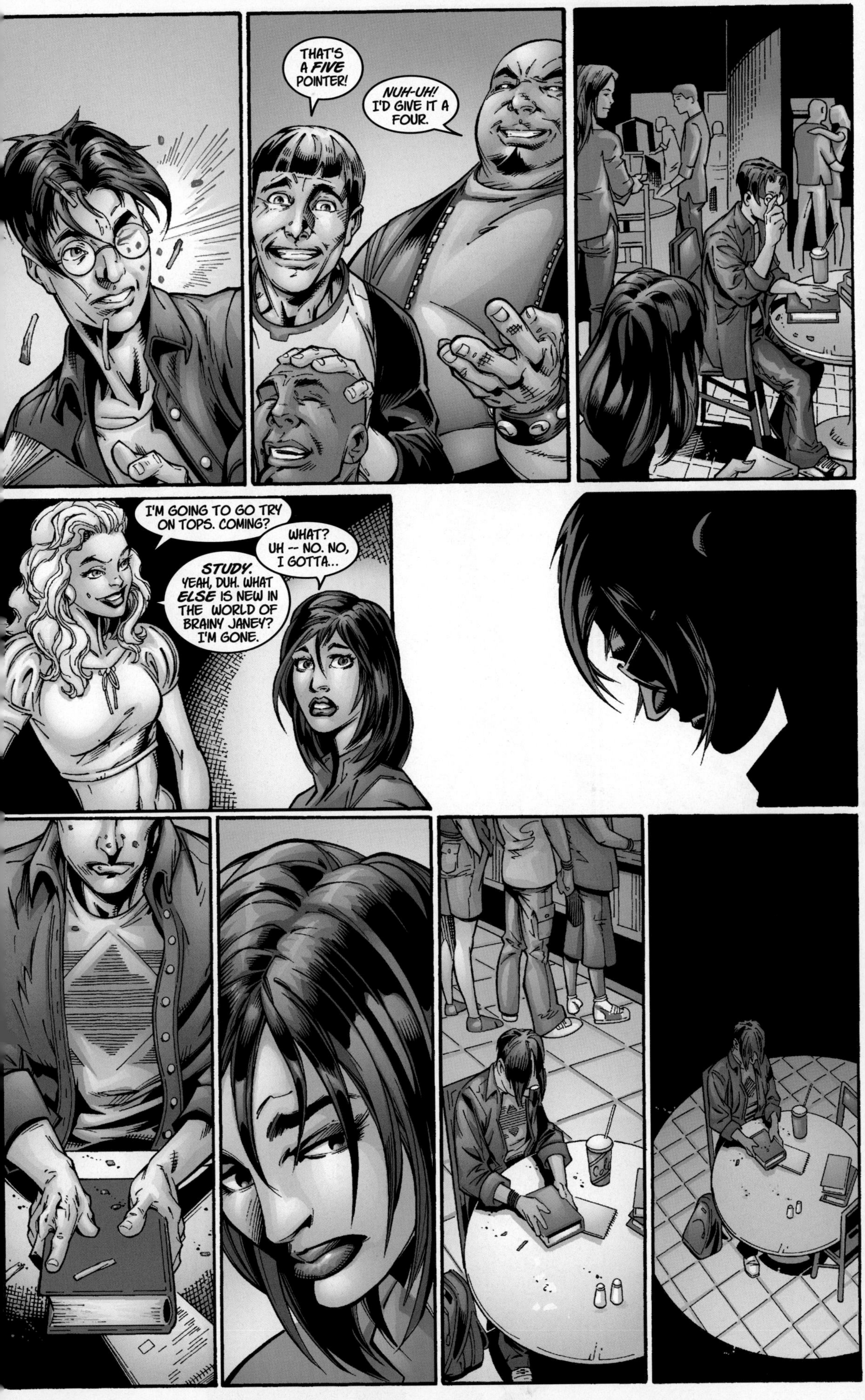
THAT'S A *FIVE* POINTER!
NUH-UH! I'D GIVE IT A FOUR.
I'M GOING TO GO TRY ON TOPS. COMING?
WHAT? UH -- NO. NO, I GOTTA...
STUDY. YEAH, DUH. WHAT *ELSE* IS NEW IN THE WORLD OF BRAINY JANEY? I'M GONE.

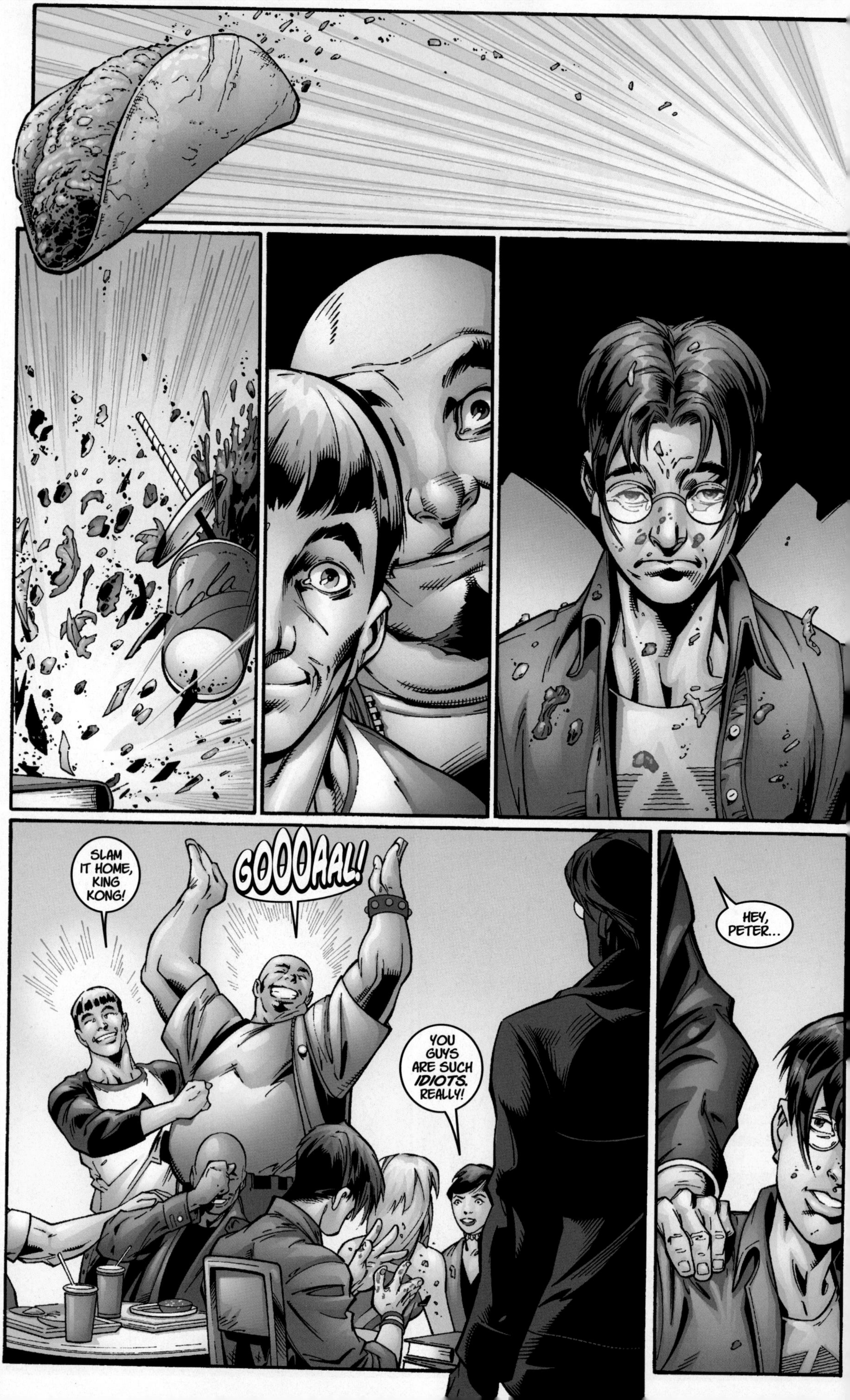
SLAM IT HOME, KING KONG!
GOOOAAL!
YOU GUYS ARE SUCH IDIOTS. REALLY!
HEY, PETER...

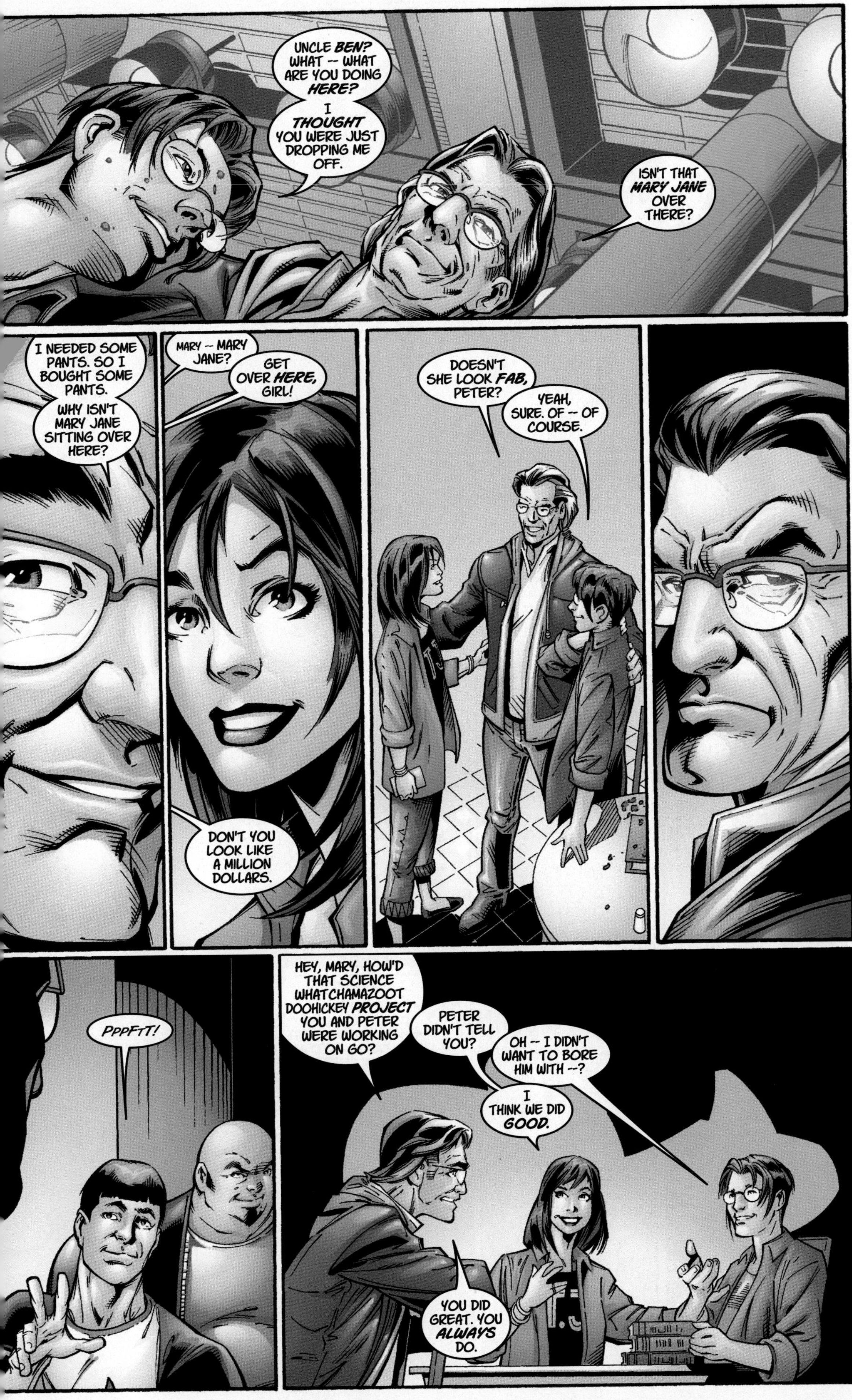
UNCLE BEN? WHAT -- WHAT ARE YOU DOING HERE?
I THOUGHT YOU WERE JUST DROPPING ME OFF.
ISN'T THAT MARY JANE OVER THERE?
I NEEDED SOME PANTS. SO I BOUGHT SOME PANTS.
WHY ISN'T MARY JANE SITTING OVER HERE?
MARY -- MARY JANE?
GET OVER HERE, GIRL!
DON'T YOU LOOK LIKE A MILLION DOLLARS.
DOESN'T SHE LOOK FAB, PETER?
YEAH, SURE. OF -- OF COURSE.
PPPFTT!
HEY, MARY, HOW'D THAT SCIENCE WHATCHAMAZOOT DOOHICKEY PROJECT YOU AND PETER WERE WORKING ON GO?
PETER DIDN'T TELL YOU?
OH -- I DIDN'T WANT TO BORE HIM WITH --?
I THINK WE DID GOOD.
YOU DID GREAT. YOU ALWAYS DO.

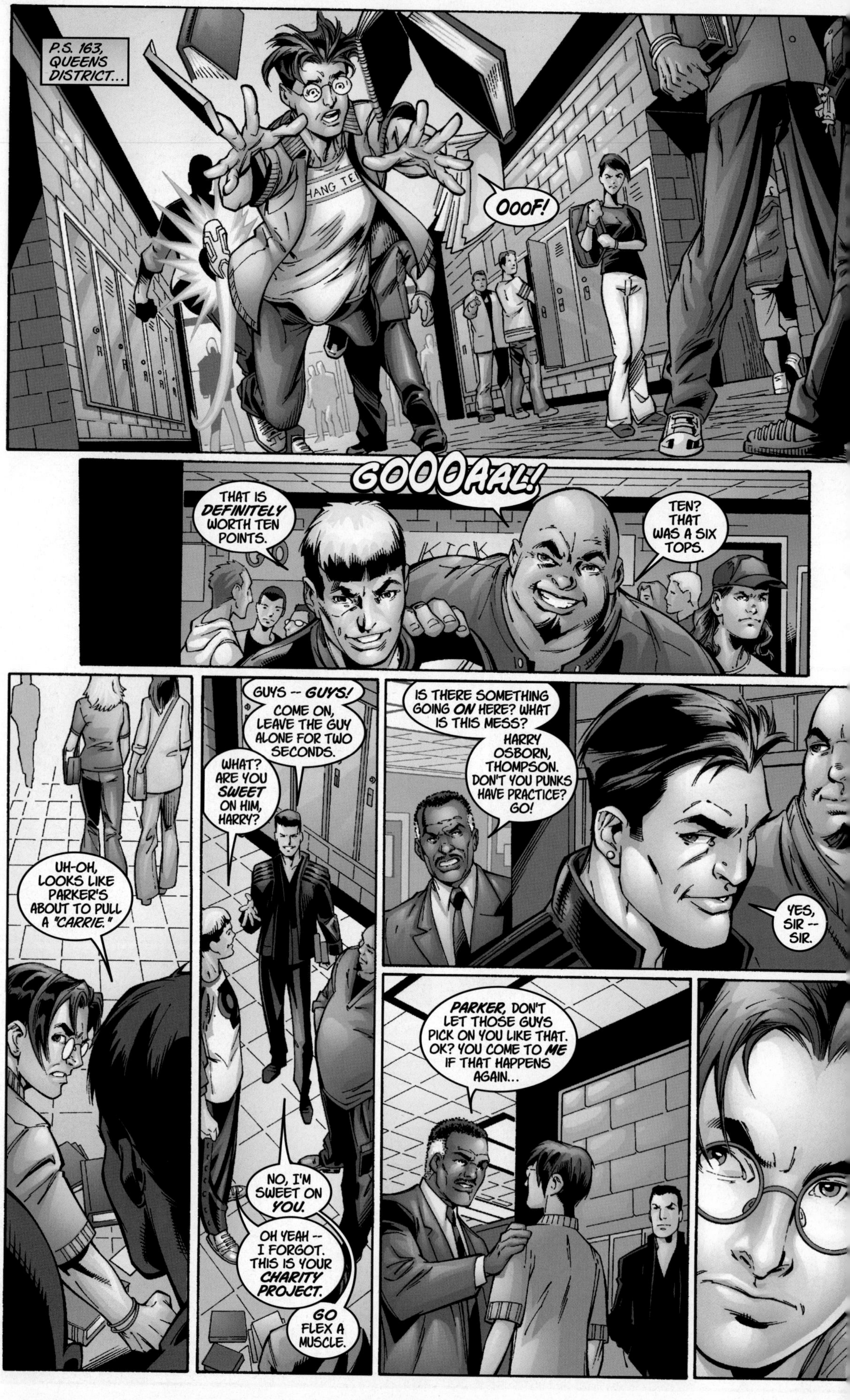
P.S. 163, QUEENS DISTRICT...
OOOF!
GOOOAAL!
THAT IS DEFINITELY WORTH TEN POINTS.
TEN? THAT WAS A SIX TOPS.
UH-OH, LOOKS LIKE PARKER'S ABOUT TO PULL A "CARRIE."
GUYS -- GUYS! COME ON, LEAVE THE GUY ALONE FOR TWO SECONDS.
WHAT? ARE YOU SWEET ON HIM, HARRY?
NO, I'M SWEET ON YOU.
OH YEAH -- I FORGOT. THIS IS YOUR CHARITY PROJECT.
GO FLEX A MUSCLE.
IS THERE SOMETHING GOING ON HERE? WHAT IS THIS MESS?
HARRY OSBORN, THOMPSON. DON'T YOU PUNKS HAVE PRACTICE? GO!
YES, SIR -- SIR.
PARKER, DON'T LET THOSE GUYS PICK ON YOU LIKE THAT. OK? YOU COME TO ME IF THAT HAPPENS AGAIN...

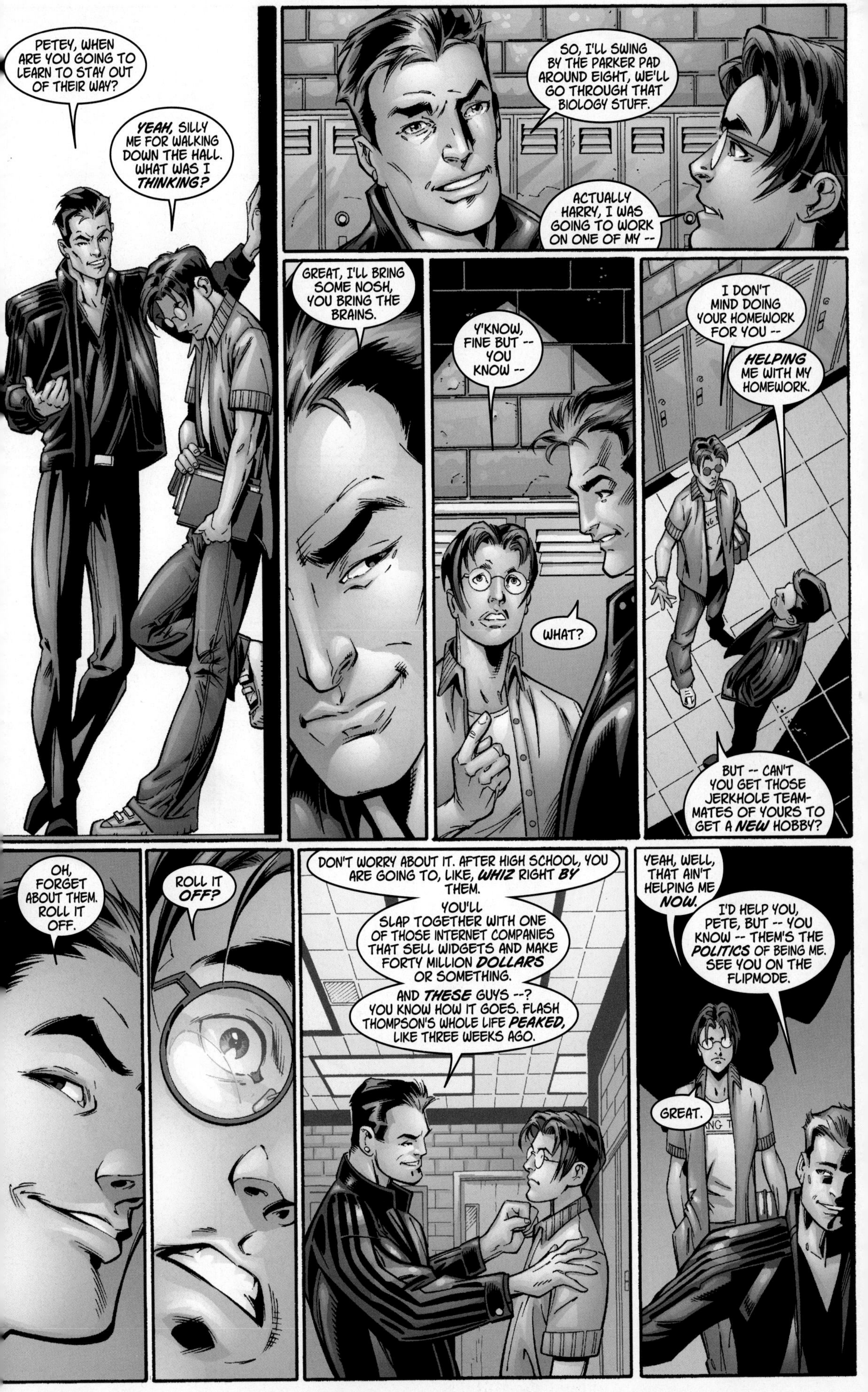
PETEY, WHEN ARE YOU GOING TO LEARN TO STAY OUT OF THEIR WAY?
YEAH, SILLY ME FOR WALKING DOWN THE HALL. WHAT WAS I THINKING?
SO, I'LL SWING BY THE PARKER PAD AROUND EIGHT, WE'LL GO THROUGH THAT BIOLOGY STUFF.
ACTUALLY HARRY, I WAS GOING TO WORK ON ONE OF MY --
GREAT, I'LL BRING SOME NOSH, YOU BRING THE BRAINS.
Y'KNOW, FINE BUT -- YOU KNOW --
WHAT?
I DON'T MIND DOING YOUR HOMEWORK FOR YOU --
HELPING ME WITH MY HOMEWORK.
BUT -- CAN'T YOU GET THOSE JERKHOLE TEAM-MATES OF YOURS TO GET A NEW HOBBY?
OH, FORGET ABOUT THEM. ROLL IT OFF.
ROLL IT OFF?
DON'T WORRY ABOUT IT. AFTER HIGH SCHOOL, YOU ARE GOING TO, LIKE, WHIZ RIGHT BY THEM.
YOU'LL SLAP TOGETHER WITH ONE OF THOSE INTERNET COMPANIES THAT SELL WIDGETS AND MAKE FORTY MILLION DOLLARS OR SOMETHING.
AND THESE GUYS --? YOU KNOW HOW IT GOES. FLASH THOMPSON'S WHOLE LIFE PEAKED, LIKE THREE WEEKS AGO.
YEAH, WELL, THAT AIN'T HELPING ME NOW.
I'D HELP YOU, PETE, BUT -- YOU KNOW -- THEM'S THE POLITICS OF BEING ME. SEE YOU ON THE FLIPMODE.
GREAT.

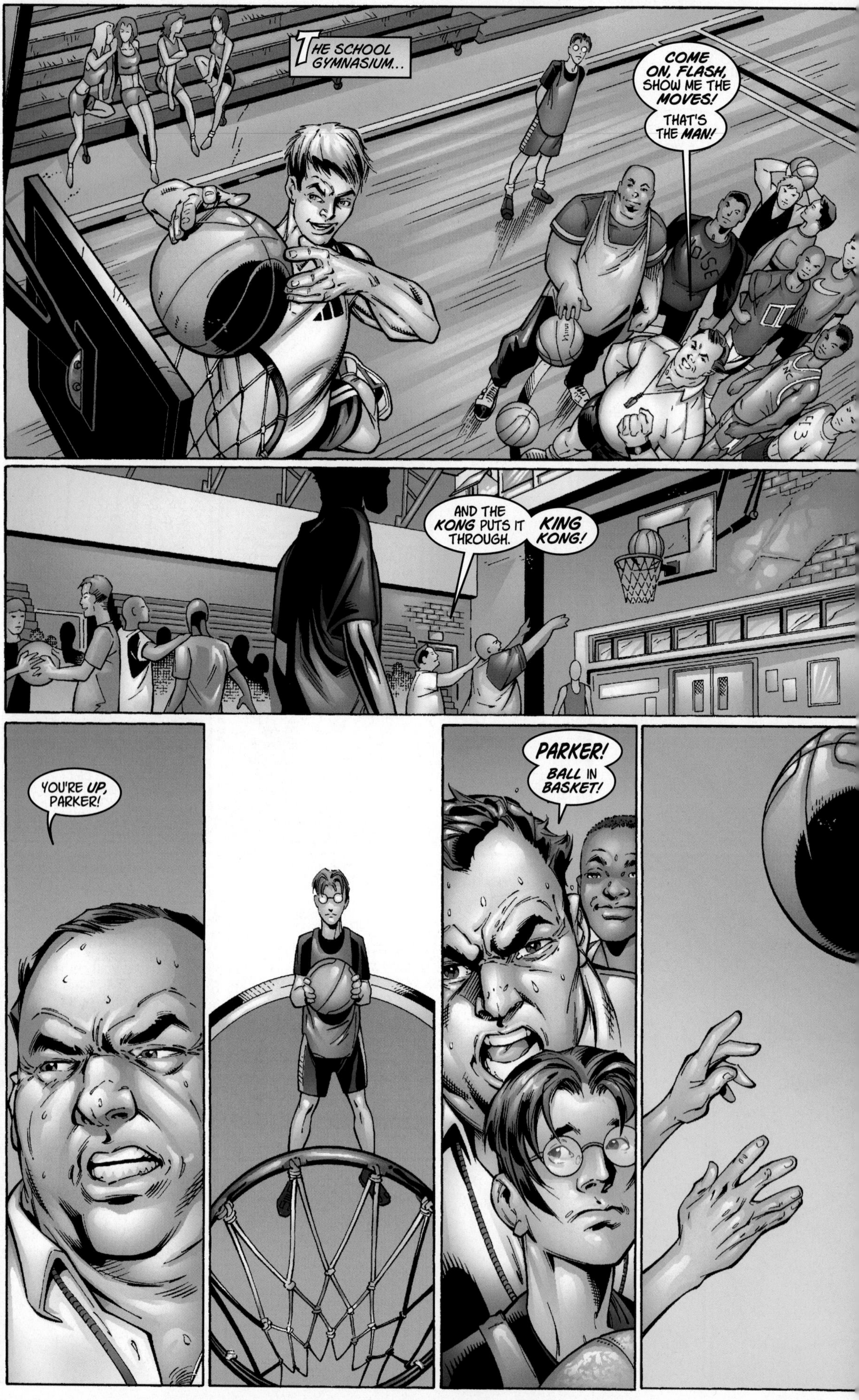
THE SCHOOL GYMNASIUM...
COME ON, FLASH, SHOW ME THE MOVES!
THAT'S THE MAN!
AND THE KONG PUTS IT THROUGH.
KING KONG!
YOU'RE UP, PARKER!
PARKER! BALL IN BASKET!

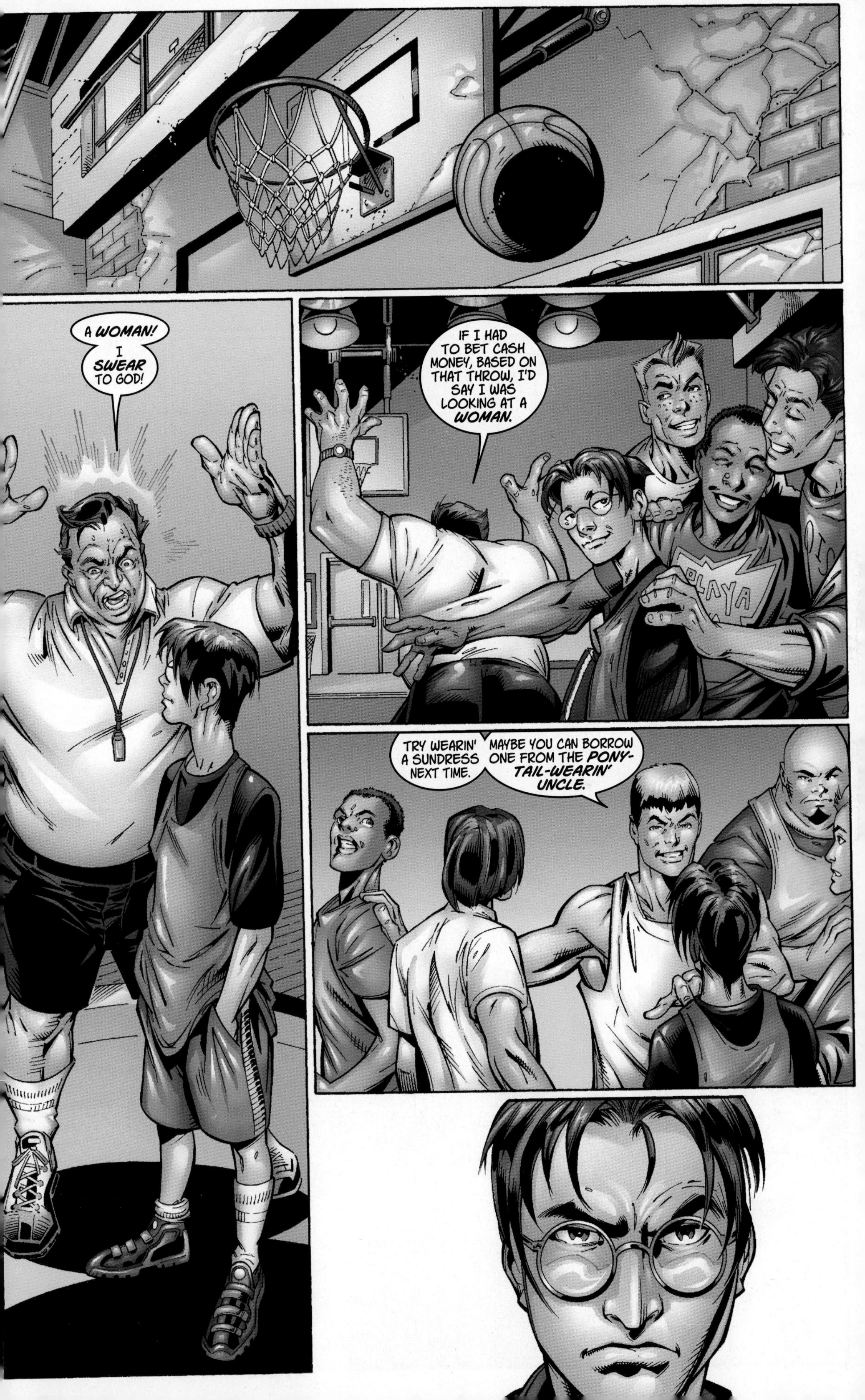
A WOMAN! I SWEAR TO GOD!
IF I HAD TO BET CASH MONEY, BASED ON THAT THROW, I'D SAY I WAS LOOKING AT A WOMAN.
PLAYA
TRY WEARIN' A SUNDRESS NEXT TIME.
MAYBE YOU CAN BORROW ONE FROM THE PONY-TAIL-WEARIN' UNCLE.

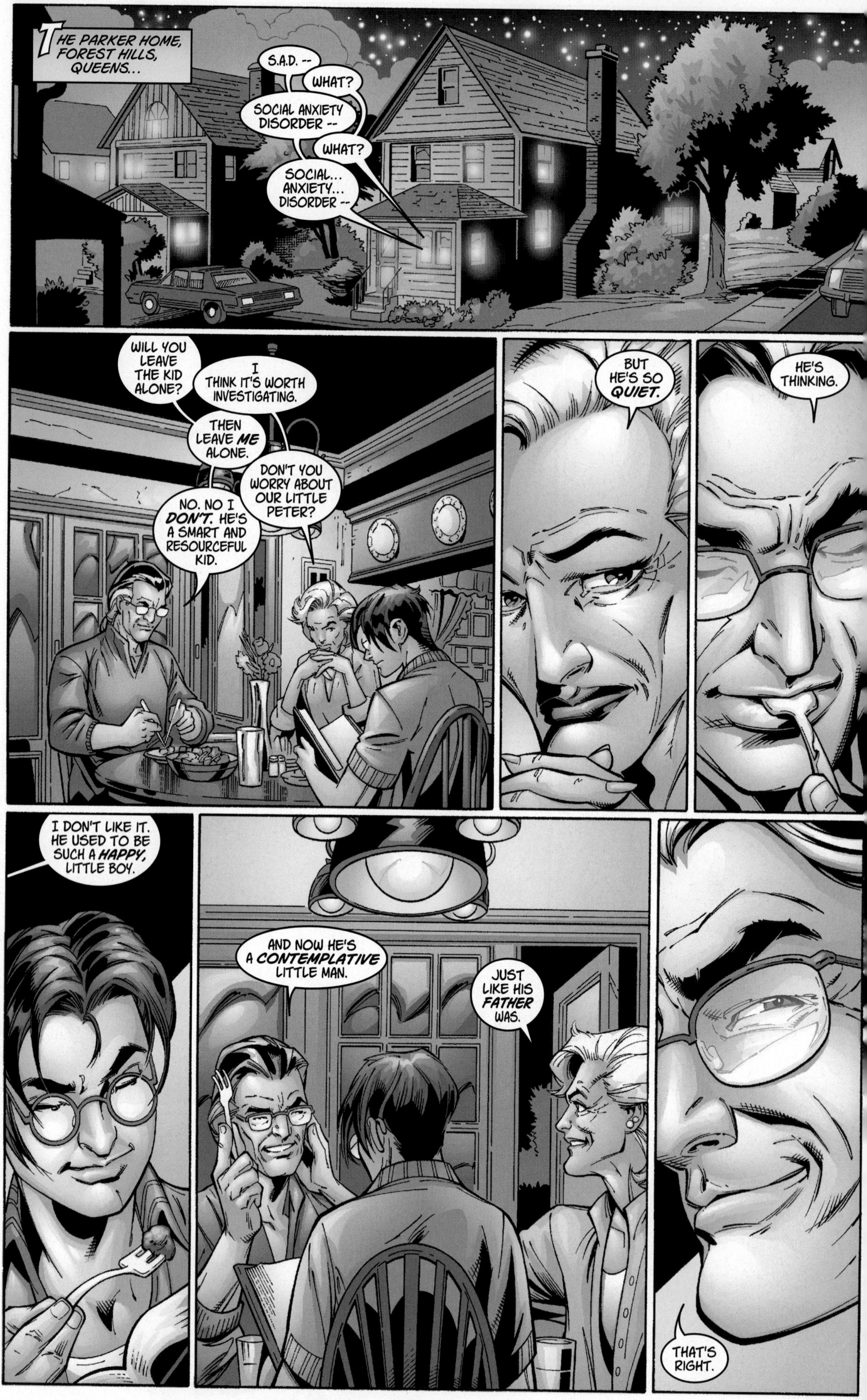
THE PARKER HOME, FOREST HILLS, QUEENS...
S.A.D. --
WHAT?
SOCIAL ANXIETY DISORDER --
WHAT?
SOCIAL... ANXIETY... DISORDER --
WILL YOU LEAVE THE KID ALONE?
I THINK IT'S WORTH INVESTIGATING.
THEN LEAVE *ME* ALONE.
DON'T YOU WORRY ABOUT OUR LITTLE PETER?
NO. NO I *DON'T.* HE'S A SMART AND RESOURCEFUL KID.
BUT HE'S SO *QUIET.*
HE'S THINKING.
I DON'T LIKE IT. HE USED TO BE SUCH A *HAPPY,* LITTLE BOY.
AND NOW HE'S A *CONTEMPLATIVE* LITTLE MAN.
JUST LIKE HIS *FATHER* WAS.
THAT'S RIGHT.

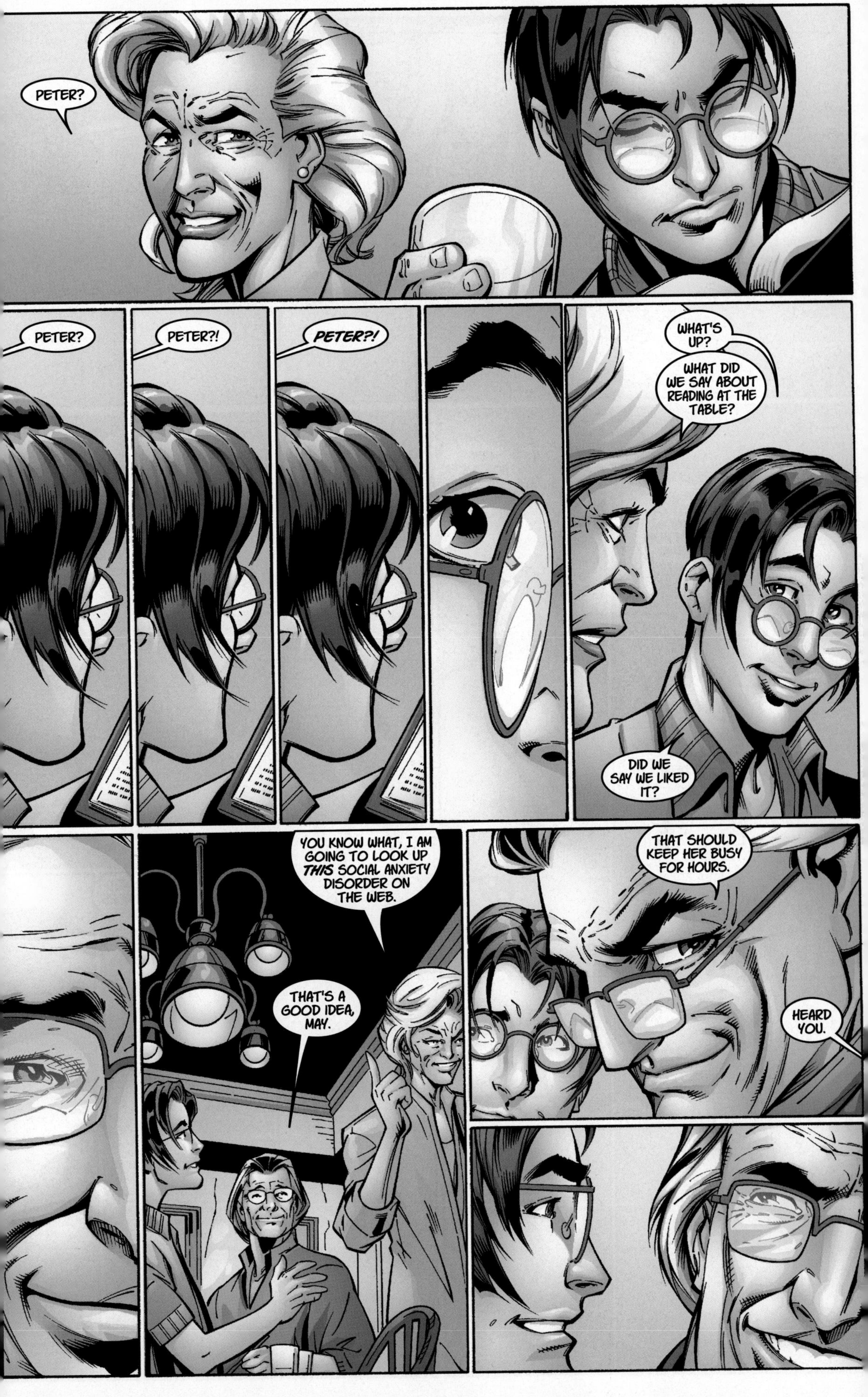
PETER?
PETER?
PETER?!
PETER?!
WHAT'S UP?
WHAT DID WE SAY ABOUT READING AT THE TABLE?
DID WE SAY WE LIKED IT?
YOU KNOW WHAT, I AM GOING TO LOOK UP THIS SOCIAL ANXIETY DISORDER ON THE WEB.
THAT'S A GOOD IDEA, MAY.
THAT SHOULD KEEP HER BUSY FOR HOURS.
HEARD YOU.

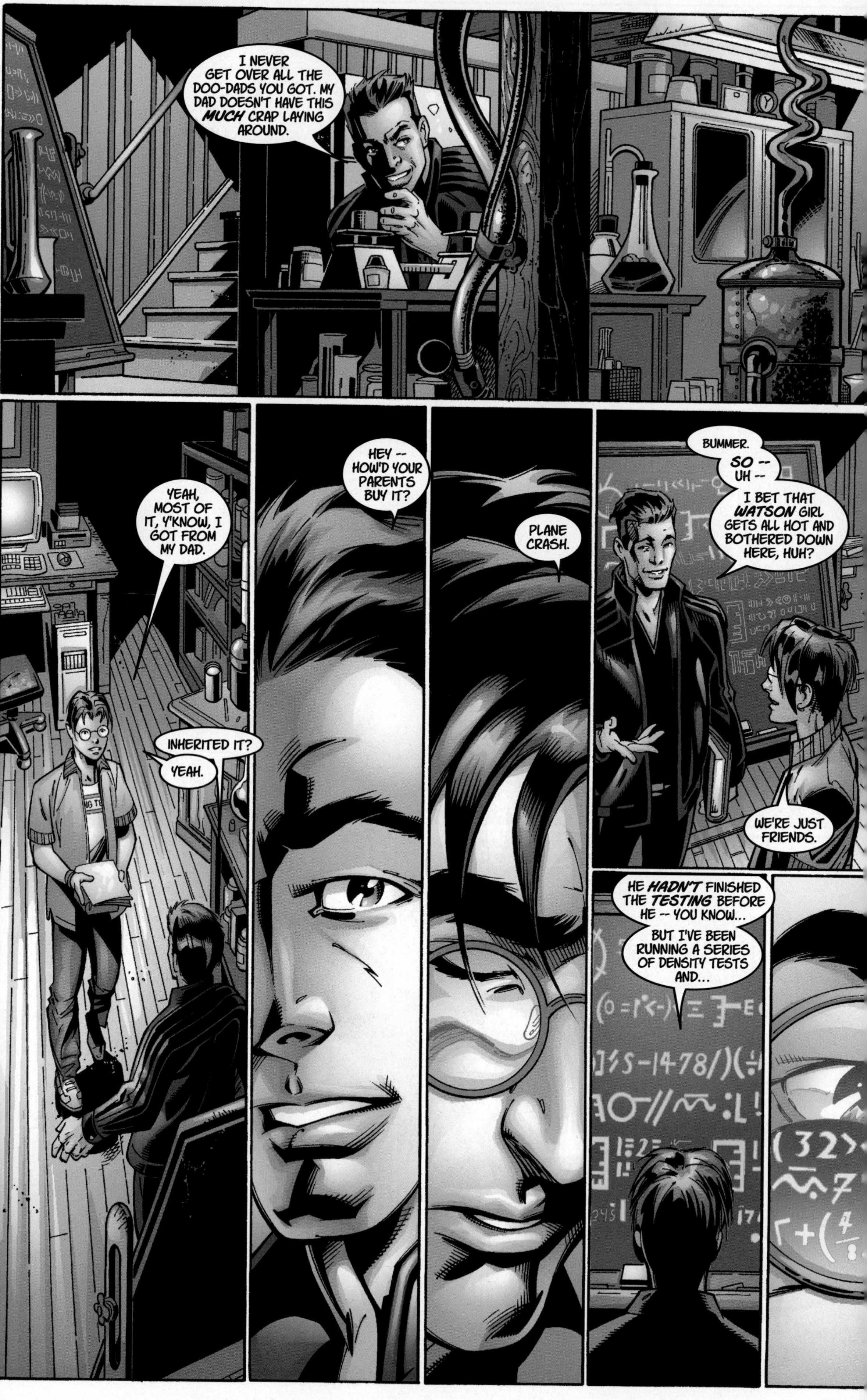
I NEVER GET OVER ALL THE DOO-DADS YOU GOT. MY DAD DOESN'T HAVE THIS MUCH CRAP LAYING AROUND.
YEAH, MOST OF IT, Y'KNOW, I GOT FROM MY DAD.
INHERITED IT?
YEAH.
HEY -- HOW'D YOUR PARENTS BUY IT?
PLANE CRASH.
BUMMER.
SO -- UH --
I BET THAT WATSON GIRL GETS ALL HOT AND BOTHERED DOWN HERE, HUH?
WE'RE JUST FRIENDS.
HE HADN'T FINISHED THE TESTING BEFORE HE -- YOU KNOW...
BUT I'VE BEEN RUNNING A SERIES OF DENSITY TESTS AND...

UH-*HUH*.

OH, NO. DON'T *DO* THAT.

SORRY. DELICATE.

WHAT *IS* ALL THIS ANYHOW?

YOU'RE NOT GOING TO BLOW UP THE SCHOOL, ARE YOU?

NO. STOP IT.

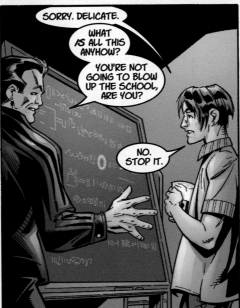

THIS IS -- IT'S REALLY -- SEE, MY *FATHER* WAS WORKING ON A COUPLE OF PATENTS --

-- THIS ONE WAS FOR THIS INTERESTING MOLECULAR ADHESIVE.

I *CAN'T* -- I HAVEN'T WRAPPED MY HEAD AROUND SOME OF THE MORE COMPLEX COMPONENTS.

...AND...

YEAH -- SO, LISTEN.

I'M GOING TO BAIL OUT OF HERE.

SO --

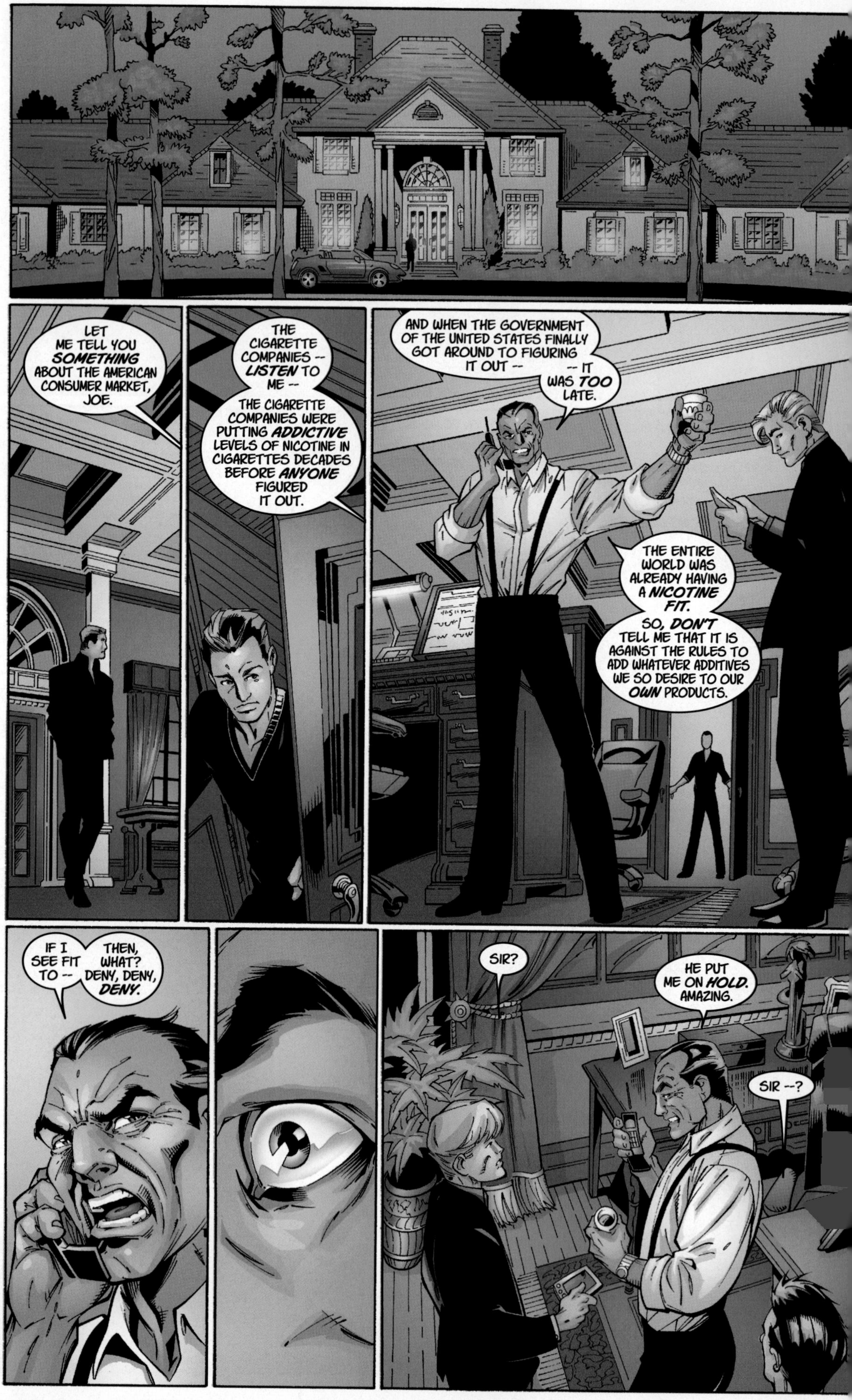
LET ME TELL YOU SOMETHING ABOUT THE AMERICAN CONSUMER MARKET, JOE.
THE CIGARETTE COMPANIES -- LISTEN TO ME --
THE CIGARETTE COMPANIES WERE PUTTING ADDICTIVE LEVELS OF NICOTINE IN CIGARETTES DECADES BEFORE ANYONE FIGURED IT OUT.
AND WHEN THE GOVERNMENT OF THE UNITED STATES FINALLY GOT AROUND TO FIGURING IT OUT --
-- IT WAS TOO LATE.
THE ENTIRE WORLD WAS ALREADY HAVING A NICOTINE FIT.
SO, DON'T TELL ME THAT IT IS AGAINST THE RULES TO ADD WHATEVER ADDITIVES WE SO DESIRE TO OUR OWN PRODUCTS.
IF I SEE FIT TO --
THEN, WHAT? DENY, DENY, DENY.
SIR?
HE PUT ME ON HOLD. AMAZING.
SIR --?

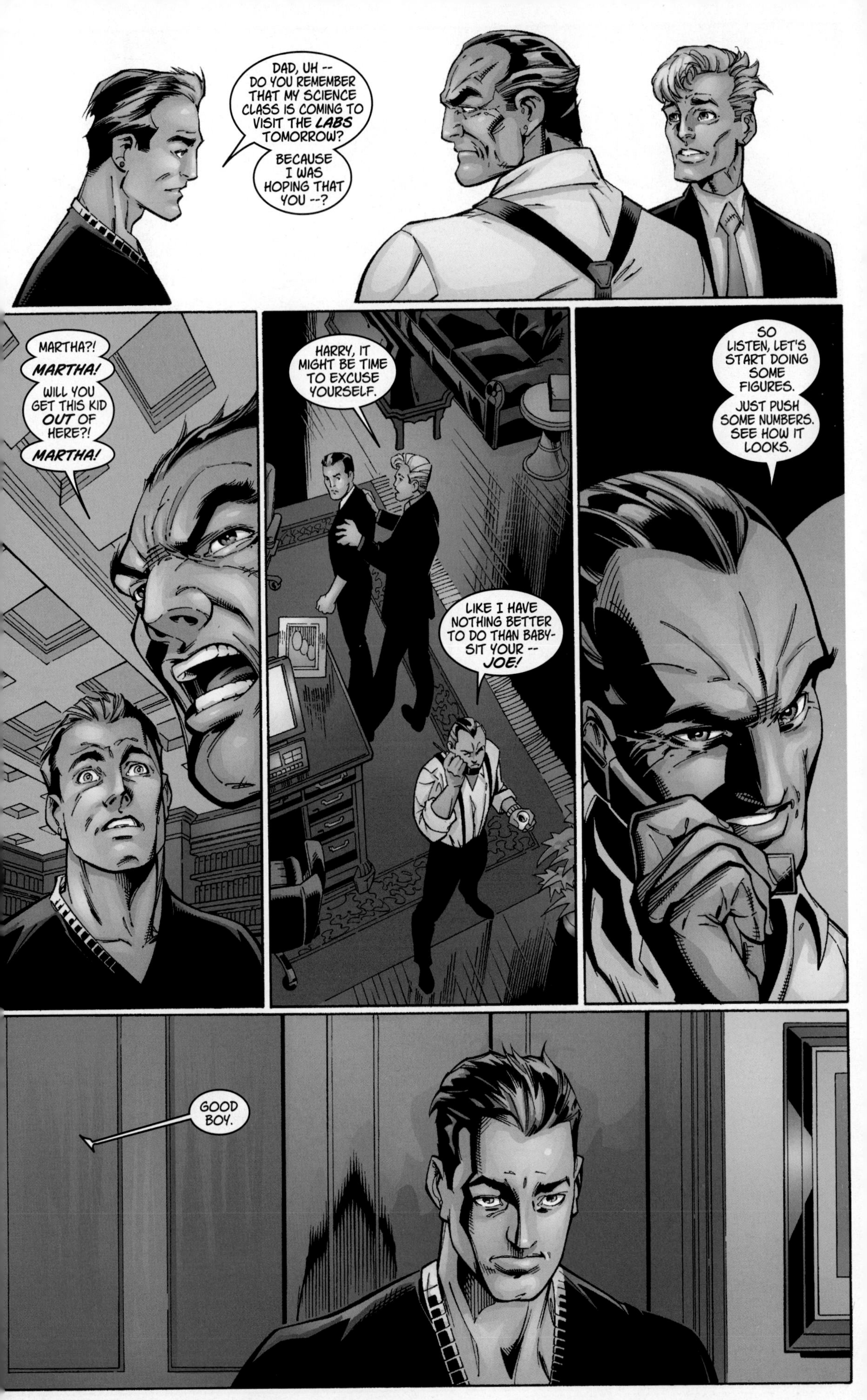

DAD, UH -- DO YOU REMEMBER THAT MY SCIENCE CLASS IS COMING TO VISIT THE *LABS* TOMORROW?
BECAUSE I WAS HOPING THAT YOU --?
MARTHA?!
MARTHA!
WILL YOU GET THIS KID ***OUT*** OF HERE?!
MARTHA!
HARRY, IT MIGHT BE TIME TO EXCUSE YOURSELF.
LIKE I HAVE NOTHING BETTER TO DO THAN BABY-SIT YOUR -- ***JOE!***
SO LISTEN, LET'S START DOING SOME FIGURES.
JUST PUSH SOME NUMBERS. SEE HOW IT LOOKS.
GOOD BOY.

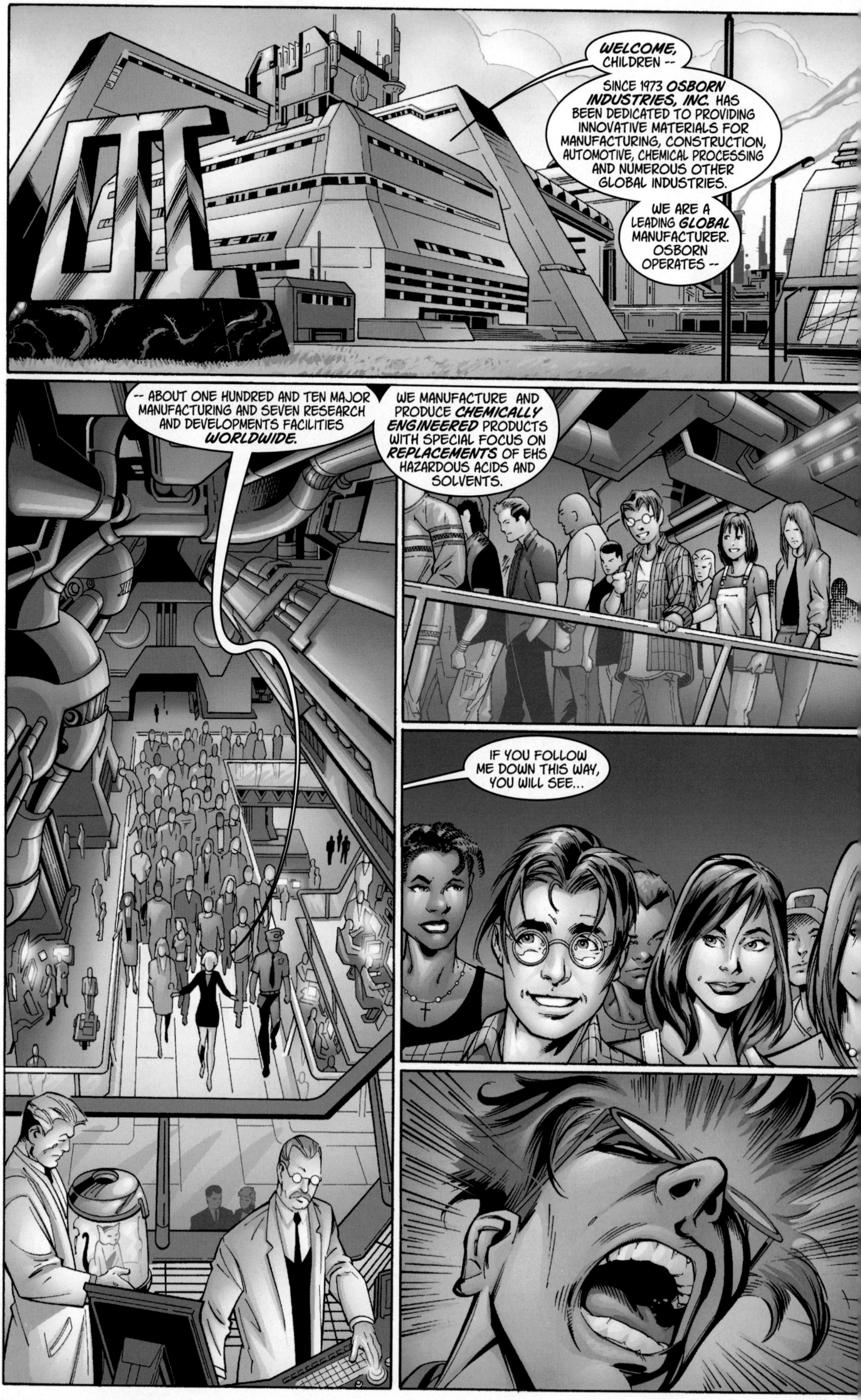
WELCOME, CHILDREN --
SINCE 1973 OSBORN INDUSTRIES, INC. HAS BEEN DEDICATED TO PROVIDING INNOVATIVE MATERIALS FOR MANUFACTURING, CONSTRUCTION, AUTOMOTIVE, CHEMICAL PROCESSING AND NUMEROUS OTHER GLOBAL INDUSTRIES.
WE ARE A LEADING GLOBAL MANUFACTURER. OSBORN OPERATES --
-- ABOUT ONE HUNDRED AND TEN MAJOR MANUFACTURING AND SEVEN RESEARCH AND DEVELOPMENTS FACILITIES WORLDWIDE.
WE MANUFACTURE AND PRODUCE CHEMICALLY ENGINEERED PRODUCTS WITH SPECIAL FOCUS ON REPLACEMENTS OF EHS HAZARDOUS ACIDS AND SOLVENTS.
IF YOU FOLLOW ME DOWN THIS WAY, YOU WILL SEE...

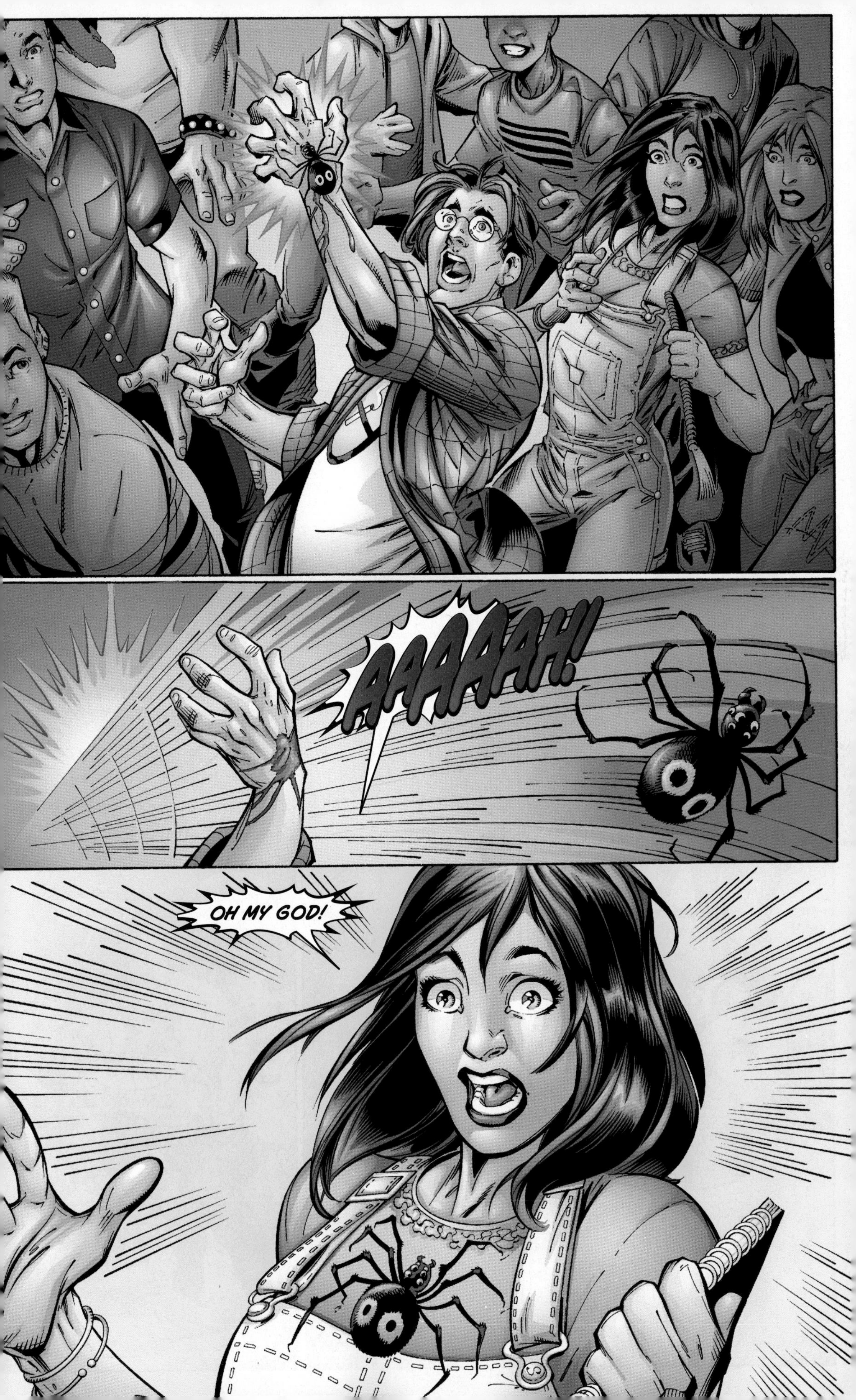
AAAAAH!
OH MY GOD!

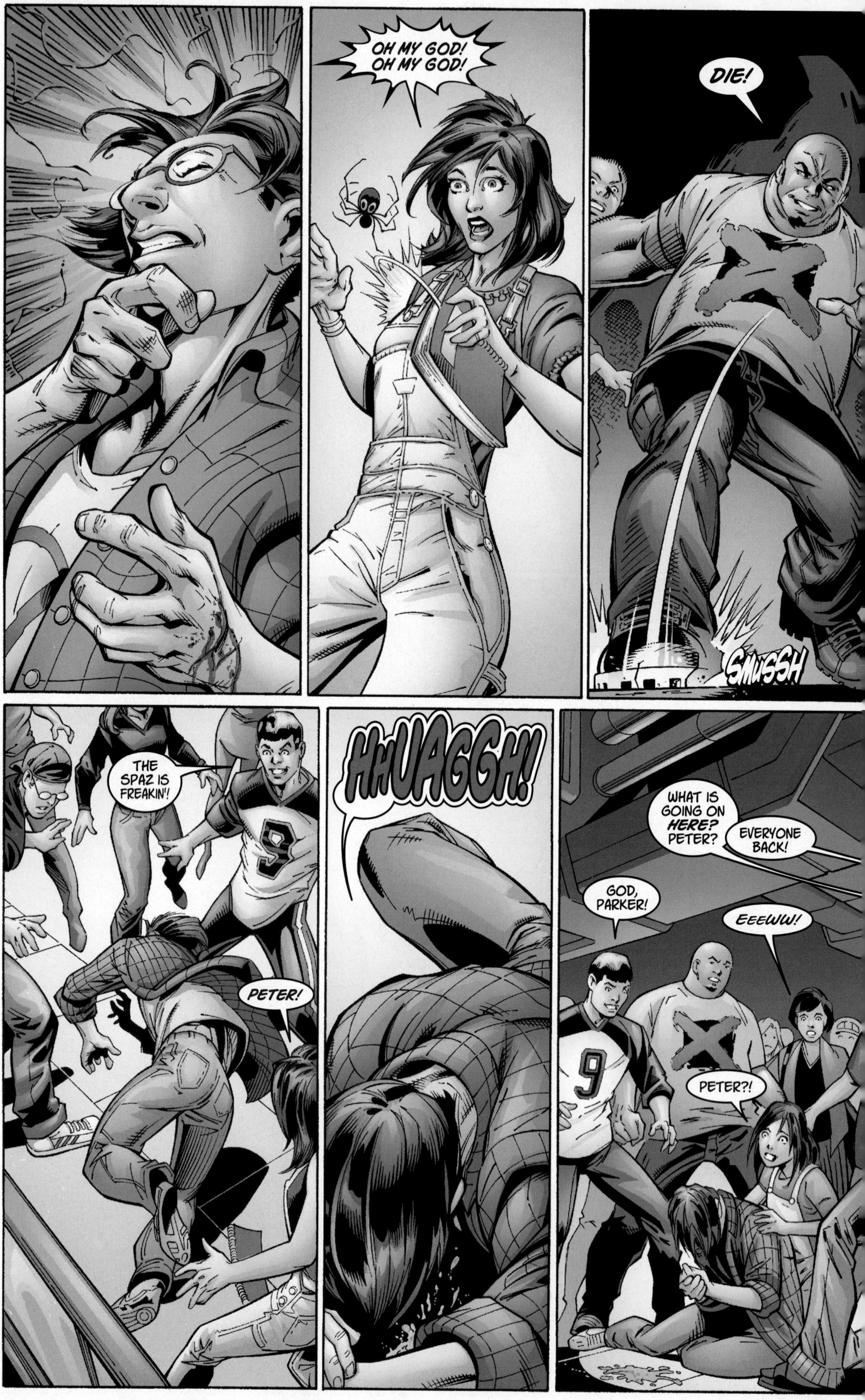
OH MY GOD!
OH MY GOD!
DIE!
SMUSSH
THE SPAZ IS FREAKIN'!
PETER!
HHUAGGH!
WHAT IS GOING ON HERE? PETER?
EVERYONE BACK!
GOD, PARKER!
EEEWW!
PETER?!

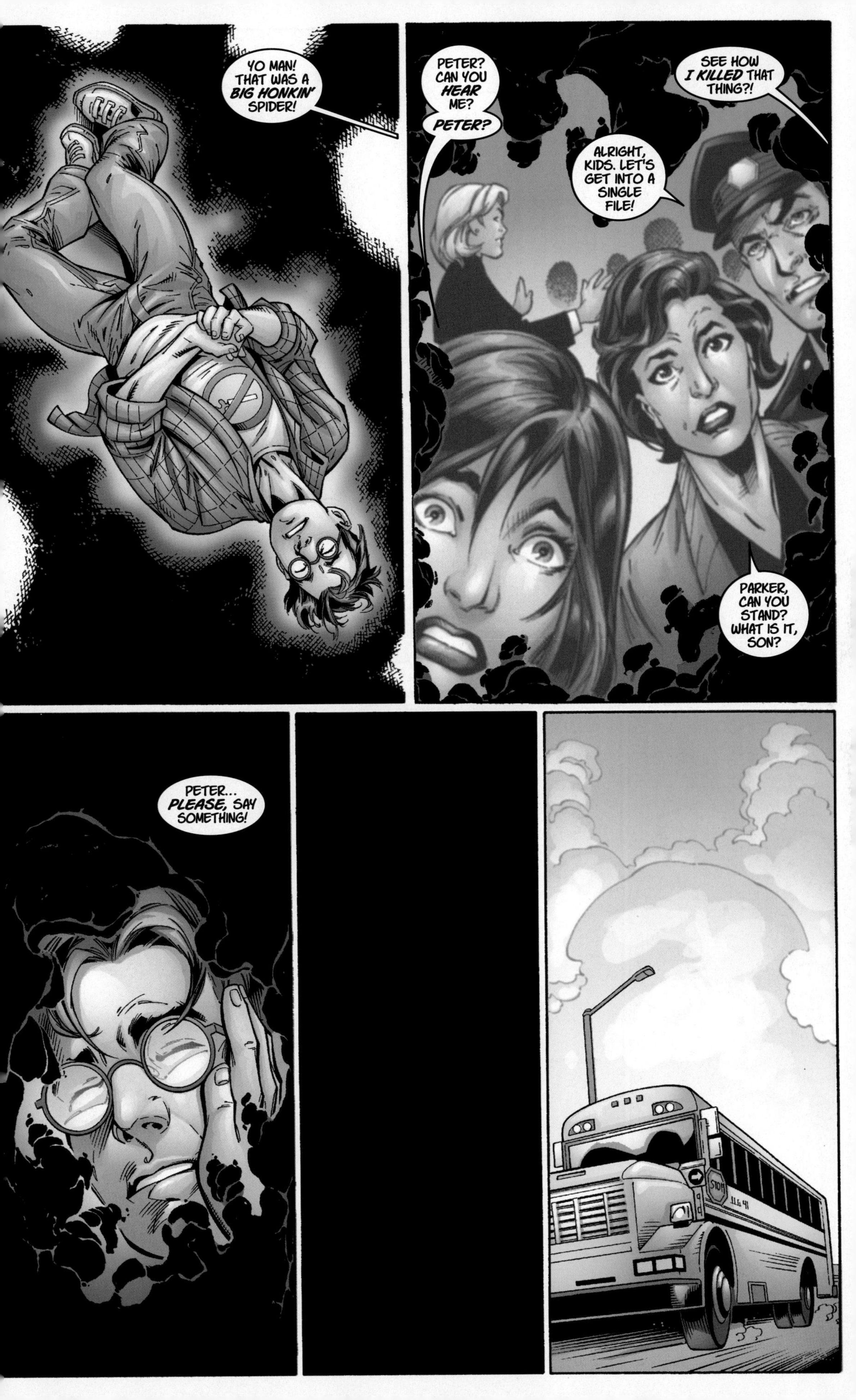
YO MAN! THAT WAS A BIG HONKIN' SPIDER!
PETER? CAN YOU HEAR ME? PETER?
SEE HOW I KILLED THAT THING?!
ALRIGHT, KIDS. LET'S GET INTO A SINGLE FILE!
PARKER, CAN YOU STAND? WHAT IS IT, SON?
PETER... PLEASE, SAY SOMETHING!
STOP

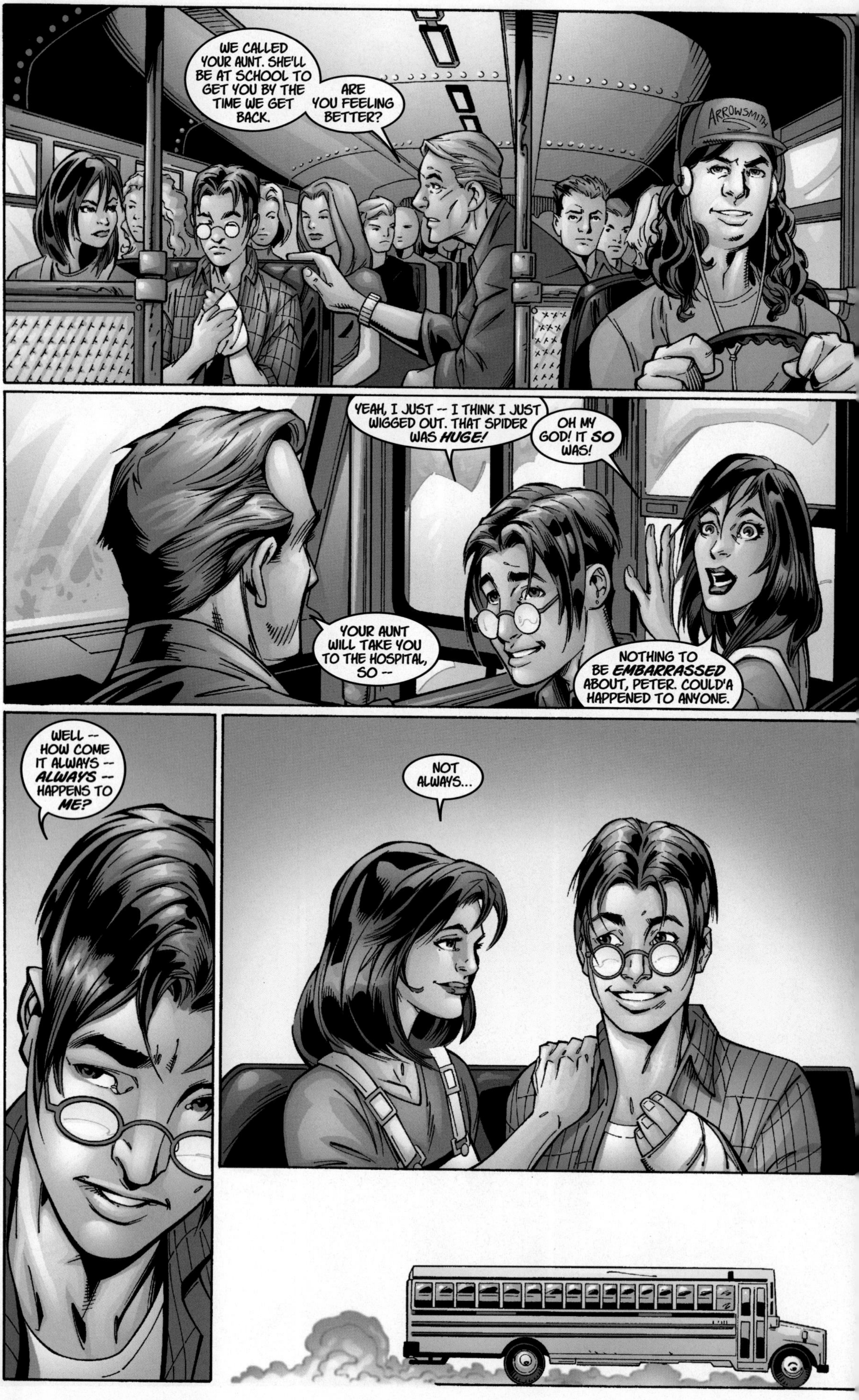
WE CALLED YOUR AUNT. SHE'LL BE AT SCHOOL TO GET YOU BY THE TIME WE GET BACK.
ARE YOU FEELING BETTER?
YEAH, I JUST -- I THINK I JUST WIGGED OUT. THAT SPIDER WAS HUGE!
OH MY GOD! IT SO WAS!
YOUR AUNT WILL TAKE YOU TO THE HOSPITAL, SO --
NOTHING TO BE EMBARRASSED ABOUT, PETER. COULD'A HAPPENED TO ANYONE.
WELL -- HOW COME IT ALWAYS -- ALWAYS -- HAPPENS TO ME?
NOT ALWAYS...

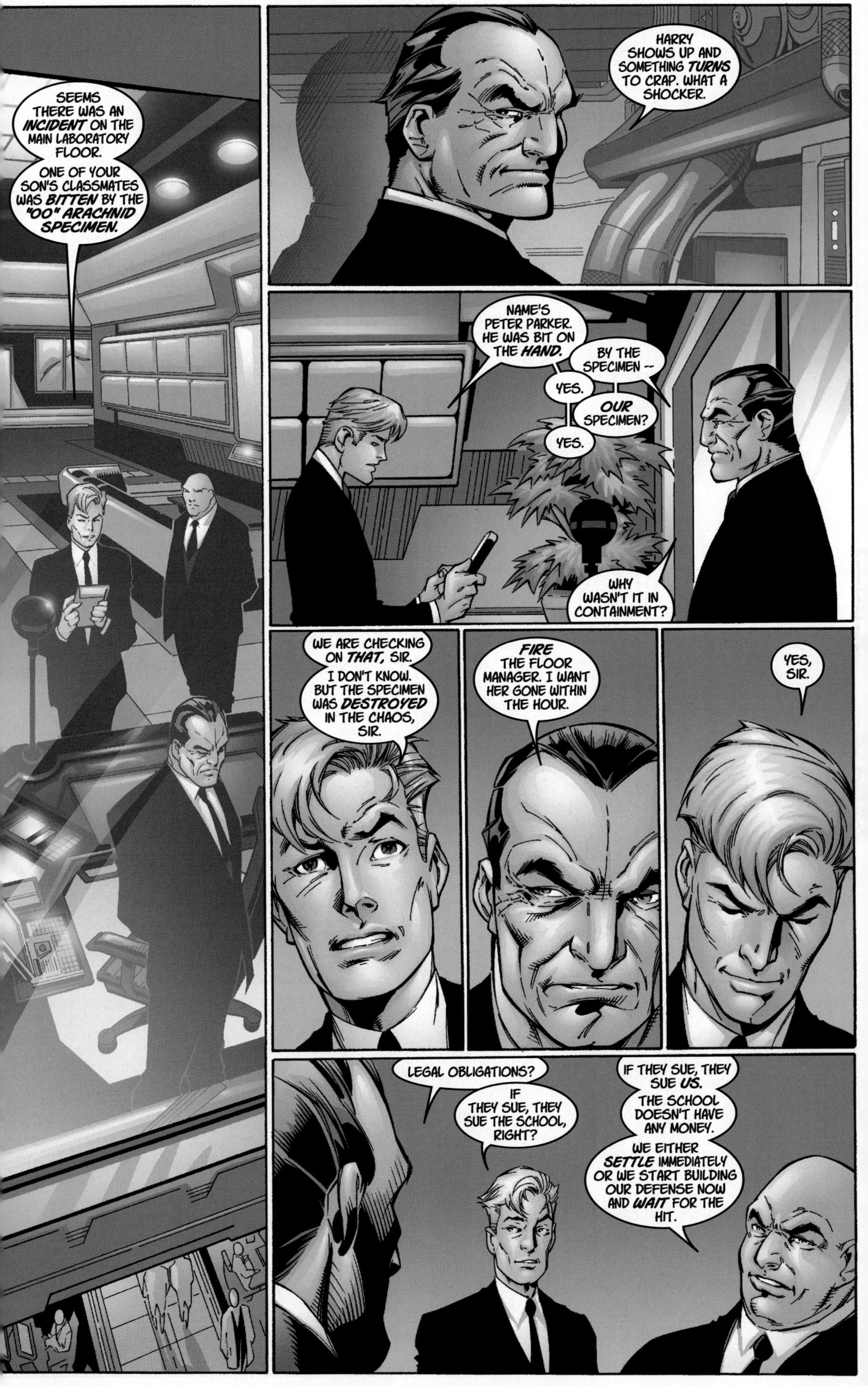

SEEMS THERE WAS AN INCIDENT ON THE MAIN LABORATORY FLOOR.
ONE OF YOUR SON'S CLASSMATES WAS BITTEN BY THE "OO" ARACHNID SPECIMEN.
HARRY SHOWS UP AND SOMETHING TURNS TO CRAP. WHAT A SHOCKER.
NAME'S PETER PARKER. HE WAS BIT ON THE HAND.
BY THE SPECIMEN --
YES.
OUR SPECIMEN?
YES.
WHY WASN'T IT IN CONTAINMENT?
WE ARE CHECKING ON THAT, SIR.
I DON'T KNOW. BUT THE SPECIMEN WAS DESTROYED IN THE CHAOS, SIR.
FIRE THE FLOOR MANAGER. I WANT HER GONE WITHIN THE HOUR.
YES, SIR.
LEGAL OBLIGATIONS?
IF THEY SUE, THEY SUE THE SCHOOL, RIGHT?
IF THEY SUE, THEY SUE US.
THE SCHOOL DOESN'T HAVE ANY MONEY.
WE EITHER SETTLE IMMEDIATELY OR WE START BUILDING OUR DEFENSE NOW AND WAIT FOR THE HIT.

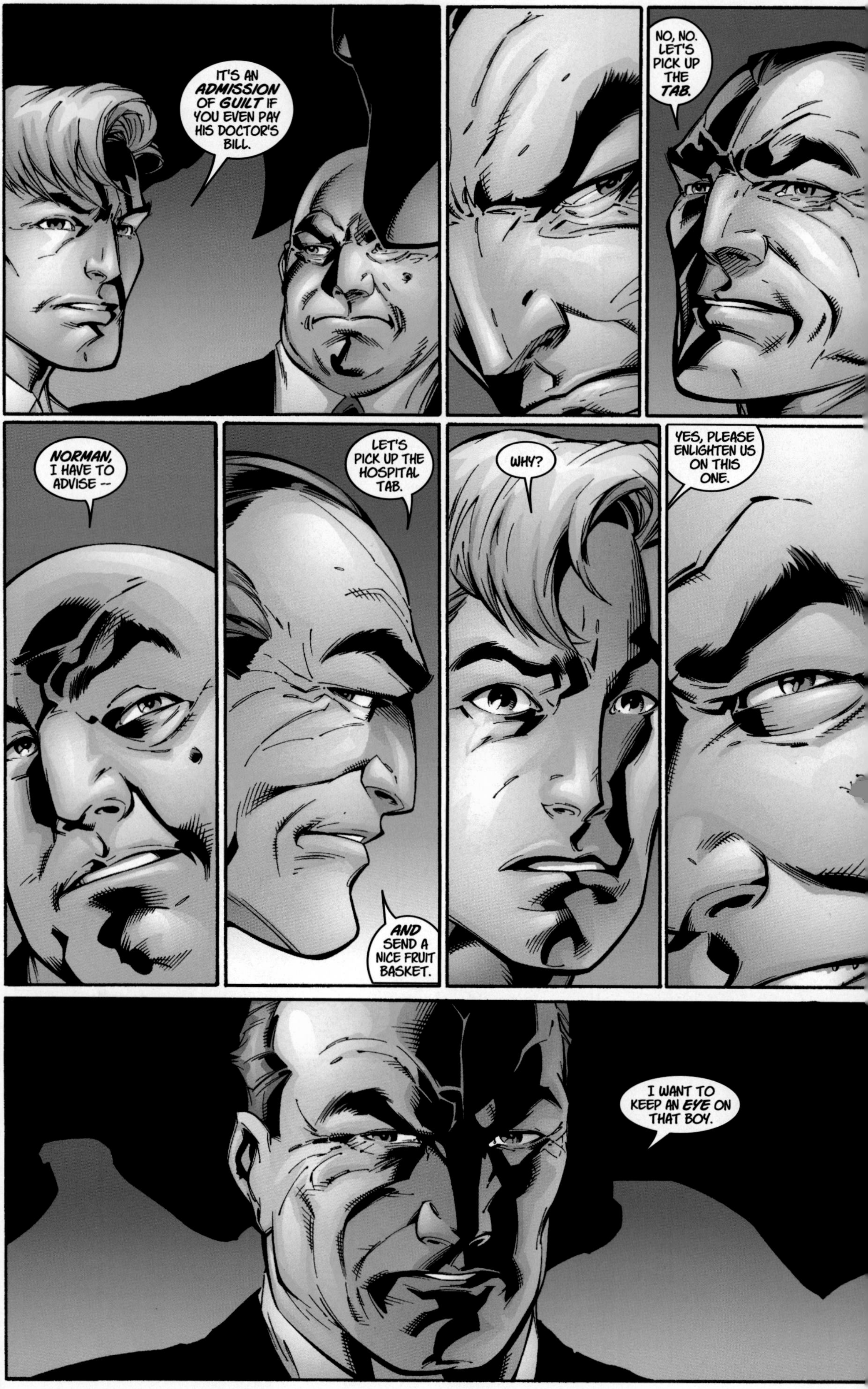
IT'S AN ADMISSION OF GUILT IF YOU EVEN PAY HIS DOCTOR'S BILL.
NO, NO. LET'S PICK UP THE TAB.
NORMAN, I HAVE TO ADVISE --
LET'S PICK UP THE HOSPITAL TAB.
AND SEND A NICE FRUIT BASKET.
WHY?
YES, PLEASE ENLIGHTEN US ON THIS ONE.
I WANT TO KEEP AN EYE ON THAT BOY.

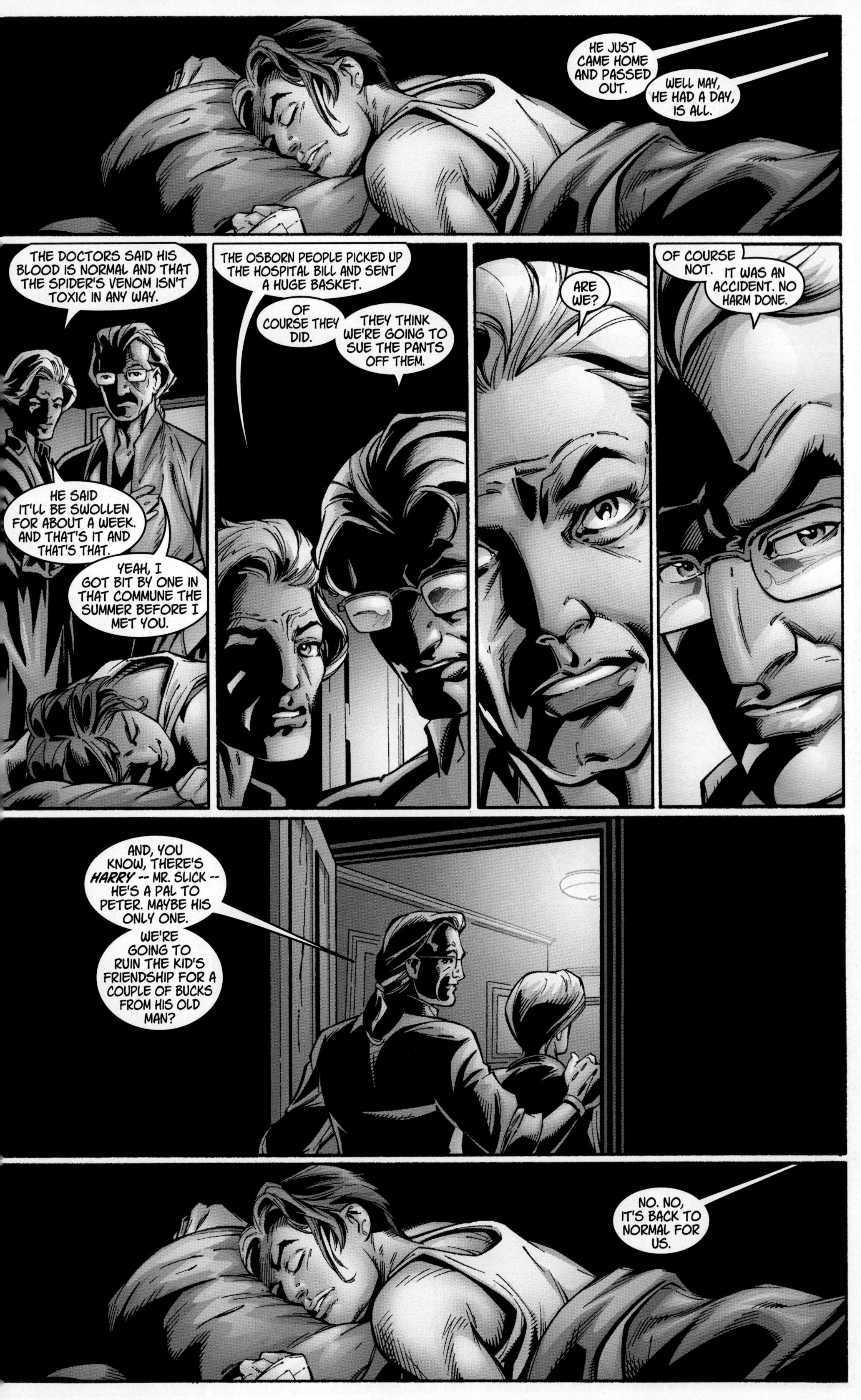
HE JUST CAME HOME AND PASSED OUT.
WELL MAY, HE HAD A DAY, IS ALL.
THE DOCTORS SAID HIS BLOOD IS NORMAL AND THAT THE SPIDER'S VENOM ISN'T TOXIC IN ANY WAY.
HE SAID IT'LL BE SWOLLEN FOR ABOUT A WEEK. AND THAT'S IT AND THAT'S THAT.
YEAH, I GOT BIT BY ONE IN THAT COMMUNE THE SUMMER BEFORE I MET YOU.
THE OSBORN PEOPLE PICKED UP THE HOSPITAL BILL AND SENT A HUGE BASKET.
OF COURSE THEY DID.
THEY THINK WE'RE GOING TO SUE THE PANTS OFF THEM.
ARE WE?
OF COURSE NOT.
IT WAS AN ACCIDENT. NO HARM DONE.
AND, YOU KNOW, THERE'S HARRY -- MR. SLICK -- HE'S A PAL TO PETER. MAYBE HIS ONLY ONE.
WE'RE GOING TO RUIN THE KID'S FRIENDSHIP FOR A COUPLE OF BUCKS FROM HIS OLD MAN?
NO. NO, IT'S BACK TO NORMAL FOR US.

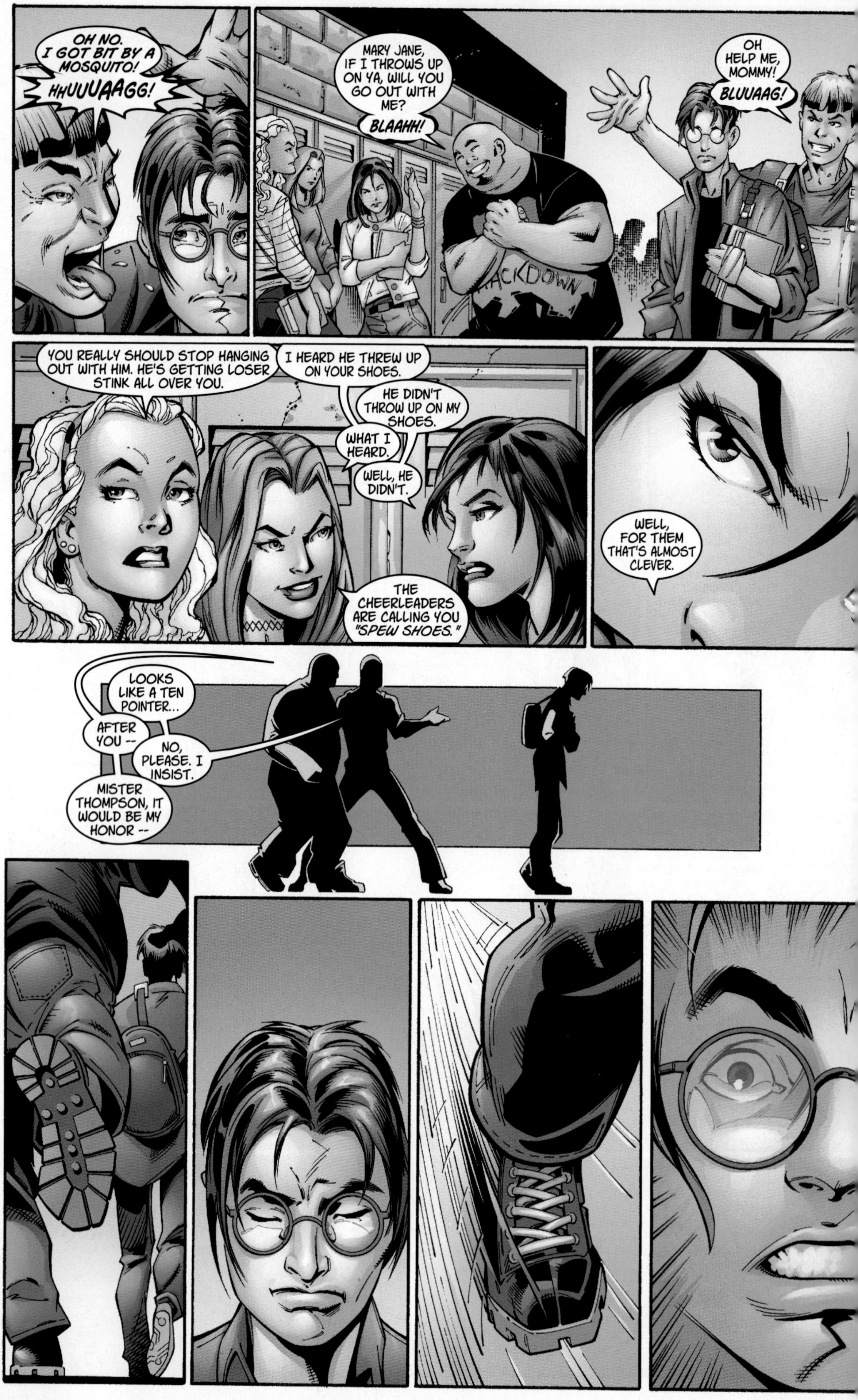
OH NO. I GOT BIT BY A MOSQUITO! HHUUUAAGG!
MARY JANE, IF I THROWS UP ON YA, WILL YOU GO OUT WITH ME? BLAAHH!
OH HELP ME, MOMMY! BLUUAAG!
YOU REALLY SHOULD STOP HANGING OUT WITH HIM. HE'S GETTING LOSER STINK ALL OVER YOU.
I HEARD HE THREW UP ON YOUR SHOES.
HE DIDN'T THROW UP ON MY SHOES.
WHAT I HEARD.
WELL, HE DIDN'T.
THE CHEERLEADERS ARE CALLING YOU "SPEW SHOES."
WELL, FOR THEM THAT'S ALMOST CLEVER.
LOOKS LIKE A TEN POINTER...
AFTER YOU --
NO, PLEASE. I INSIST.
MISTER THOMPSON, IT WOULD BE MY HONOR --

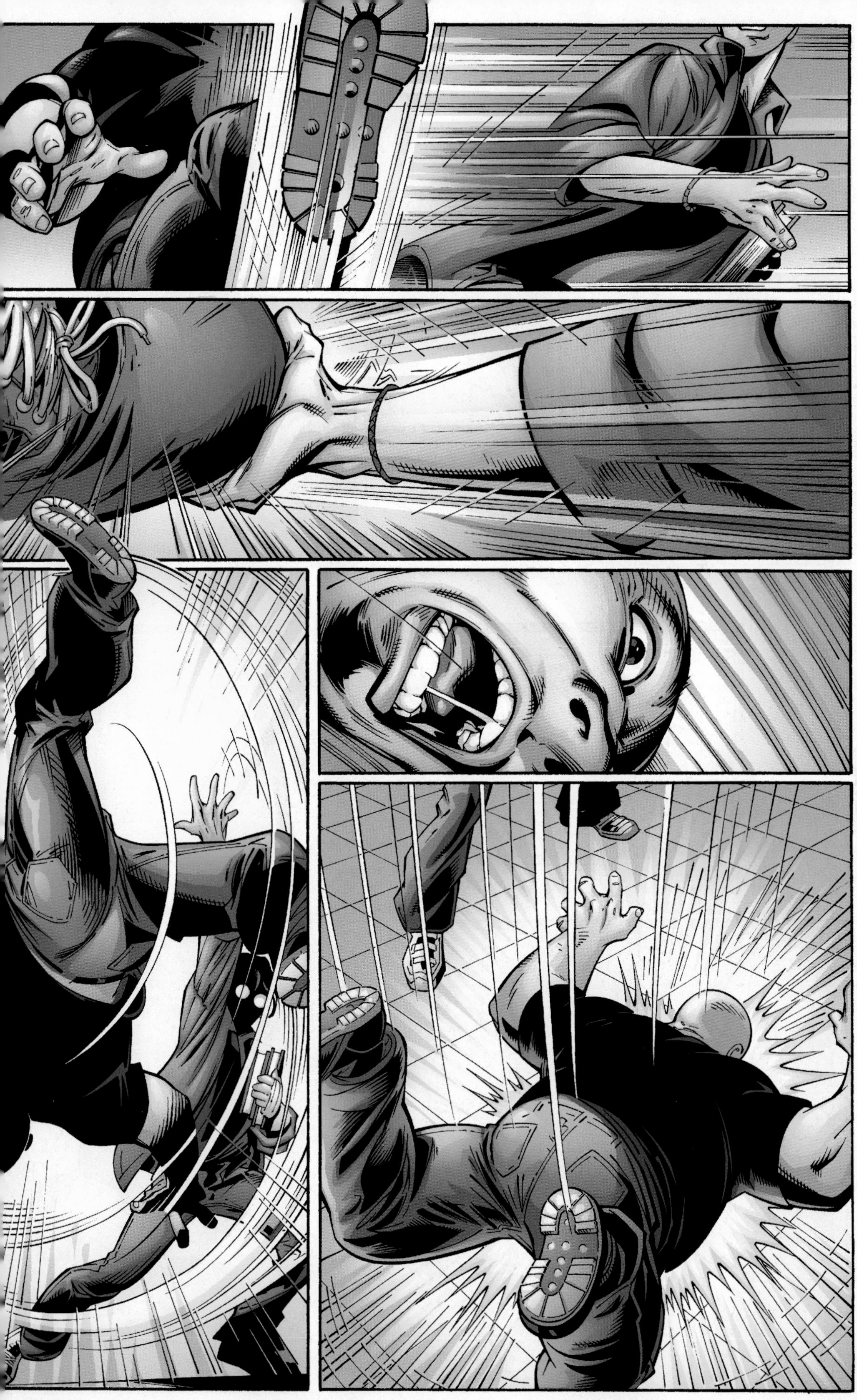

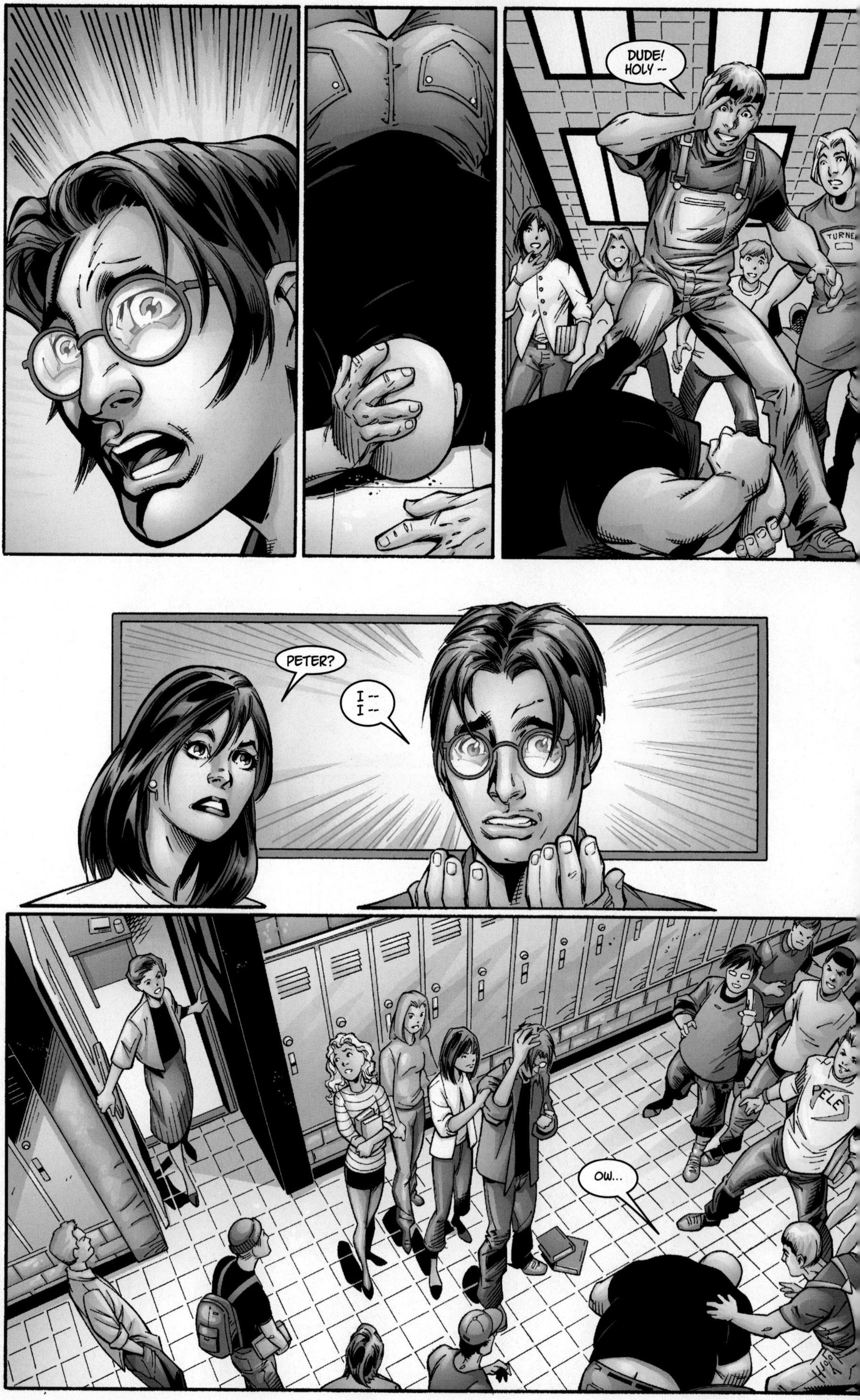
DUDE! HOLY --
PETER?
I -- I --
OW...

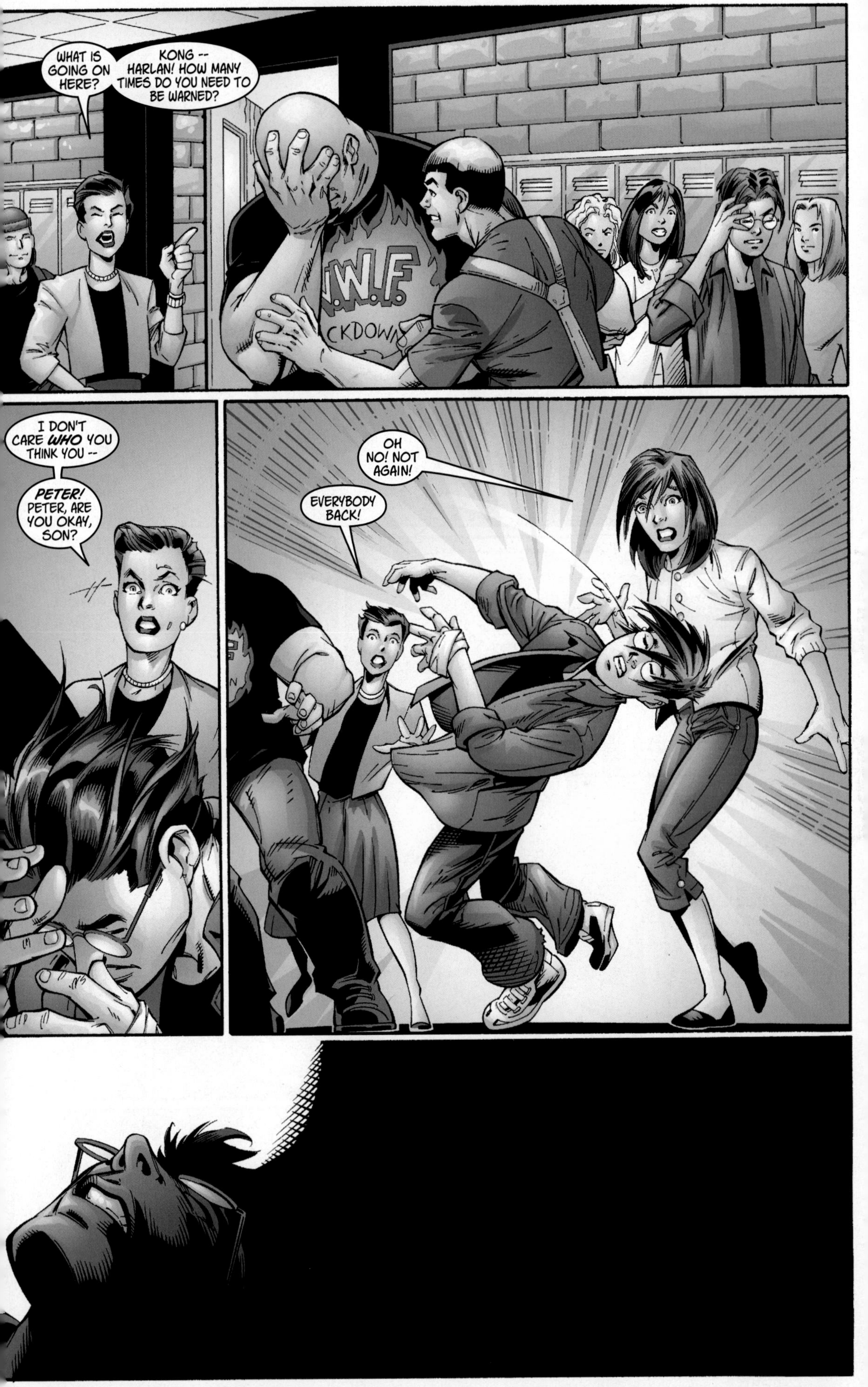
WHAT IS GOING ON HERE?
KONG -- HARLAN! HOW MANY TIMES DO YOU NEED TO BE WARNED?
N.W.F.
CKDOWN
I DON'T CARE **WHO** YOU THINK YOU --
PETER! PETER, ARE YOU OKAY, SON?
OH NO! NOT AGAIN!
EVERYBODY BACK!

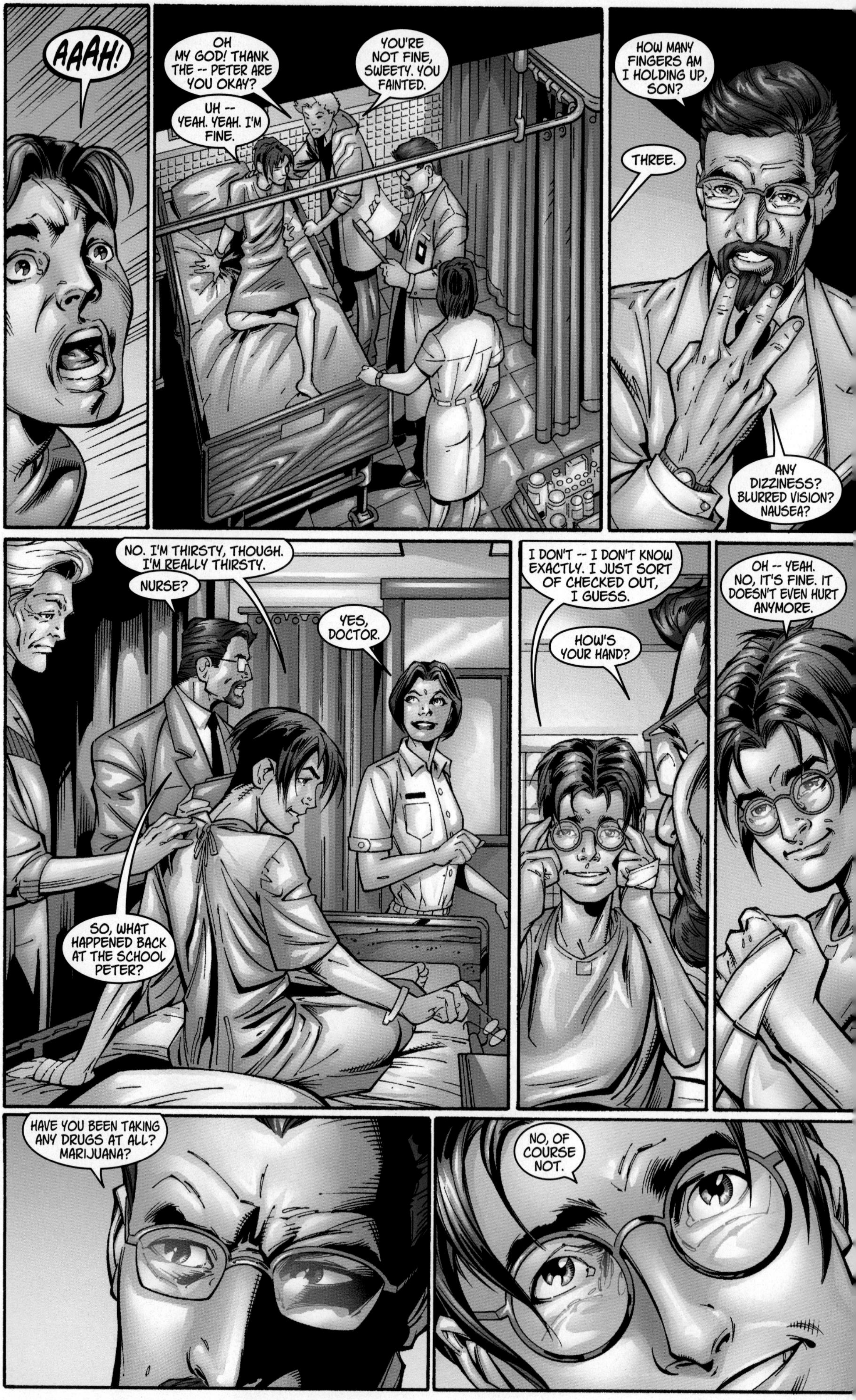
AAAH!
OH MY GOD! THANK THE -- PETER ARE YOU OKAY?
UH -- YEAH. YEAH. I'M FINE.
YOU'RE NOT FINE, SWEETY. YOU FAINTED.
HOW MANY FINGERS AM I HOLDING UP, SON?
THREE.
ANY DIZZINESS? BLURRED VISION? NAUSEA?
NO. I'M THIRSTY, THOUGH. I'M REALLY THIRSTY.
NURSE?
YES, DOCTOR.
SO, WHAT HAPPENED BACK AT THE SCHOOL PETER?
I DON'T -- I DON'T KNOW EXACTLY. I JUST SORT OF CHECKED OUT, I GUESS.
HOW'S YOUR HAND?
OH -- YEAH. NO, IT'S FINE. IT DOESN'T EVEN HURT ANYMORE.
HAVE YOU BEEN TAKING ANY DRUGS AT ALL? MARIJUANA?
NO, OF COURSE NOT.

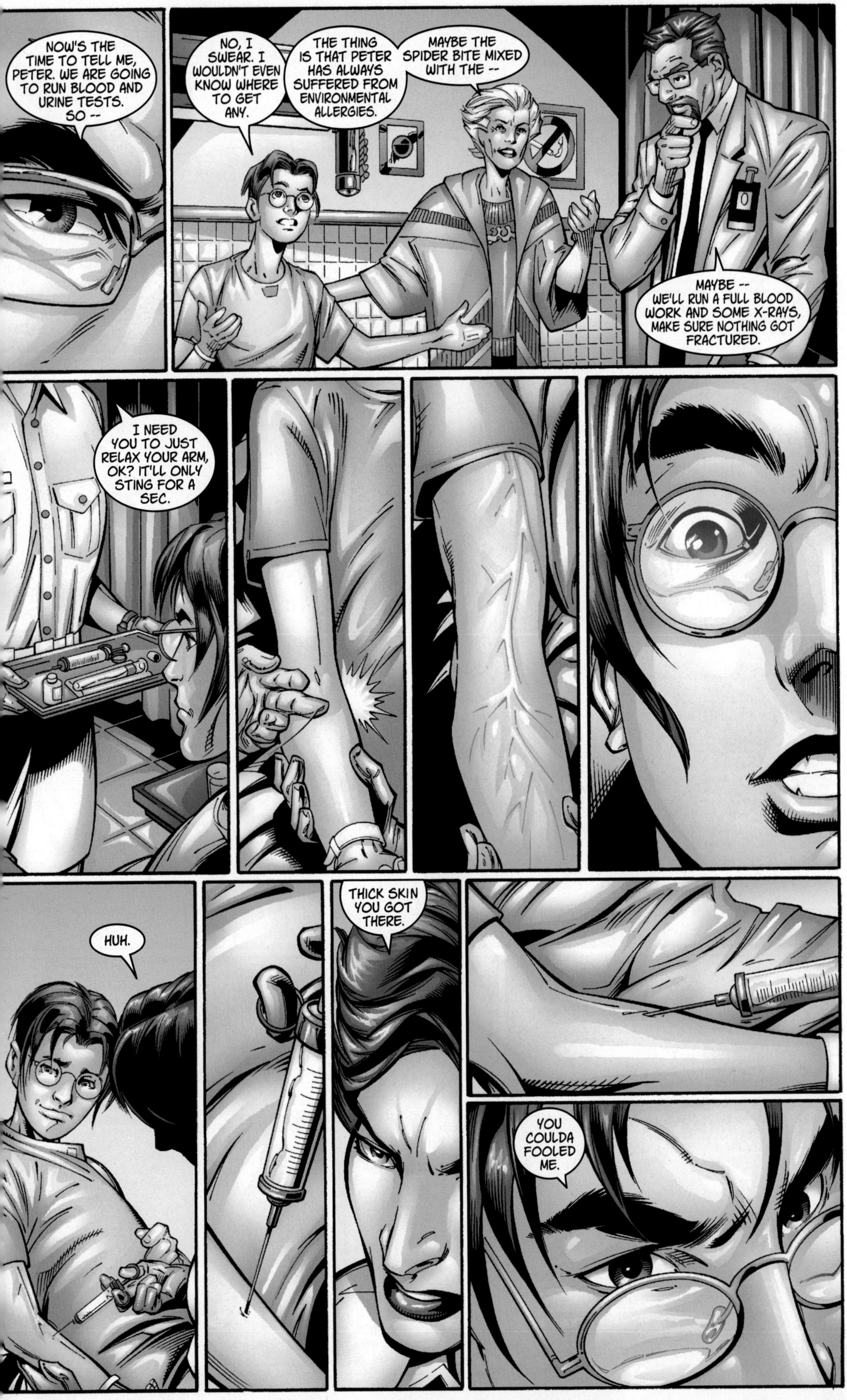
NOW'S THE TIME TO TELL ME, PETER. WE ARE GOING TO RUN BLOOD AND URINE TESTS. SO --
NO, I SWEAR. I WOULDN'T EVEN KNOW WHERE TO GET ANY.
THE THING IS THAT PETER HAS ALWAYS SUFFERED FROM ENVIRONMENTAL ALLERGIES.
MAYBE THE SPIDER BITE MIXED WITH THE --
MAYBE -- WE'LL RUN A FULL BLOOD WORK AND SOME X-RAYS, MAKE SURE NOTHING GOT FRACTURED.
I NEED YOU TO JUST RELAX YOUR ARM, OK? IT'LL ONLY STING FOR A SEC.
HUH.
THICK SKIN YOU GOT THERE.
YOU COULDA FOOLED ME.

HI, COULD YOU TAKE THIS TO THE LAB AND HAVE THEM DO AN EXPRESS ON THIS ONE?

THEY'RE WAITING. HE'S A CUTE KID. THANKS.

WHATEVER.

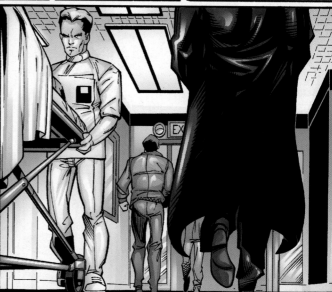

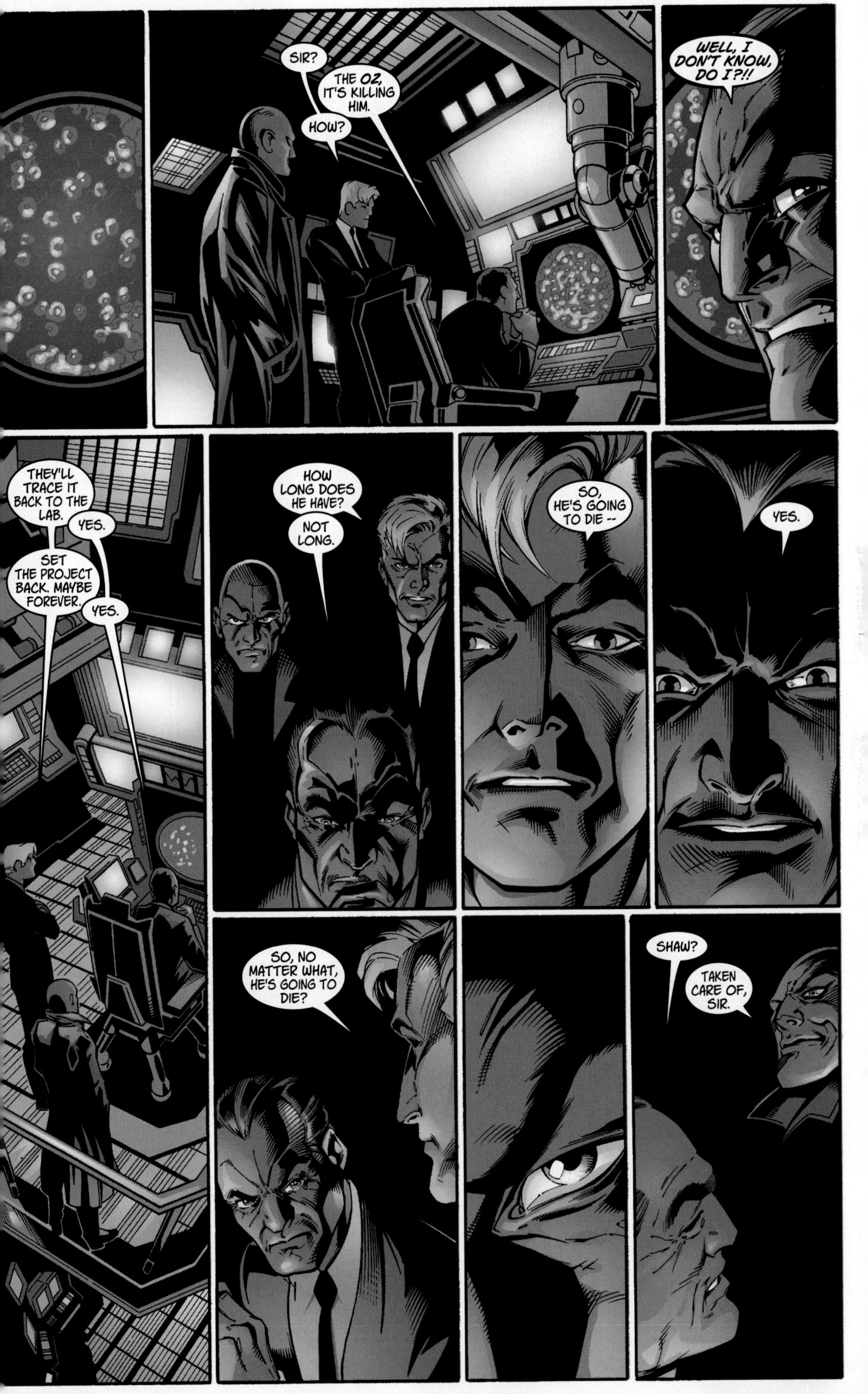
SIR?
THE OZ, IT'S KILLING HIM.
HOW?
WELL, I DON'T KNOW, DO I?!!
THEY'LL TRACE IT BACK TO THE LAB.
YES.
SET THE PROJECT BACK. MAYBE FOREVER.
YES.
HOW LONG DOES HE HAVE?
NOT LONG.
SO, HE'S GOING TO DIE --
YES.
SO, NO MATTER WHAT, HE'S GOING TO DIE?
SHAW?
TAKEN CARE OF, SIR.

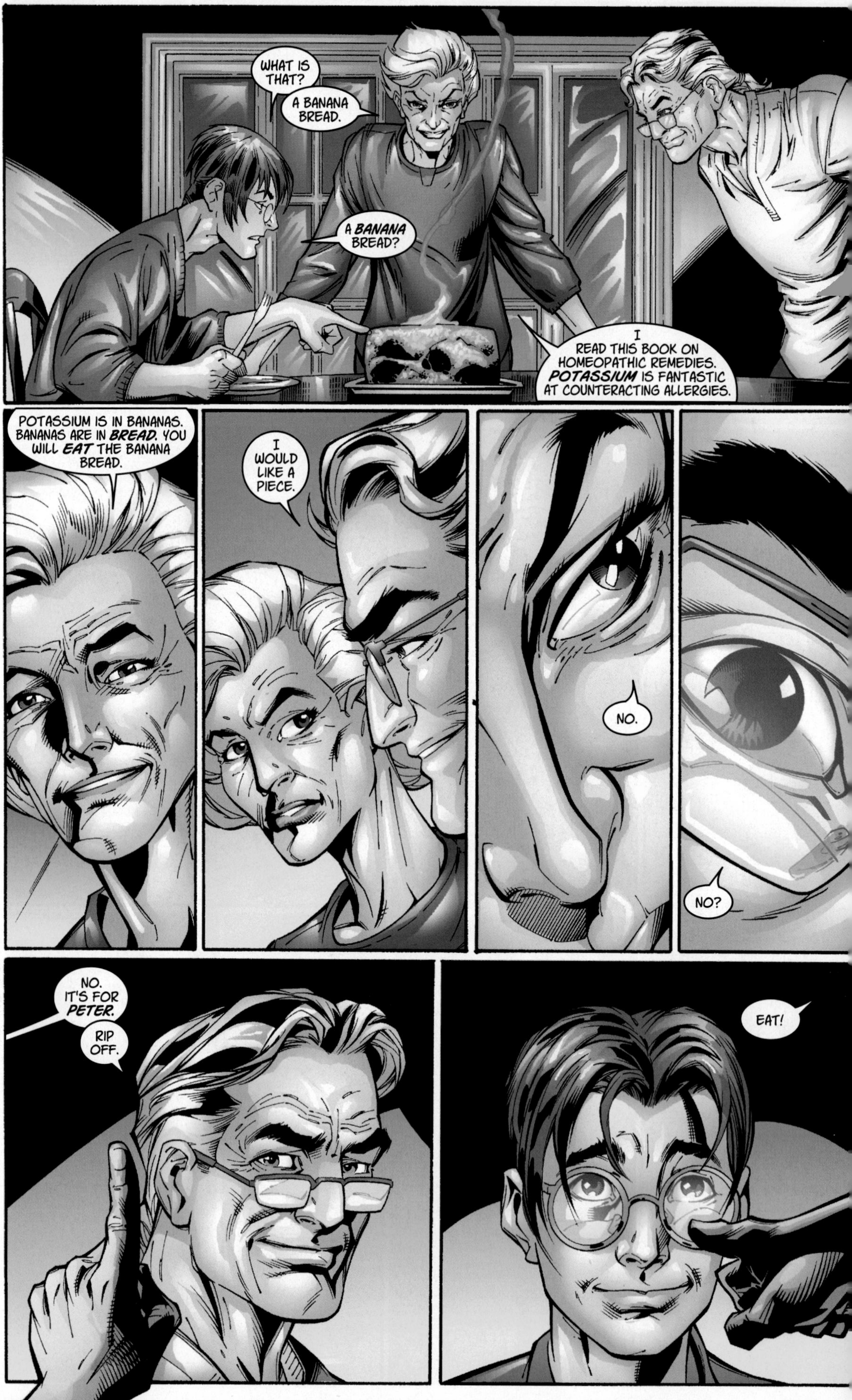
WHAT IS THAT?
A BANANA BREAD.
A BANANA BREAD?
I READ THIS BOOK ON HOMEOPATHIC REMEDIES. POTASSIUM IS FANTASTIC AT COUNTERACTING ALLERGIES.
POTASSIUM IS IN BANANAS. BANANAS ARE IN BREAD. YOU WILL EAT THE BANANA BREAD.
I WOULD LIKE A PIECE.
NO.
NO?
NO. IT'S FOR PETER.
RIP OFF.
EAT!

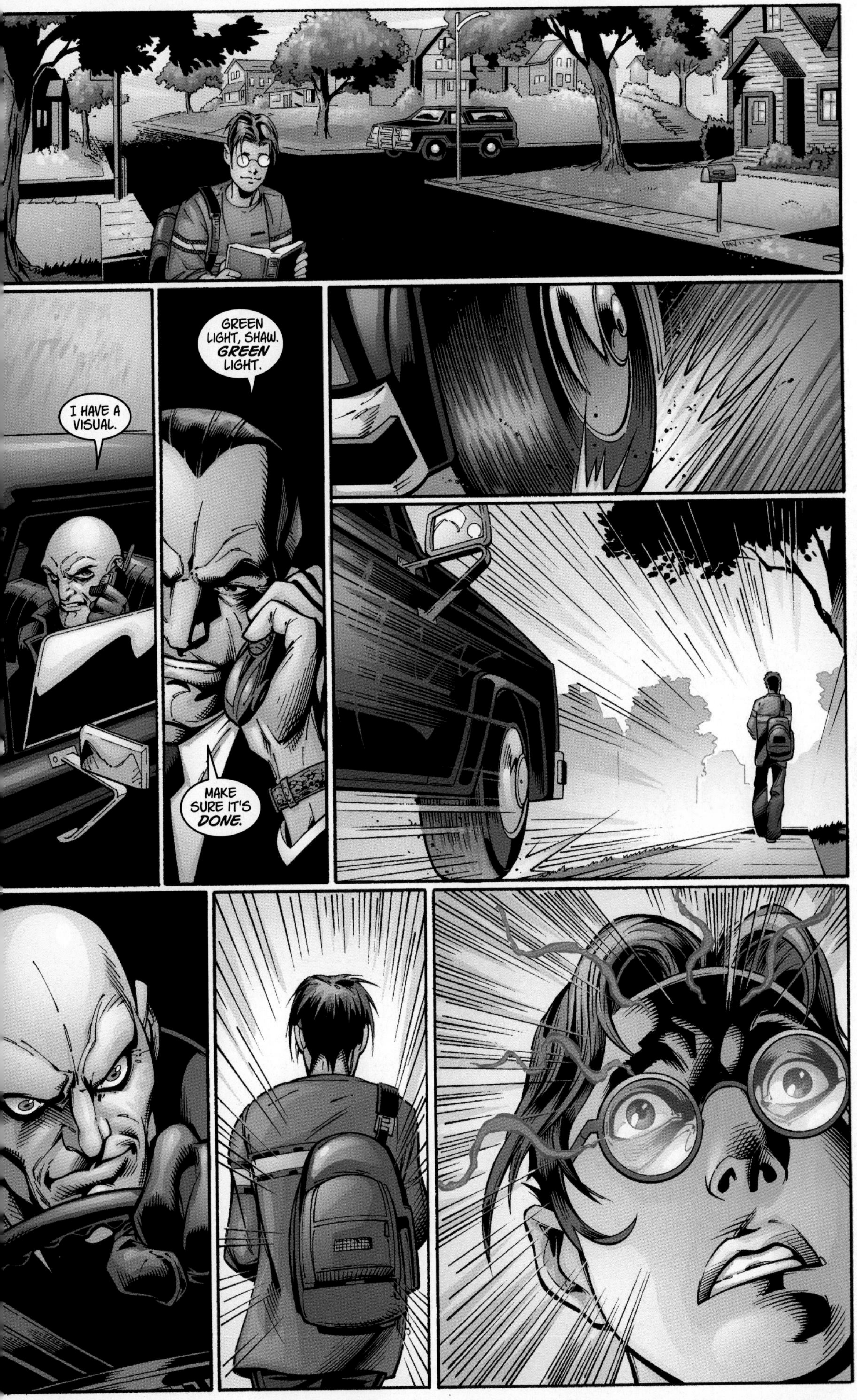

I HAVE A VISUAL.
GREEN LIGHT, SHAW. GREEN LIGHT.
MAKE SURE IT'S DONE.

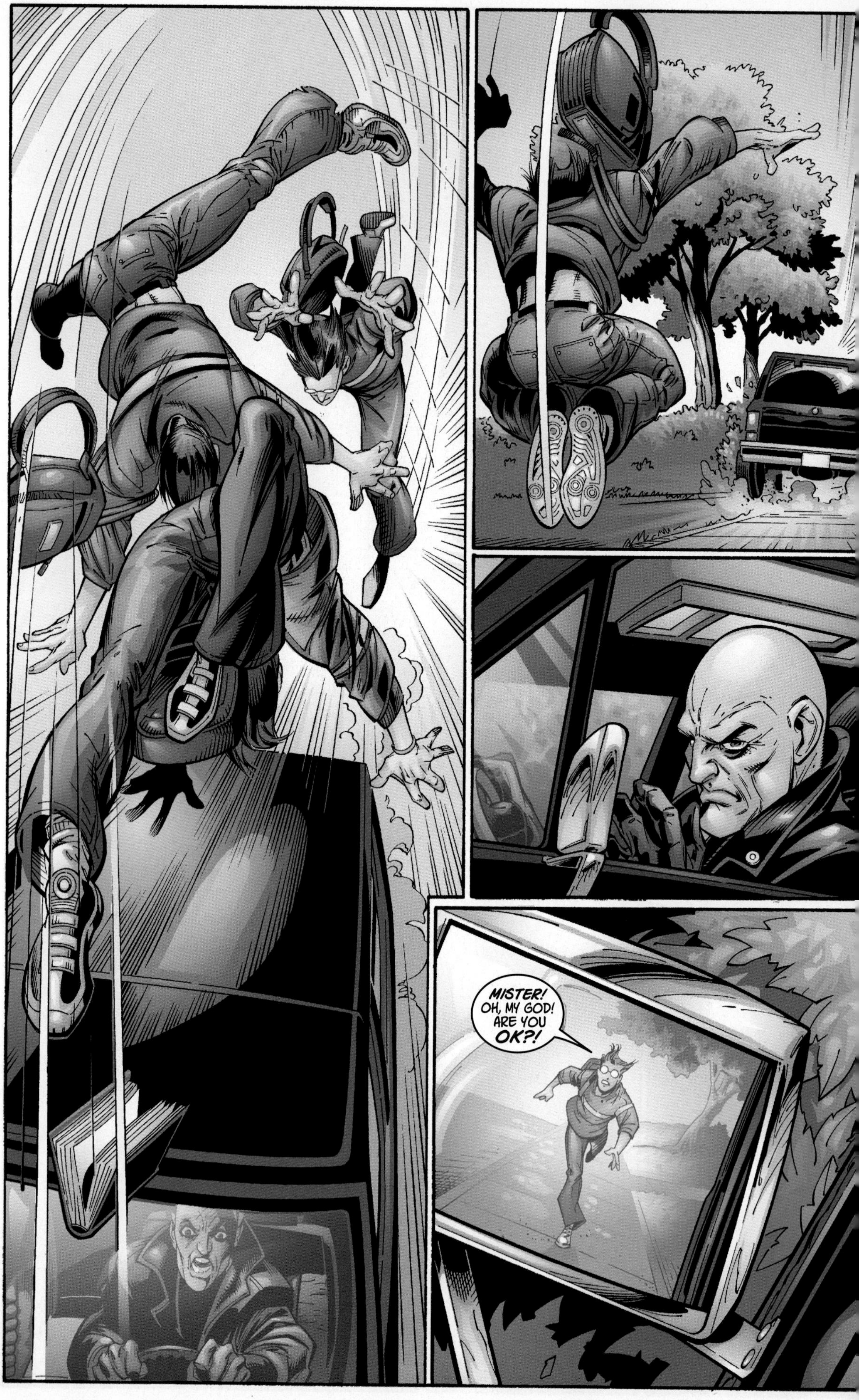
MISTER! OH, MY GOD! ARE YOU OK?!

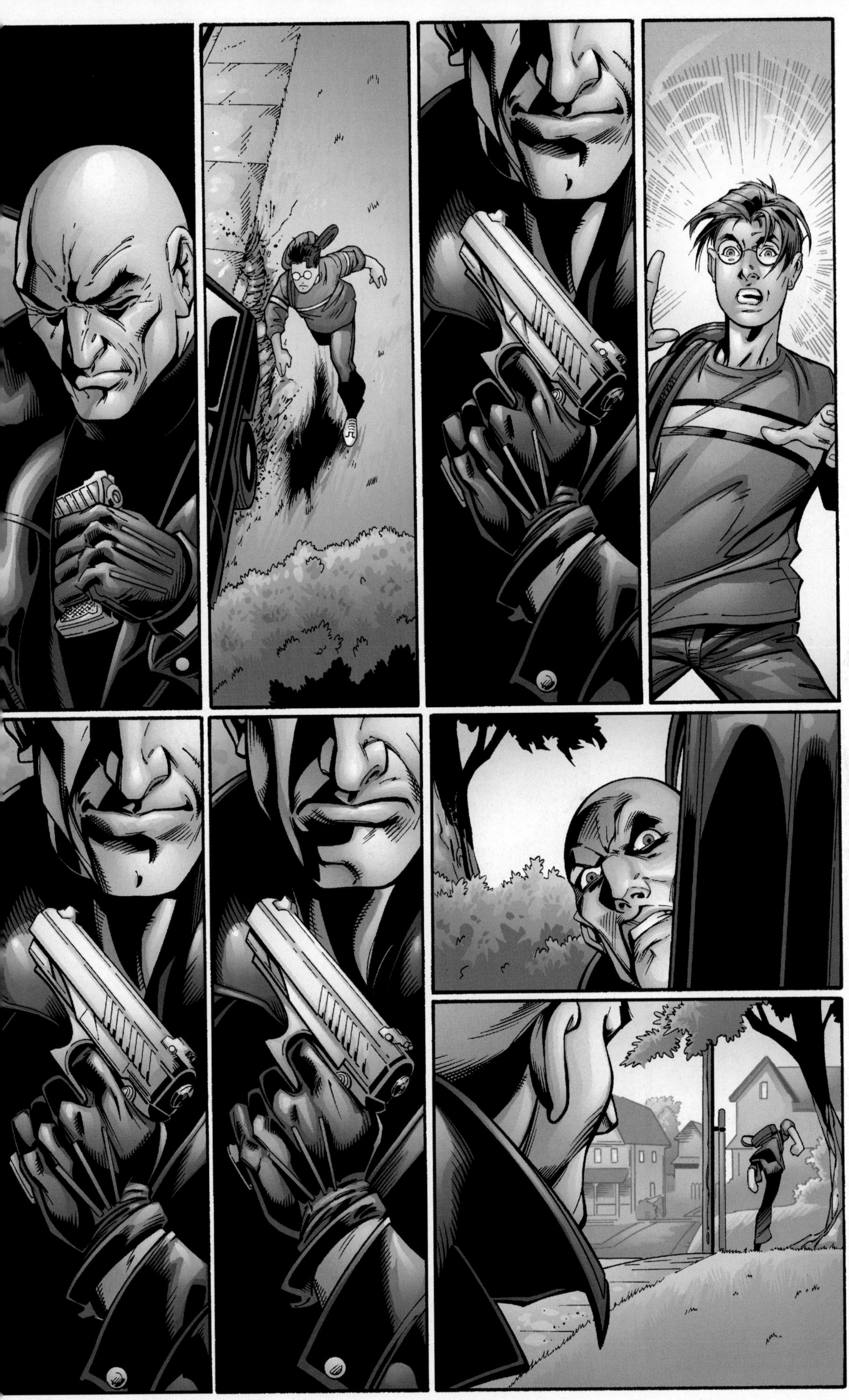

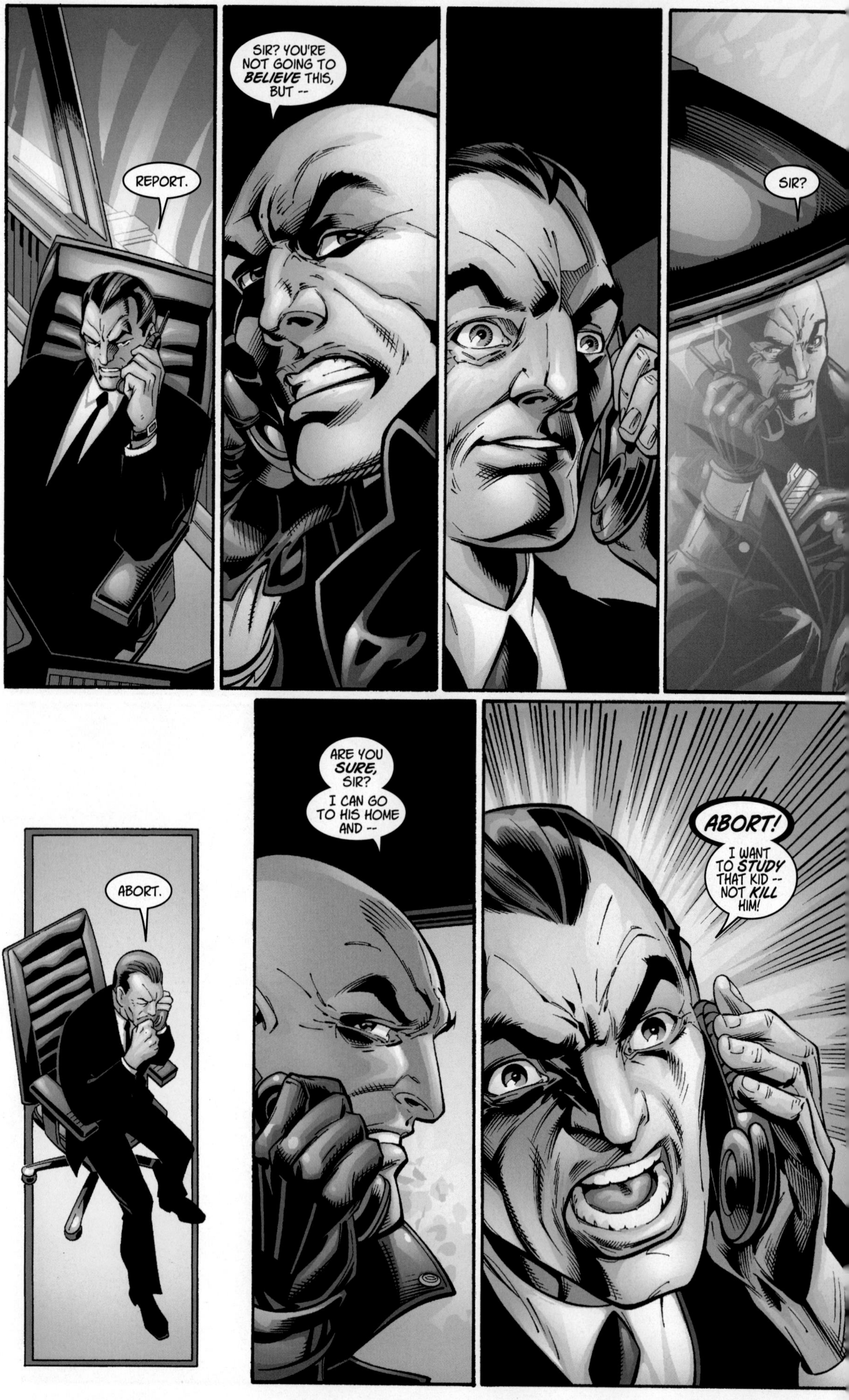
REPORT.
SIR? YOU'RE NOT GOING TO BELIEVE THIS, BUT --
SIR?
ABORT.
ARE YOU SURE, SIR?
I CAN GO TO HIS HOME AND --
ABORT!
I WANT TO STUDY THAT KID -- NOT KILL HIM!

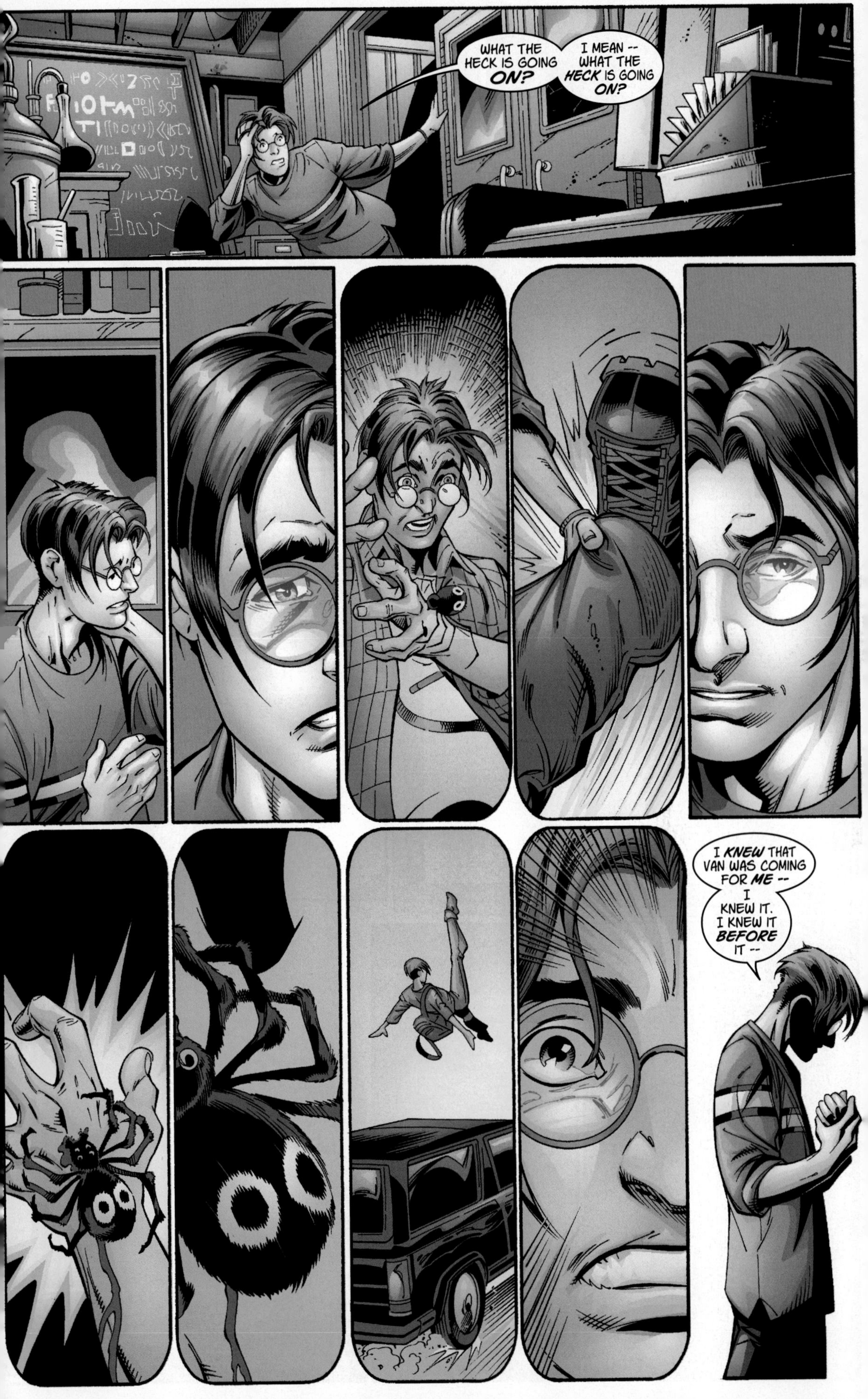
WHAT THE HECK IS GOING ON?
I MEAN -- WHAT THE HECK IS GOING ON?
I KNEW THAT VAN WAS COMING FOR ME -- I KNEW IT. I KNEW IT BEFORE IT --

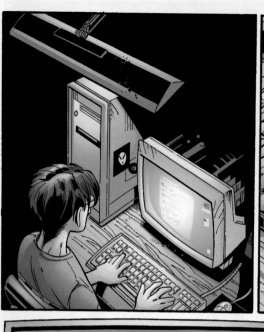

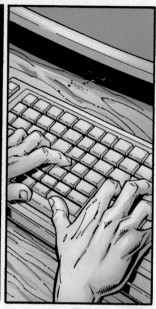

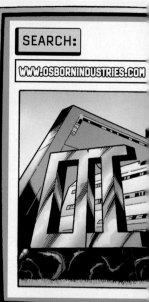

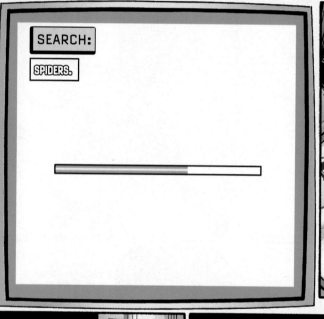

SEARCH:
WWW.OSBORNINDUSTRIES.COM
SEARCH:
SPIDERS.
MANY PEOPLE CONFUSE SPIDERS WITH INSECTS. BOTH BELONG TO THE PHYLUM ARTHROPODA IN THE ANIMAL KINGDOM --
WELL, WHADDAYA THINK OF THAT.

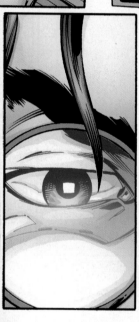

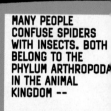

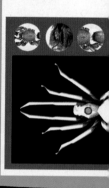

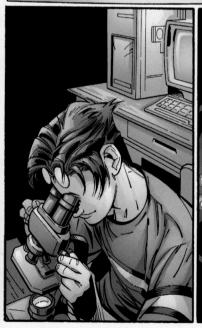

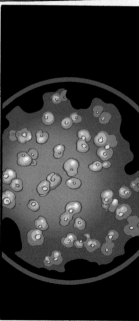

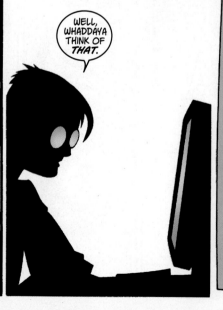

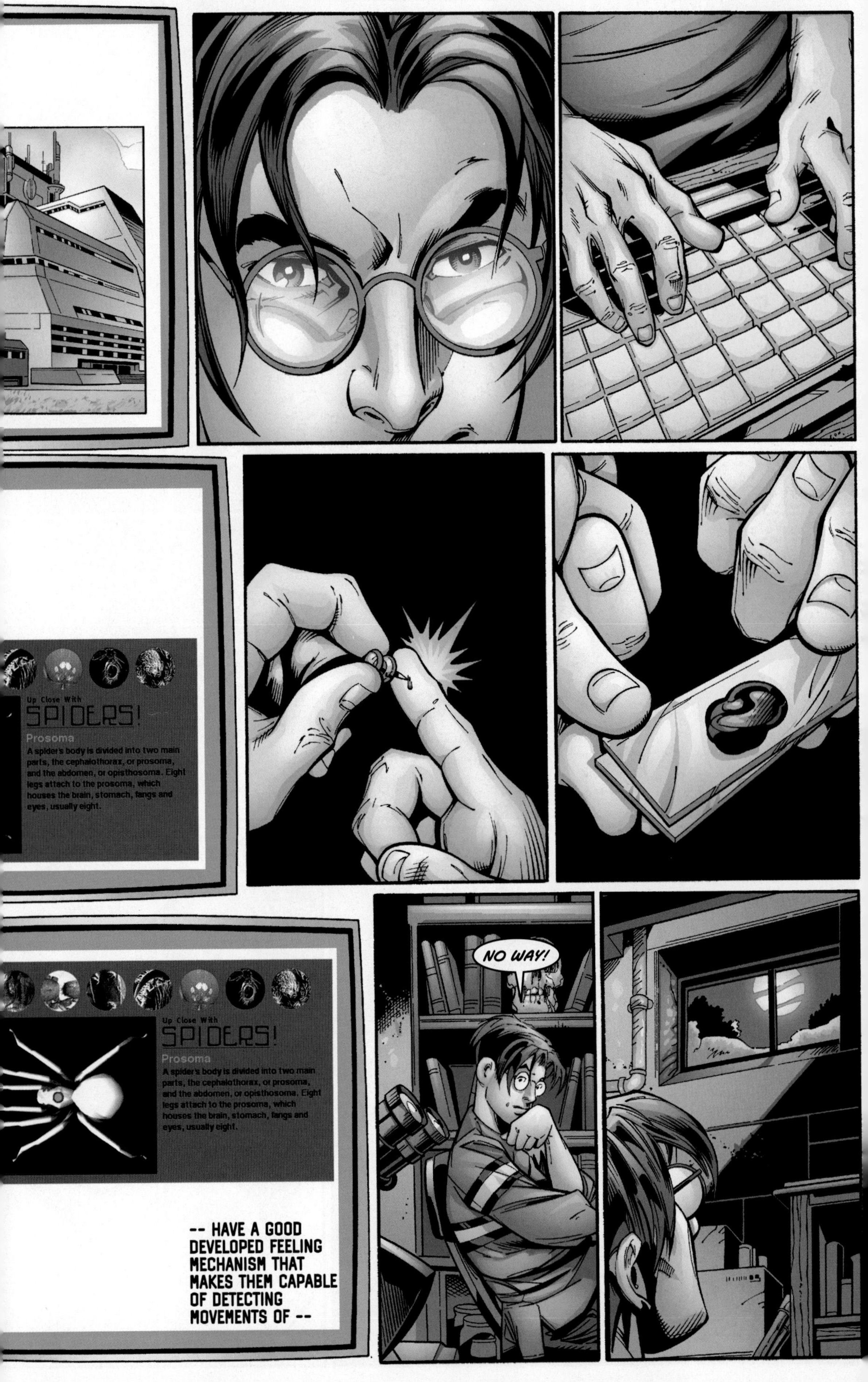
Up Close With
SPIDERS!
Prosoma
A spider's body is divided into two main parts, the cephalothorax, or prosoma, and the abdomen, or opisthosoma. Eight legs attach to the prosoma, which houses the brain, stomach, fangs and eyes, usually eight.
Up Close With
SPIDERS!
Prosoma
A spider's body is divided into two main parts, the cephalothorax, or prosoma, and the abdomen, or opisthosoma. Eight legs attach to the prosoma, which houses the brain, stomach, fangs and eyes, usually eight.
-- HAVE A GOOD DEVELOPED FEELING MECHANISM THAT MAKES THEM CAPABLE OF DETECTING MOVEMENTS OF --
NO WAY!

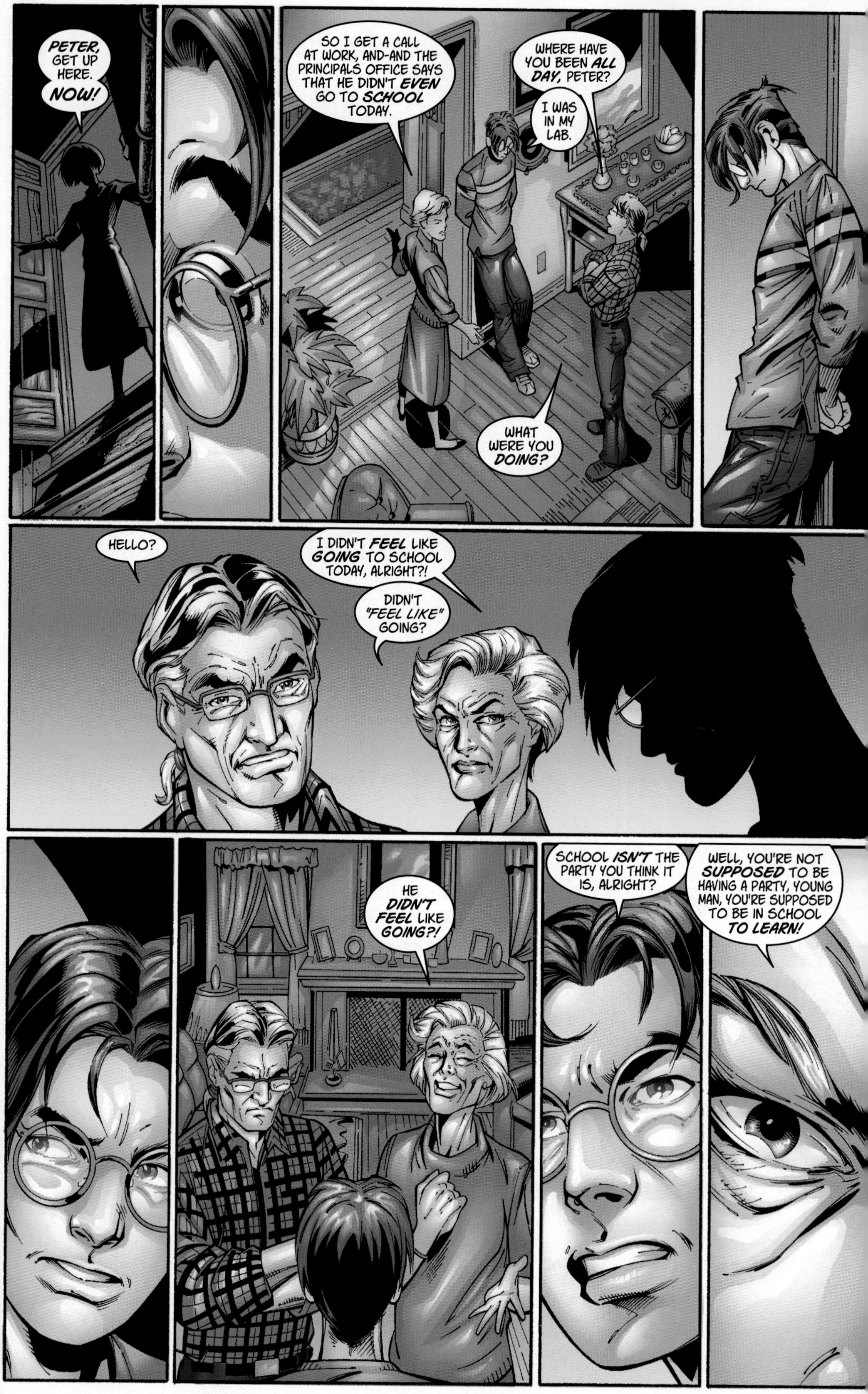
PETER, GET UP HERE. NOW!
SO I GET A CALL AT WORK, AND-AND THE PRINCIPALS OFFICE SAYS THAT HE DIDN'T EVEN GO TO SCHOOL TODAY.
WHERE HAVE YOU BEEN ALL DAY, PETER?
I WAS IN MY LAB.
WHAT WERE YOU DOING?
HELLO?
I DIDN'T FEEL LIKE GOING TO SCHOOL TODAY, ALRIGHT?!
DIDN'T "FEEL LIKE" GOING?
HE DIDN'T FEEL LIKE GOING?!
SCHOOL ISN'T THE PARTY YOU THINK IT IS, ALRIGHT?
WELL, YOU'RE NOT SUPPOSED TO BE HAVING A PARTY, YOUNG MAN, YOU'RE SUPPOSED TO BE IN SCHOOL TO LEARN!

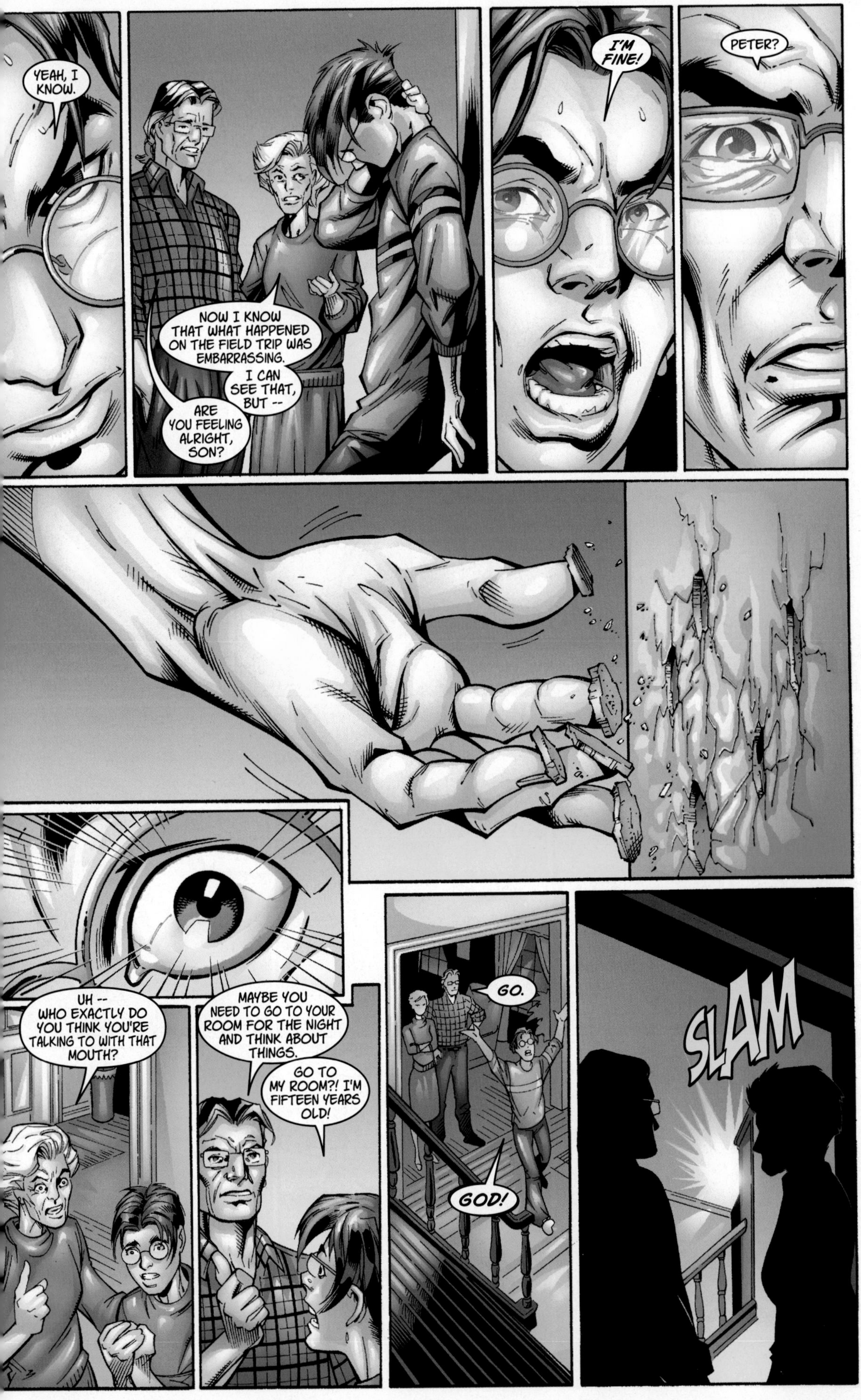
YEAH, I KNOW.
NOW I KNOW THAT WHAT HAPPENED ON THE FIELD TRIP WAS EMBARRASSING.
I CAN SEE THAT, BUT --
ARE YOU FEELING ALRIGHT, SON?
I'M FINE!
PETER?
UH -- WHO EXACTLY DO YOU THINK YOU'RE TALKING TO WITH THAT MOUTH?
MAYBE YOU NEED TO GO TO YOUR ROOM FOR THE NIGHT AND THINK ABOUT THINGS.
GO TO MY ROOM?! I'M FIFTEEN YEARS OLD!
GO.
GOD!
SLAM

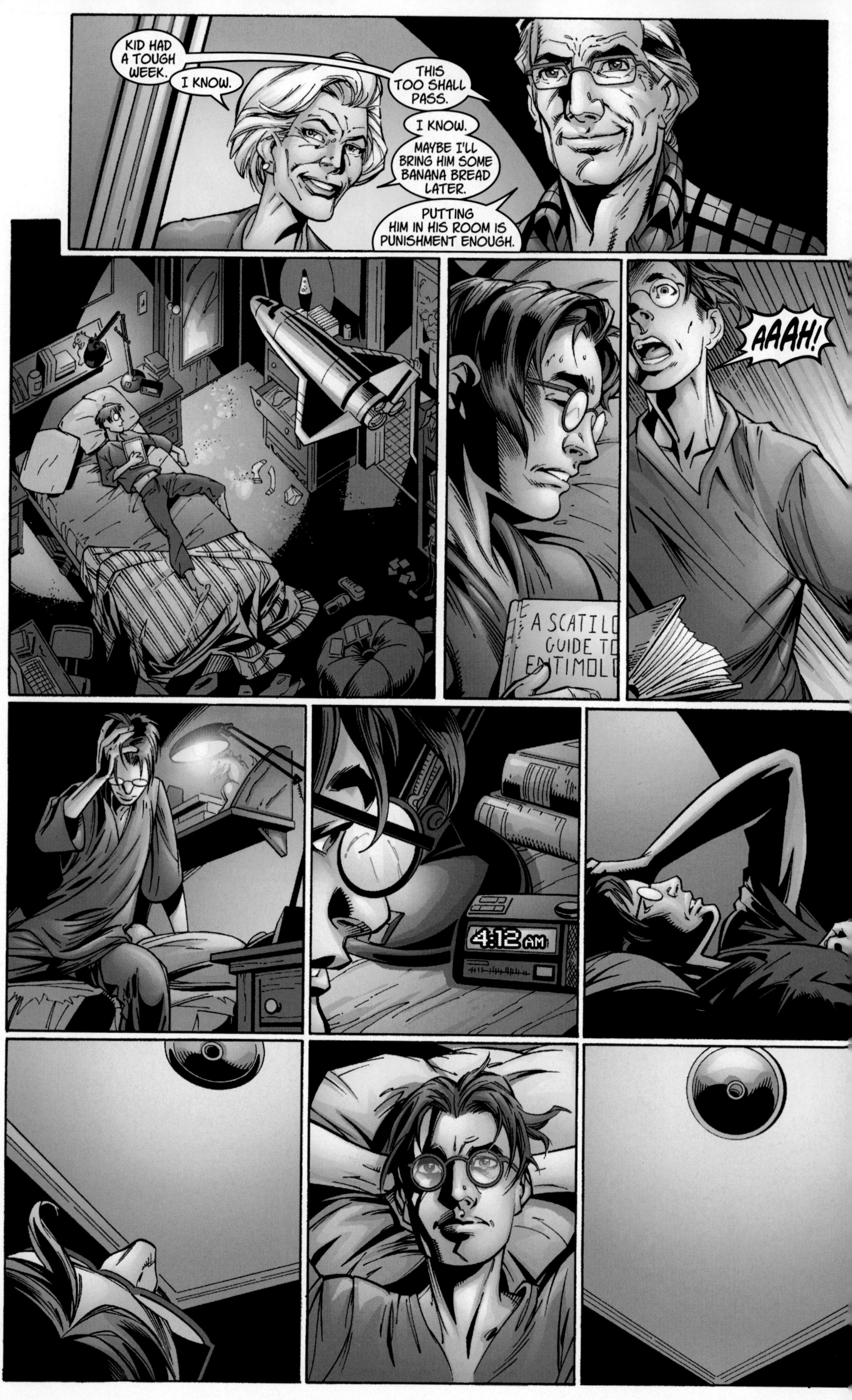
KID HAD A TOUGH WEEK.
I KNOW.
THIS TOO SHALL PASS.
I KNOW.
MAYBE I'LL BRING HIM SOME BANANA BREAD LATER.
PUTTING HIM IN HIS ROOM IS PUNISHMENT ENOUGH.
A SCATILO GUIDE TO ENTIMOLO
AAAH!
4:12 AM

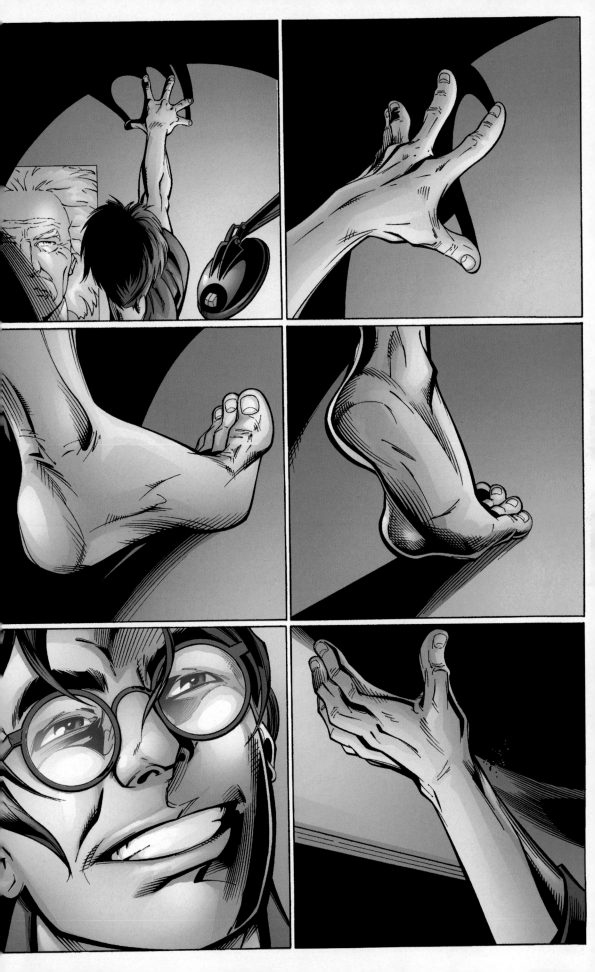

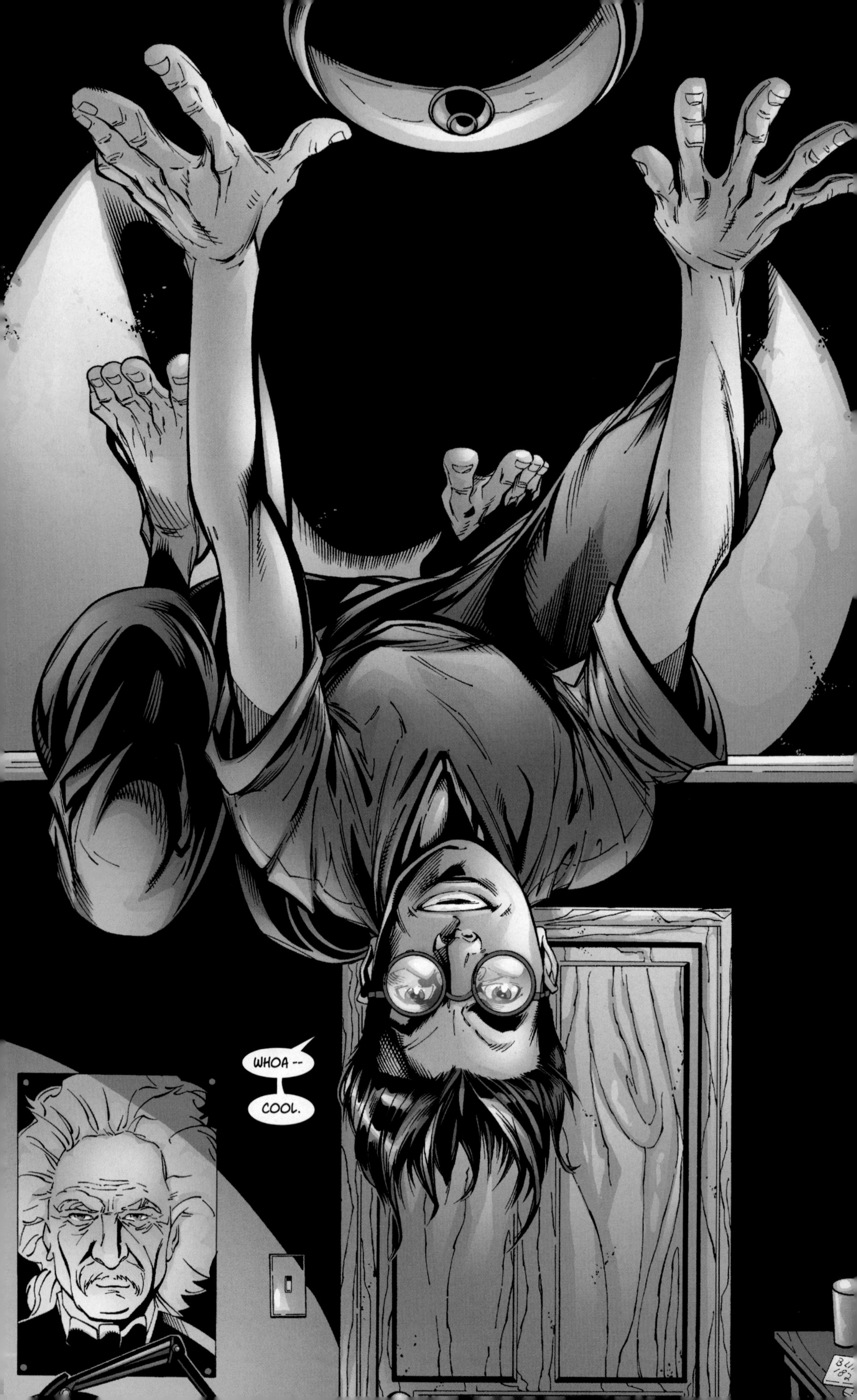
WHOA --
COOL.

2

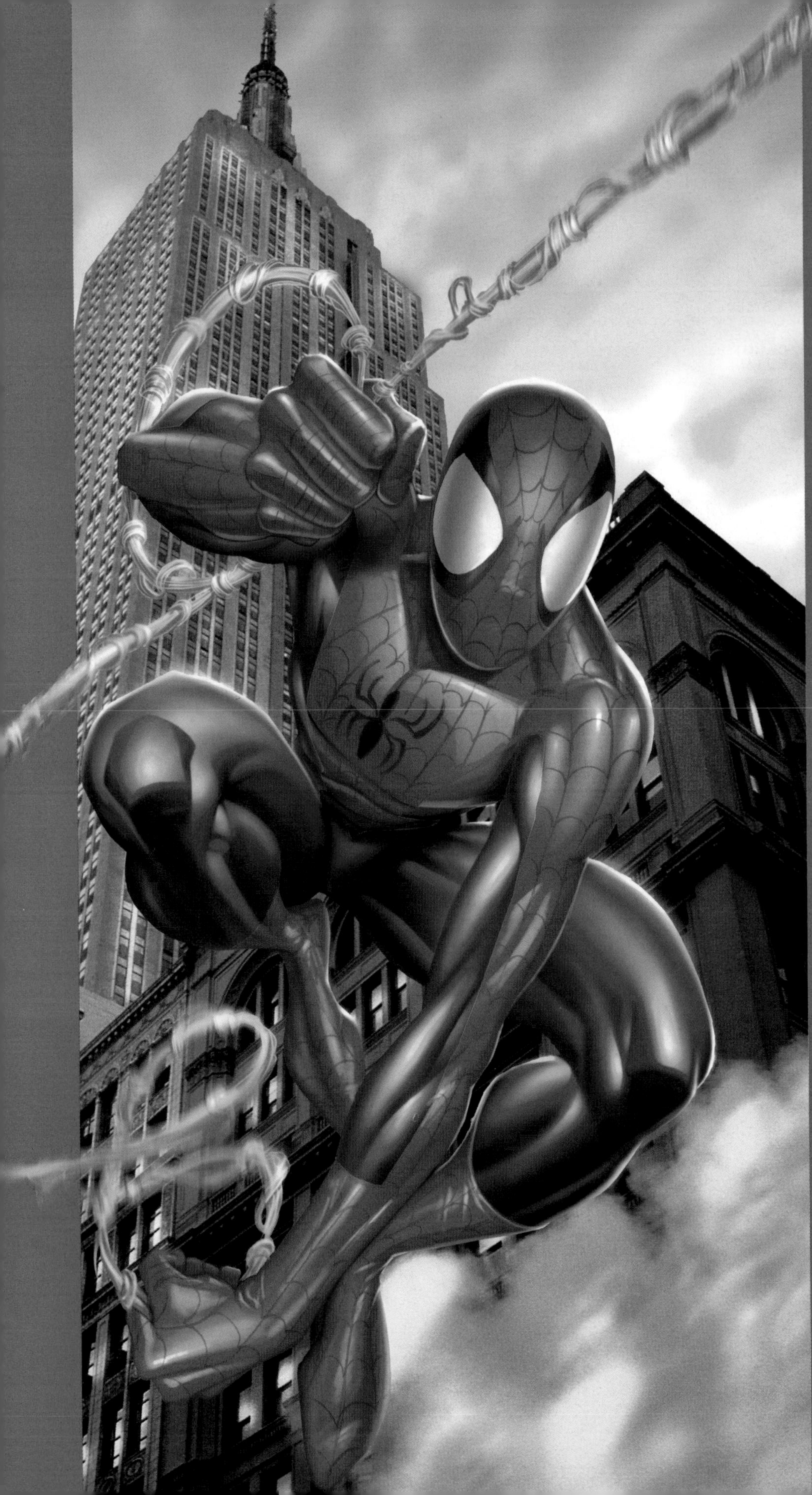

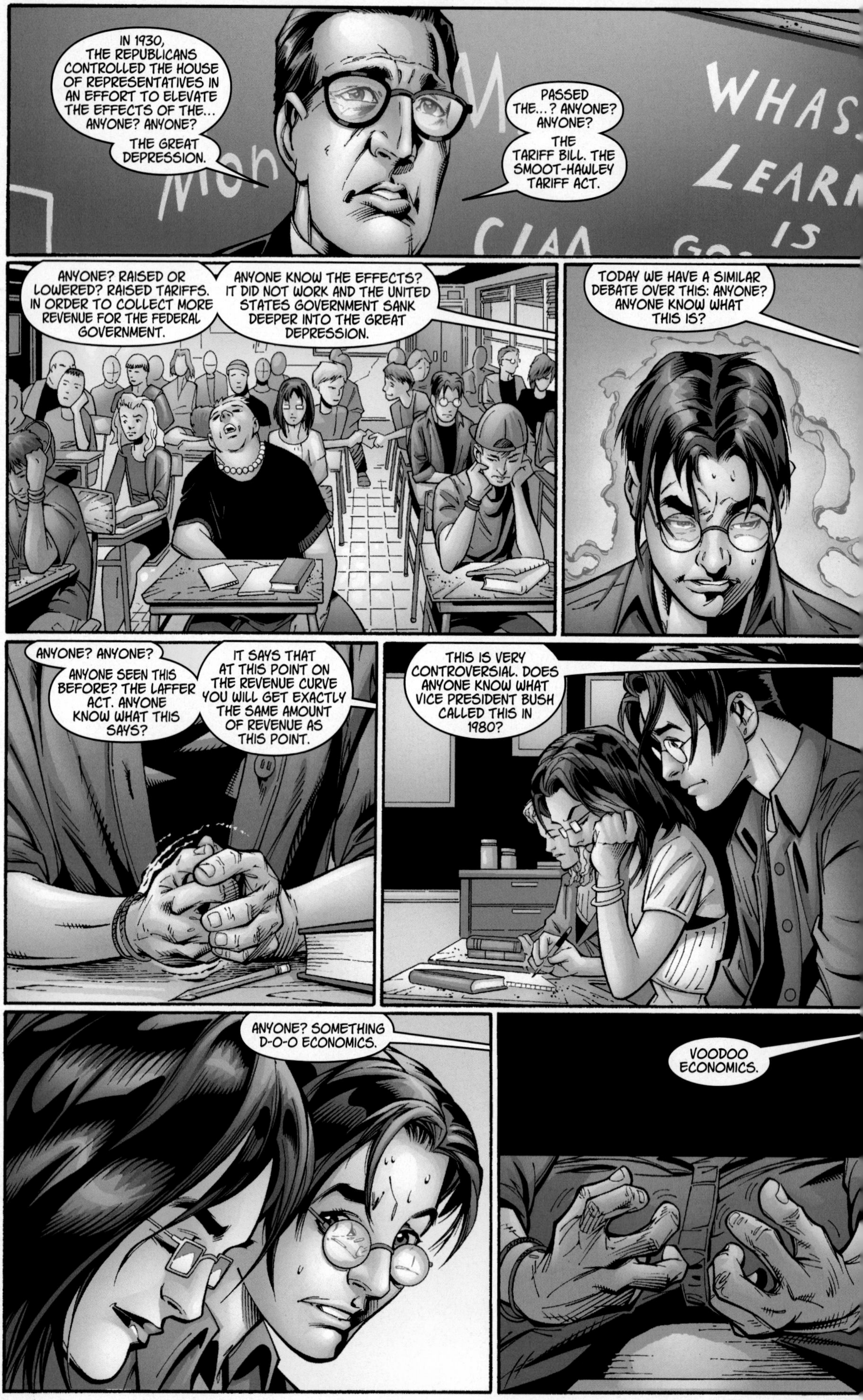
IN 1930, THE REPUBLICANS CONTROLLED THE HOUSE OF REPRESENTATIVES IN AN EFFORT TO ELEVATE THE EFFECTS OF THE... ANYONE? ANYONE?
THE GREAT DEPRESSION.
PASSED THE...? ANYONE? ANYONE?
THE TARIFF BILL. THE SMOOT-HAWLEY TARIFF ACT.
WHASS
LEARN
IS
ANYONE? RAISED OR LOWERED? RAISED TARIFFS. IN ORDER TO COLLECT MORE REVENUE FOR THE FEDERAL GOVERNMENT.
ANYONE KNOW THE EFFECTS? IT DID NOT WORK AND THE UNITED STATES GOVERNMENT SANK DEEPER INTO THE GREAT DEPRESSION.
TODAY WE HAVE A SIMILAR DEBATE OVER THIS: ANYONE? ANYONE KNOW WHAT THIS IS?
ANYONE? ANYONE?
ANYONE SEEN THIS BEFORE? THE LAFFER ACT. ANYONE KNOW WHAT THIS SAYS?
IT SAYS THAT AT THIS POINT ON THE REVENUE CURVE YOU WILL GET EXACTLY THE SAME AMOUNT OF REVENUE AS THIS POINT.
THIS IS VERY CONTROVERSIAL. DOES ANYONE KNOW WHAT VICE PRESIDENT BUSH CALLED THIS IN 1980?
ANYONE? SOMETHING D-O-O ECONOMICS.
VOODOO ECONOMICS.

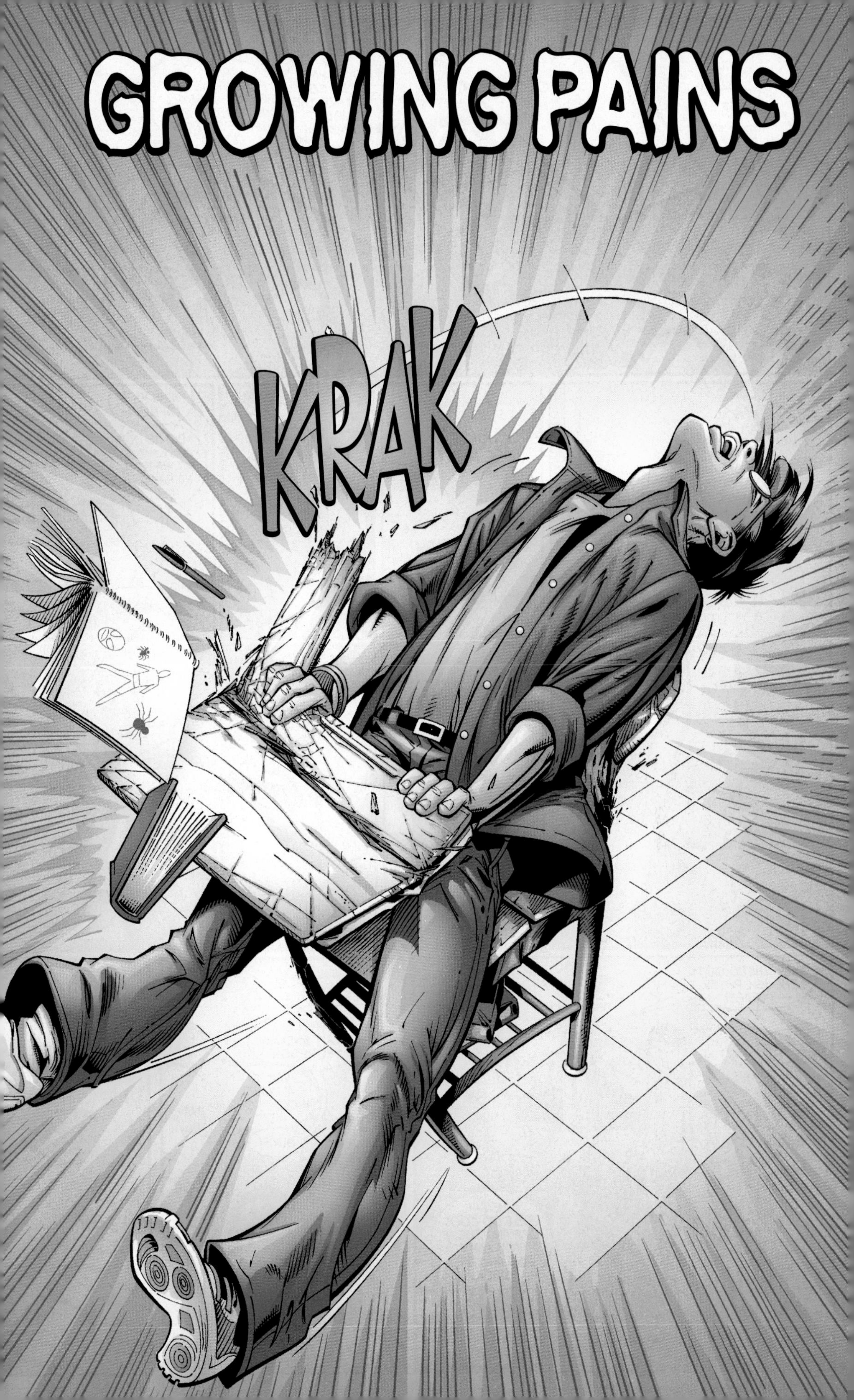
GROWING PAINS
KRAK

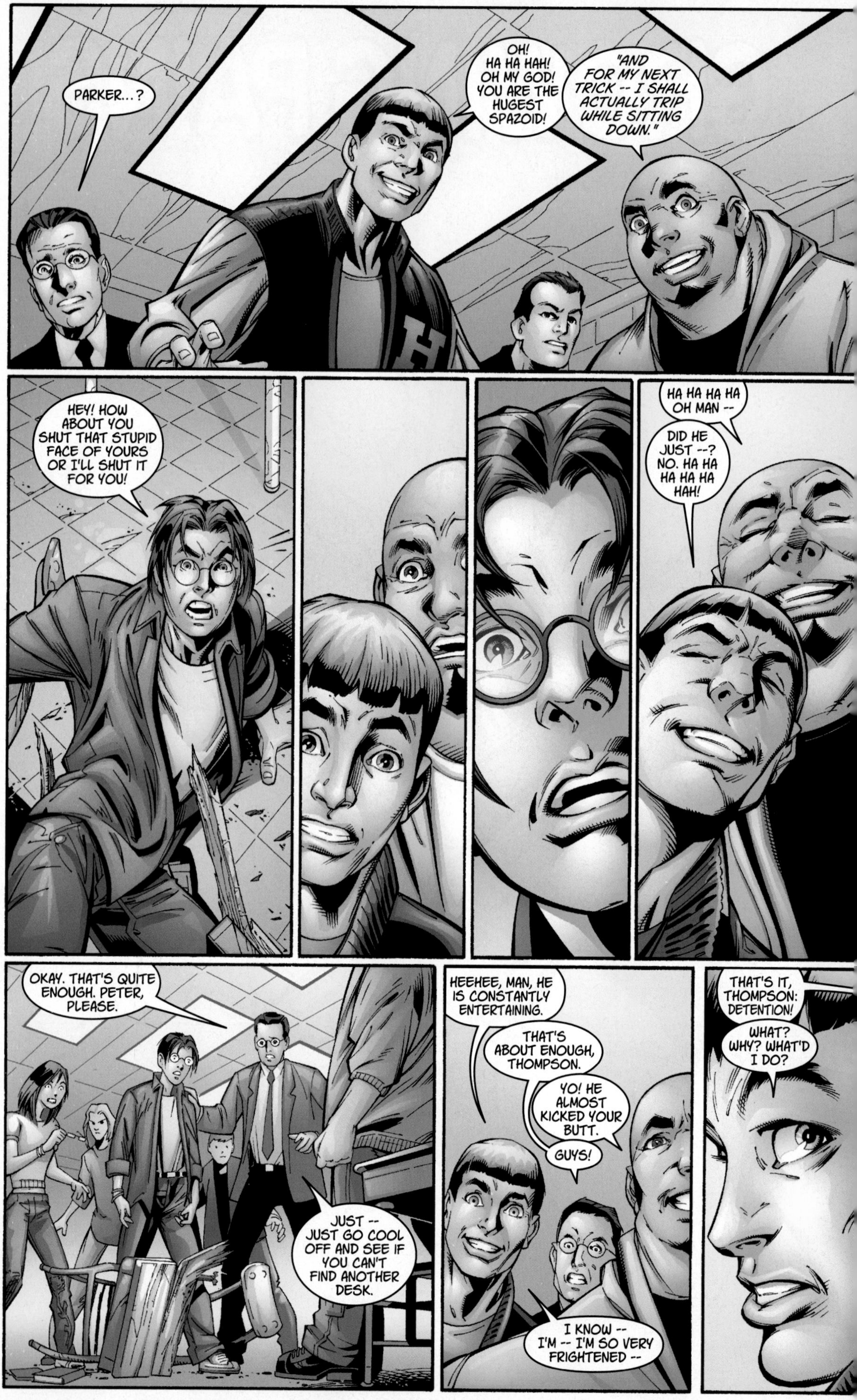
PARKER...?
OH! HA HA HAH! OH MY GOD! YOU ARE THE HUGEST SPAZOID!
"AND FOR MY NEXT TRICK -- I SHALL ACTUALLY TRIP WHILE SITTING DOWN."
HEY! HOW ABOUT YOU SHUT THAT STUPID FACE OF YOURS OR I'LL SHUT IT FOR YOU!
HA HA HA HA OH MAN --
DID HE JUST --? NO. HA HA HA HA HA HAH!
OKAY. THAT'S QUITE ENOUGH. PETER, PLEASE.
JUST -- JUST GO COOL OFF AND SEE IF YOU CAN'T FIND ANOTHER DESK.
HEEHEE, MAN, HE IS CONSTANTLY ENTERTAINING.
THAT'S ABOUT ENOUGH, THOMPSON.
YO! HE ALMOST KICKED YOUR BUTT.
GUYS!
I KNOW -- I'M -- I'M SO VERY FRIGHTENED --
THAT'S IT, THOMPSON: DETENTION!
WHAT? WHY? WHAT'D I DO?

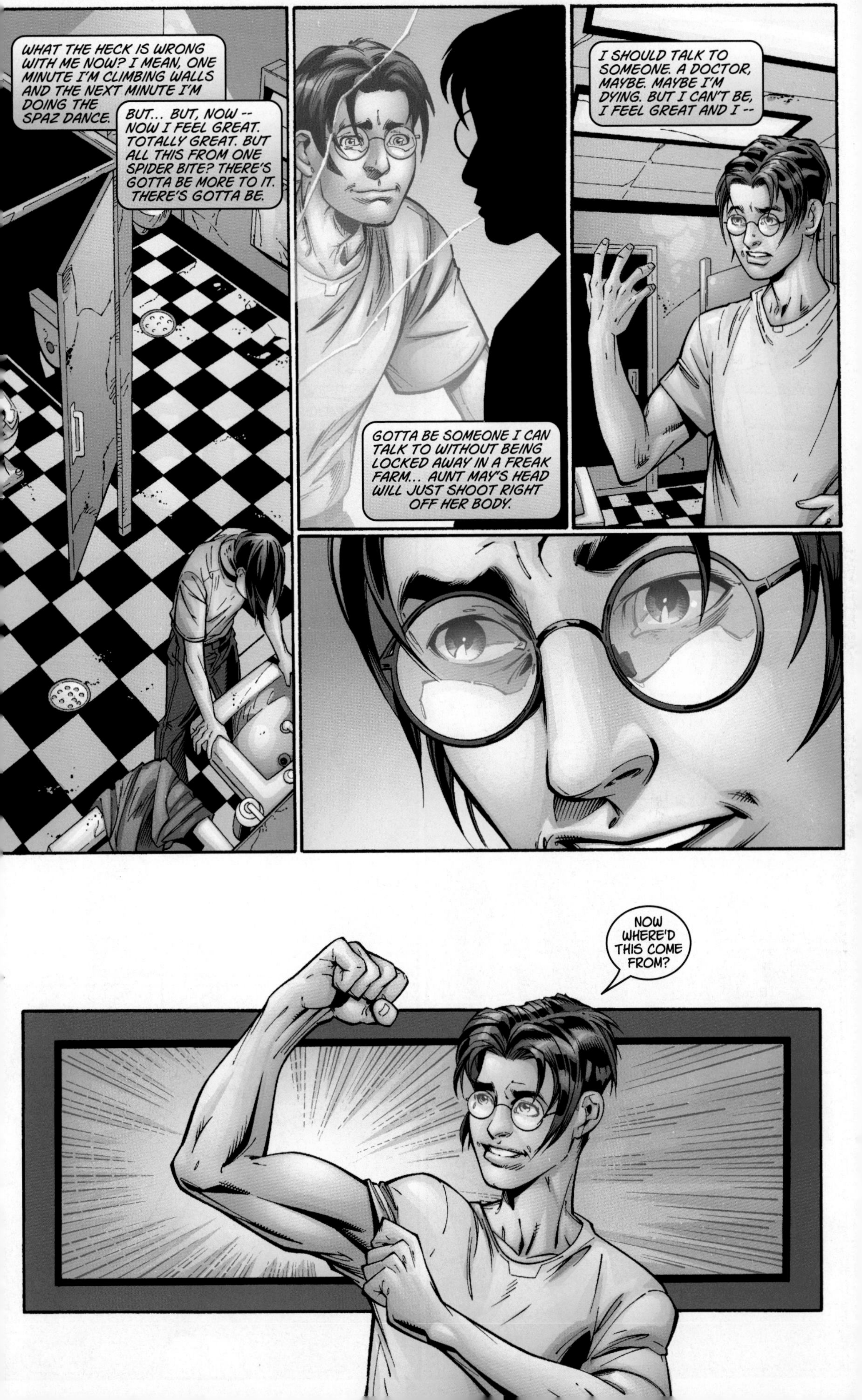
WHAT THE HECK IS WRONG WITH ME NOW? I MEAN, ONE MINUTE I'M CLIMBING WALLS AND THE NEXT MINUTE I'M DOING THE SPAZ DANCE.
BUT... BUT, NOW -- NOW I FEEL GREAT. TOTALLY GREAT. BUT ALL THIS FROM ONE SPIDER BITE? THERE'S GOTTA BE MORE TO IT. THERE'S GOTTA BE.
GOTTA BE SOMEONE I CAN TALK TO WITHOUT BEING LOCKED AWAY IN A FREAK FARM... AUNT MAY'S HEAD WILL JUST SHOOT RIGHT OFF HER BODY.
I SHOULD TALK TO SOMEONE. A DOCTOR, MAYBE. MAYBE I'M DYING. BUT I CAN'T BE, I FEEL GREAT AND I --
NOW WHERE'D THIS COME FROM?

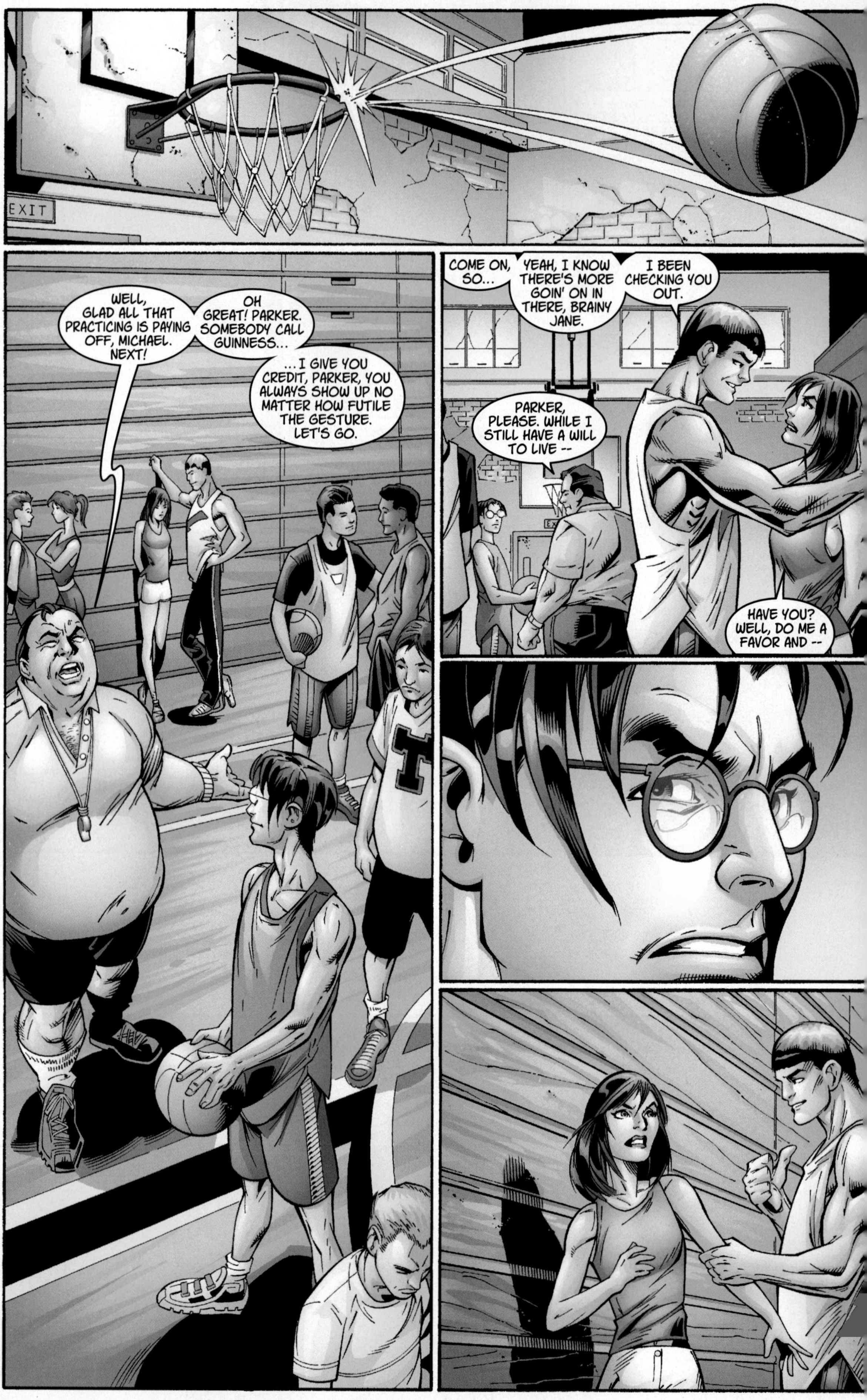
EXIT
WELL, GLAD ALL THAT PRACTICING IS PAYING OFF, MICHAEL. NEXT!
OH GREAT! PARKER. SOMEBODY CALL GUINNESS...
...I GIVE YOU CREDIT, PARKER, YOU ALWAYS SHOW UP NO MATTER HOW FUTILE THE GESTURE. LET'S GO.
COME ON, SO...
YEAH, I KNOW THERE'S MORE GOIN' ON IN THERE, BRAINY JANE.
I BEEN CHECKING YOU OUT.
PARKER, PLEASE. WHILE I STILL HAVE A WILL TO LIVE --
HAVE YOU? WELL, DO ME A FAVOR AND --

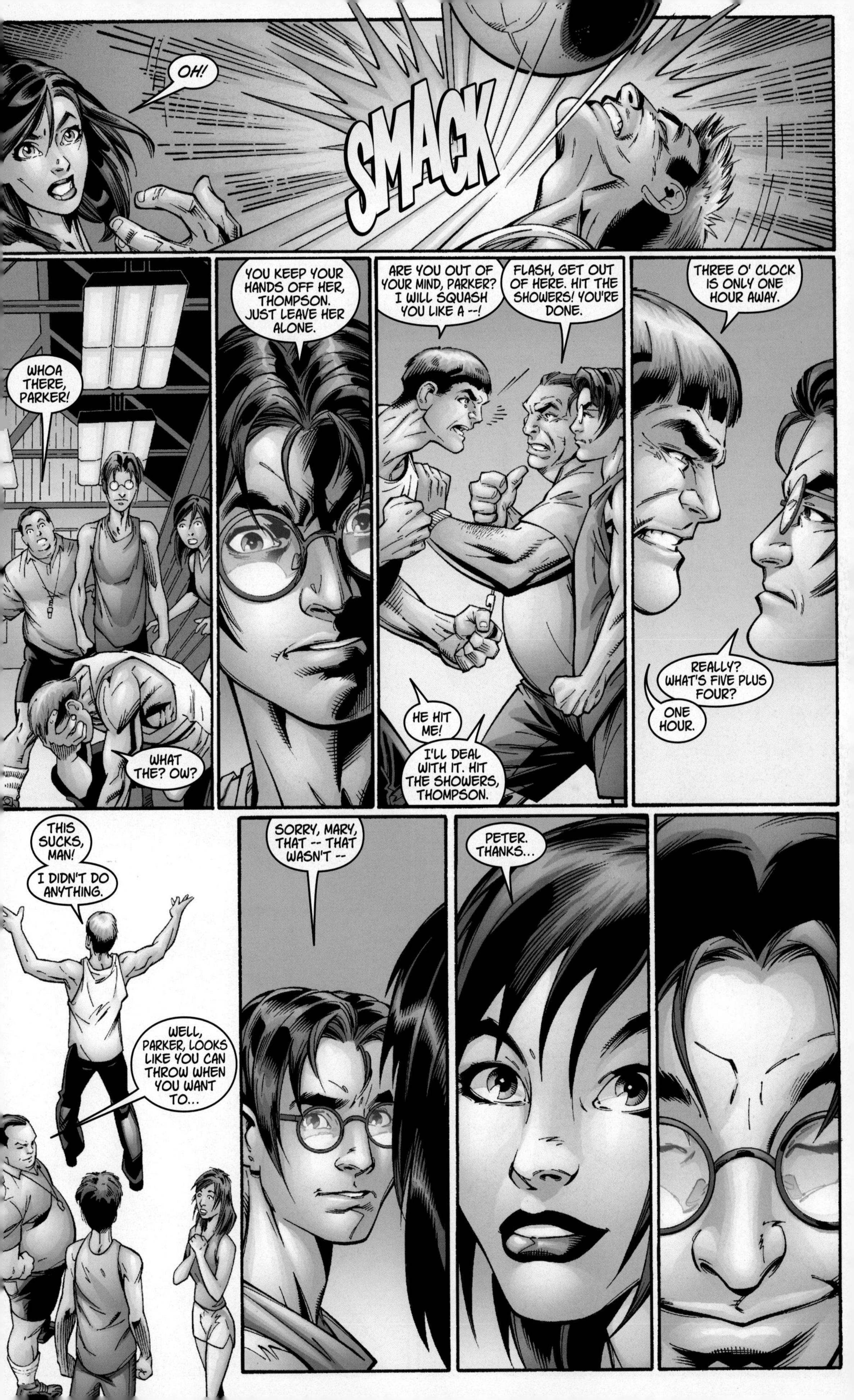
OH!
SMACK
WHOA THERE, PARKER!
WHAT THE? OW?
YOU KEEP YOUR HANDS OFF HER, THOMPSON. JUST LEAVE HER ALONE.
ARE YOU OUT OF YOUR MIND, PARKER? I WILL SQUASH YOU LIKE A --!
FLASH, GET OUT OF HERE. HIT THE SHOWERS! YOU'RE DONE.
HE HIT ME!
I'LL DEAL WITH IT. HIT THE SHOWERS, THOMPSON.
THREE O' CLOCK IS ONLY ONE HOUR AWAY.
REALLY? WHAT'S FIVE PLUS FOUR?
ONE HOUR.
THIS SUCKS, MAN!
I DIDN'T DO ANYTHING.
WELL, PARKER, LOOKS LIKE YOU CAN THROW WHEN YOU WANT TO...
SORRY, MARY, THAT -- THAT WASN'T --
PETER. THANKS...

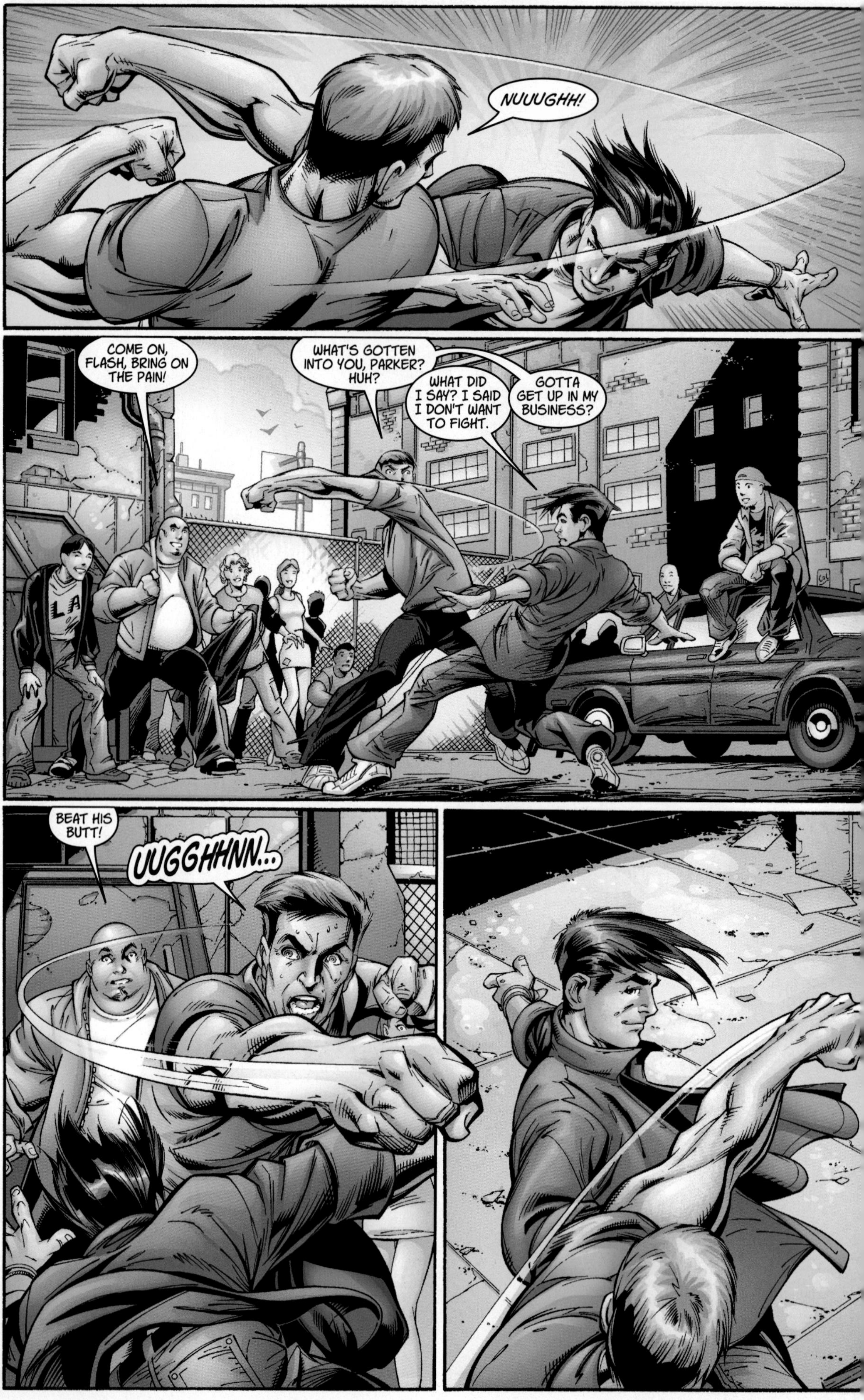
NUUUGHH!
COME ON, FLASH, BRING ON THE PAIN!
WHAT'S GOTTEN INTO YOU, PARKER? HUH?
WHAT DID I SAY? I SAID I DON'T WANT TO FIGHT.
GOTTA GET UP IN MY BUSINESS?
BEAT HIS BUTT!
UUGGHHNN...

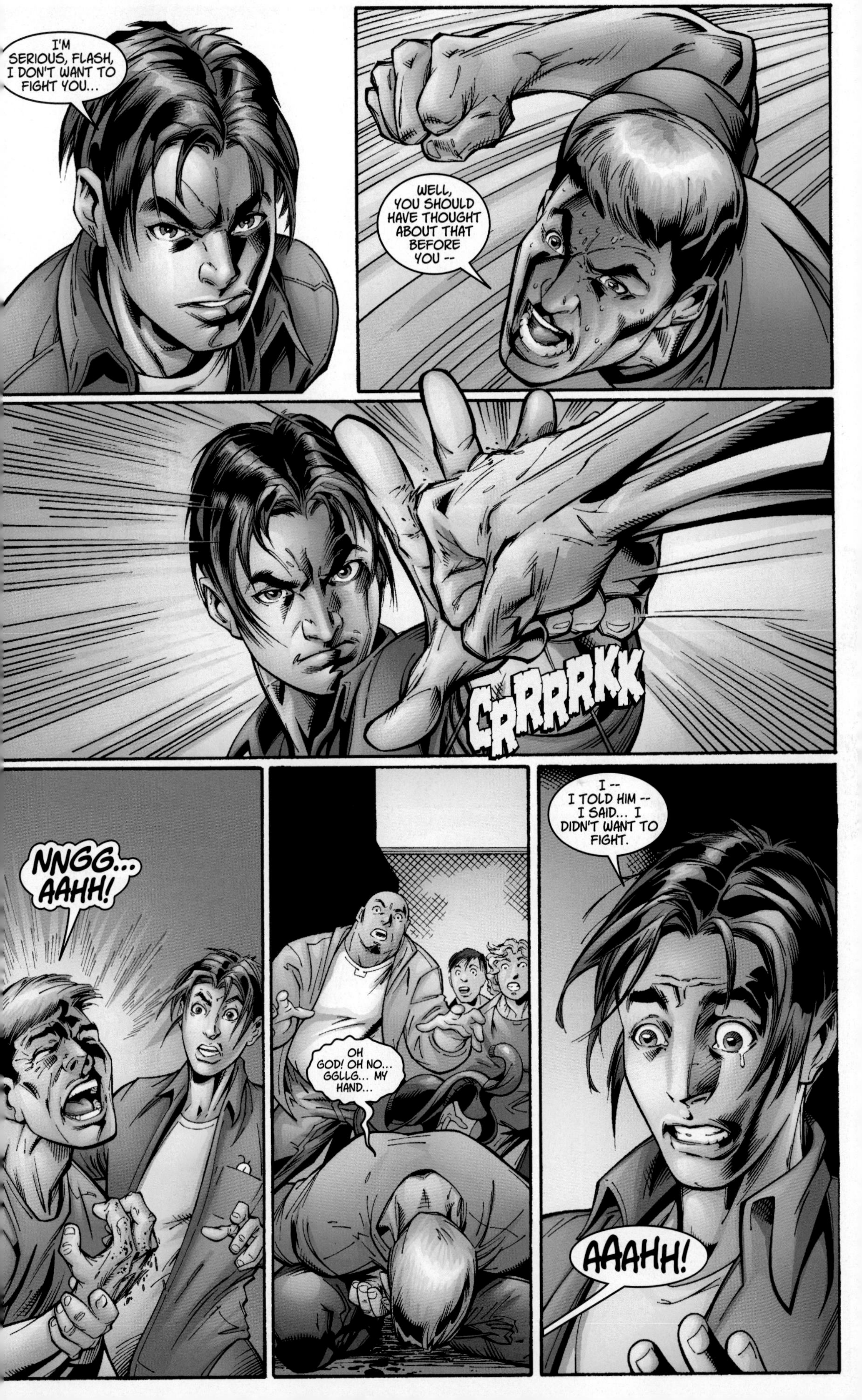
I'M SERIOUS, FLASH, I DON'T WANT TO FIGHT YOU...
WELL, YOU SHOULD HAVE THOUGHT ABOUT THAT BEFORE YOU --
CRRRRKK
NNGG... AAHH!
OH GOD! OH NO... GGLLG... MY HAND...
I -- I TOLD HIM -- I SAID... I DIDN'T WANT TO FIGHT.
AAAHH!

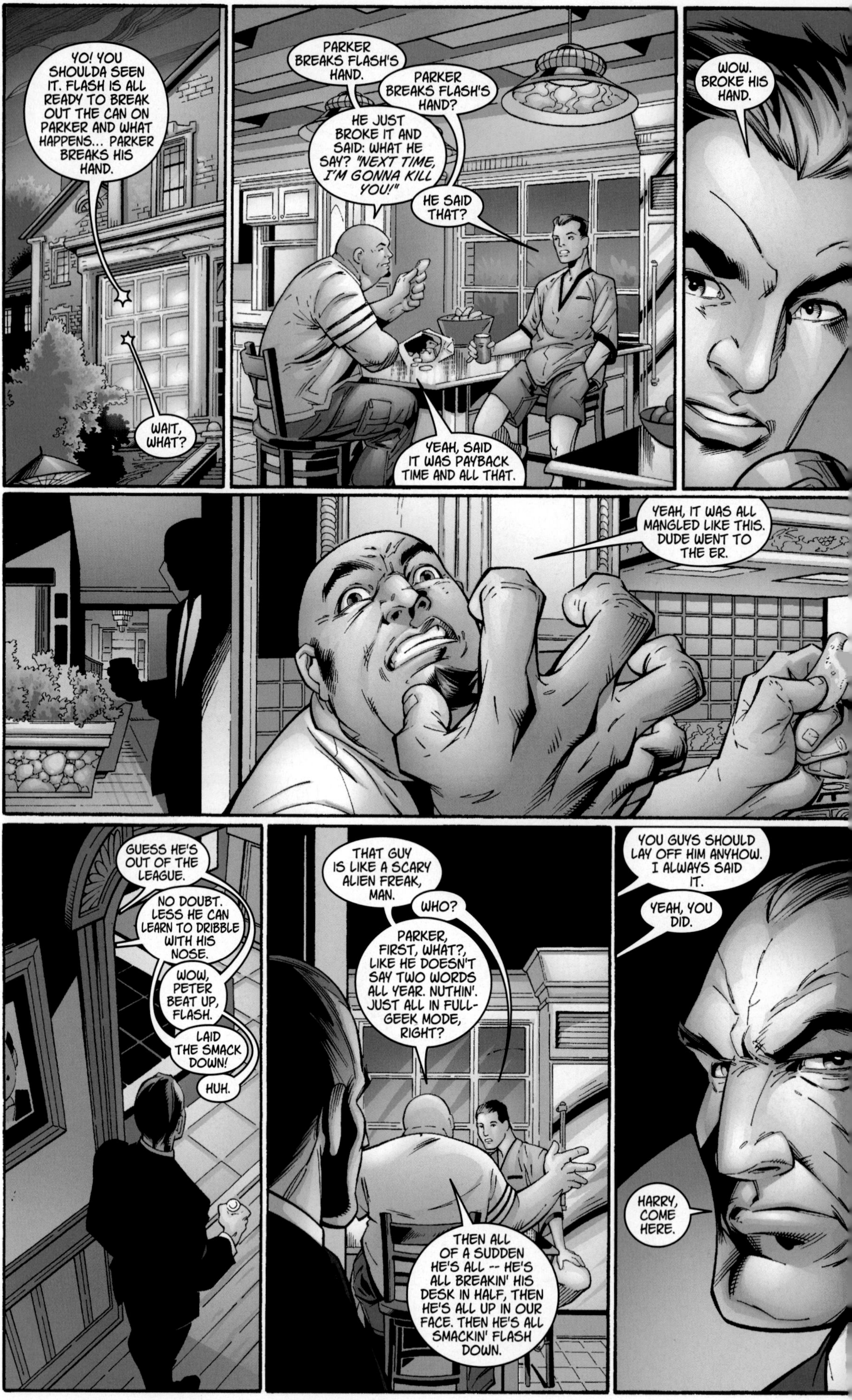
YO! YOU SHOULDA SEEN IT. FLASH IS ALL READY TO BREAK OUT THE CAN ON PARKER AND WHAT HAPPENS... PARKER BREAKS HIS HAND.
WAIT, WHAT?
PARKER BREAKS FLASH'S HAND.
PARKER BREAKS FLASH'S HAND?
HE JUST BROKE IT AND SAID: WHAT HE SAY? "NEXT TIME, I'M GONNA KILL YOU!"
HE SAID THAT?
YEAH, SAID IT WAS PAYBACK TIME AND ALL THAT.
WOW. BROKE HIS HAND.
YEAH, IT WAS ALL MANGLED LIKE THIS. DUDE WENT TO THE ER.
GUESS HE'S OUT OF THE LEAGUE.
NO DOUBT. LESS HE CAN LEARN TO DRIBBLE WITH HIS NOSE.
WOW, PETER BEAT UP, FLASH.
LAID THE SMACK DOWN!
HUH.
THAT GUY IS LIKE A SCARY ALIEN FREAK, MAN.
WHO?
PARKER, FIRST, WHAT?, LIKE HE DOESN'T SAY TWO WORDS ALL YEAR. NUTHIN'. JUST ALL IN FULL-GEEK MODE, RIGHT?
THEN ALL OF A SUDDEN HE'S ALL -- HE'S ALL BREAKIN' HIS DESK IN HALF, THEN HE'S ALL UP IN OUR FACE. THEN HE'S ALL SMACKIN' FLASH DOWN.
YOU GUYS SHOULD LAY OFF HIM ANYHOW. I ALWAYS SAID IT.
YEAH, YOU DID.
HARRY, COME HERE.

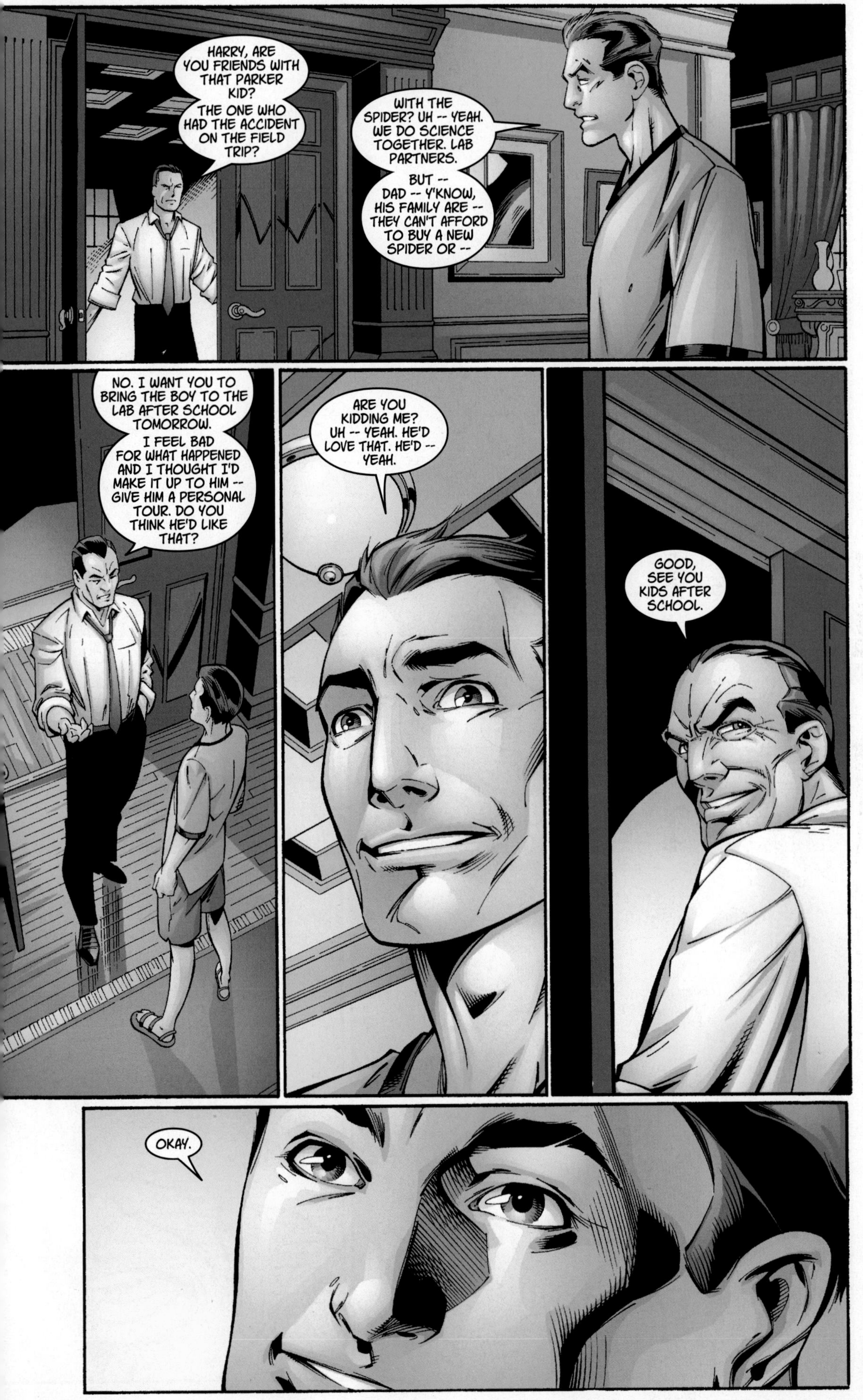
HARRY, ARE YOU FRIENDS WITH THAT PARKER KID?
THE ONE WHO HAD THE ACCIDENT ON THE FIELD TRIP?
WITH THE SPIDER? UH -- YEAH. WE DO SCIENCE TOGETHER. LAB PARTNERS.
BUT -- DAD -- Y'KNOW, HIS FAMILY ARE -- THEY CAN'T AFFORD TO BUY A NEW SPIDER OR --
NO. I WANT YOU TO BRING THE BOY TO THE LAB AFTER SCHOOL TOMORROW.
I FEEL BAD FOR WHAT HAPPENED AND I THOUGHT I'D MAKE IT UP TO HIM -- GIVE HIM A PERSONAL TOUR. DO YOU THINK HE'D LIKE THAT?
ARE YOU KIDDING ME? UH -- YEAH. HE'D LOVE THAT. HE'D -- YEAH.
GOOD, SEE YOU KIDS AFTER SCHOOL.
OKAY.

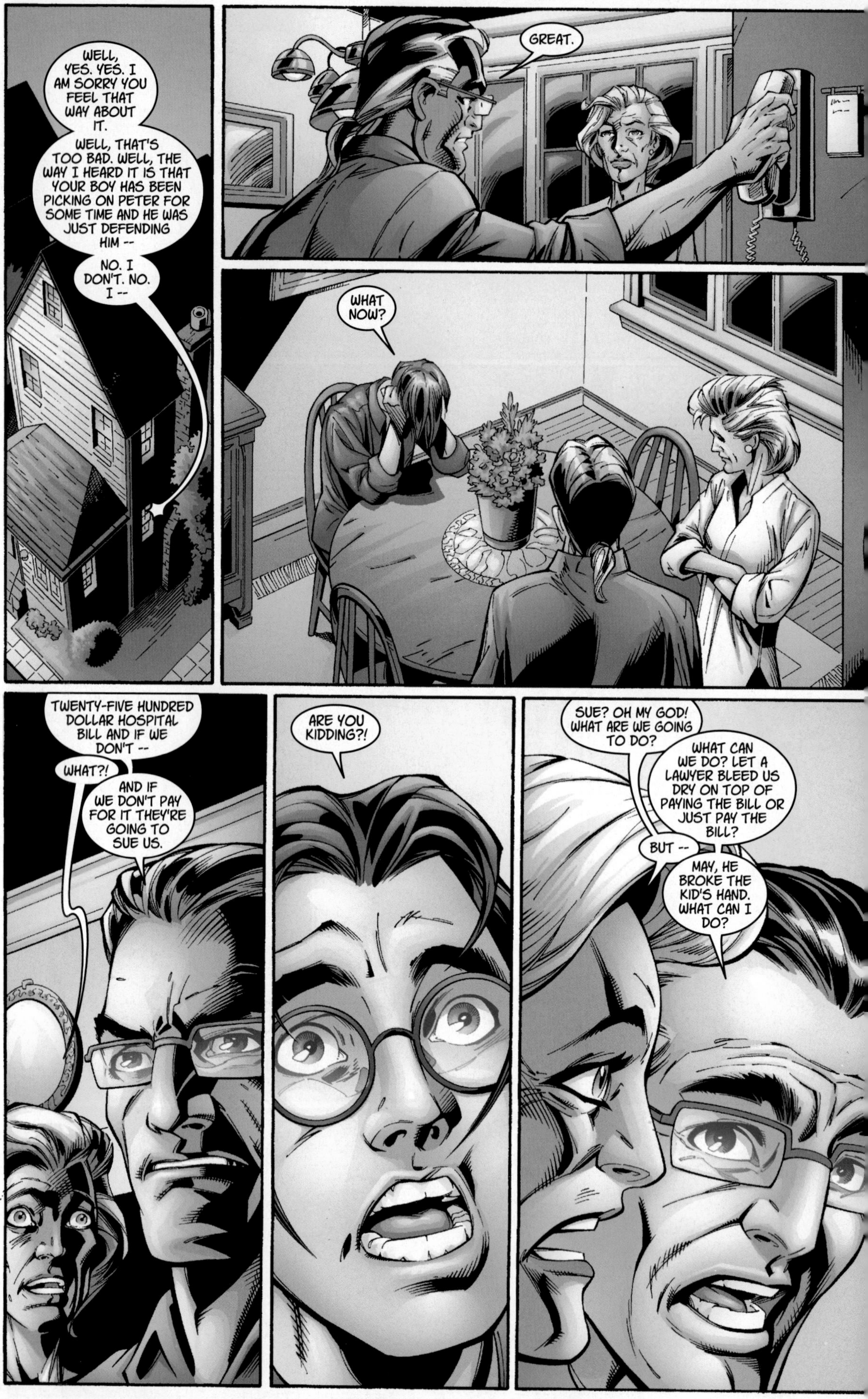
WELL, YES. YES. I AM SORRY YOU FEEL THAT WAY ABOUT IT.
WELL, THAT'S TOO BAD. WELL, THE WAY I HEARD IT IS THAT YOUR BOY HAS BEEN PICKING ON PETER FOR SOME TIME AND HE WAS JUST DEFENDING HIM --
NO. I DON'T. NO. I --
GREAT.
WHAT NOW?
TWENTY-FIVE HUNDRED DOLLAR HOSPITAL BILL AND IF WE DON'T --
WHAT?!
AND IF WE DON'T PAY FOR IT THEY'RE GOING TO SUE US.
ARE YOU KIDDING?!
SUE? OH MY GOD! WHAT ARE WE GOING TO DO?
WHAT CAN WE DO? LET A LAWYER BLEED US DRY ON TOP OF PAYING THE BILL OR JUST PAY THE BILL?
BUT --
MAY, HE BROKE THE KID'S HAND. WHAT CAN I DO?

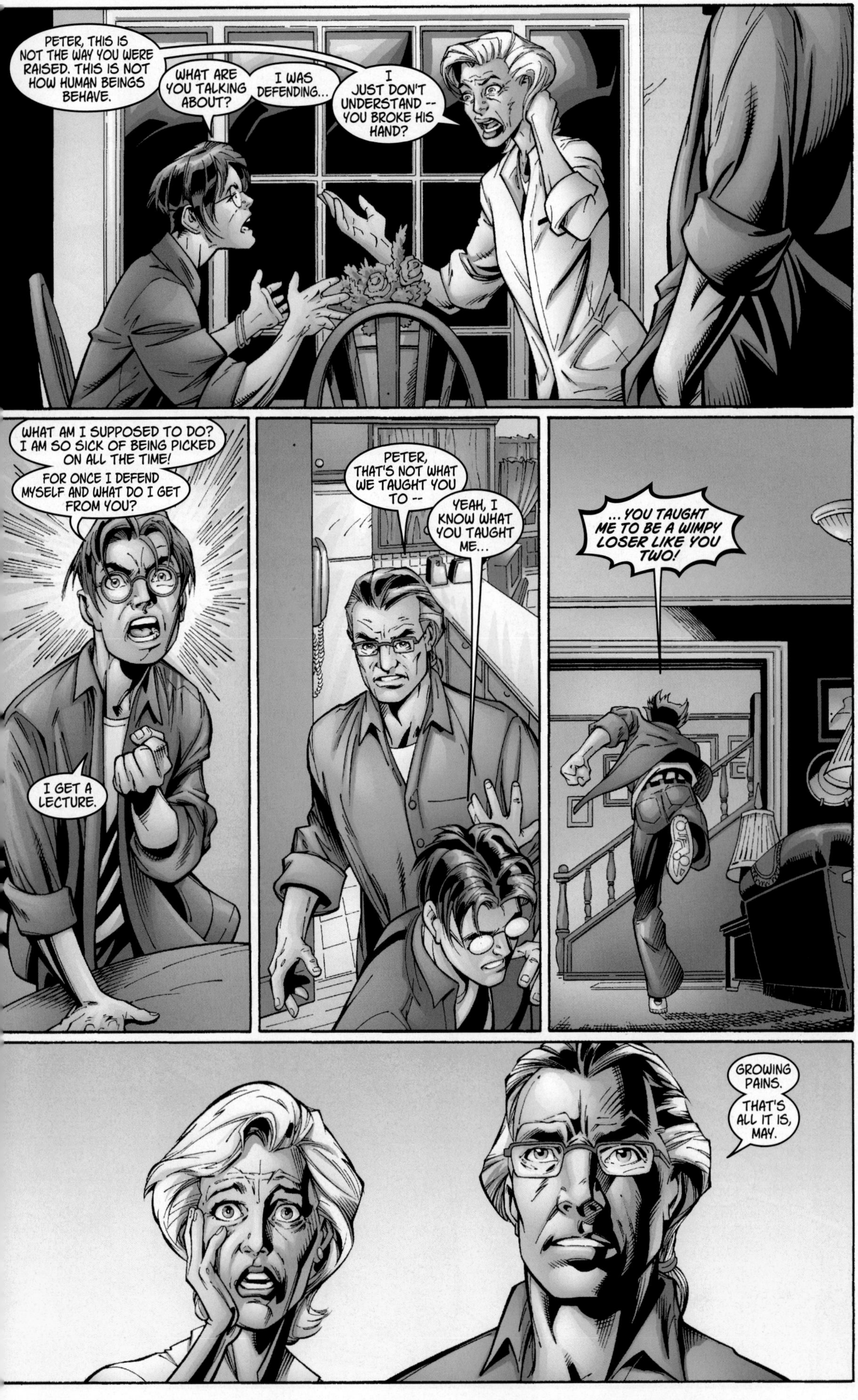
PETER, THIS IS NOT THE WAY YOU WERE RAISED. THIS IS NOT HOW HUMAN BEINGS BEHAVE.
WHAT ARE YOU TALKING ABOUT?
I WAS DEFENDING...
I JUST DON'T UNDERSTAND -- YOU BROKE HIS HAND?
WHAT AM I SUPPOSED TO DO? I AM SO SICK OF BEING PICKED ON ALL THE TIME!
FOR ONCE I DEFEND MYSELF AND WHAT DO I GET FROM YOU?
I GET A LECTURE.
PETER, THAT'S NOT WHAT WE TAUGHT YOU TO --
YEAH, I KNOW WHAT YOU TAUGHT ME...
...YOU TAUGHT ME TO BE A WIMPY LOSER LIKE YOU TWO!
GROWING PAINS.
THAT'S ALL IT IS, MAY.

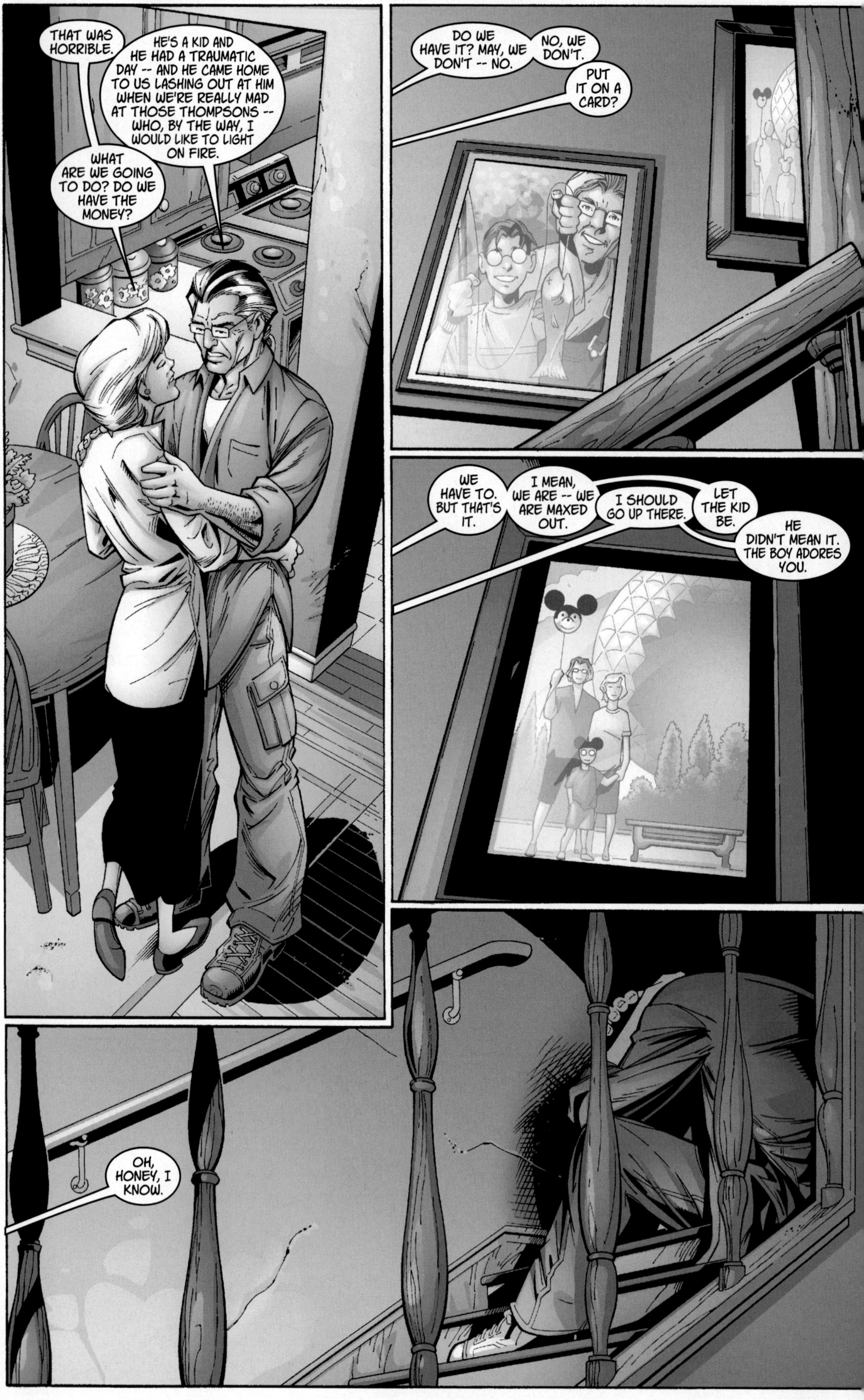
THAT WAS HORRIBLE.
HE'S A KID AND HE HAD A TRAUMATIC DAY -- AND HE CAME HOME TO US LASHING OUT AT HIM WHEN WE'RE REALLY MAD AT THOSE THOMPSONS -- WHO, BY THE WAY, I WOULD LIKE TO LIGHT ON FIRE.
WHAT ARE WE GOING TO DO? DO WE HAVE THE MONEY?
DO WE HAVE IT? MAY, WE DON'T -- NO.
NO, WE DON'T.
PUT IT ON A CARD?
WE HAVE TO. BUT THAT'S IT.
I MEAN, WE ARE -- WE ARE MAXED OUT.
I SHOULD GO UP THERE.
LET THE KID BE.
HE DIDN'T MEAN IT. THE BOY ADORES YOU.
OH, HONEY, I KNOW.

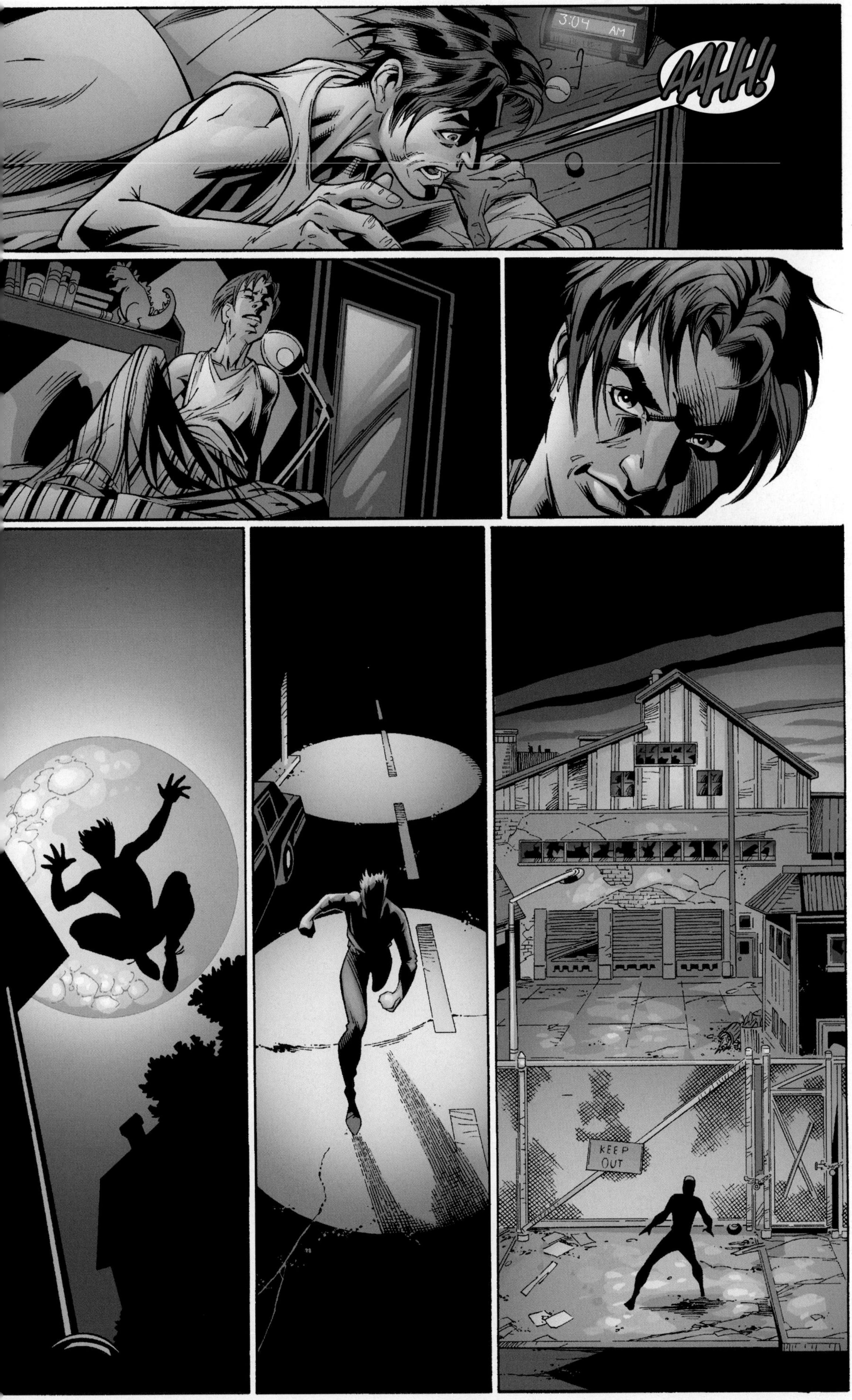
3:04 AM
AAHH!
KEEP OUT

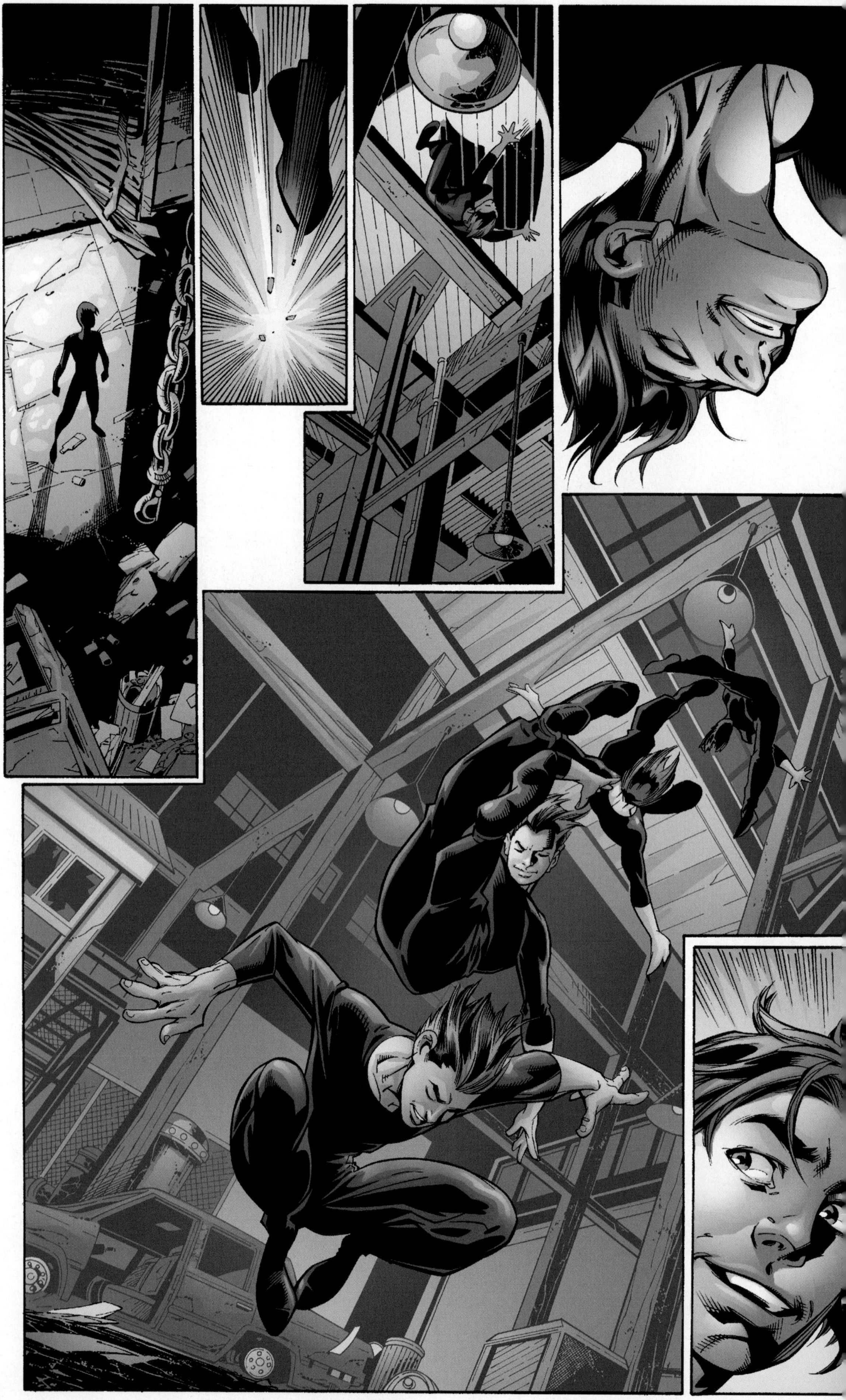

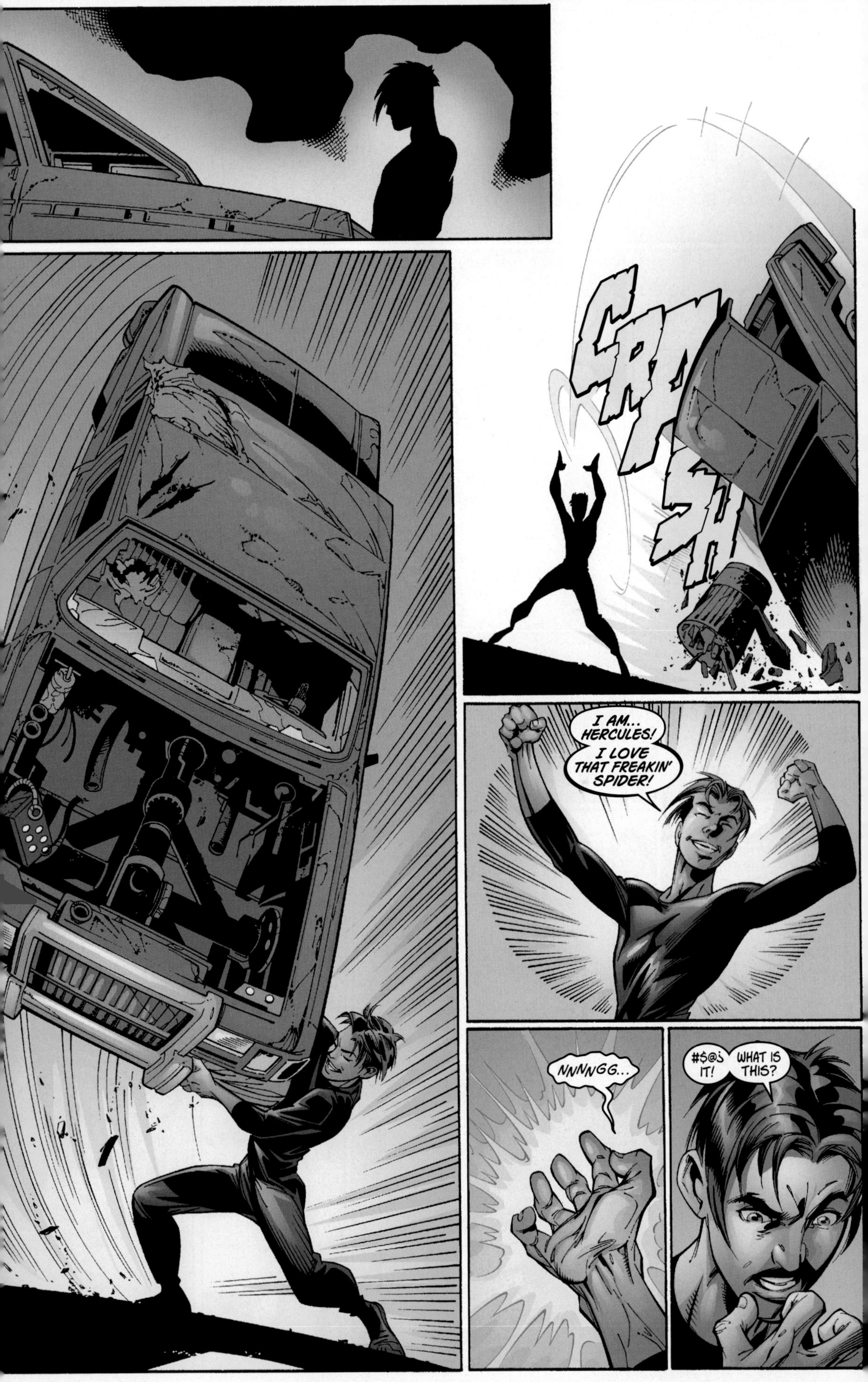
CRASH
I AM... HERCULES! I LOVE THAT FREAKIN' SPIDER!
NNNNGG...
#$@¿ IT!
WHAT IS THIS?

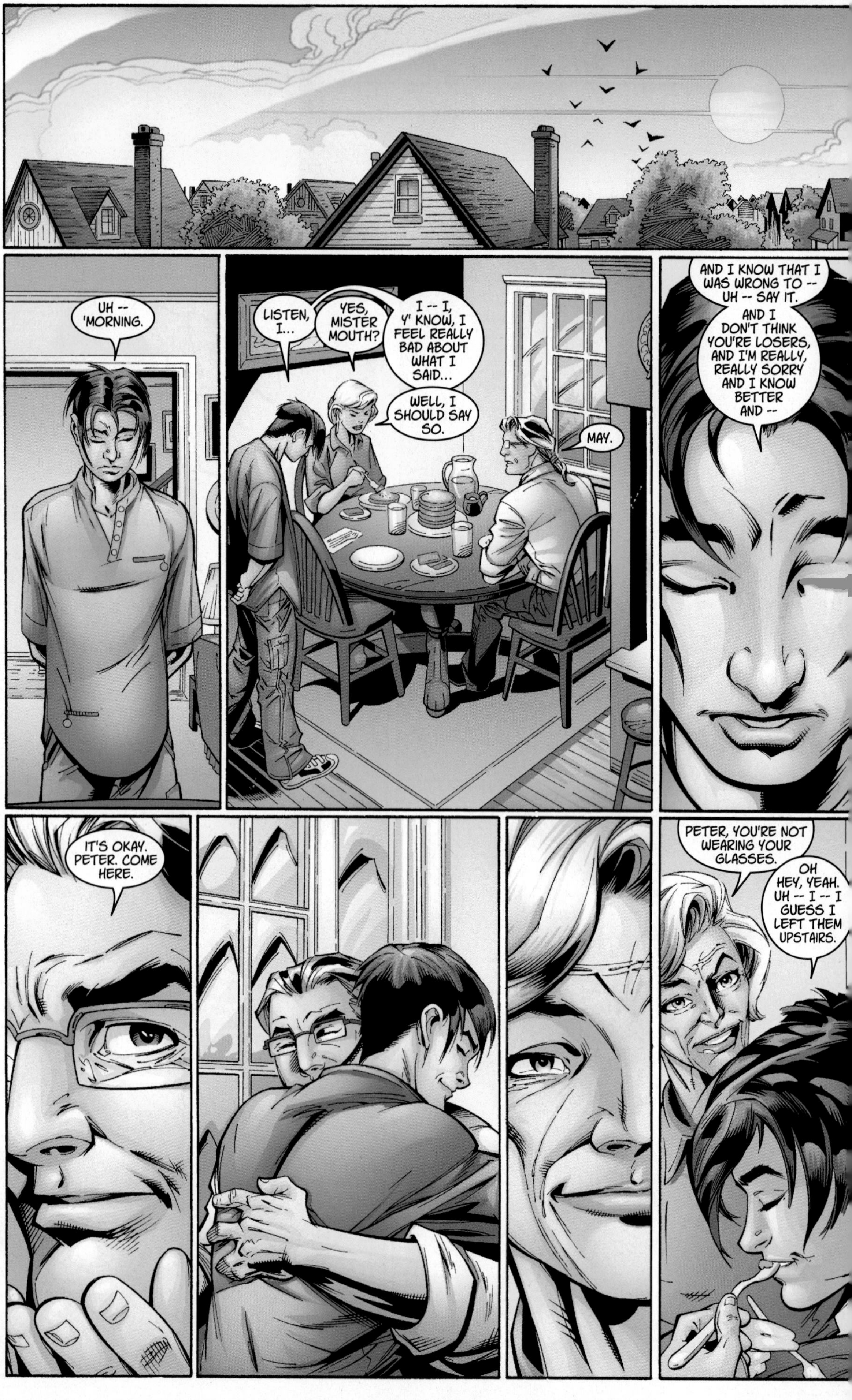
UH -- 'MORNING.
LISTEN, I...
YES, MISTER MOUTH?
I -- I, Y' KNOW, I FEEL REALLY BAD ABOUT WHAT I SAID...
WELL, I SHOULD SAY SO.
MAY.
AND I KNOW THAT I WAS WRONG TO -- UH -- SAY IT.
AND I DON'T THINK YOU'RE LOSERS, AND I'M REALLY, REALLY SORRY AND I KNOW BETTER AND --
IT'S OKAY. PETER. COME HERE.
PETER, YOU'RE NOT WEARING YOUR GLASSES.
OH HEY, YEAH. UH -- I -- I GUESS I LEFT THEM UPSTAIRS.

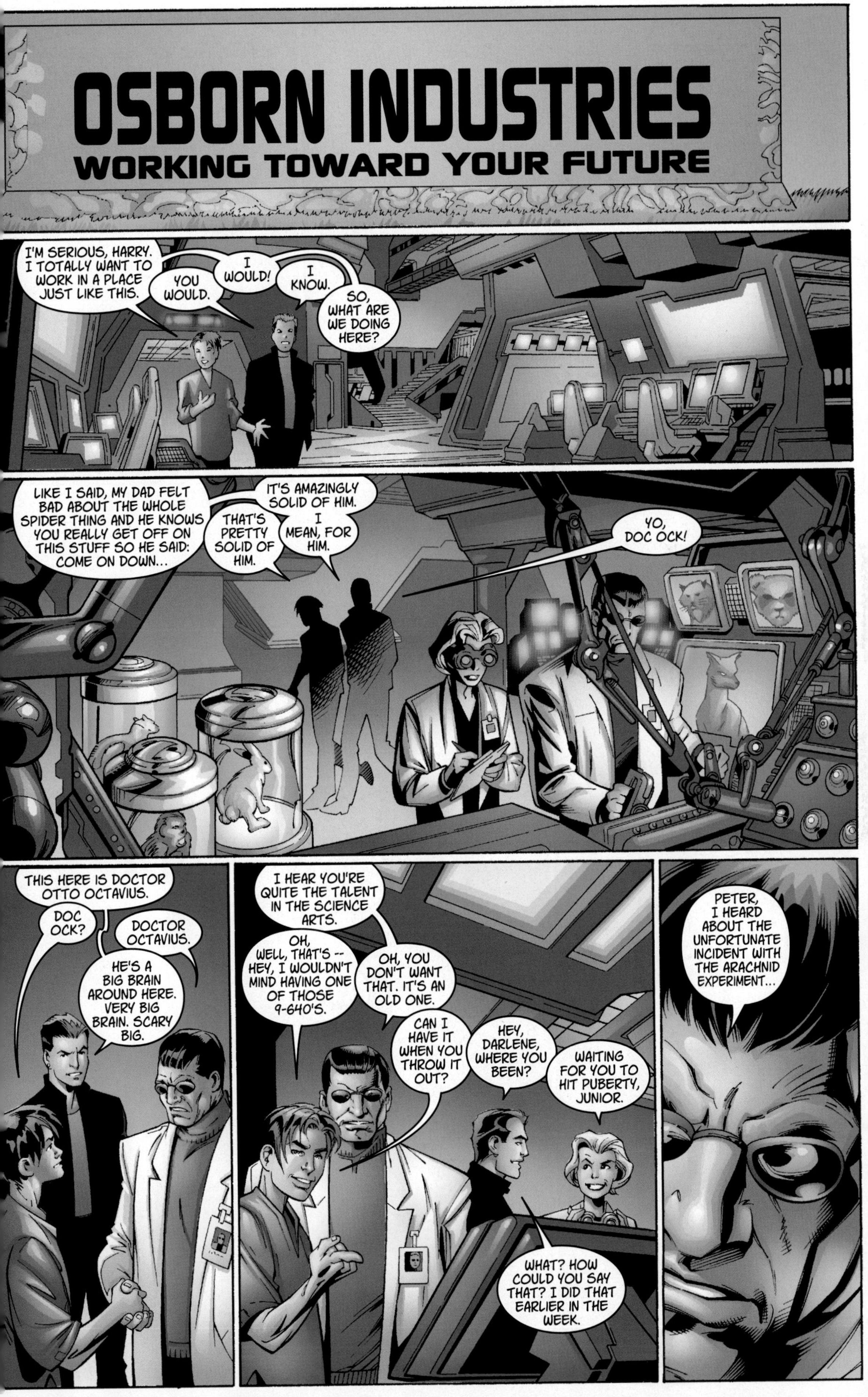
OSBORN INDUSTRIES
WORKING TOWARD YOUR FUTURE
I'M SERIOUS, HARRY. I TOTALLY WANT TO WORK IN A PLACE JUST LIKE THIS.
YOU WOULD.
I WOULD!
I KNOW.
SO, WHAT ARE WE DOING HERE?
LIKE I SAID, MY DAD FELT BAD ABOUT THE WHOLE SPIDER THING AND HE KNOWS YOU REALLY GET OFF ON THIS STUFF SO HE SAID: COME ON DOWN...
THAT'S PRETTY SOLID OF HIM.
IT'S AMAZINGLY SOLID OF HIM.
I MEAN, FOR HIM.
YO, DOC OCK!
THIS HERE IS DOCTOR OTTO OCTAVIUS.
DOC OCK?
DOCTOR OCTAVIUS.
HE'S A BIG BRAIN AROUND HERE. VERY BIG BRAIN. SCARY BIG.
I HEAR YOU'RE QUITE THE TALENT IN THE SCIENCE ARTS.
OH, WELL, THAT'S -- HEY, I WOULDN'T MIND HAVING ONE OF THOSE 9-640'S.
OH, YOU DON'T WANT THAT. IT'S AN OLD ONE.
CAN I HAVE IT WHEN YOU THROW IT OUT?
HEY, DARLENE, WHERE YOU BEEN?
WAITING FOR YOU TO HIT PUBERTY, JUNIOR.
WHAT? HOW COULD YOU SAY THAT? I DID THAT EARLIER IN THE WEEK.
PETER, I HEARD ABOUT THE UNFORTUNATE INCIDENT WITH THE ARACHNID EXPERIMENT...

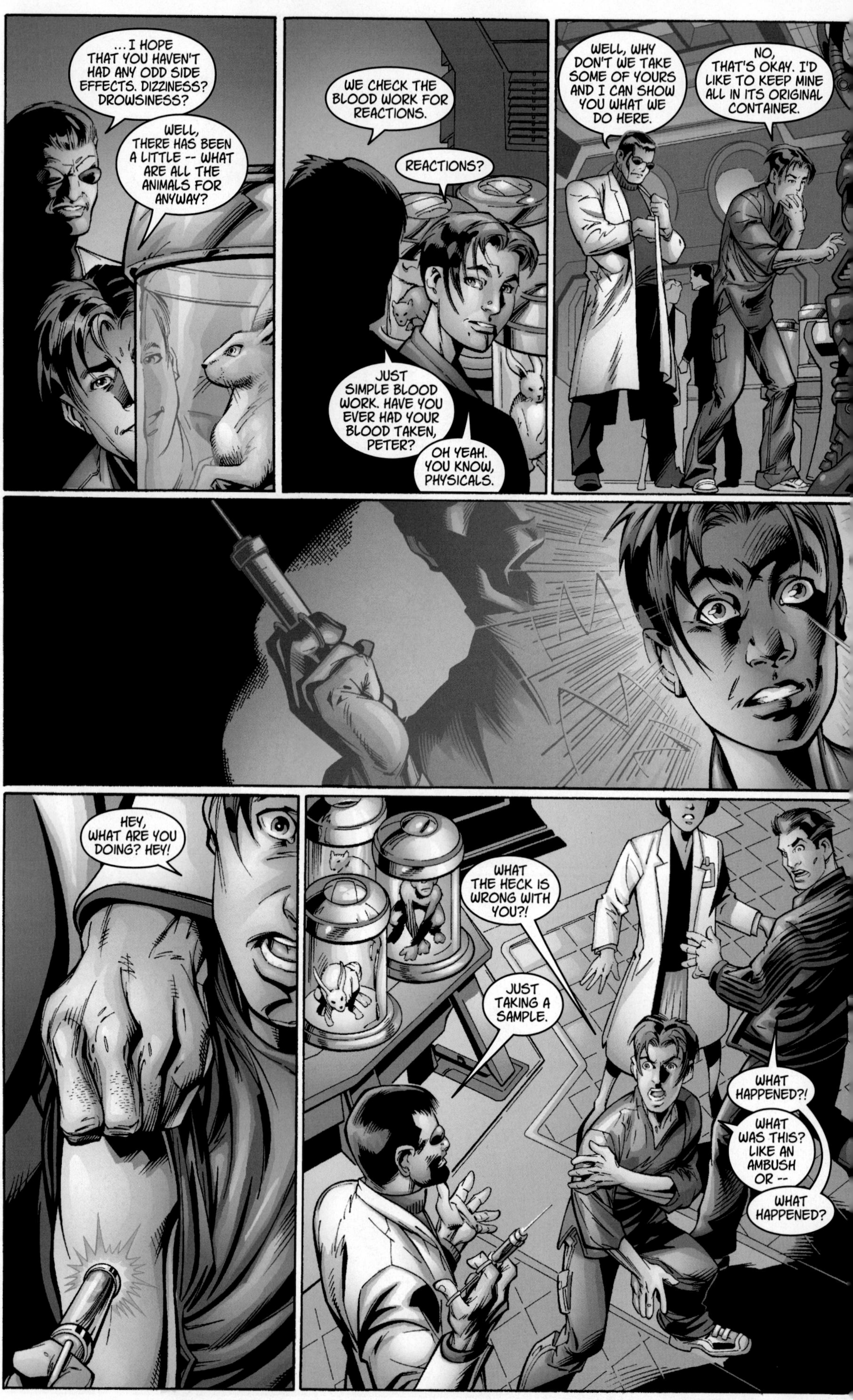
...I HOPE THAT YOU HAVEN'T HAD ANY ODD SIDE EFFECTS. DIZZINESS? DROWSINESS?
WELL, THERE HAS BEEN A LITTLE -- WHAT ARE ALL THE ANIMALS FOR ANYWAY?
WE CHECK THE BLOOD WORK FOR REACTIONS.
REACTIONS?
JUST SIMPLE BLOOD WORK. HAVE YOU EVER HAD YOUR BLOOD TAKEN, PETER?
OH YEAH. YOU KNOW, PHYSICALS.
WELL, WHY DON'T WE TAKE SOME OF YOURS AND I CAN SHOW YOU WHAT WE DO HERE.
NO, THAT'S OKAY. I'D LIKE TO KEEP MINE ALL IN ITS ORIGINAL CONTAINER.
HEY, WHAT ARE YOU DOING? HEY!
WHAT THE HECK IS WRONG WITH YOU?!
JUST TAKING A SAMPLE.
WHAT HAPPENED?!
WHAT WAS THIS? LIKE AN AMBUSH OR --
WHAT HAPPENED?

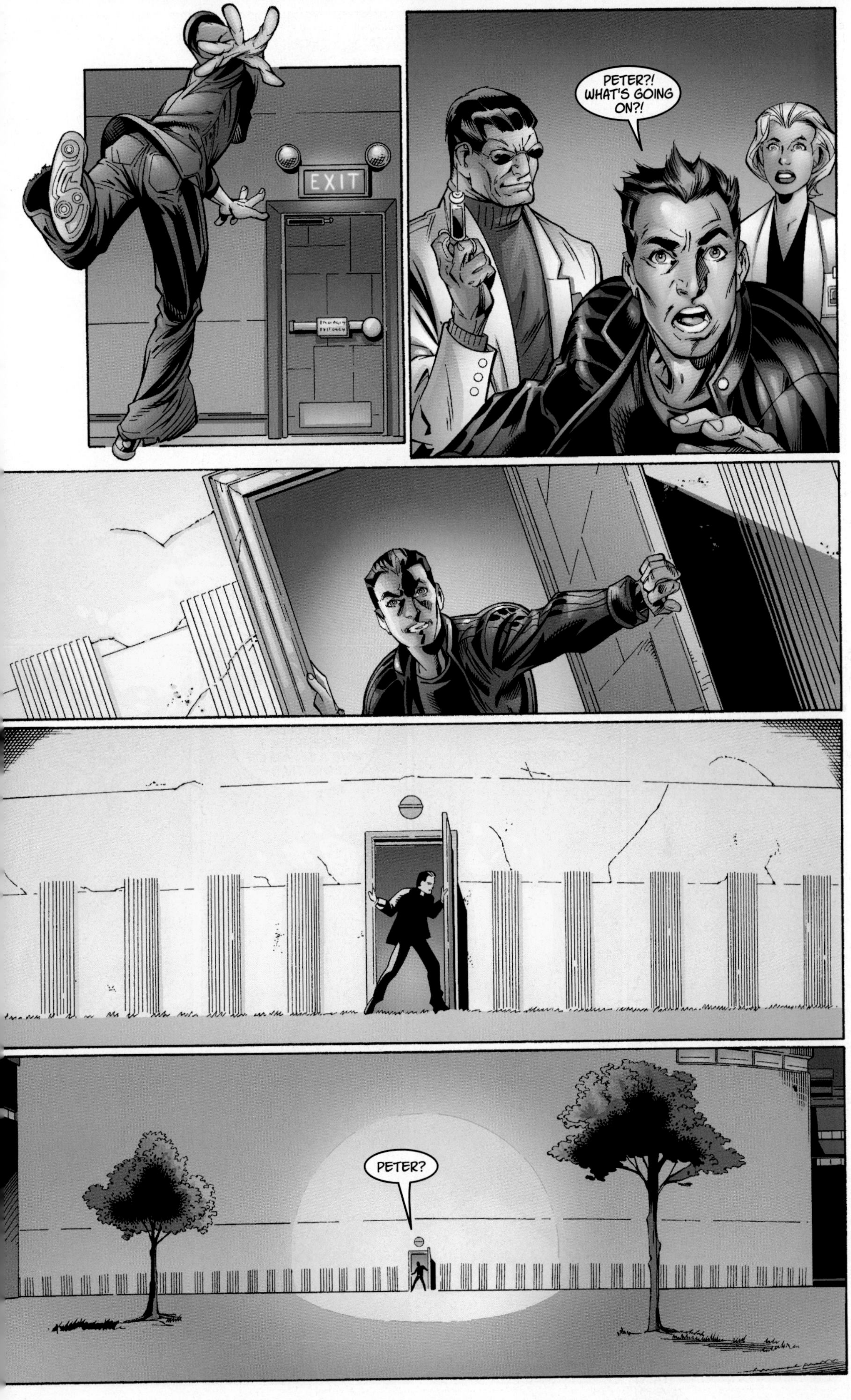
EXIT
PETER?! WHAT'S GOING ON?!
PETER?

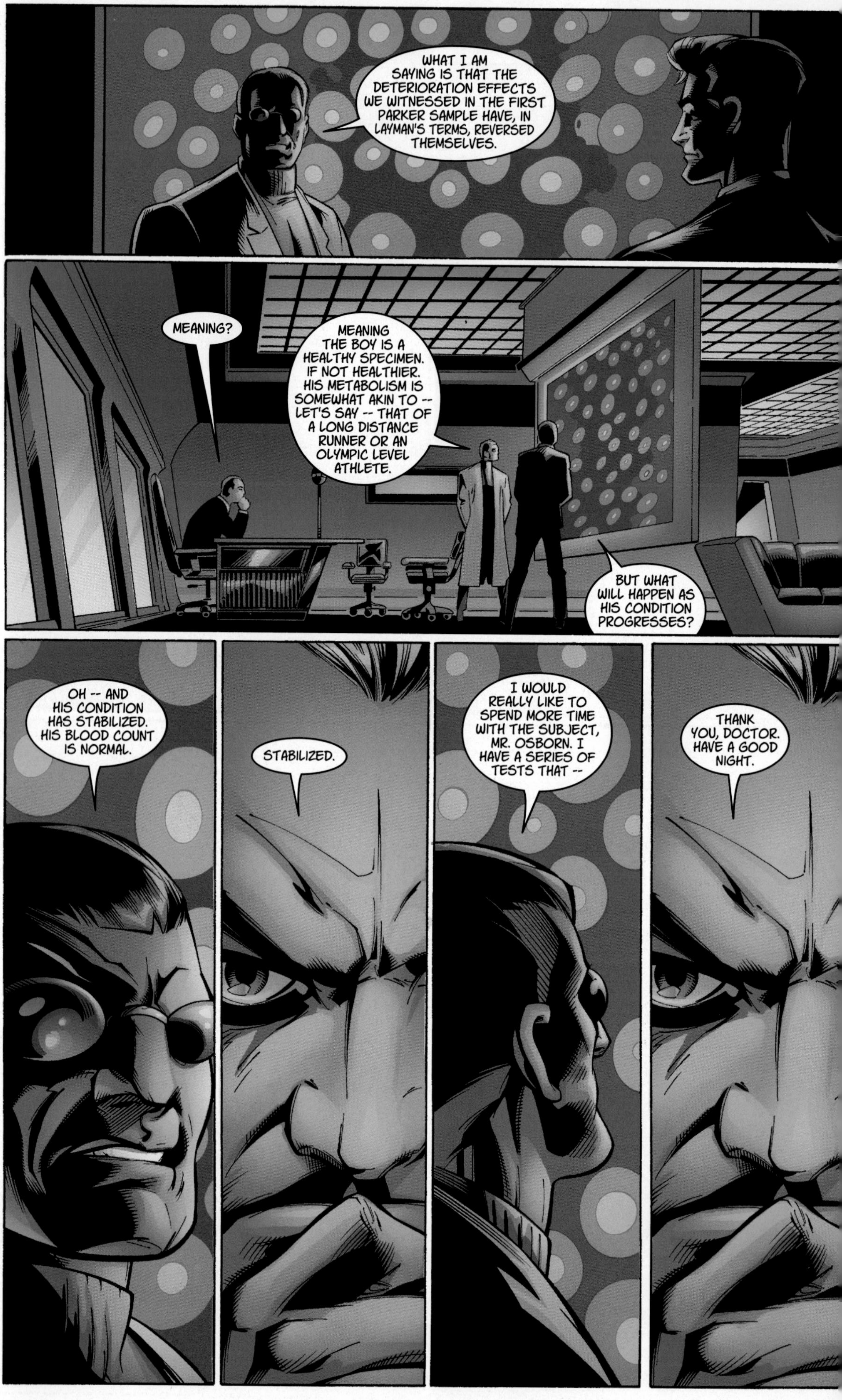
WHAT I AM SAYING IS THAT THE DETERIORATION EFFECTS WE WITNESSED IN THE FIRST PARKER SAMPLE HAVE, IN LAYMAN'S TERMS, REVERSED THEMSELVES.
MEANING?
MEANING THE BOY IS A HEALTHY SPECIMEN. IF NOT HEALTHIER. HIS METABOLISM IS SOMEWHAT AKIN TO -- LET'S SAY -- THAT OF A LONG DISTANCE RUNNER OR AN OLYMPIC LEVEL ATHLETE.
BUT WHAT WILL HAPPEN AS HIS CONDITION PROGRESSES?
OH -- AND HIS CONDITION HAS STABILIZED. HIS BLOOD COUNT IS NORMAL.
STABILIZED.
I WOULD REALLY LIKE TO SPEND MORE TIME WITH THE SUBJECT, MR. OSBORN. I HAVE A SERIES OF TESTS THAT --
THANK YOU, DOCTOR. HAVE A GOOD NIGHT.

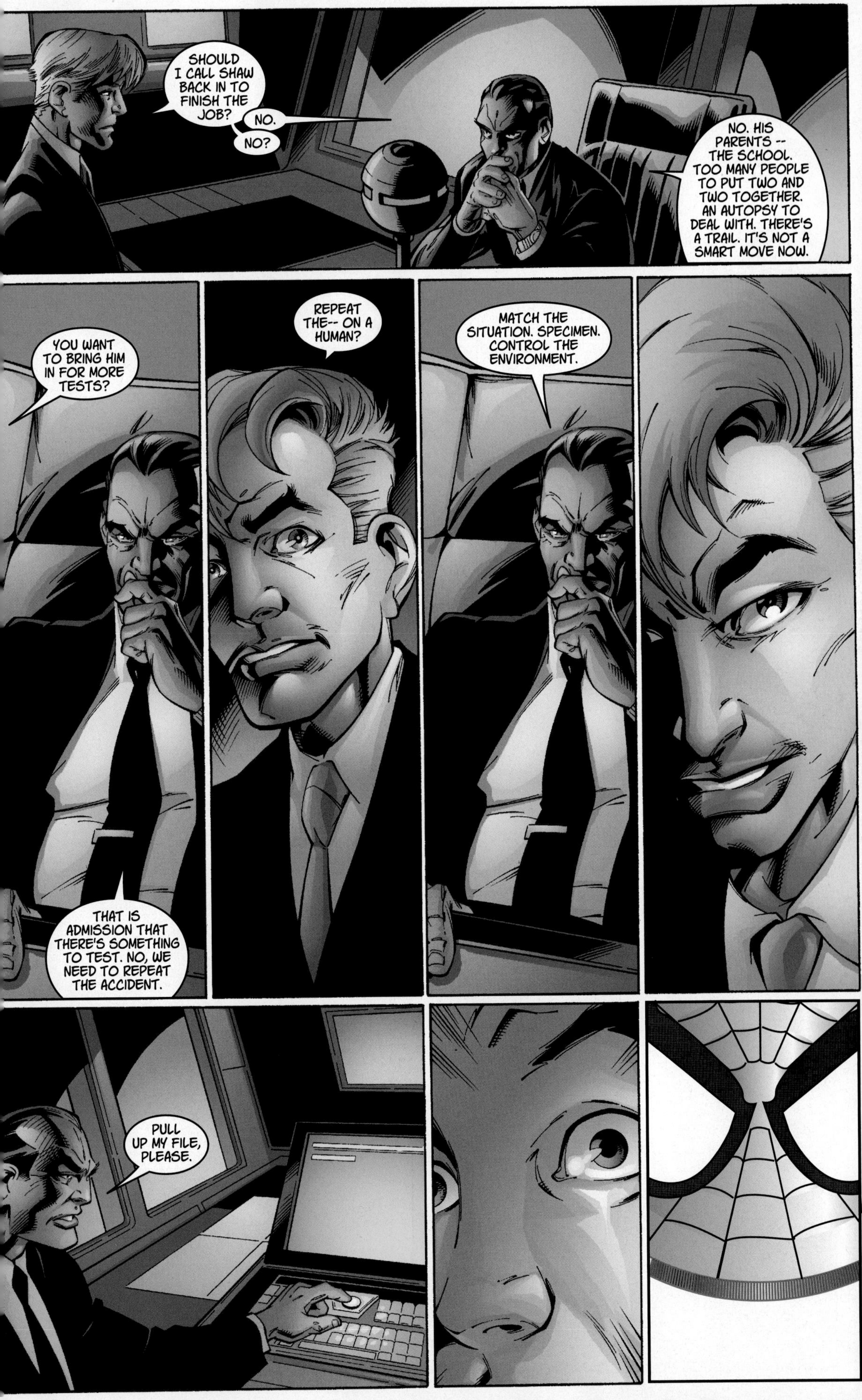
SHOULD I CALL SHAW BACK IN TO FINISH THE JOB?
NO.
NO?
NO. HIS PARENTS -- THE SCHOOL. TOO MANY PEOPLE TO PUT TWO AND TWO TOGETHER. AN AUTOPSY TO DEAL WITH. THERE'S A TRAIL. IT'S NOT A SMART MOVE NOW.
YOU WANT TO BRING HIM IN FOR MORE TESTS?
THAT IS ADMISSION THAT THERE'S SOMETHING TO TEST. NO, WE NEED TO REPEAT THE ACCIDENT.
REPEAT THE-- ON A HUMAN?
MATCH THE SITUATION. SPECIMEN. CONTROL THE ENVIRONMENT.
PULL UP MY FILE, PLEASE.

3

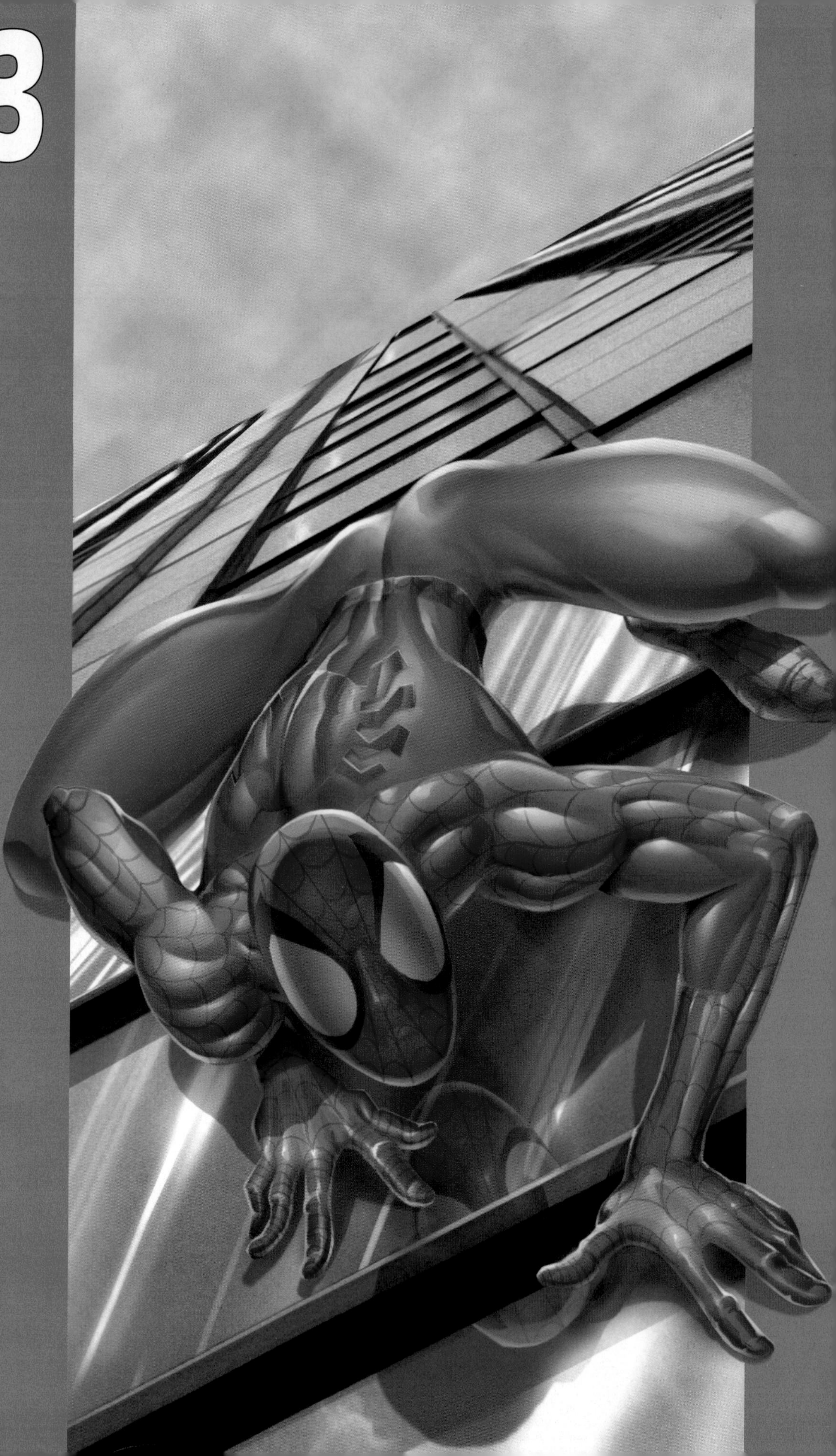

"RIGHT THERE -- YES.

"RIGHT THERE WE CAN SEE WHERE THE ARACHNID OZ EXPERIMENT NUMBER "OO" BIT THAT PARKER BOY.

"INITIALLY, THE BIOLOGICAL EFFECTS TO THE PARKER BOY WERE NEGATIVE. VERY NEGATIVE.

"AND HIS CHANCE FOR SURVIVAL WAS VERY SLIM. FATAL.

"BUT WE NOW BELIEVE THAT IT WAS THE MIXTURE OF SPIDER VENOM WITH THE OZ THAT CREATED THE ADVERSE EFFECTS TO THE BOY'S SYSTEM.

"BUT EVEN WITH THE UNTESTED MIXTURE OF TOXINS AND GENEALOGY --

"-- THE OZ WAS ABLE TO DOMINATE THE STRUCTURAL COMPOUNDS AND THE RESULTS TO THE BOY'S SYSTEM WERE NOTHING SHORT OF REVOLUTIONARY.

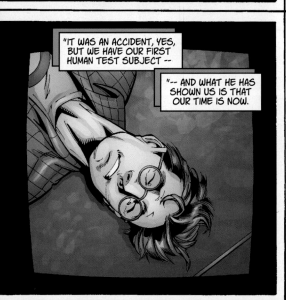

"IT WAS AN ACCIDENT, YES, BUT WE HAVE OUR FIRST HUMAN TEST SUBJECT --

"-- AND WHAT HE HAS SHOWN US IS THAT OUR TIME IS NOW.

"TURN IT OFF, PLEASE."

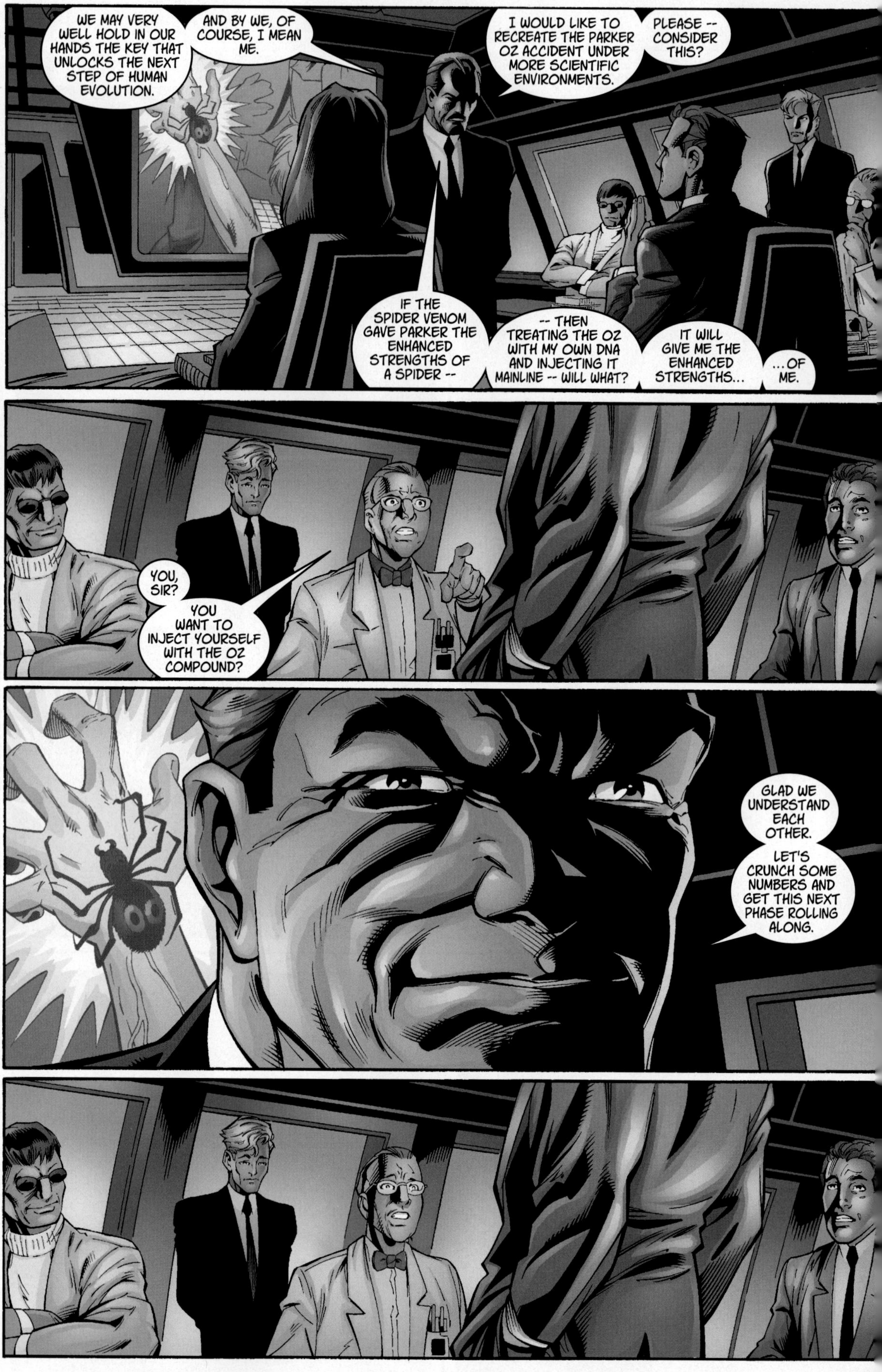
WE MAY VERY WELL HOLD IN OUR HANDS THE KEY THAT UNLOCKS THE NEXT STEP OF HUMAN EVOLUTION.
AND BY WE, OF COURSE, I MEAN ME.
I WOULD LIKE TO RECREATE THE PARKER OZ ACCIDENT UNDER MORE SCIENTIFIC ENVIRONMENTS.
PLEASE -- CONSIDER THIS?
IF THE SPIDER VENOM GAVE PARKER THE ENHANCED STRENGTHS OF A SPIDER --
-- THEN TREATING THE OZ WITH MY OWN DNA AND INJECTING IT MAINLINE -- WILL WHAT?
IT WILL GIVE ME THE ENHANCED STRENGTHS...
...OF ME.
YOU, SIR?
YOU WANT TO INJECT YOURSELF WITH THE OZ COMPOUND?
GLAD WE UNDERSTAND EACH OTHER.
LET'S CRUNCH SOME NUMBERS AND GET THIS NEXT PHASE ROLLING ALONG.

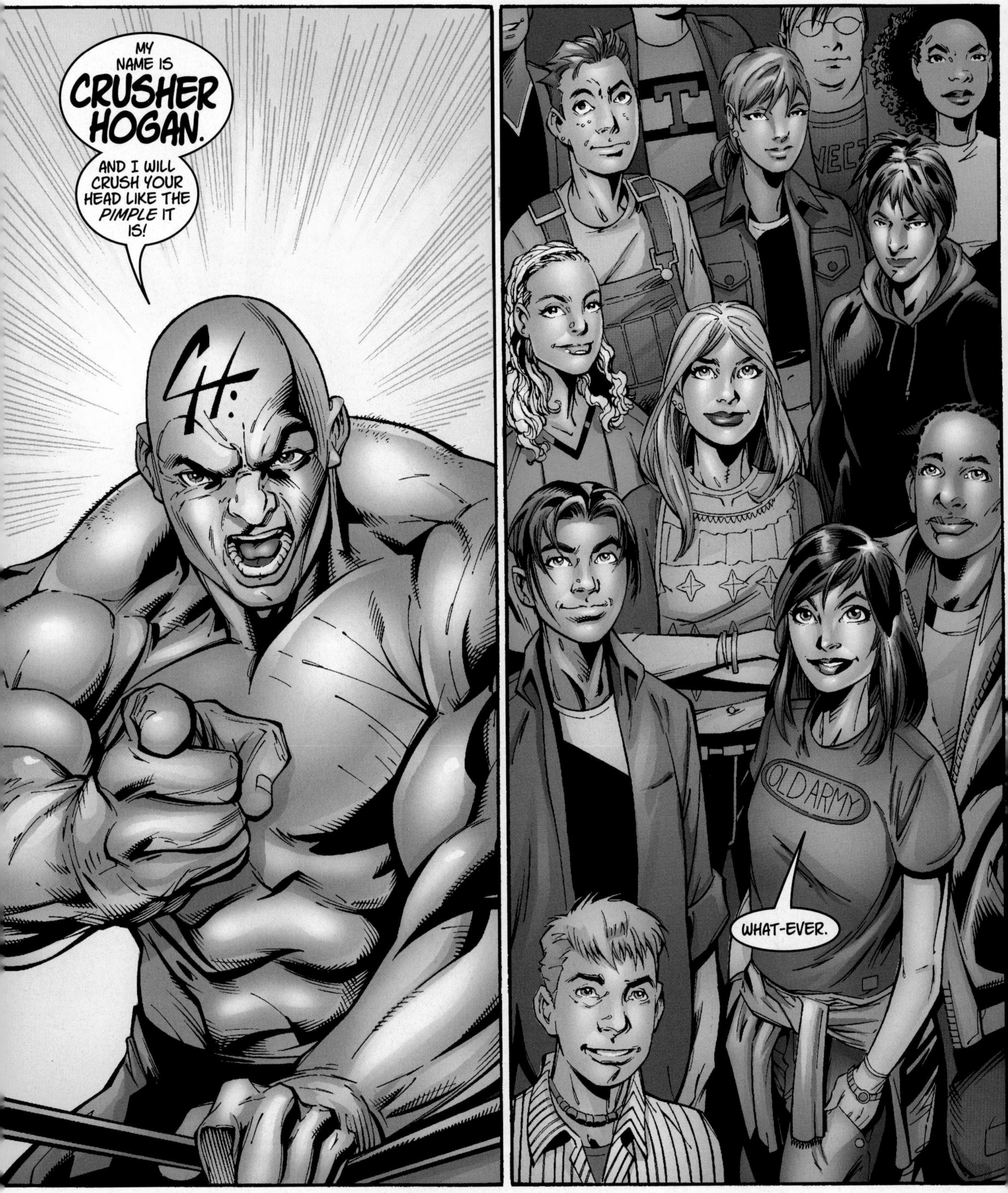
MY NAME IS CRUSHER HOGAN.
AND I WILL CRUSH YOUR HEAD LIKE THE *PIMPLE* IT IS!
OLD ARMY
WHAT-EVER.

WANNABE

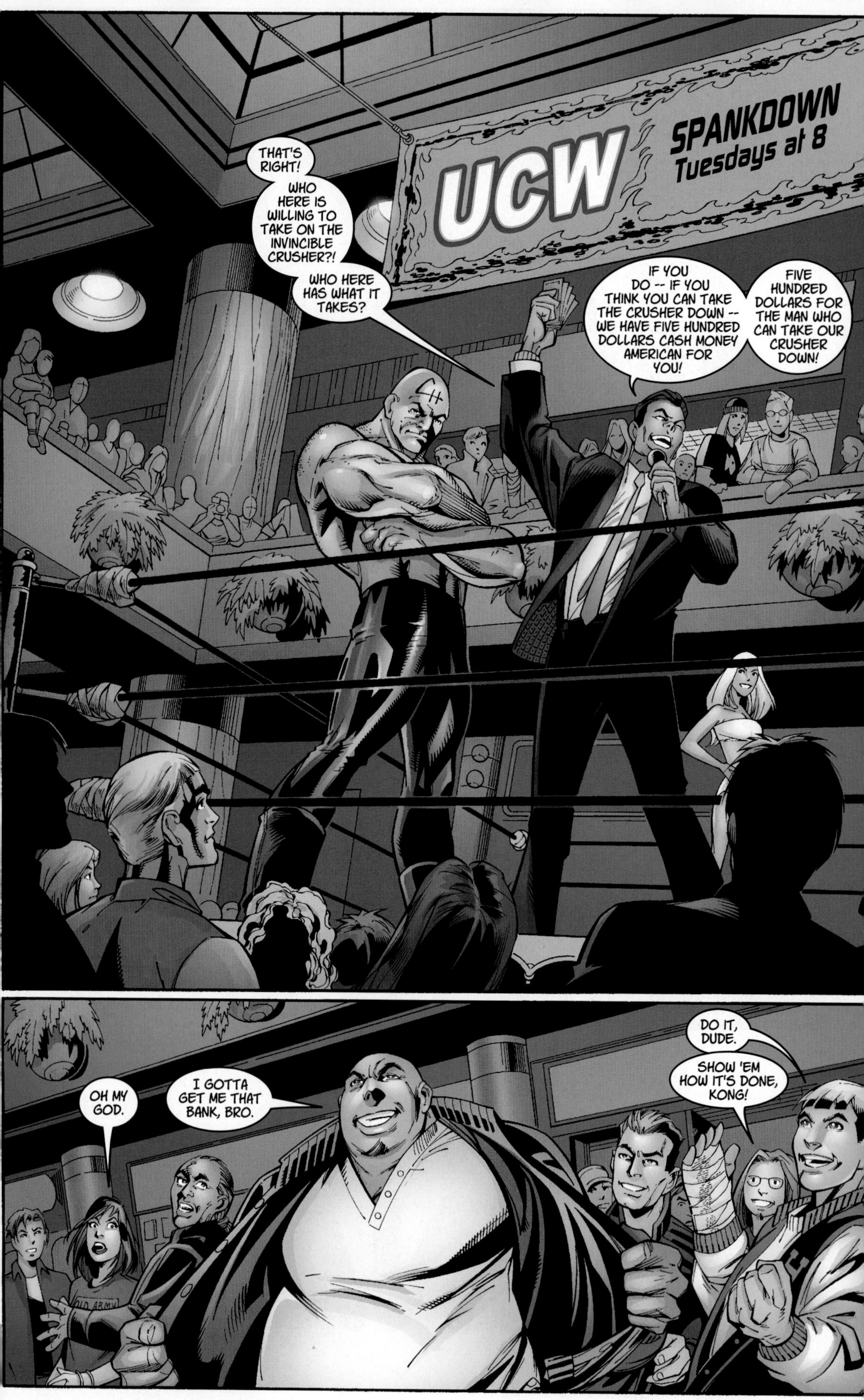
UCW
SPANKDOWN Tuesdays at 8
THAT'S RIGHT!
WHO HERE IS WILLING TO TAKE ON THE INVINCIBLE CRUSHER?!
WHO HERE HAS WHAT IT TAKES?
IF YOU DO -- IF YOU THINK YOU CAN TAKE THE CRUSHER DOWN -- WE HAVE FIVE HUNDRED DOLLARS CASH MONEY AMERICAN FOR YOU!
FIVE HUNDRED DOLLARS FOR THE MAN WHO CAN TAKE OUR CRUSHER DOWN!
OH MY GOD.
I GOTTA GET ME THAT BANK, BRO.
DO IT, DUDE.
SHOW 'EM HOW IT'S DONE, KONG!
OLD ARMY

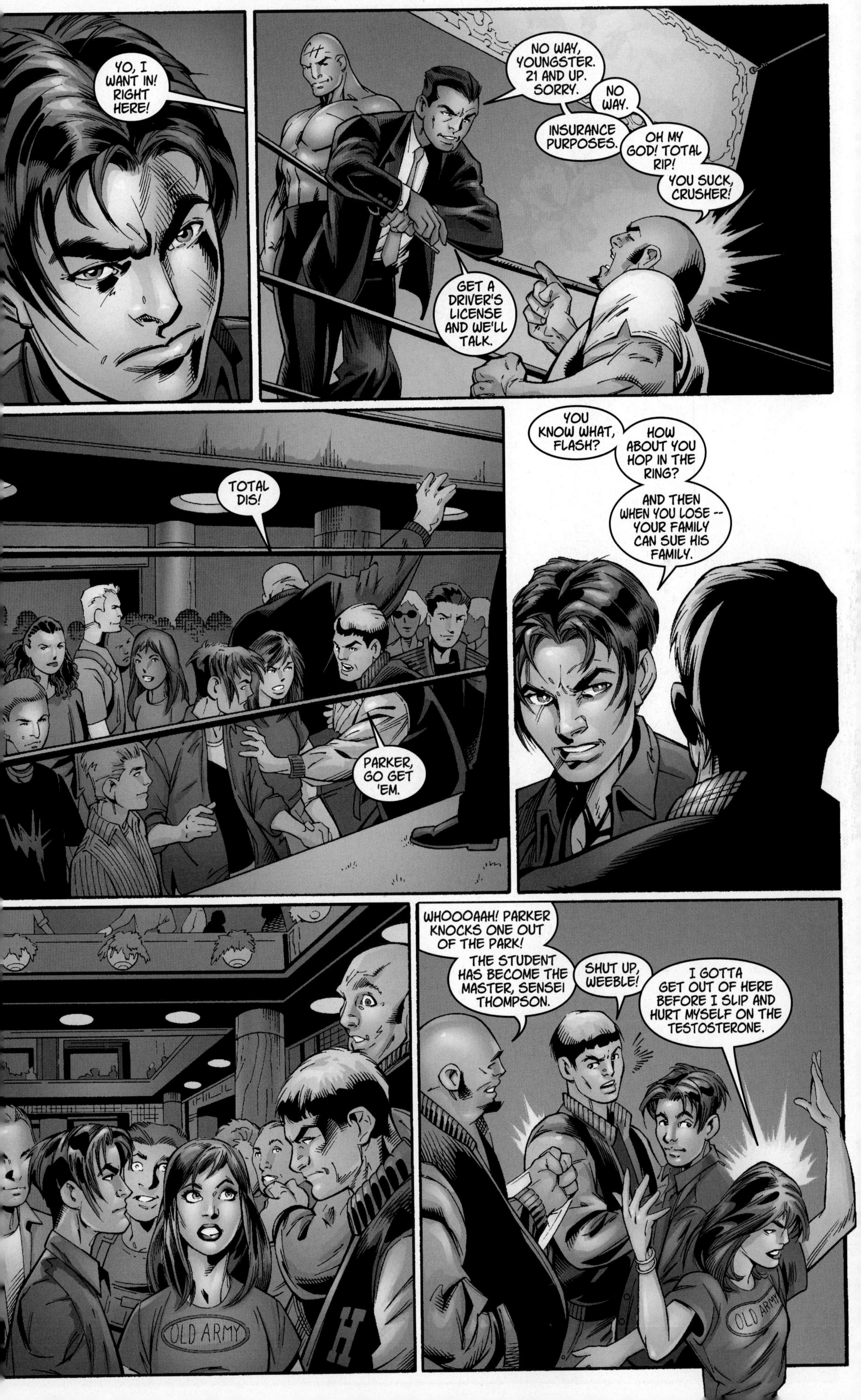

YO, I WANT IN! RIGHT HERE!
NO WAY, YOUNGSTER. 21 AND UP. SORRY.
INSURANCE PURPOSES.
NO WAY.
OH MY GOD! TOTAL RIP!
YOU SUCK, CRUSHER!
GET A DRIVER'S LICENSE AND WE'LL TALK.
TOTAL DIS!
PARKER, GO GET 'EM.
YOU KNOW WHAT, FLASH?
HOW ABOUT YOU HOP IN THE RING?
AND THEN WHEN YOU LOSE -- YOUR FAMILY CAN SUE HIS FAMILY.
WHOOOAAH! PARKER KNOCKS ONE OUT OF THE PARK!
THE STUDENT HAS BECOME THE MASTER, SENSEI THOMPSON.
SHUT UP, WEEBLE!
I GOTTA GET OUT OF HERE BEFORE I SLIP AND HURT MYSELF ON THE TESTOSTERONE.
OLD ARMY
OLD ARMY

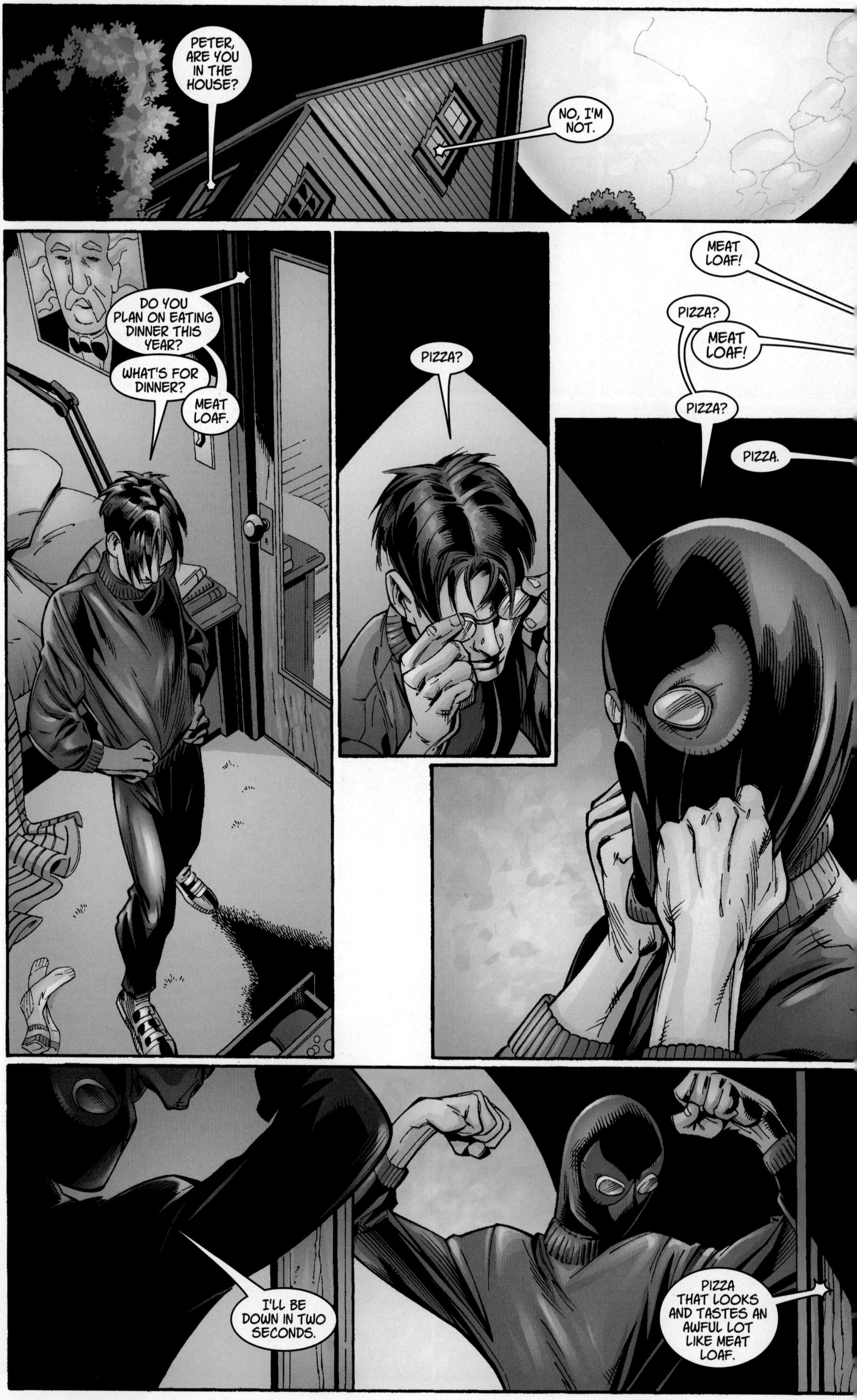

PETER, ARE YOU IN THE HOUSE?
NO, I'M NOT.
DO YOU PLAN ON EATING DINNER THIS YEAR?
WHAT'S FOR DINNER?
MEAT LOAF.
PIZZA?
MEAT LOAF!
PIZZA?
MEAT LOAF!
PIZZA?
PIZZA.
I'LL BE DOWN IN TWO SECONDS.
PIZZA THAT LOOKS AND TASTES AN AWFUL LOT LIKE MEAT LOAF.

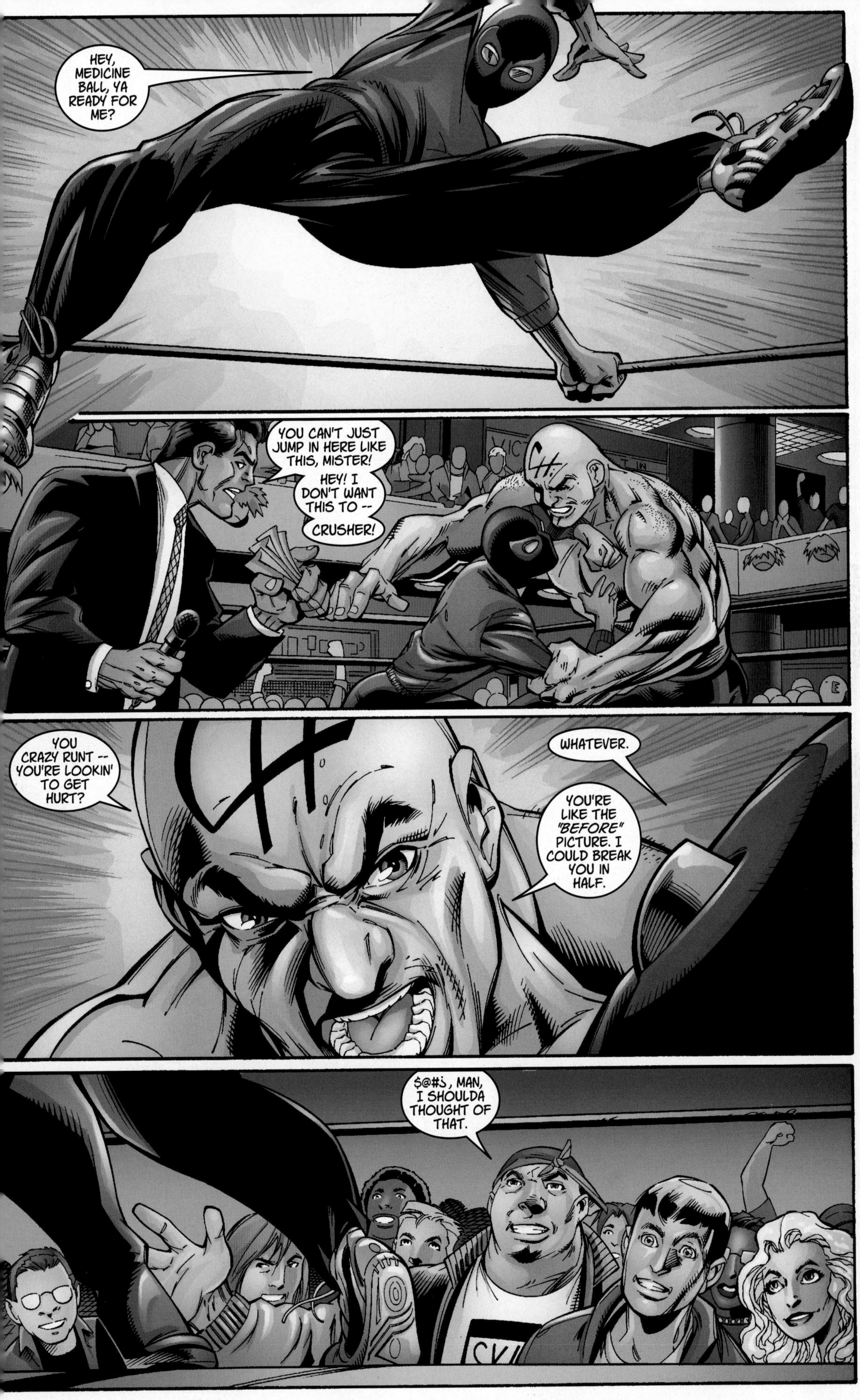
HEY, MEDICINE BALL, YA READY FOR ME?
YOU CAN'T JUST JUMP IN HERE LIKE THIS, MISTER!
HEY! I DON'T WANT THIS TO --
CRUSHER!
YOU CRAZY RUNT -- YOU'RE LOOKIN' TO GET HURT?
WHATEVER.
YOU'RE LIKE THE "BEFORE" PICTURE. I COULD BREAK YOU IN HALF.
$@#$, MAN, I SHOULDA THOUGHT OF THAT.

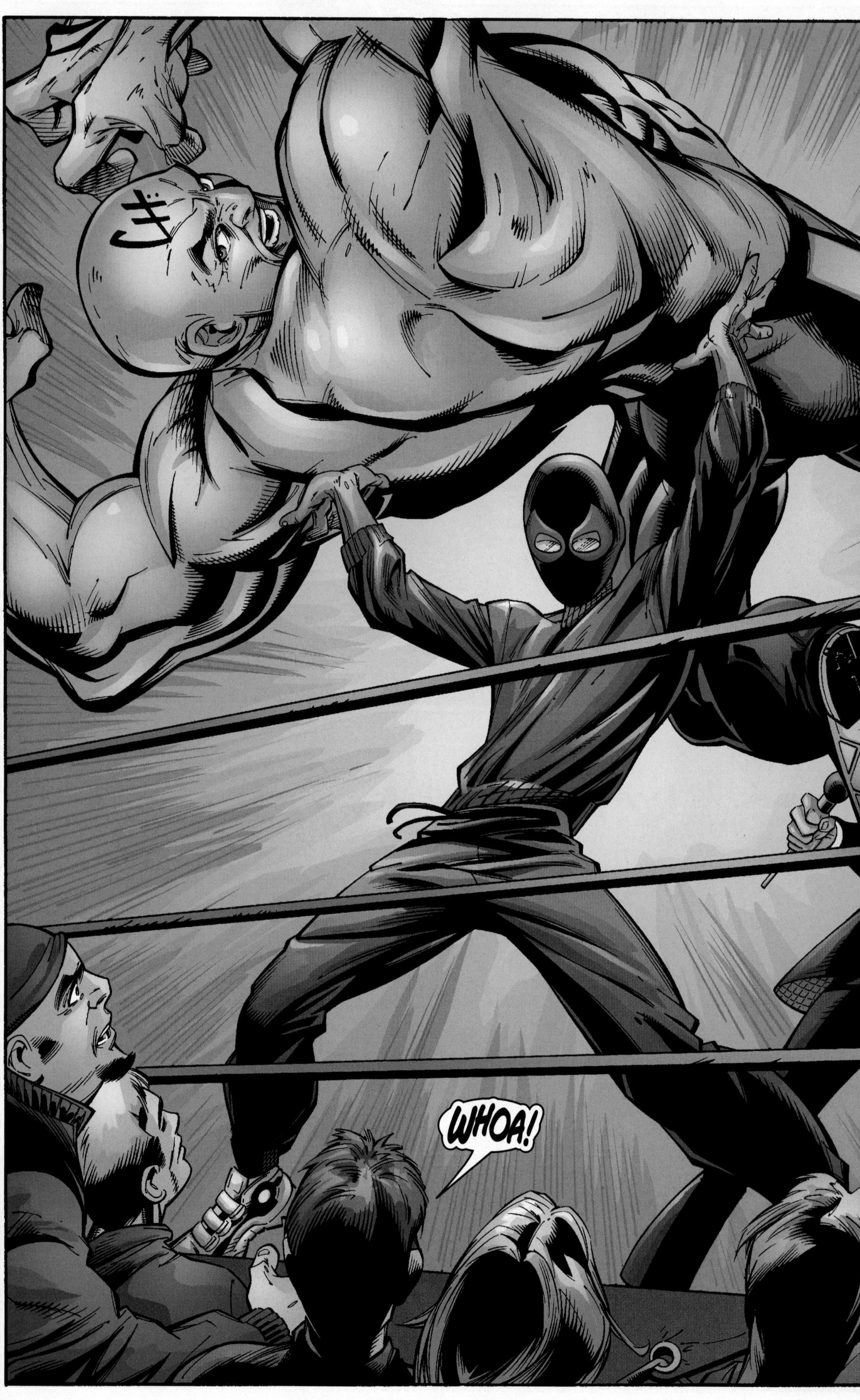
WHOA!

HEY! HEY!

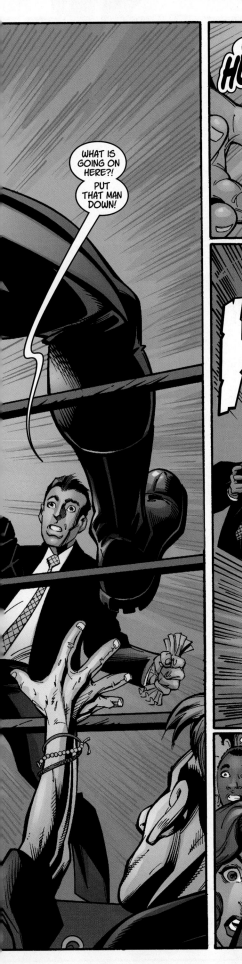

WHAT IS GOING ON HERE?! PUT THAT MAN DOWN!

WHAM

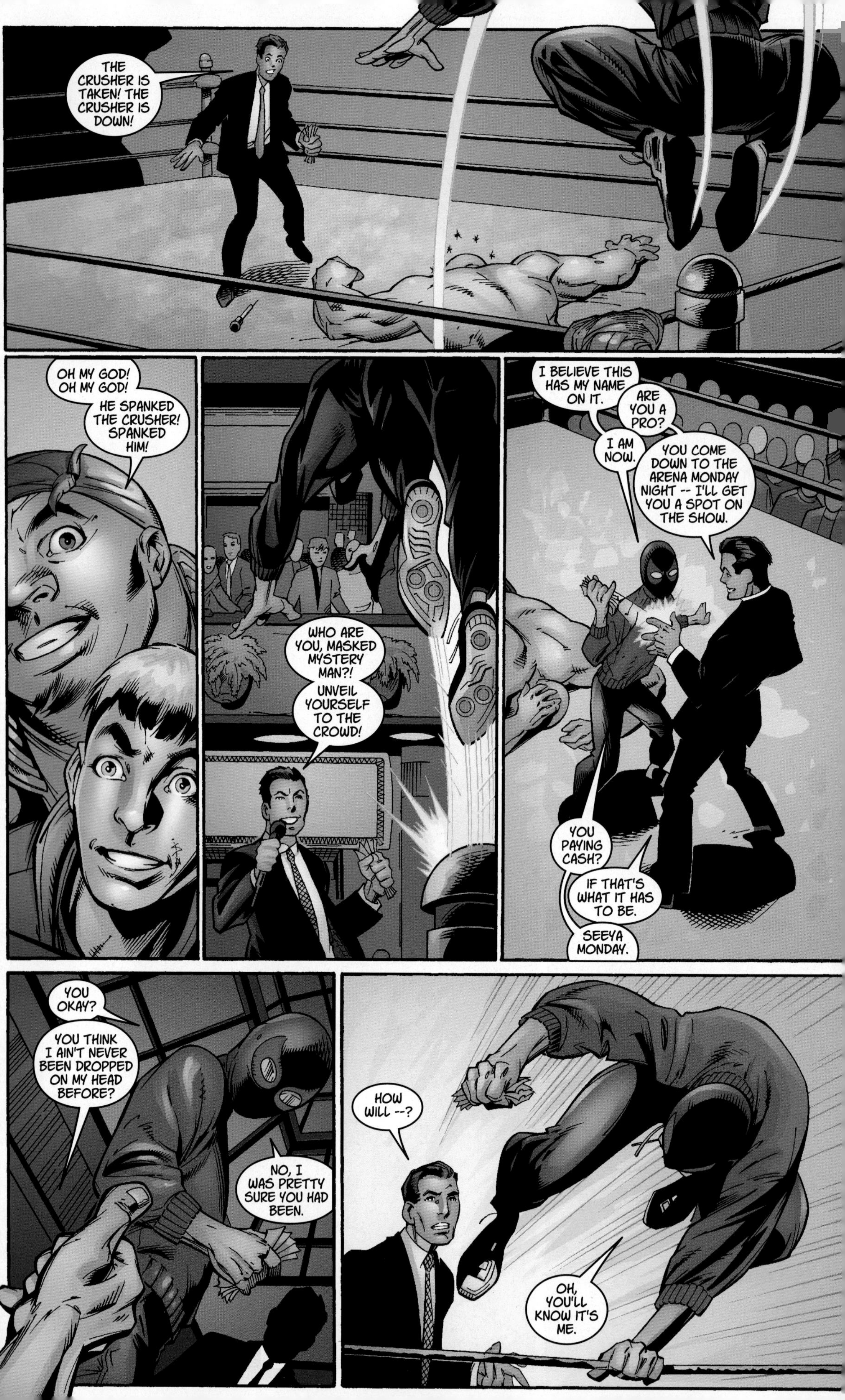
THE CRUSHER IS TAKEN! THE CRUSHER IS DOWN!
OH MY GOD! OH MY GOD!
HE SPANKED THE CRUSHER! SPANKED HIM!
WHO ARE YOU, MASKED MYSTERY MAN?!
UNVEIL YOURSELF TO THE CROWD!
I BELIEVE THIS HAS MY NAME ON IT.
ARE YOU A PRO?
I AM NOW.
YOU COME DOWN TO THE ARENA MONDAY NIGHT -- I'LL GET YOU A SPOT ON THE SHOW.
YOU PAYING CASH?
IF THAT'S WHAT IT HAS TO BE.
SEEYA MONDAY.
YOU OKAY?
YOU THINK I AIN'T NEVER BEEN DROPPED ON MY HEAD BEFORE?
NO, I WAS PRETTY SURE YOU HAD BEEN.
HOW WILL --?
OH, YOU'LL KNOW IT'S ME.

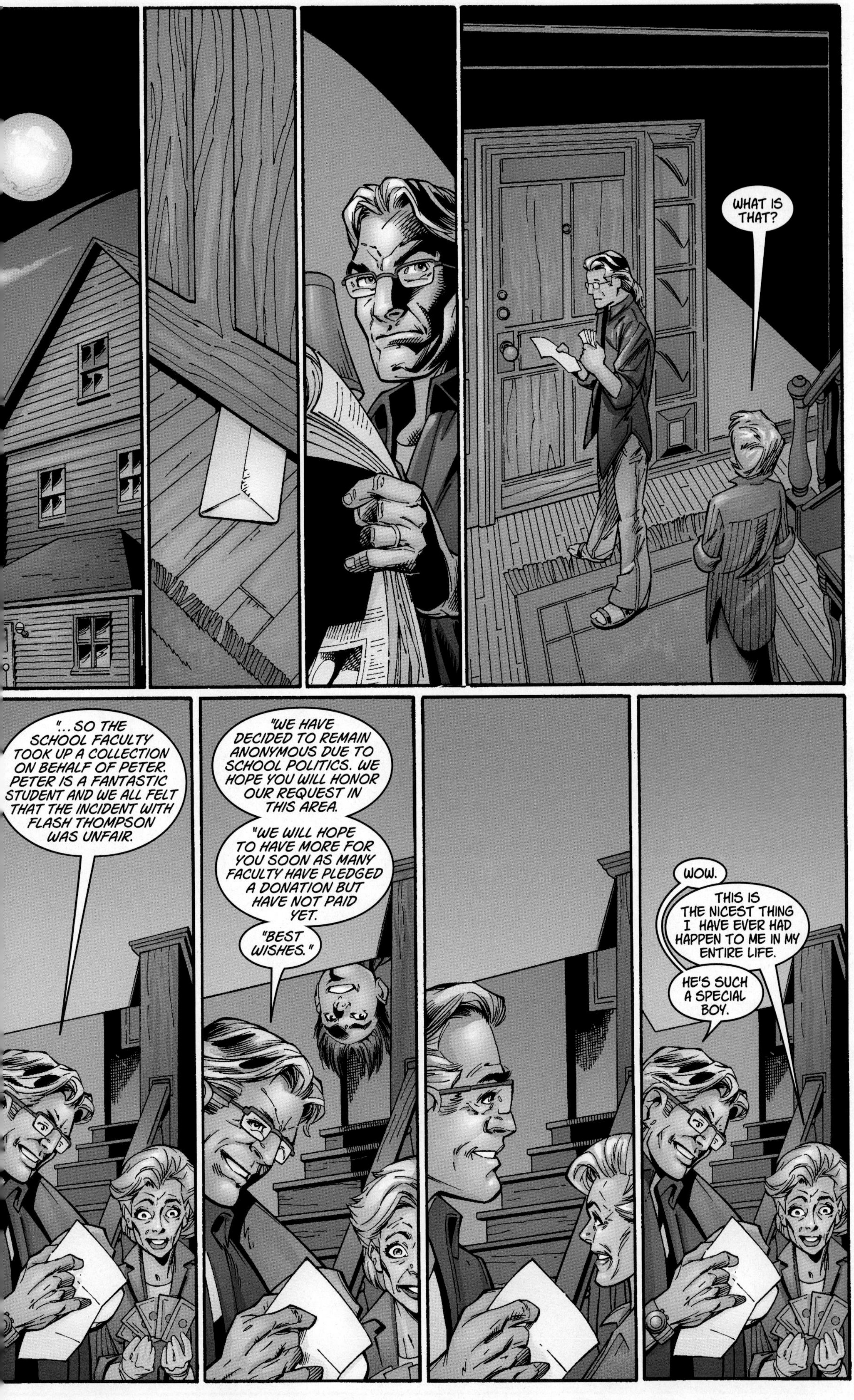
WHAT IS THAT?
"...SO THE SCHOOL FACULTY TOOK UP A COLLECTION ON BEHALF OF PETER. PETER IS A FANTASTIC STUDENT AND WE ALL FELT THAT THE INCIDENT WITH FLASH THOMPSON WAS UNFAIR.
"WE HAVE DECIDED TO REMAIN ANONYMOUS DUE TO SCHOOL POLITICS. WE HOPE YOU WILL HONOR OUR REQUEST IN THIS AREA.
"WE WILL HOPE TO HAVE MORE FOR YOU SOON AS MANY FACULTY HAVE PLEDGED A DONATION BUT HAVE NOT PAID YET.
"BEST WISHES."
WOW.
THIS IS THE NICEST THING I HAVE EVER HAD HAPPEN TO ME IN MY ENTIRE LIFE.
HE'S SUCH A SPECIAL BOY.

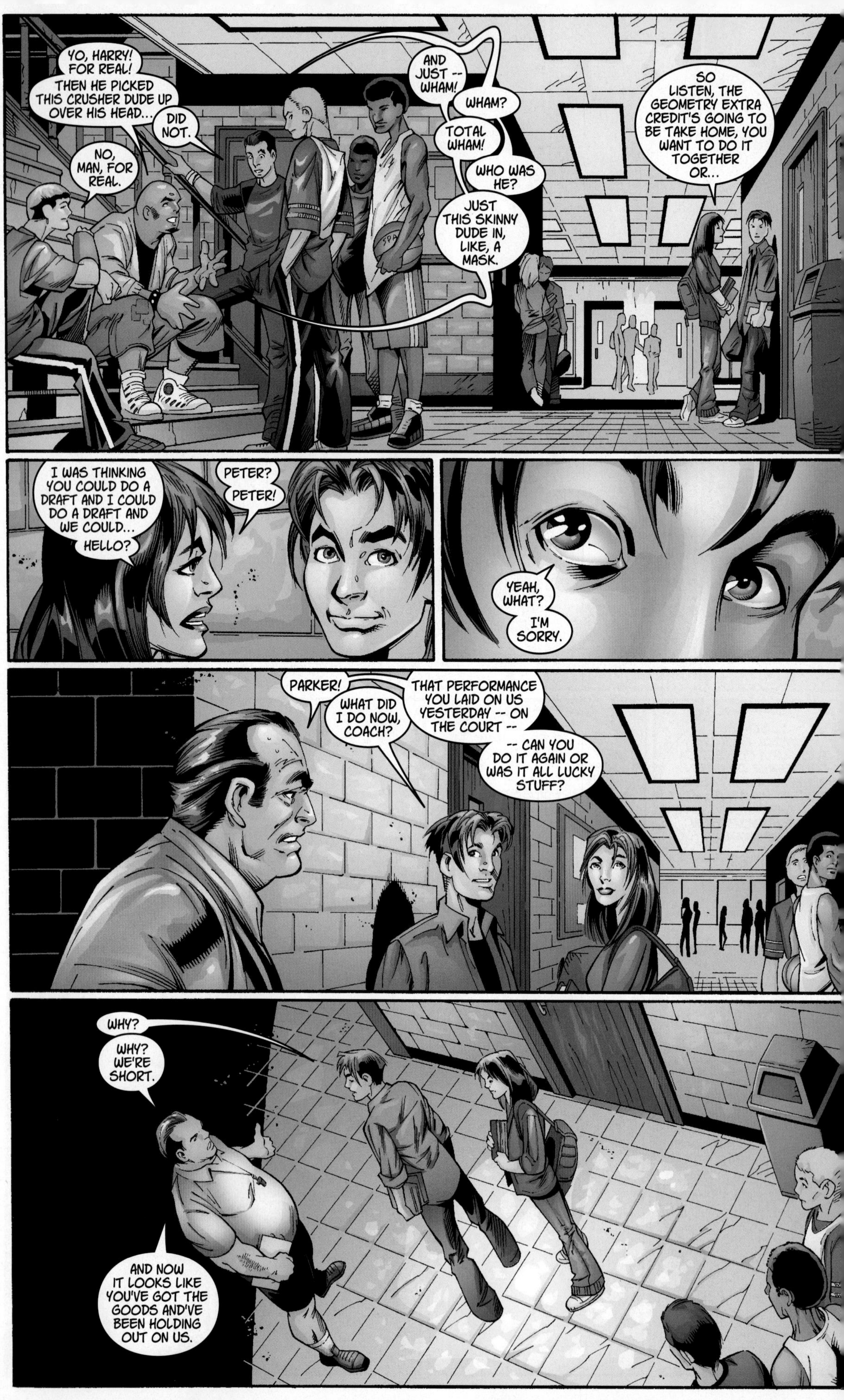
YO, HARRY! FOR REAL! THEN HE PICKED THIS CRUSHER DUDE UP OVER HIS HEAD...
DID NOT.
NO, MAN, FOR REAL.
AND JUST -- WHAM!
WHAM?
TOTAL WHAM!
WHO WAS HE?
JUST THIS SKINNY DUDE IN, LIKE, A MASK.
SO LISTEN, THE GEOMETRY EXTRA CREDIT'S GOING TO BE TAKE HOME, YOU WANT TO DO IT TOGETHER OR...
I WAS THINKING YOU COULD DO A DRAFT AND I COULD DO A DRAFT AND WE COULD...
HELLO?
PETER?
PETER!
YEAH, WHAT?
I'M SORRY.
PARKER!
WHAT DID I DO NOW, COACH?
THAT PERFORMANCE YOU LAID ON US YESTERDAY -- ON THE COURT --
-- CAN YOU DO IT AGAIN OR WAS IT ALL LUCKY STUFF?
WHY?
WHY? WE'RE SHORT.
AND NOW IT LOOKS LIKE YOU'VE GOT THE GOODS AND'VE BEEN HOLDING OUT ON US.

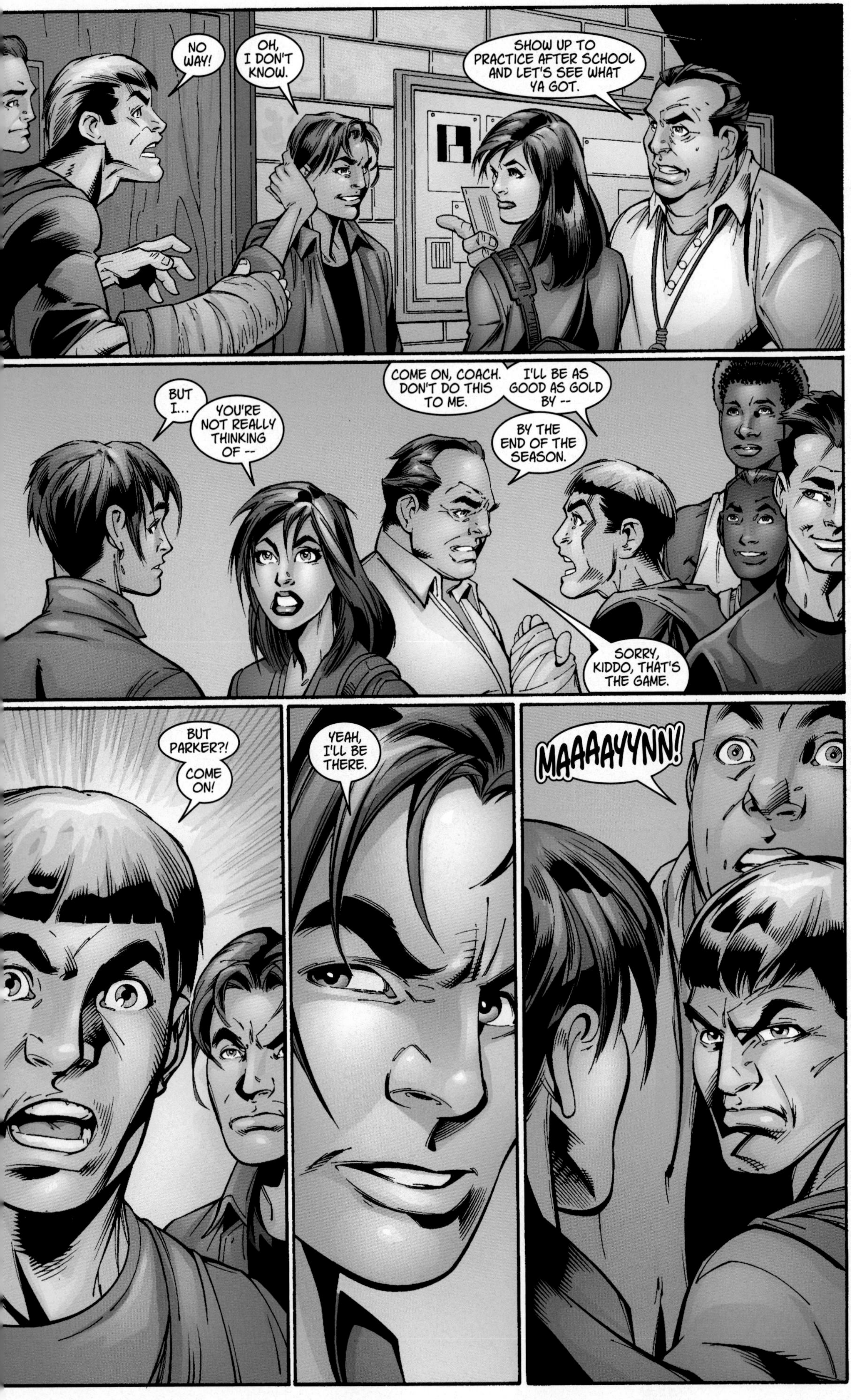
NO WAY!
OH, I DON'T KNOW.
SHOW UP TO PRACTICE AFTER SCHOOL AND LET'S SEE WHAT YA GOT.
BUT I...
YOU'RE NOT REALLY THINKING OF --
COME ON, COACH. DON'T DO THIS TO ME.
I'LL BE AS GOOD AS GOLD BY --
BY THE END OF THE SEASON.
SORRY, KIDDO, THAT'S THE GAME.
BUT PARKER?!
COME ON!
YEAH, I'LL BE THERE.
MAAAAYYNN!

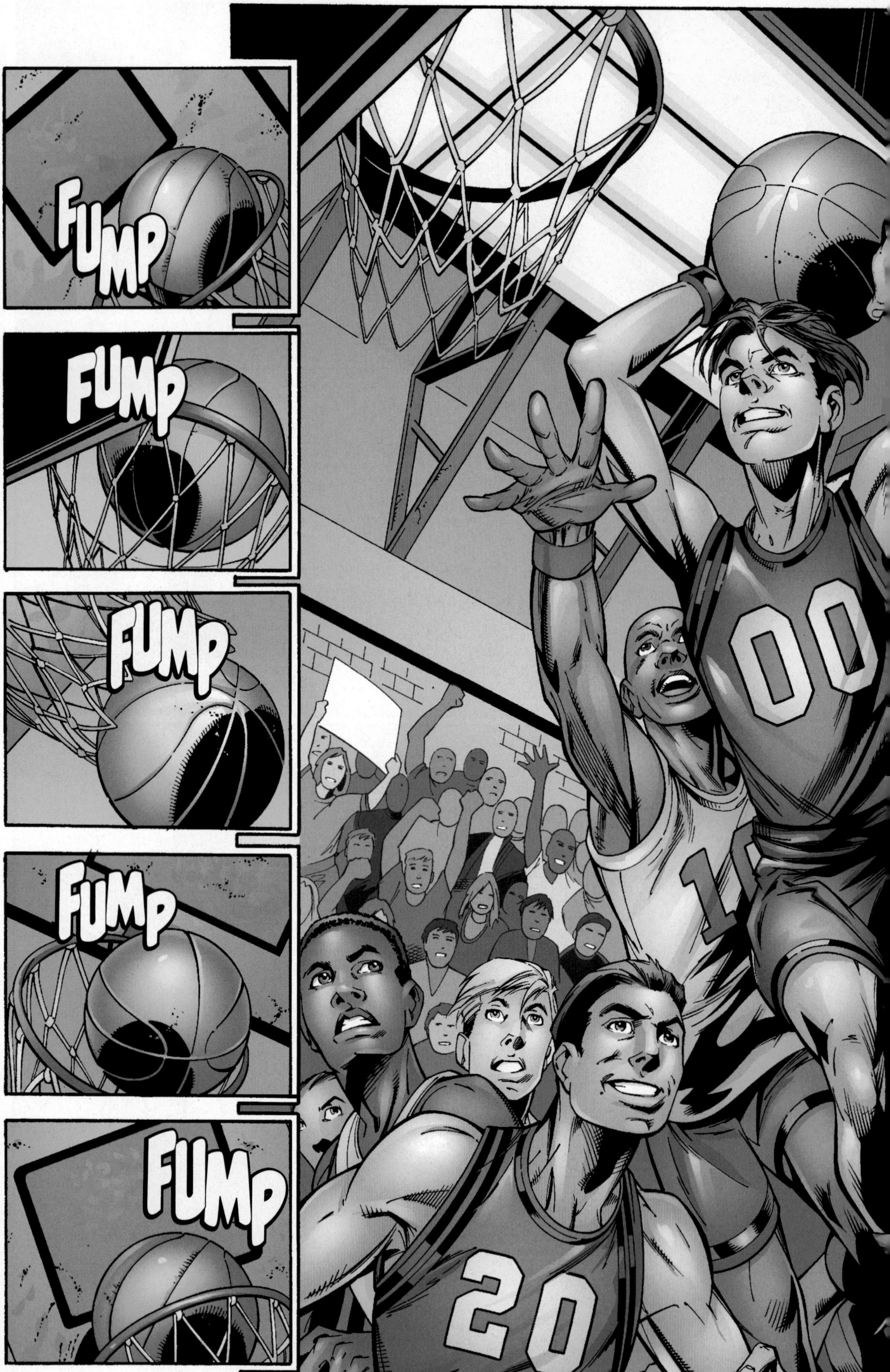
FUMP
FUMP
FUMP
FUMP
FUMP

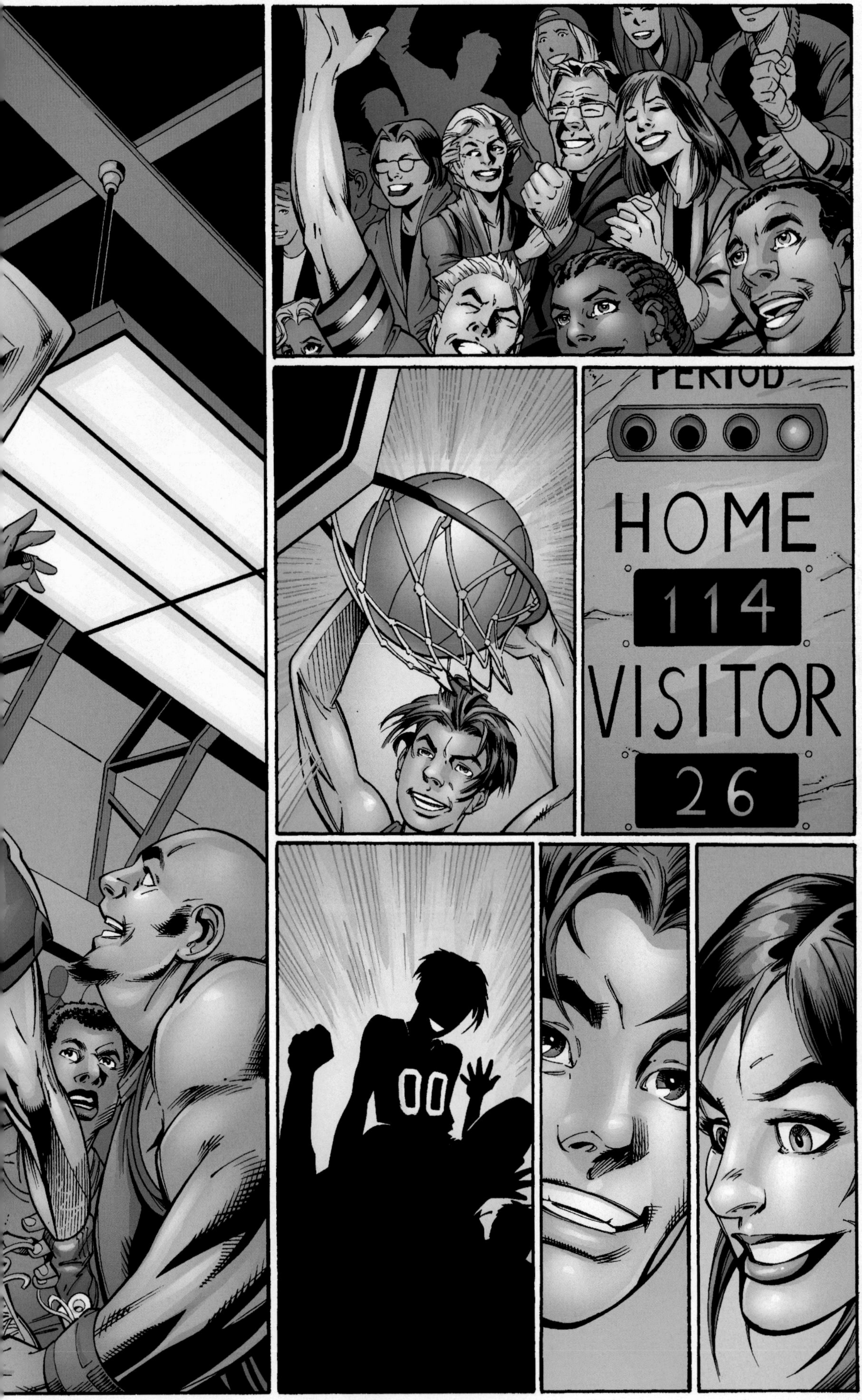
HOME
114
VISITOR
26
00

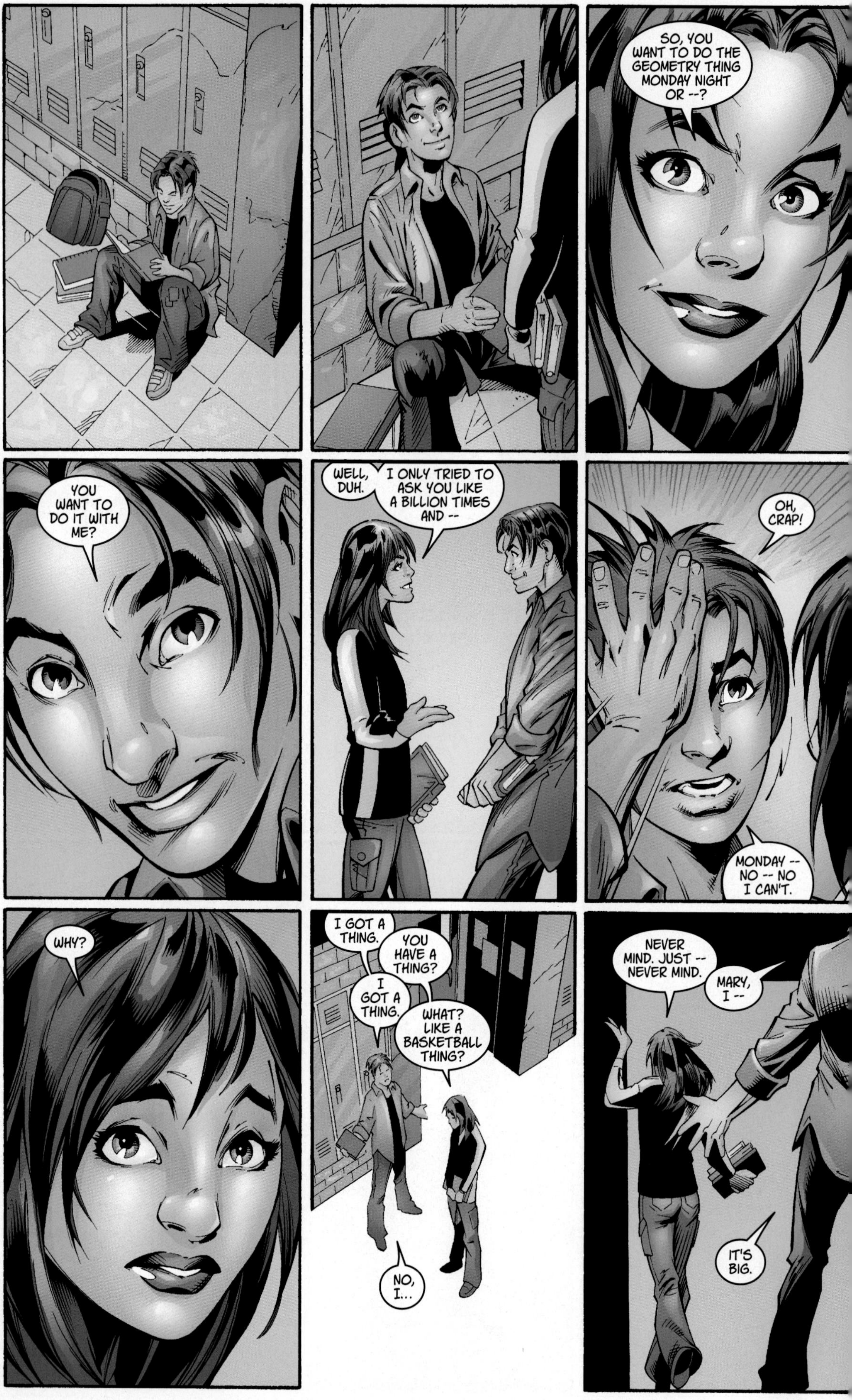
SO, YOU WANT TO DO THE GEOMETRY THING MONDAY NIGHT OR --?
YOU WANT TO DO IT WITH ME?
WELL, DUH.
I ONLY TRIED TO ASK YOU LIKE A BILLION TIMES AND --
OH, CRAP!
MONDAY -- NO -- NO I CAN'T.
WHY?
I GOT A THING.
YOU HAVE A THING?
I GOT A THING.
WHAT? LIKE A BASKETBALL THING?
NO, I...
NEVER MIND. JUST -- NEVER MIND.
MARY, I --
IT'S BIG.

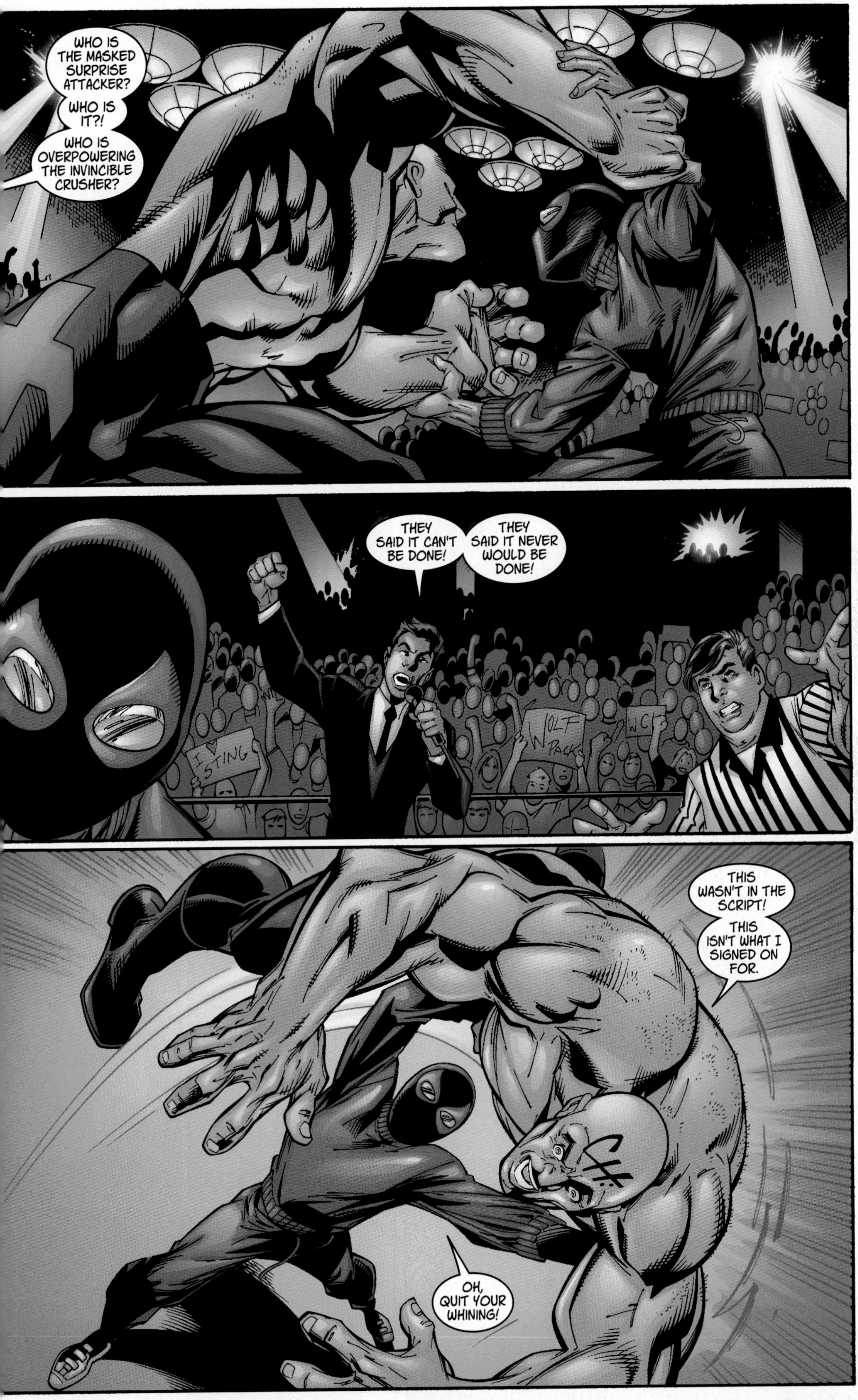
WHO IS THE MASKED SURPRISE ATTACKER?
WHO IS IT?!
WHO IS OVERPOWERING THE INVINCIBLE CRUSHER?
THEY SAID IT CAN'T BE DONE!
THEY SAID IT NEVER WOULD BE DONE!
I ♥ STING
WOLF PACK
WC
THIS WASN'T IN THE SCRIPT!
THIS ISN'T WHAT I SIGNED ON FOR.
OH, QUIT YOUR WHINING!

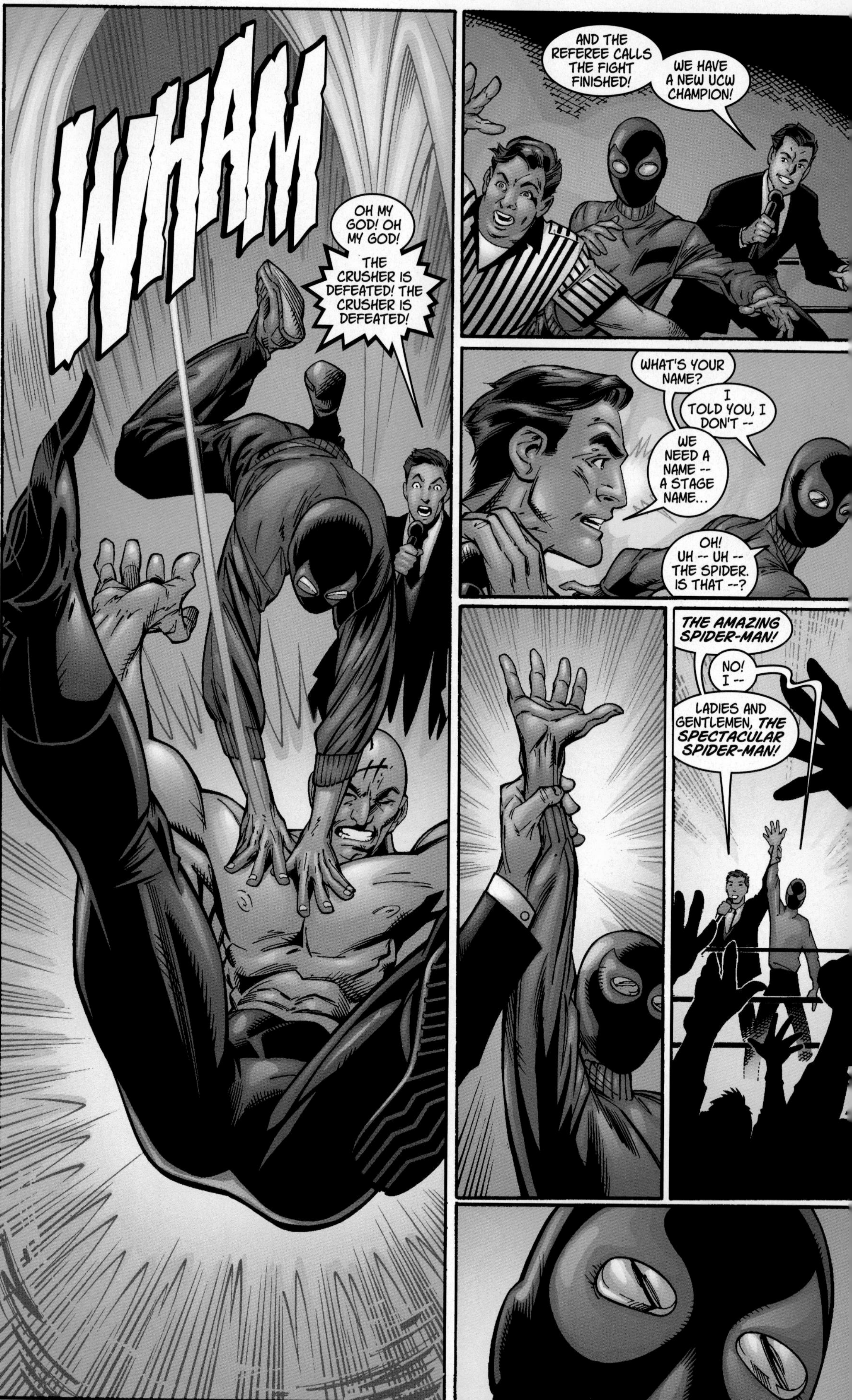
WHAM
OH MY GOD! OH MY GOD!
THE CRUSHER IS DEFEATED! THE CRUSHER IS DEFEATED!
AND THE REFEREE CALLS THE FIGHT FINISHED!
WE HAVE A NEW UCW CHAMPION!
WHAT'S YOUR NAME?
I TOLD YOU, I DON'T --
WE NEED A NAME -- A STAGE NAME...
OH! UH -- UH -- THE SPIDER. IS THAT --?
THE AMAZING SPIDER-MAN!
NO! I --
LADIES AND GENTLEMEN, THE SPECTACULAR SPIDER-MAN!

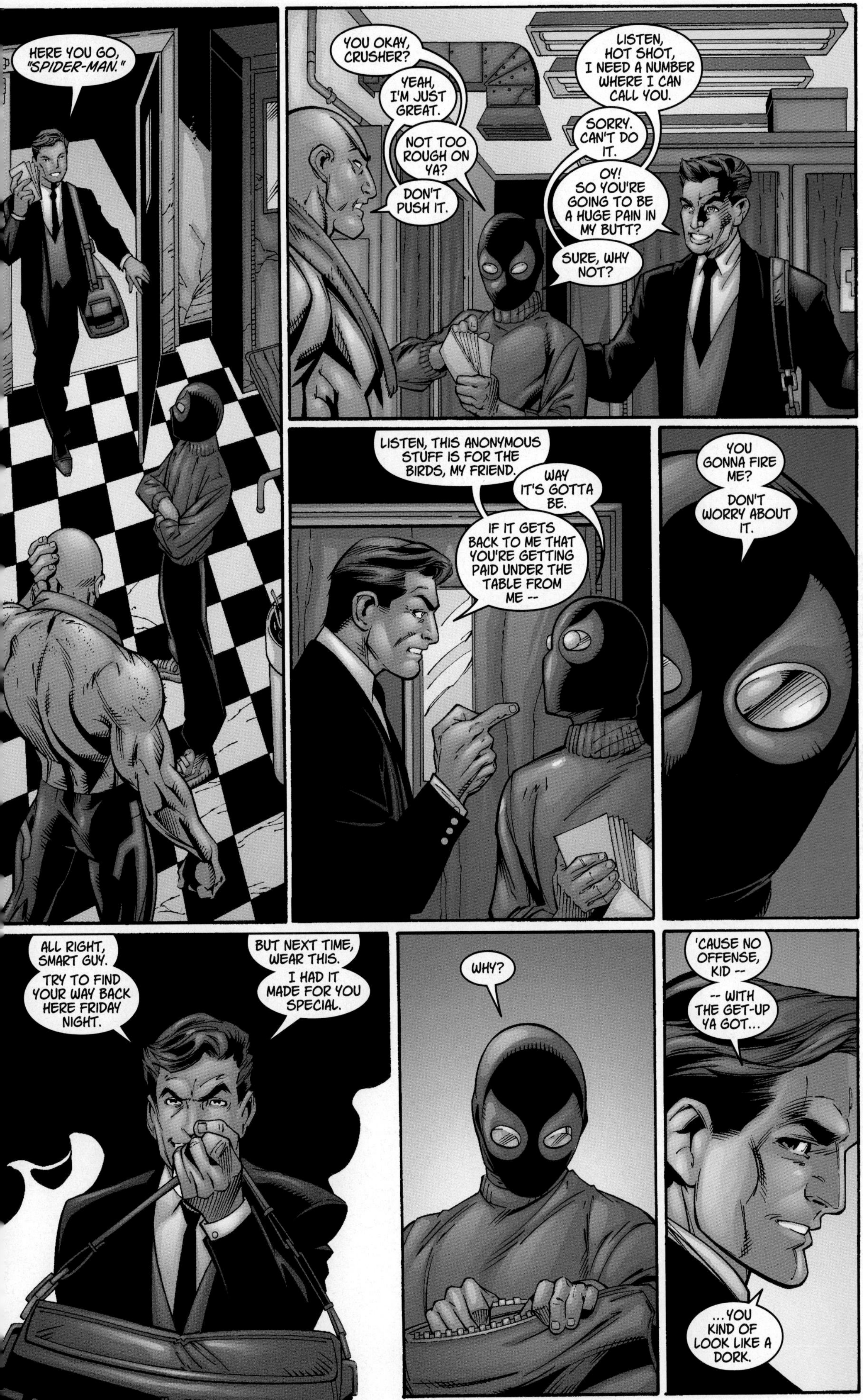
HERE YOU GO, "SPIDER-MAN."
YOU OKAY, CRUSHER?
YEAH, I'M JUST GREAT.
NOT TOO ROUGH ON YA?
DON'T PUSH IT.
LISTEN, HOT SHOT, I NEED A NUMBER WHERE I CAN CALL YOU.
SORRY. CAN'T DO IT.
OY! SO YOU'RE GOING TO BE A HUGE PAIN IN MY BUTT?
SURE, WHY NOT?
LISTEN, THIS ANONYMOUS STUFF IS FOR THE BIRDS, MY FRIEND.
WAY IT'S GOTTA BE.
IF IT GETS BACK TO ME THAT YOU'RE GETTING PAID UNDER THE TABLE FROM ME --
YOU GONNA FIRE ME?
DON'T WORRY ABOUT IT.
ALL RIGHT, SMART GUY.
TRY TO FIND YOUR WAY BACK HERE FRIDAY NIGHT.
BUT NEXT TIME, WEAR THIS.
I HAD IT MADE FOR YOU SPECIAL.
WHY?
'CAUSE NO OFFENSE, KID --
-- WITH THE GET-UP YA GOT...
...YOU KIND OF LOOK LIKE A DORK.

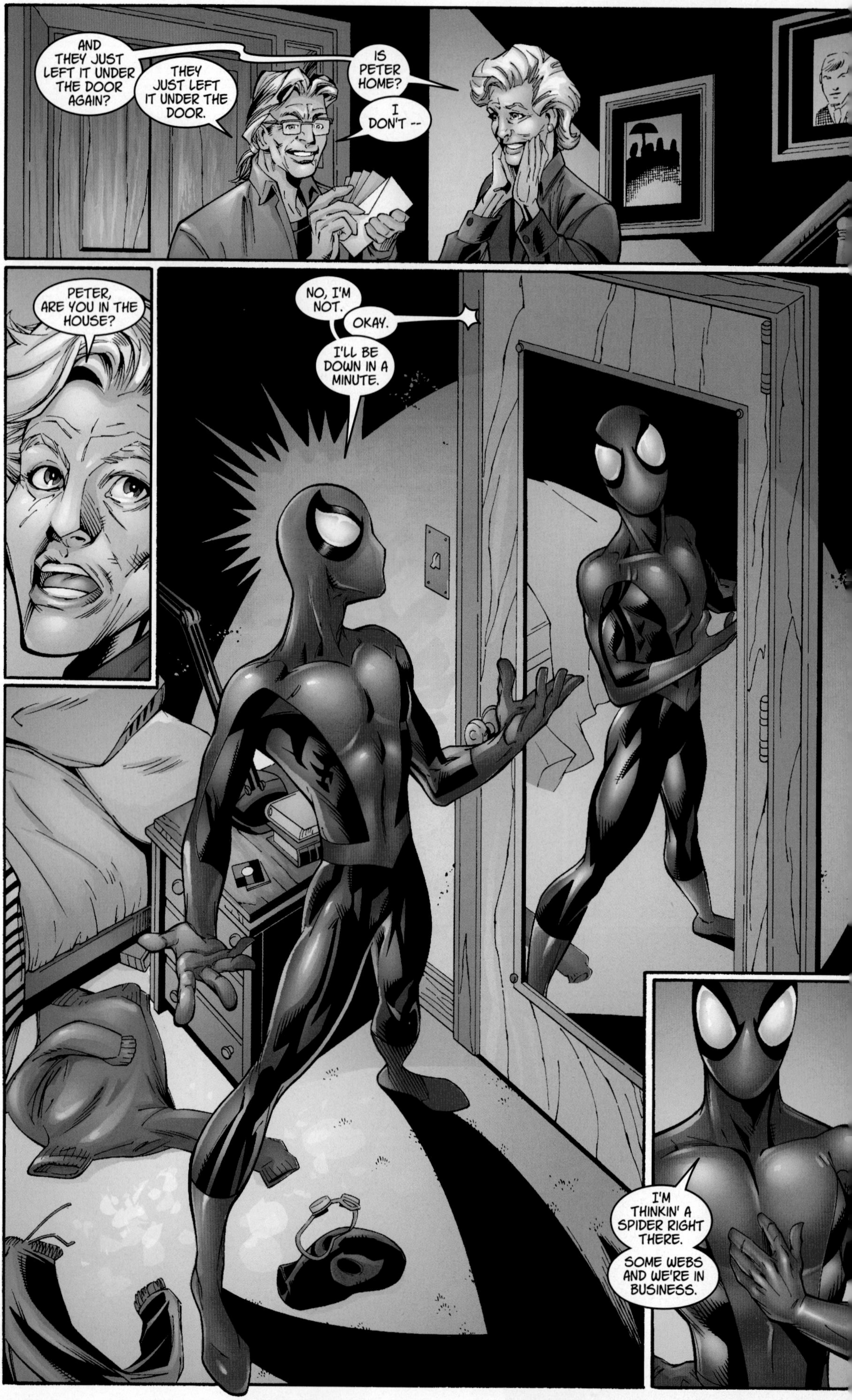
AND THEY JUST LEFT IT UNDER THE DOOR AGAIN?
THEY JUST LEFT IT UNDER THE DOOR.
IS PETER HOME?
I DON'T --
PETER, ARE YOU IN THE HOUSE?
NO, I'M NOT.
OKAY.
I'LL BE DOWN IN A MINUTE.
I'M THINKIN' A SPIDER RIGHT THERE.
SOME WEBS AND WE'RE IN BUSINESS.

4

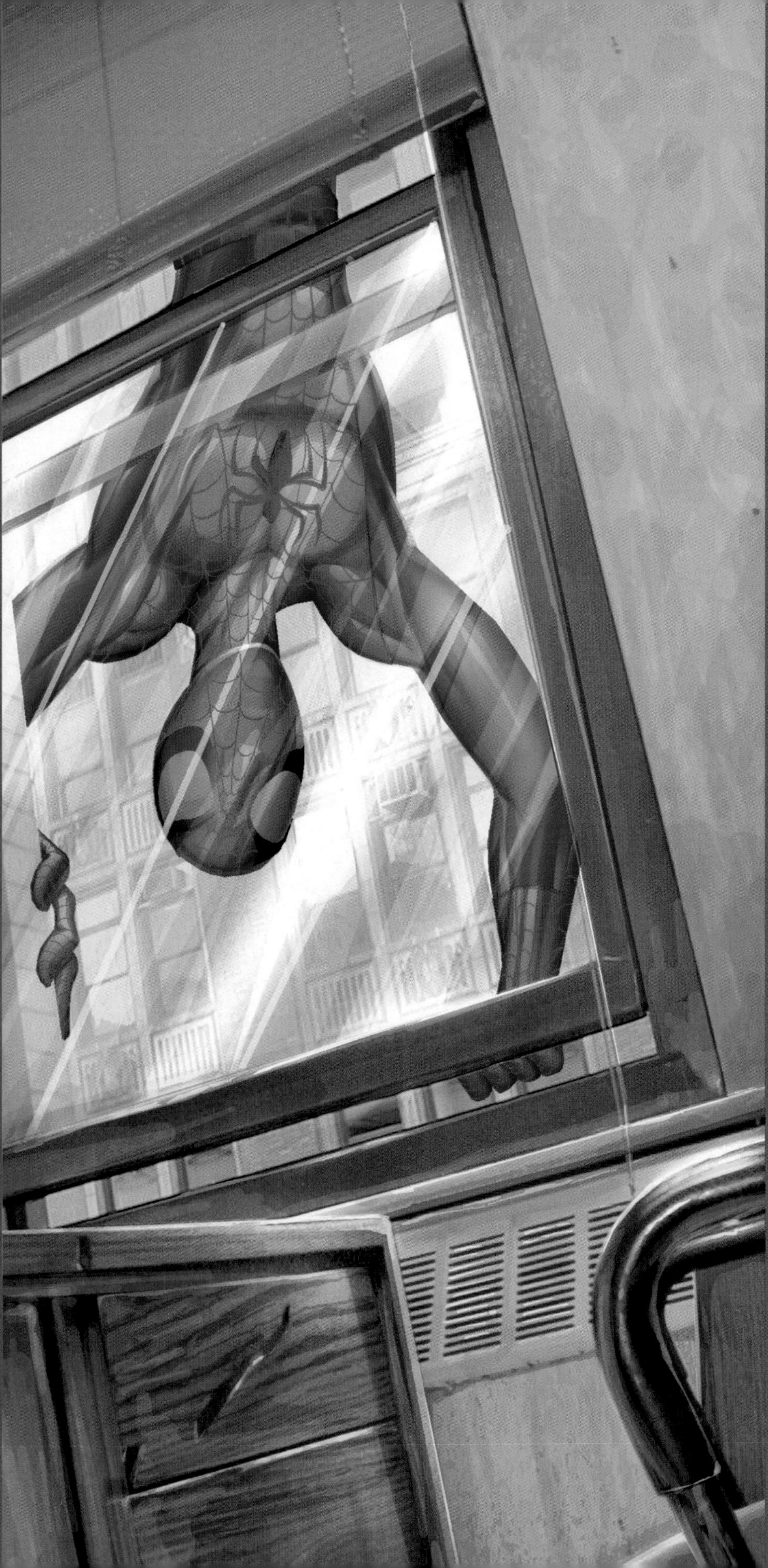

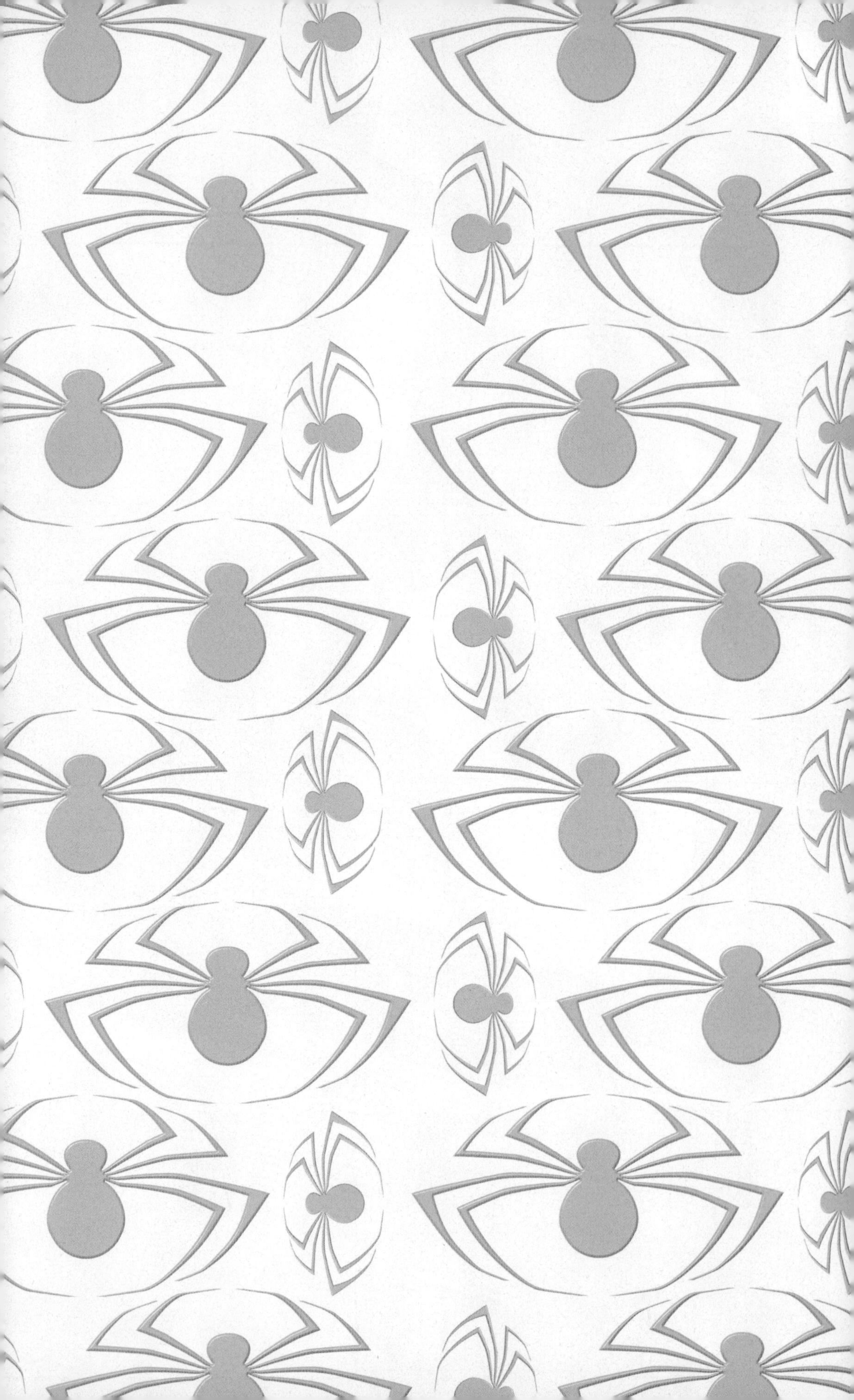

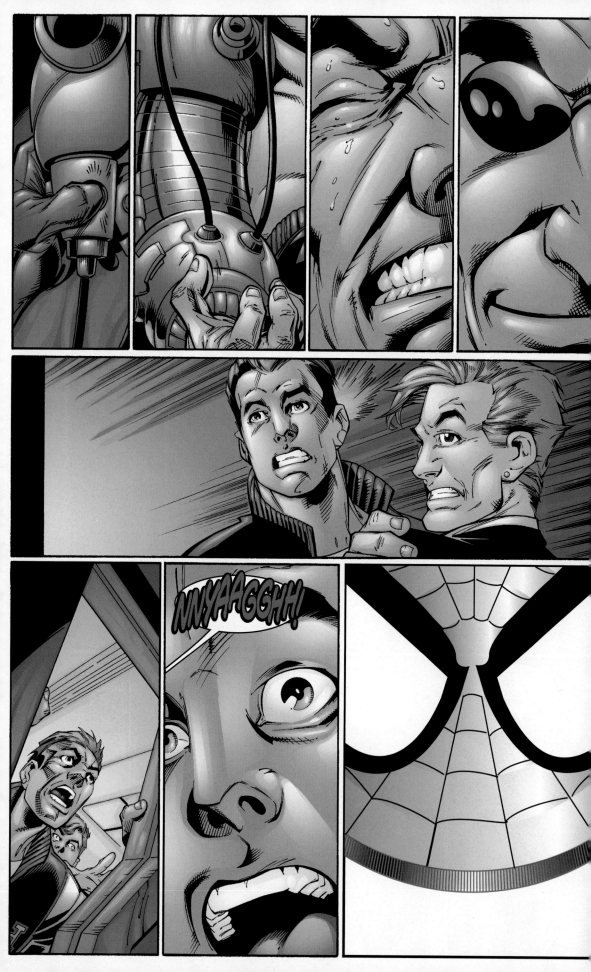

NNYAAGGHH!

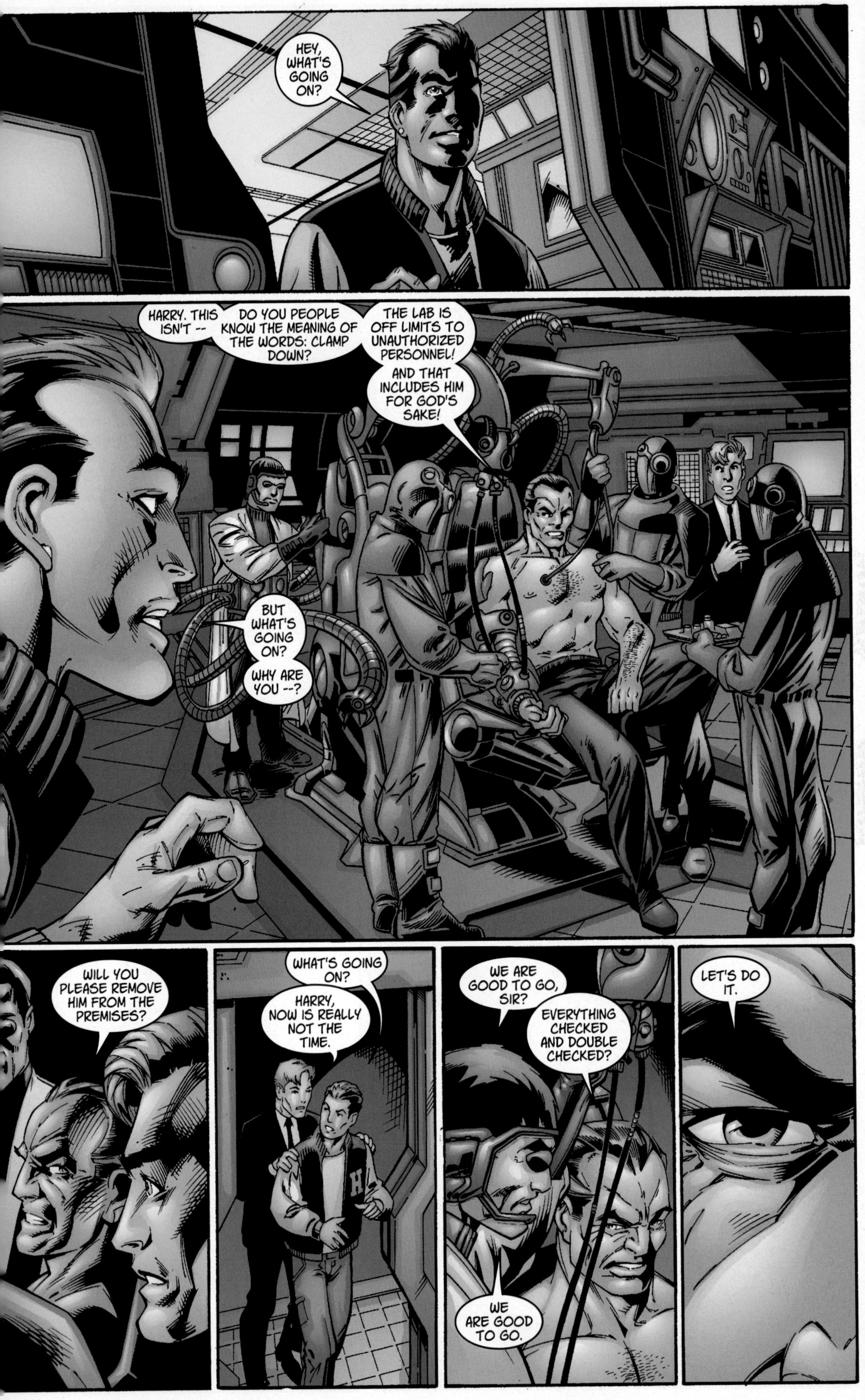
HEY, WHAT'S GOING ON?
HARRY. THIS ISN'T --
DO YOU PEOPLE KNOW THE MEANING OF THE WORDS: CLAMP DOWN?
THE LAB IS OFF LIMITS TO UNAUTHORIZED PERSONNEL!
AND THAT INCLUDES HIM FOR GOD'S SAKE!
BUT WHAT'S GOING ON?
WHY ARE YOU --?
WILL YOU PLEASE REMOVE HIM FROM THE PREMISES?
WHAT'S GOING ON?
HARRY, NOW IS REALLY NOT THE TIME.
WE ARE GOOD TO GO, SIR?
EVERYTHING CHECKED AND DOUBLE CHECKED?
WE ARE GOOD TO GO.
LET'S DO IT.

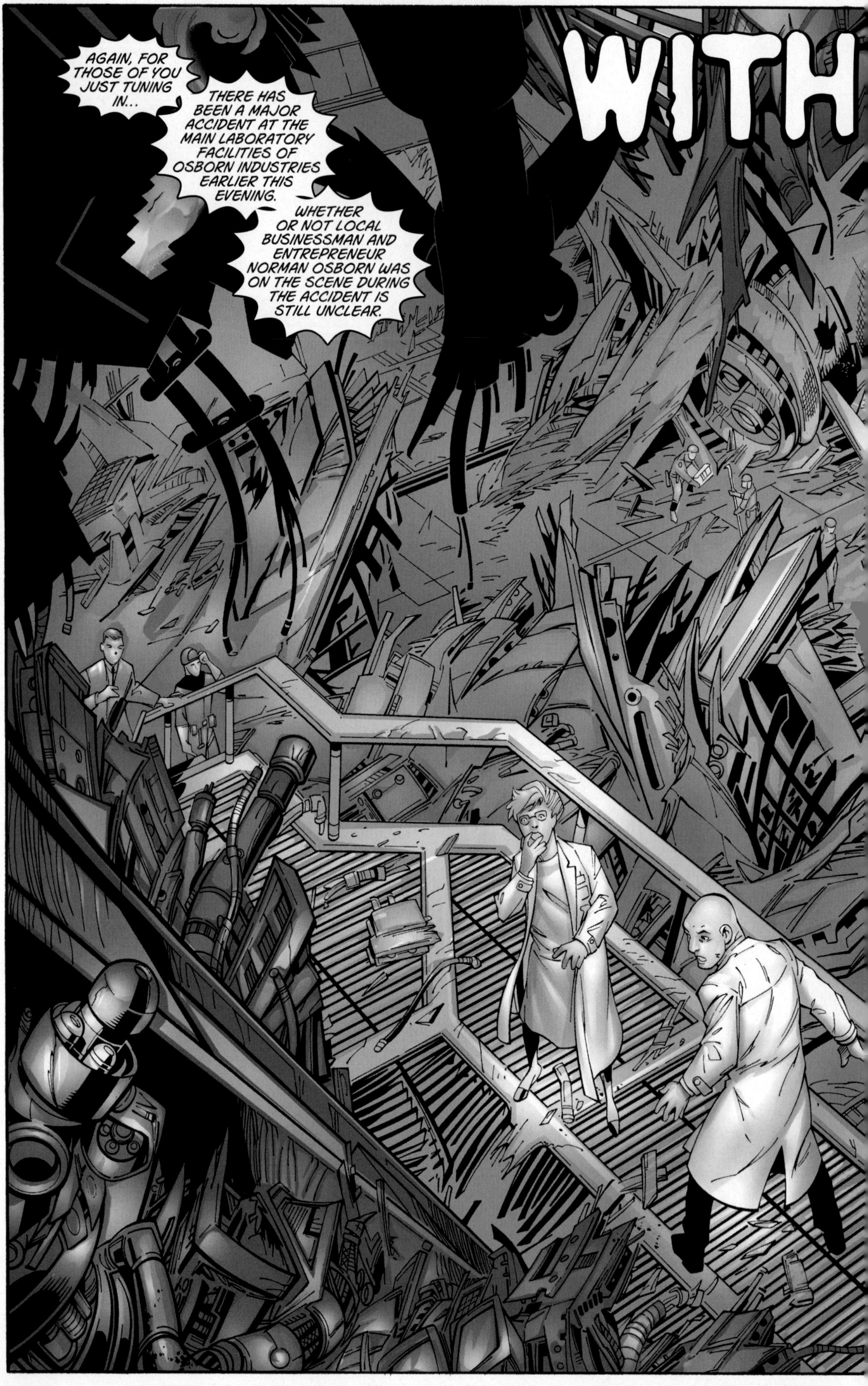
AGAIN, FOR THOSE OF YOU JUST TUNING IN...
THERE HAS BEEN A MAJOR ACCIDENT AT THE MAIN LABORATORY FACILITIES OF OSBORN INDUSTRIES EARLIER THIS EVENING.
WHETHER OR NOT LOCAL BUSINESSMAN AND ENTREPRENEUR NORMAN OSBORN WAS ON THE SCENE DURING THE ACCIDENT IS STILL UNCLEAR.
WITH

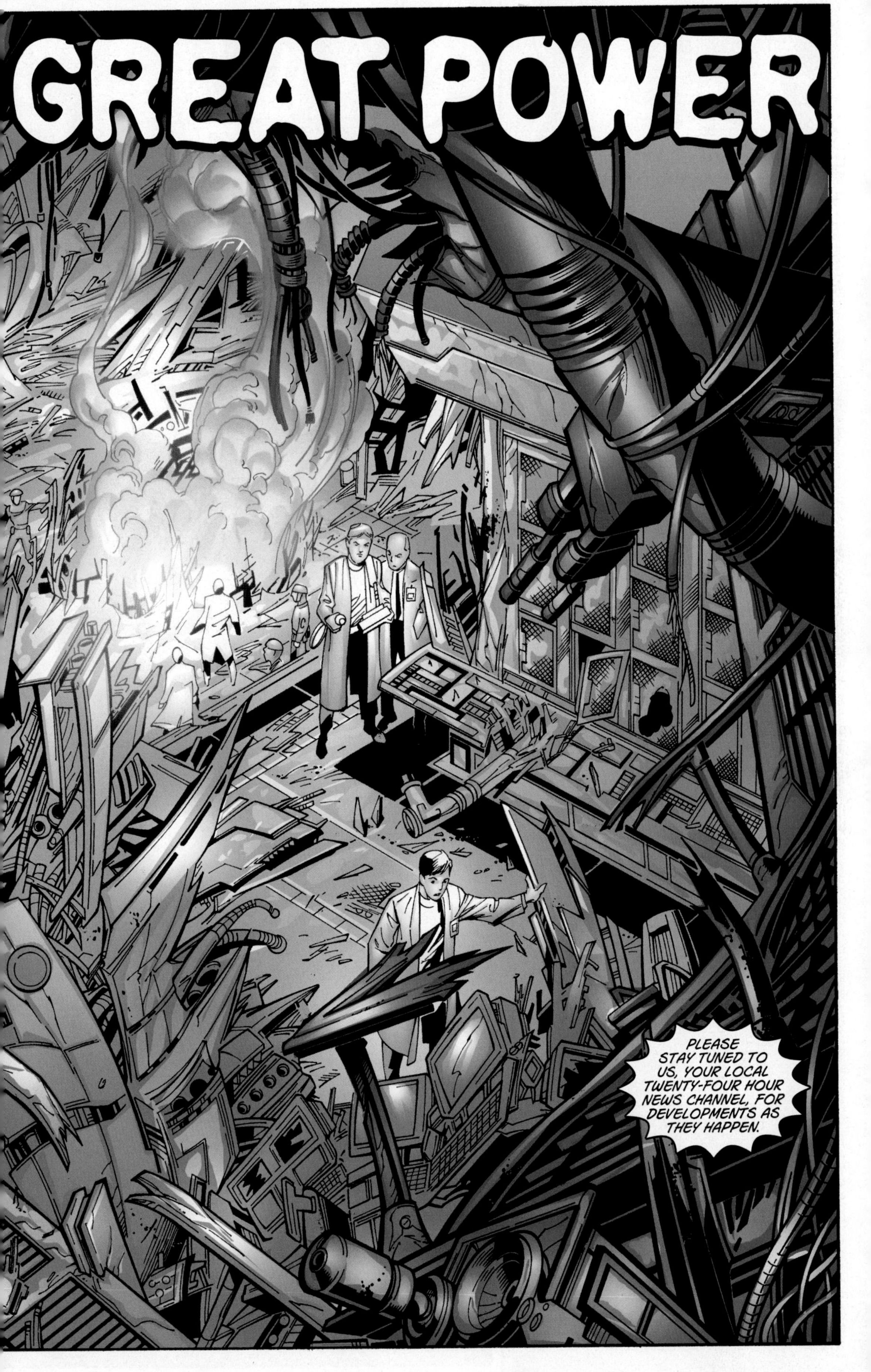
GREAT POWER
PLEASE STAY TUNED TO US, YOUR LOCAL TWENTY-FOUR HOUR NEWS CHANNEL, FOR DEVELOPMENTS AS THEY HAPPEN.

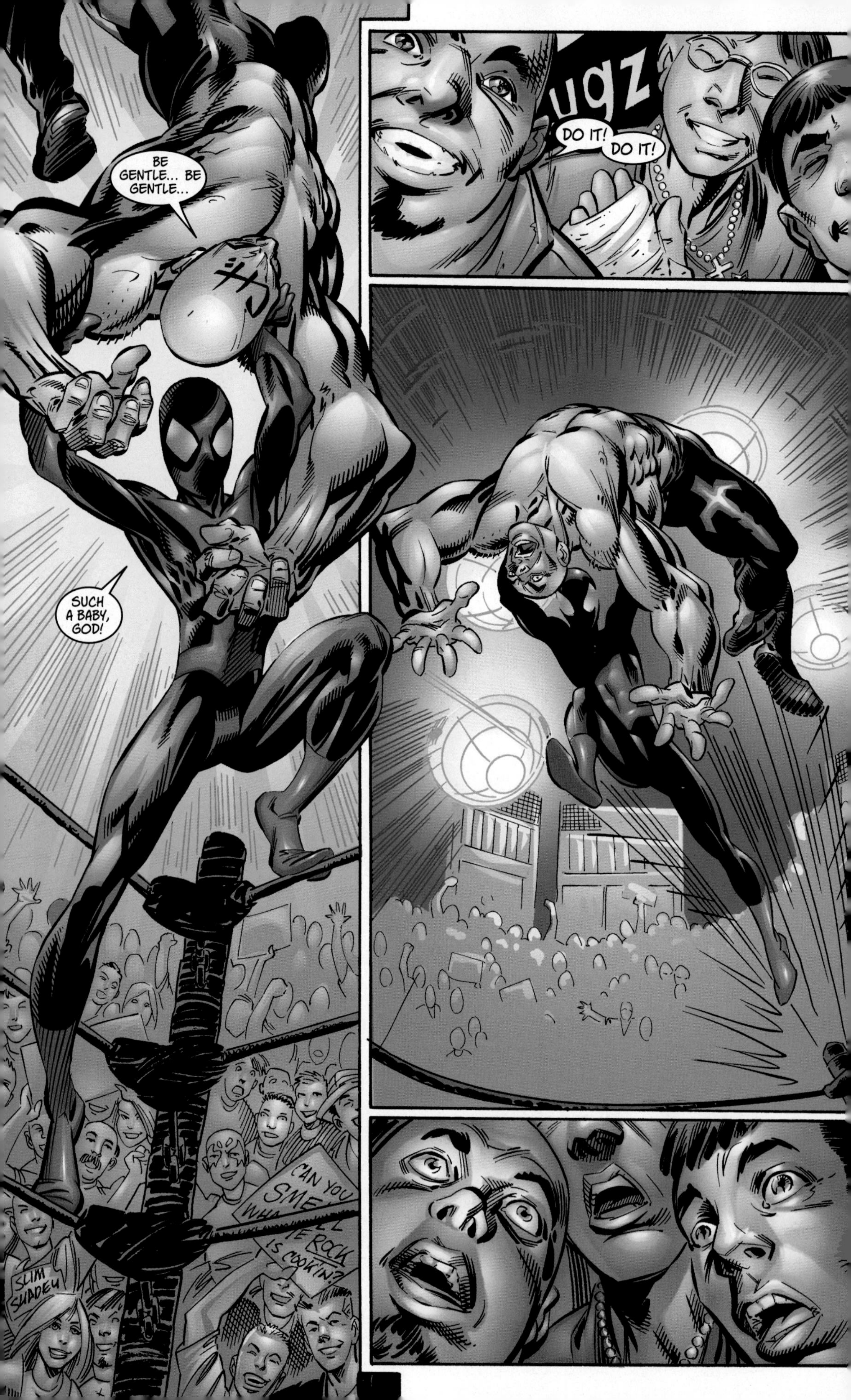
BE GENTLE... BE GENTLE...
SUCH A BABY, GOD!
DO IT!
DO IT!
SLIM SHADEY

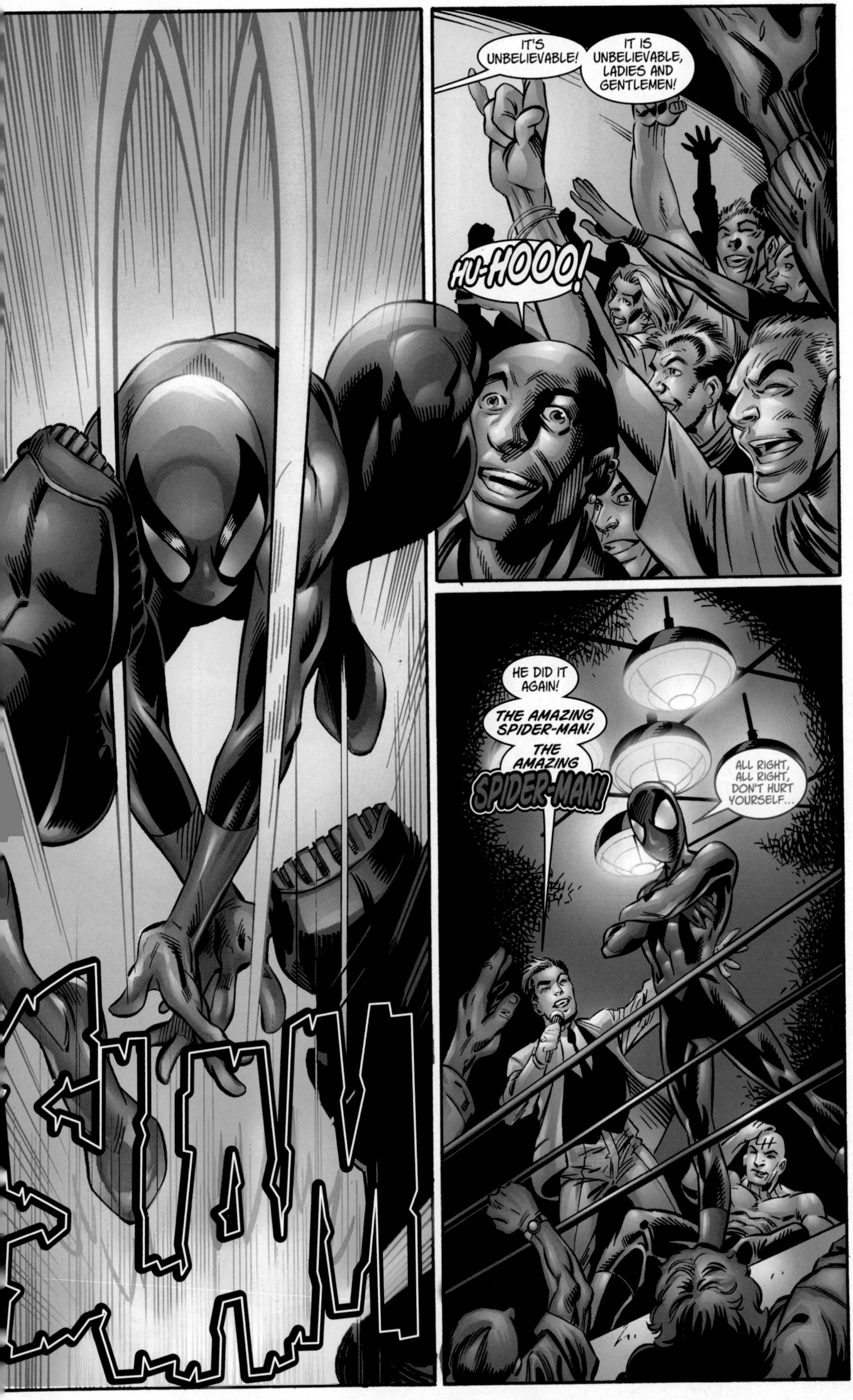
SLAM
IT'S UNBELIEVABLE!
IT IS UNBELIEVABLE, LADIES AND GENTLEMEN!
HU-HOOO!
HE DID IT AGAIN!
THE AMAZING SPIDER-MAN!
THE AMAZING SPIDER-MAN!
ALL RIGHT, ALL RIGHT, DON'T HURT YOURSELF...

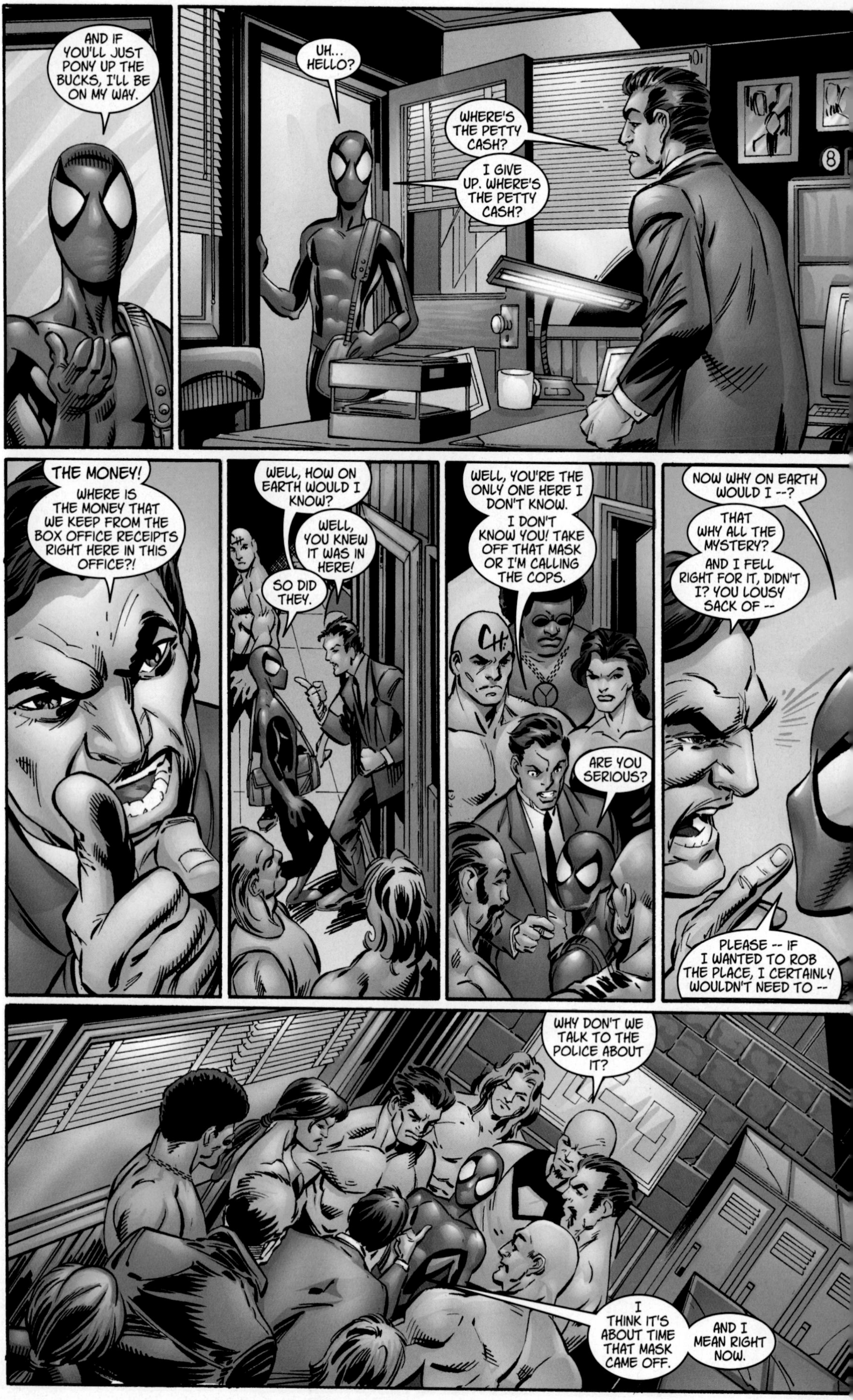
AND IF YOU'LL JUST PONY UP THE BUCKS, I'LL BE ON MY WAY.
UH... HELLO?
WHERE'S THE PETTY CASH?
I GIVE UP. WHERE'S THE PETTY CASH?
THE MONEY! WHERE IS THE MONEY THAT WE KEEP FROM THE BOX OFFICE RECEIPTS RIGHT HERE IN THIS OFFICE?!
WELL, HOW ON EARTH WOULD I KNOW?
WELL, YOU KNEW IT WAS IN HERE!
SO DID THEY.
WELL, YOU'RE THE ONLY ONE HERE I DON'T KNOW.
I DON'T KNOW YOU! TAKE OFF THAT MASK OR I'M CALLING THE COPS.
ARE YOU SERIOUS?
NOW WHY ON EARTH WOULD I --?
THAT WHY ALL THE MYSTERY?
AND I FELL RIGHT FOR IT, DIDN'T I? YOU LOUSY SACK OF --
PLEASE -- IF I WANTED TO ROB THE PLACE, I CERTAINLY WOULDN'T NEED TO --
WHY DON'T WE TALK TO THE POLICE ABOUT IT?
I THINK IT'S ABOUT TIME THAT MASK CAME OFF.
AND I MEAN RIGHT NOW.

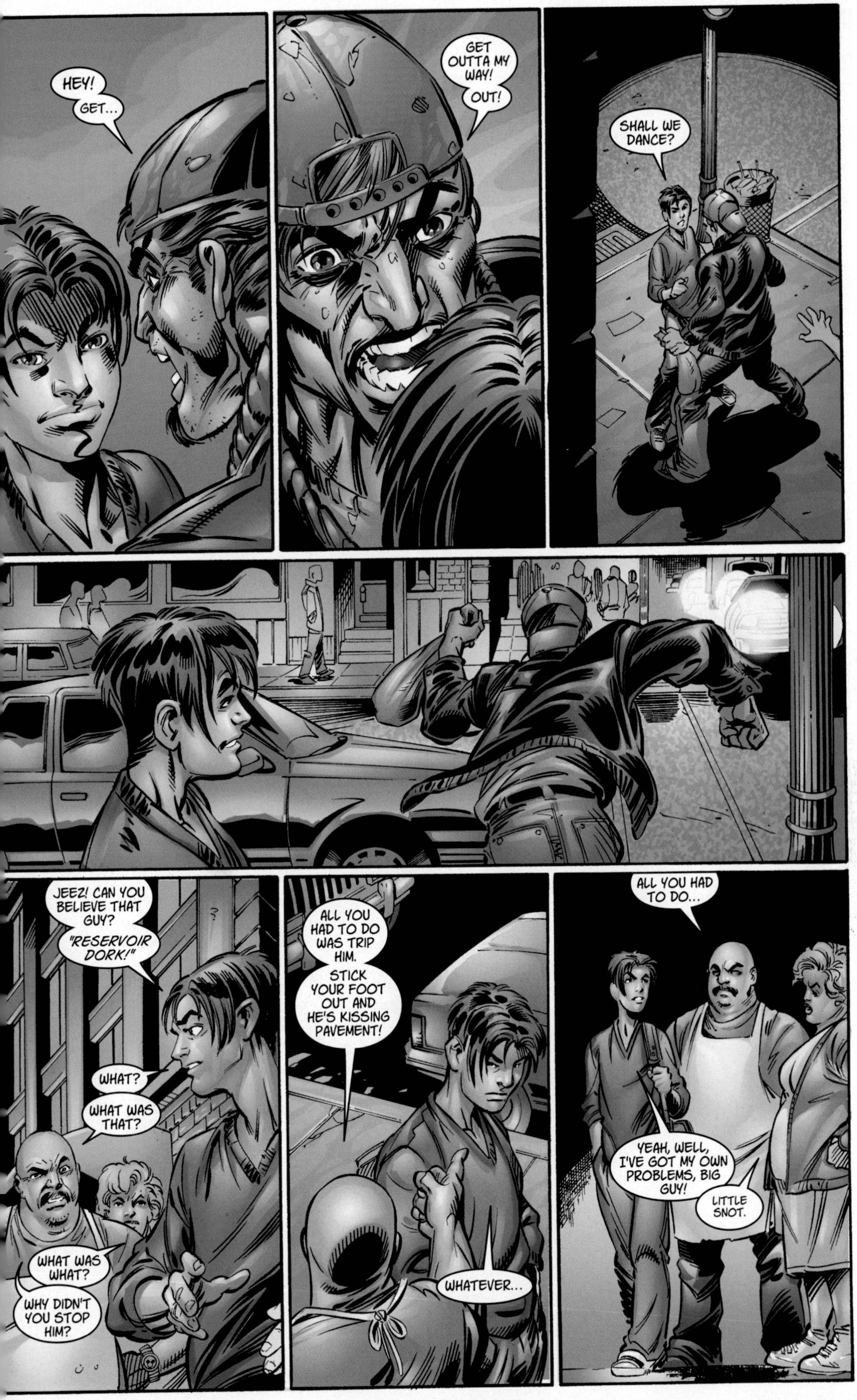
HEY!
GET...
GET OUTTA MY WAY!
OUT!
SHALL WE DANCE?
JEEZ! CAN YOU BELIEVE THAT GUY?
"RESERVOIR DORK!"
WHAT?
WHAT WAS THAT?
WHAT WAS WHAT?
WHY DIDN'T YOU STOP HIM?
ALL YOU HAD TO DO WAS TRIP HIM.
STICK YOUR FOOT OUT AND HE'S KISSING PAVEMENT!
WHATEVER...
ALL YOU HAD TO DO...
YEAH, WELL, I'VE GOT MY OWN PROBLEMS, BIG GUY!
LITTLE SNOT.

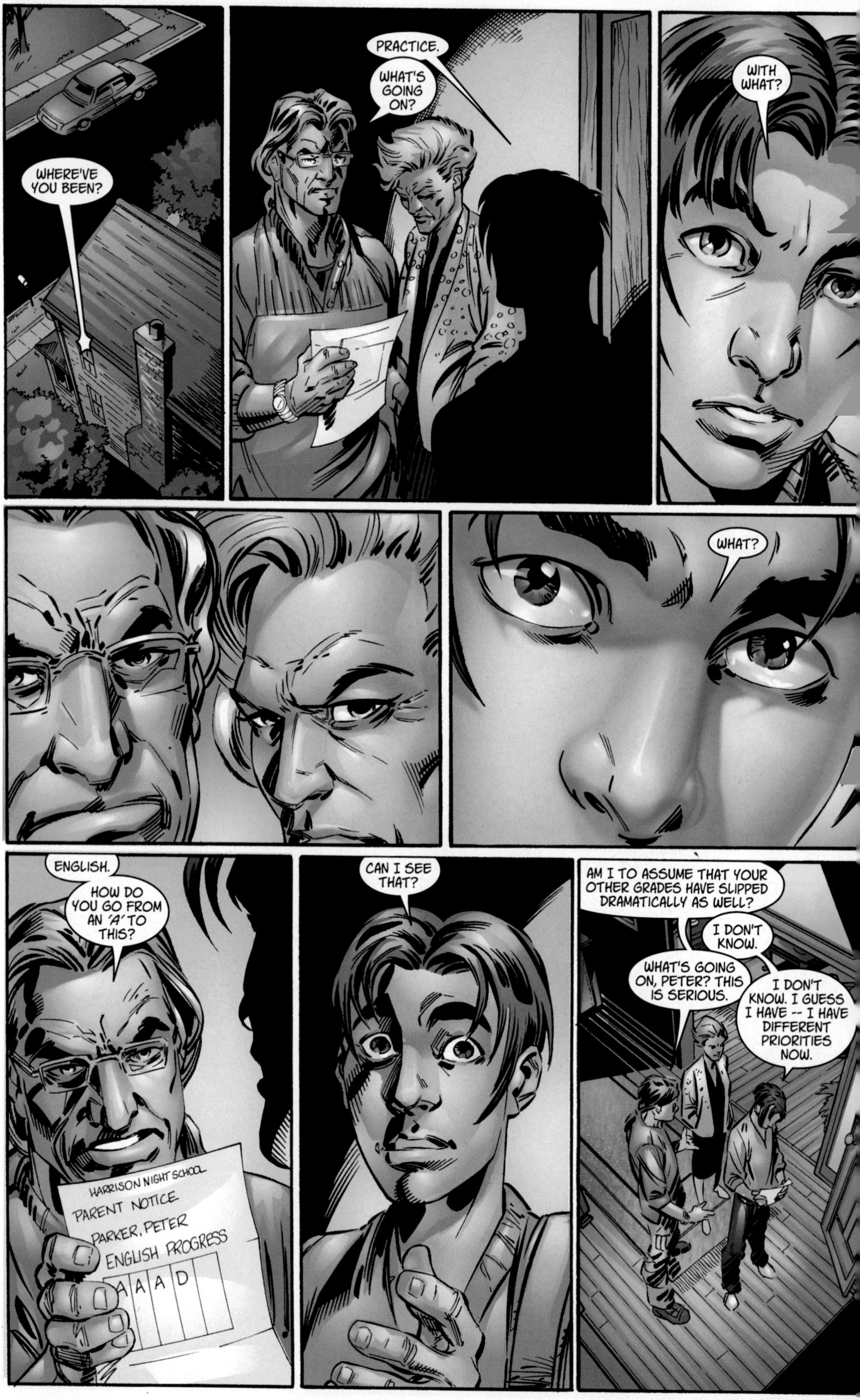
WHERE'VE YOU BEEN?
PRACTICE.
WHAT'S GOING ON?
WITH WHAT?
WHAT?
ENGLISH.
HOW DO YOU GO FROM AN 'A' TO THIS?
HARRISON NIGHT SCHOOL
PARENT NOTICE
PARKER, PETER
ENGLISH PROGRESS
A A A D
CAN I SEE THAT?
AM I TO ASSUME THAT YOUR OTHER GRADES HAVE SLIPPED DRAMATICALLY AS WELL?
I DON'T KNOW.
WHAT'S GOING ON, PETER? THIS IS SERIOUS.
I DON'T KNOW. I GUESS I HAVE -- I HAVE DIFFERENT PRIORITIES NOW.

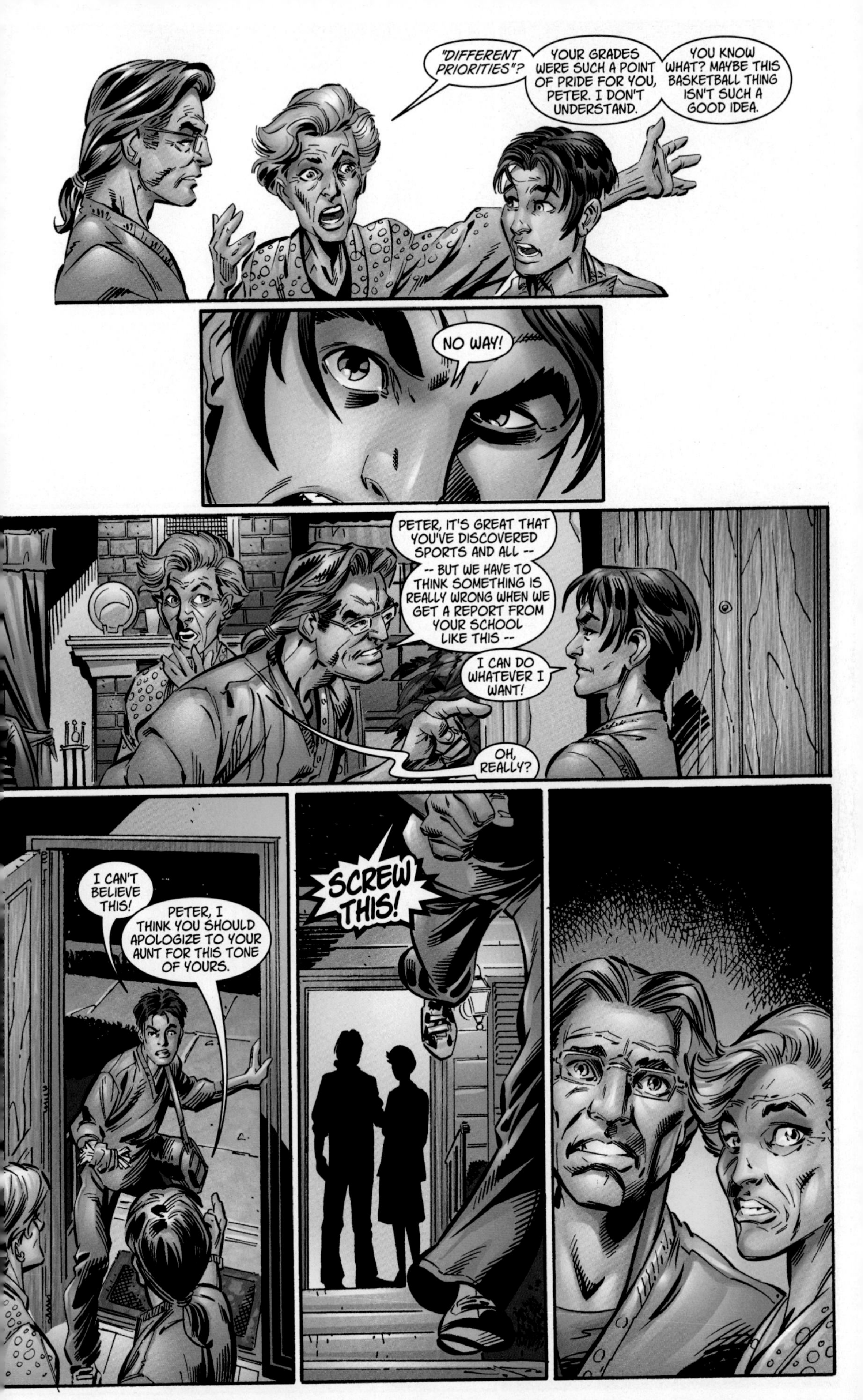
"DIFFERENT PRIORITIES"?
YOUR GRADES WERE SUCH A POINT OF PRIDE FOR YOU, PETER. I DON'T UNDERSTAND.
YOU KNOW WHAT? MAYBE THIS BASKETBALL THING ISN'T SUCH A GOOD IDEA.
NO WAY!
PETER, IT'S GREAT THAT YOU'VE DISCOVERED SPORTS AND ALL --
-- BUT WE HAVE TO THINK SOMETHING IS REALLY WRONG WHEN WE GET A REPORT FROM YOUR SCHOOL LIKE THIS --
I CAN DO WHATEVER I WANT!
OH, REALLY?
I CAN'T BELIEVE THIS!
PETER, I THINK YOU SHOULD APOLOGIZE TO YOUR AUNT FOR THIS TONE OF YOURS.
SCREW THIS!

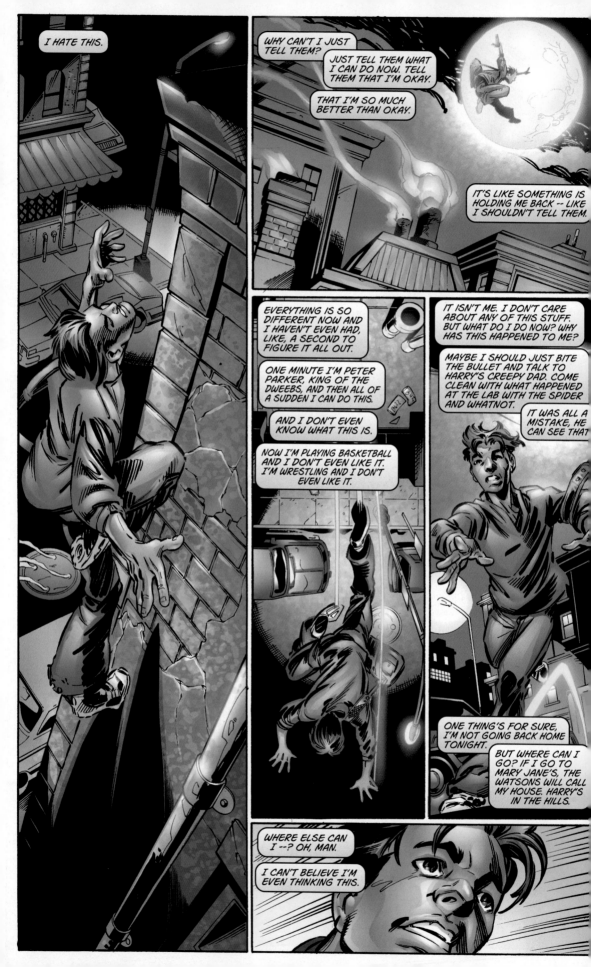

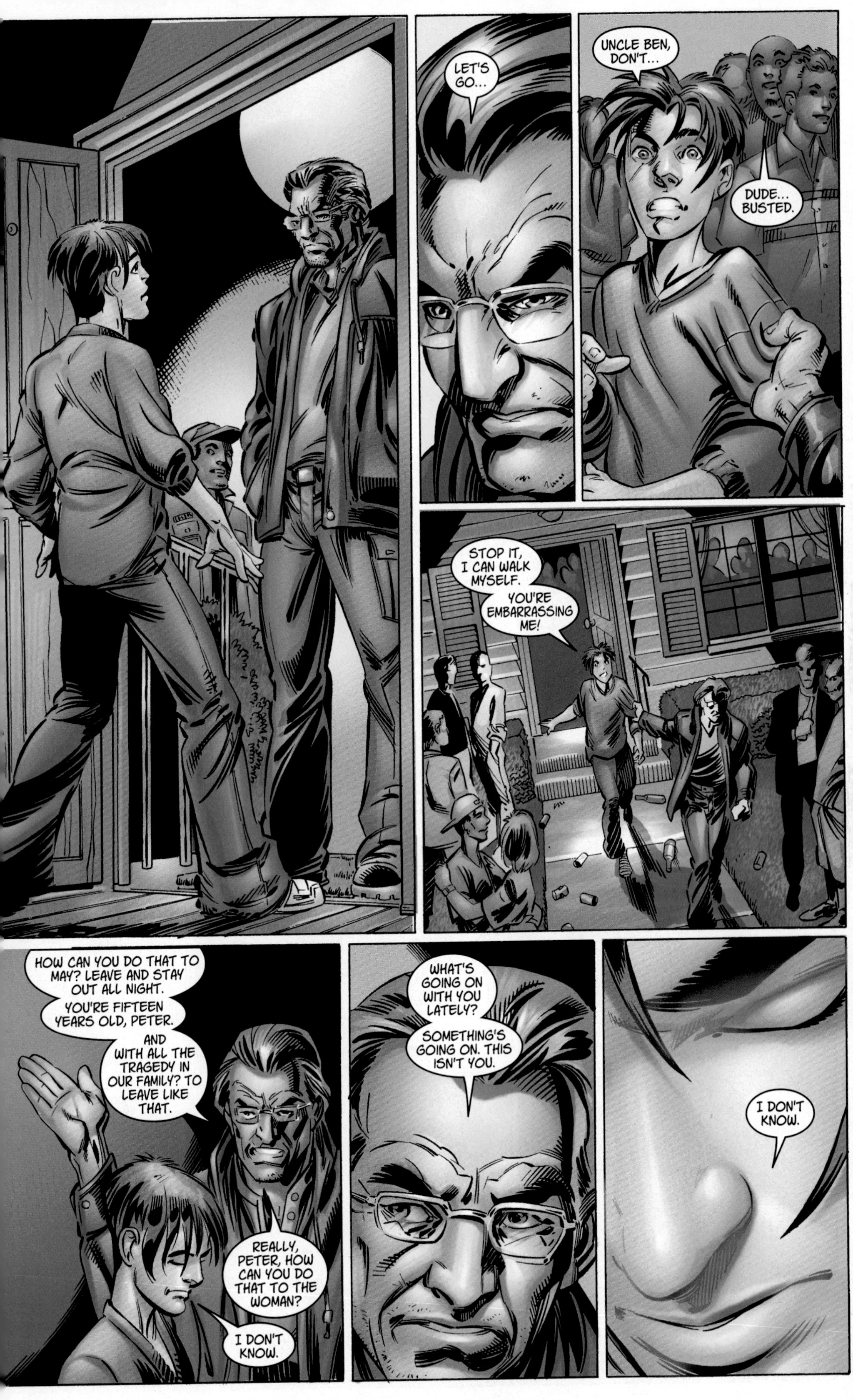
LET'S GO...
UNCLE BEN, DON'T...
DUDE... BUSTED.
STOP IT, I CAN WALK MYSELF.
YOU'RE EMBARRASSING ME!
HOW CAN YOU DO THAT TO MAY? LEAVE AND STAY OUT ALL NIGHT.
YOU'RE FIFTEEN YEARS OLD, PETER.
AND WITH ALL THE TRAGEDY IN OUR FAMILY? TO LEAVE LIKE THAT.
REALLY, PETER, HOW CAN YOU DO THAT TO THE WOMAN?
I DON'T KNOW.
WHAT'S GOING ON WITH YOU LATELY?
SOMETHING'S GOING ON. THIS ISN'T YOU.
I DON'T KNOW.

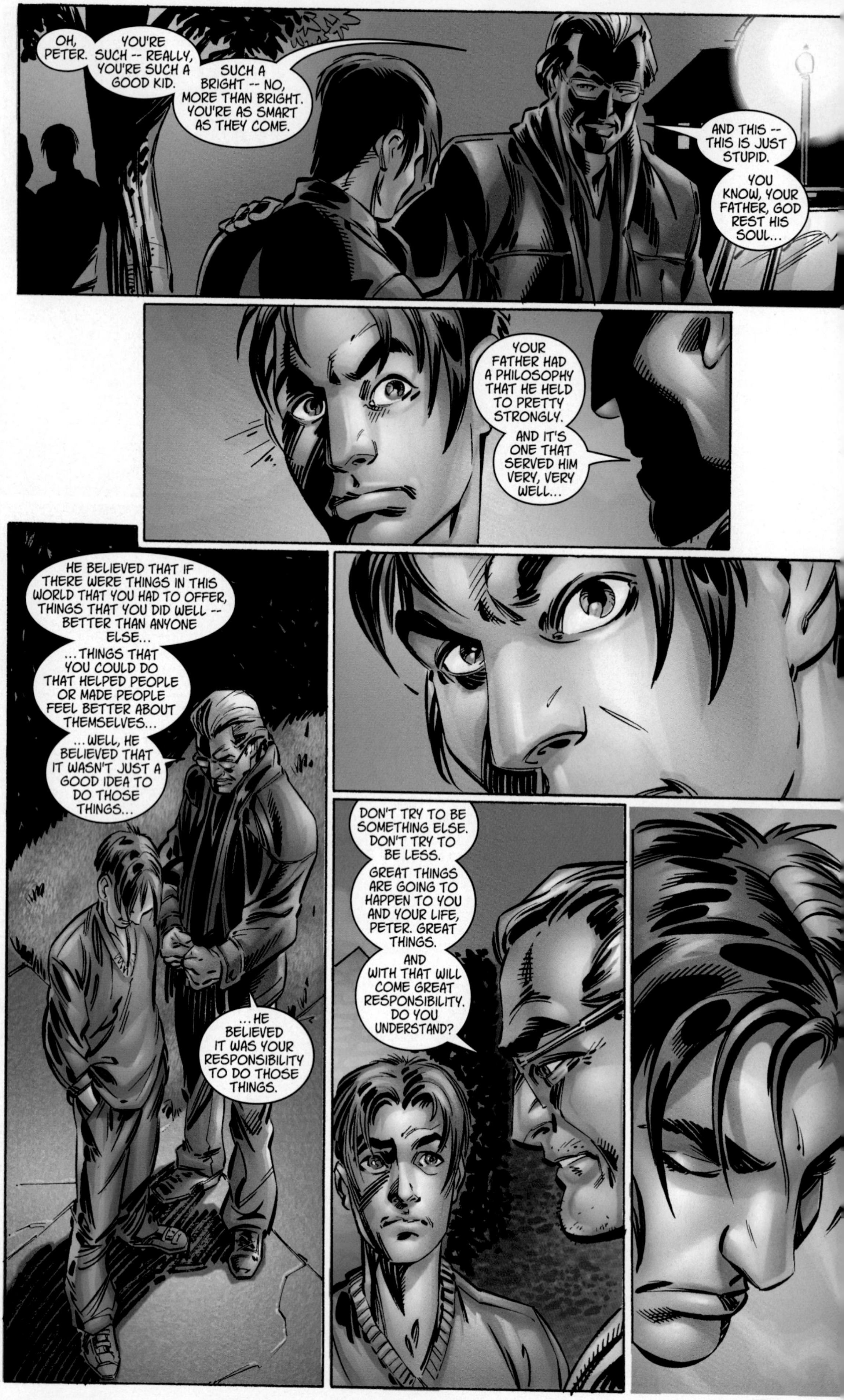
OH, PETER.
YOU'RE SUCH -- REALLY, YOU'RE SUCH A GOOD KID.
SUCH A BRIGHT -- NO, MORE THAN BRIGHT. YOU'RE AS SMART AS THEY COME.
AND THIS -- THIS IS JUST STUPID.
YOU KNOW, YOUR FATHER, GOD REST HIS SOUL...
YOUR FATHER HAD A PHILOSOPHY THAT HE HELD TO PRETTY STRONGLY.
AND IT'S ONE THAT SERVED HIM VERY, VERY WELL...
HE BELIEVED THAT IF THERE WERE THINGS IN THIS WORLD THAT YOU HAD TO OFFER, THINGS THAT YOU DID WELL -- BETTER THAN ANYONE ELSE...
...THINGS THAT YOU COULD DO THAT HELPED PEOPLE OR MADE PEOPLE FEEL BETTER ABOUT THEMSELVES...
...WELL, HE BELIEVED THAT IT WASN'T JUST A GOOD IDEA TO DO THOSE THINGS...
...HE BELIEVED IT WAS YOUR RESPONSIBILITY TO DO THOSE THINGS.
DON'T TRY TO BE SOMETHING ELSE. DON'T TRY TO BE LESS.
GREAT THINGS ARE GOING TO HAPPEN TO YOU AND YOUR LIFE, PETER. GREAT THINGS.
AND WITH THAT WILL COME GREAT RESPONSIBILITY. DO YOU UNDERSTAND?

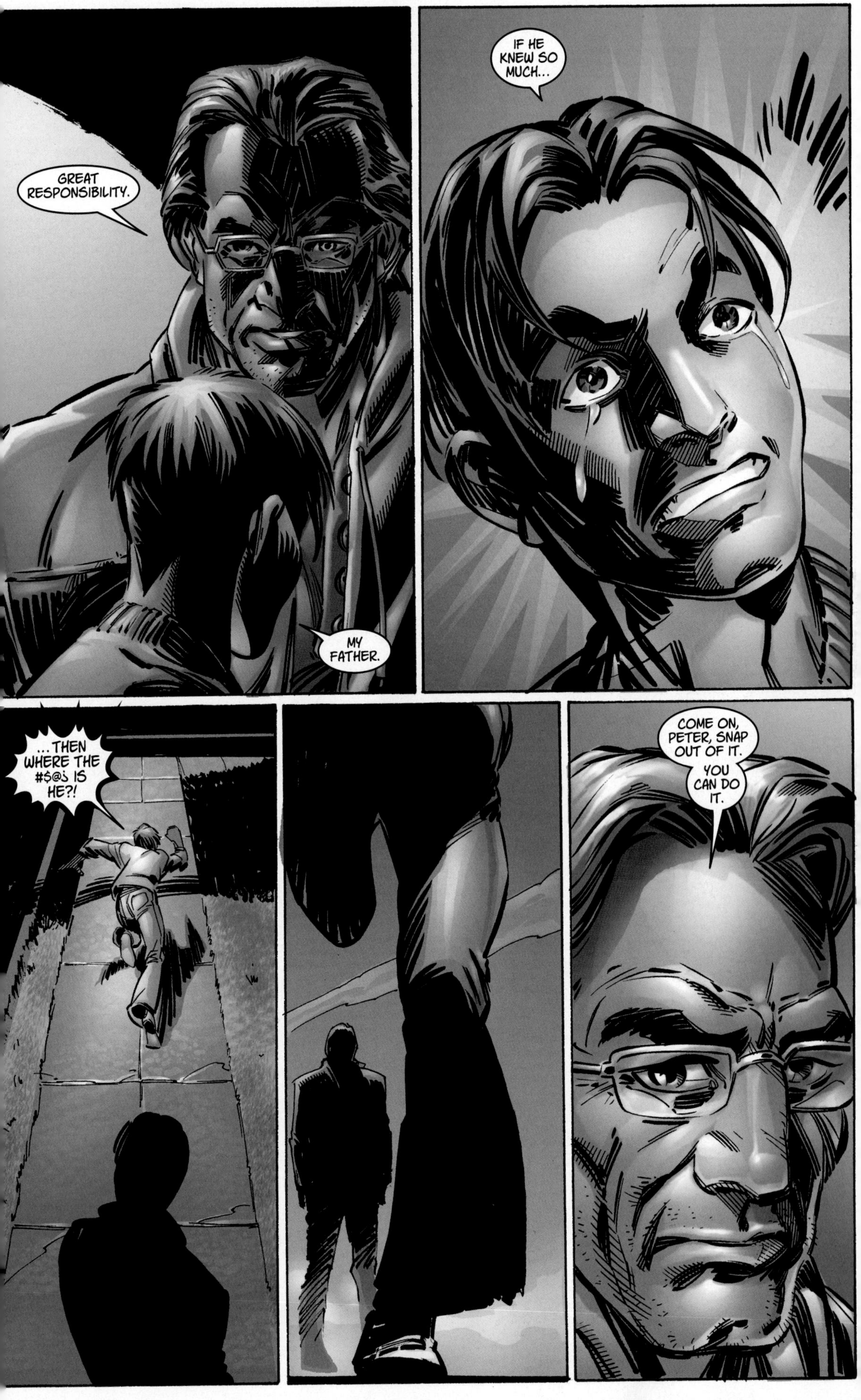
GREAT RESPONSIBILITY.
MY FATHER.
IF HE KNEW SO MUCH...
...THEN WHERE THE #$@$ IS HE?!
COME ON, PETER, SNAP OUT OF IT.
YOU CAN DO IT.

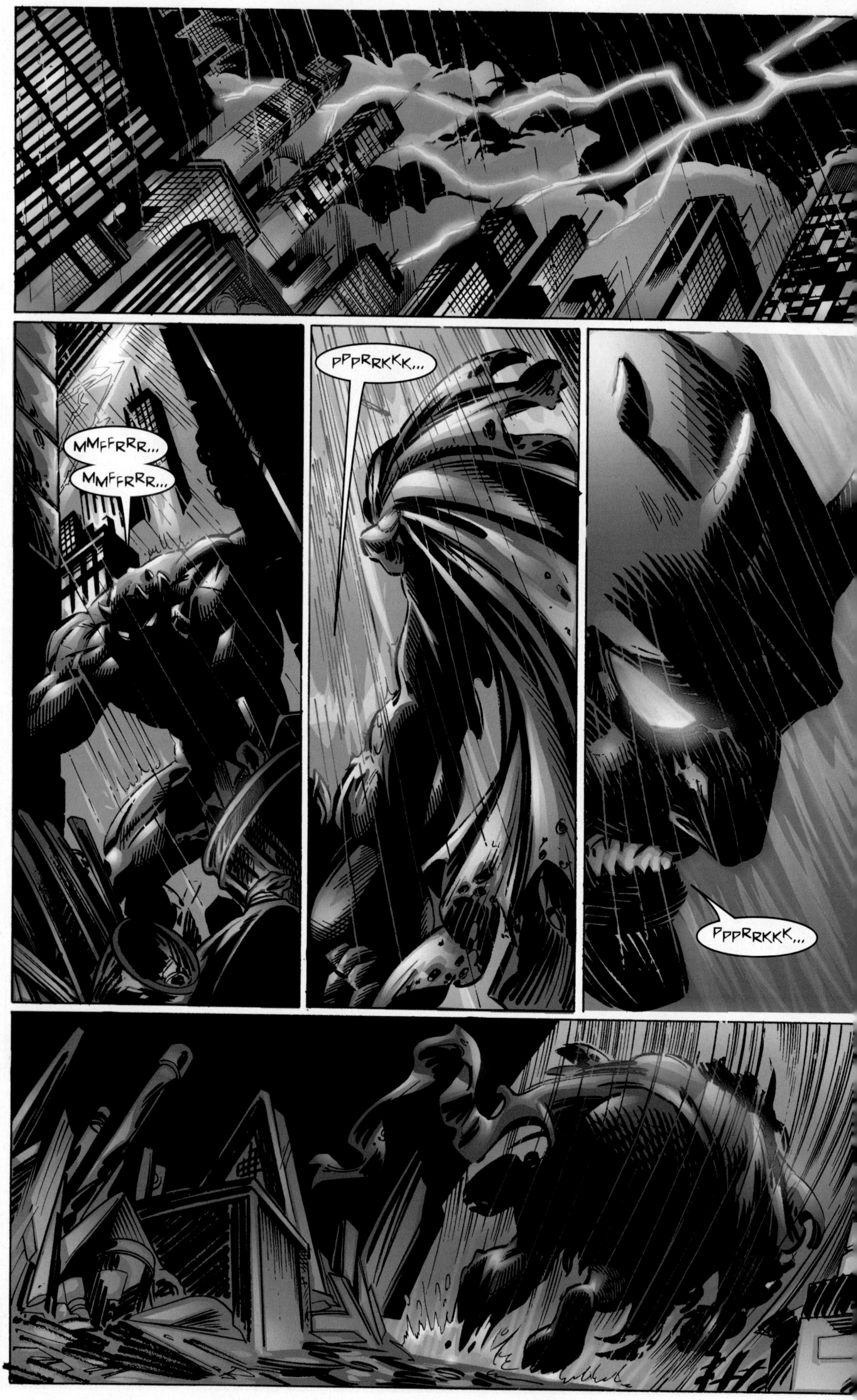
MMFFRRR...
MMFFRRR...
PPPRRKKK...
PPPRRKKK...

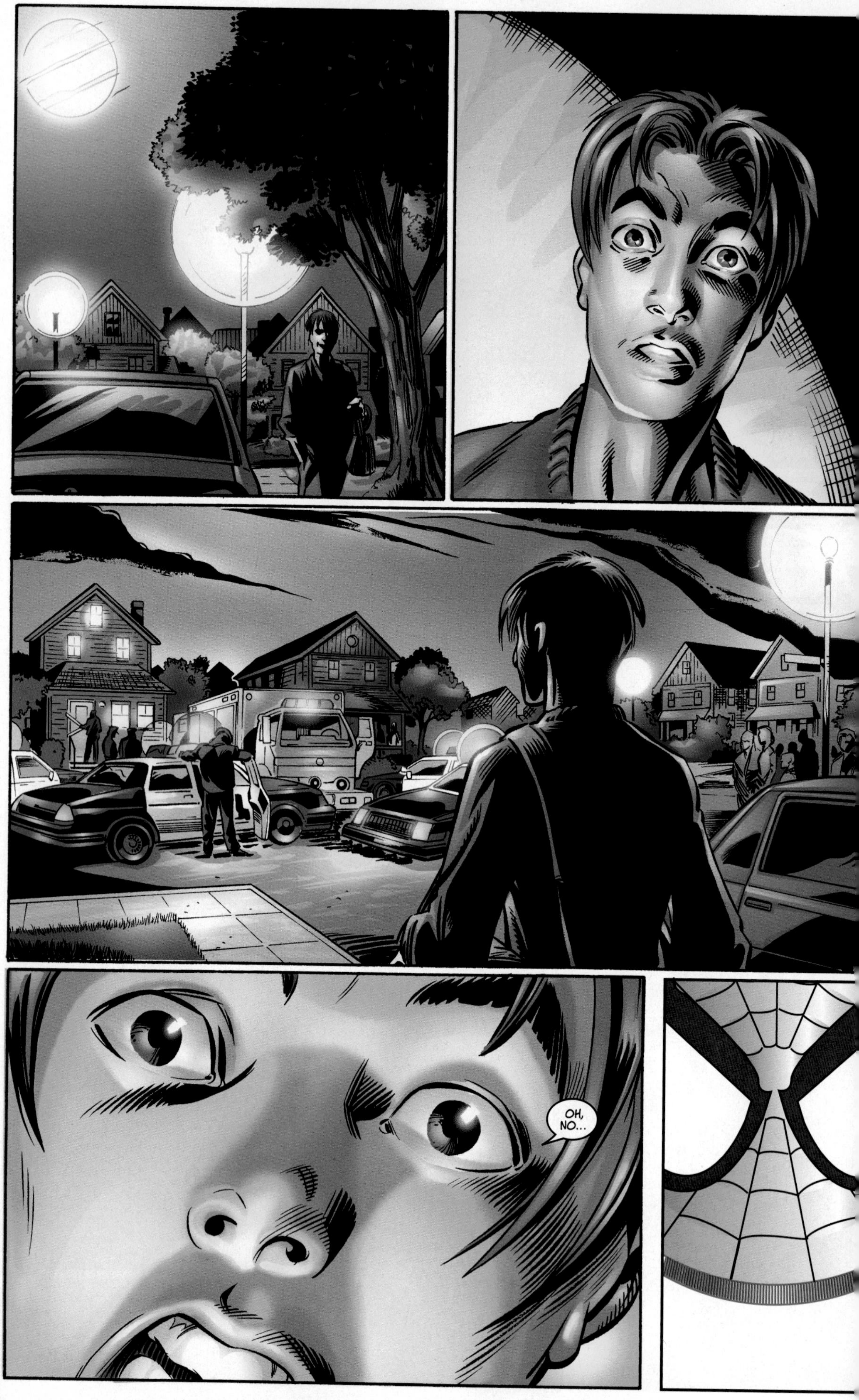
OH, NO...

5

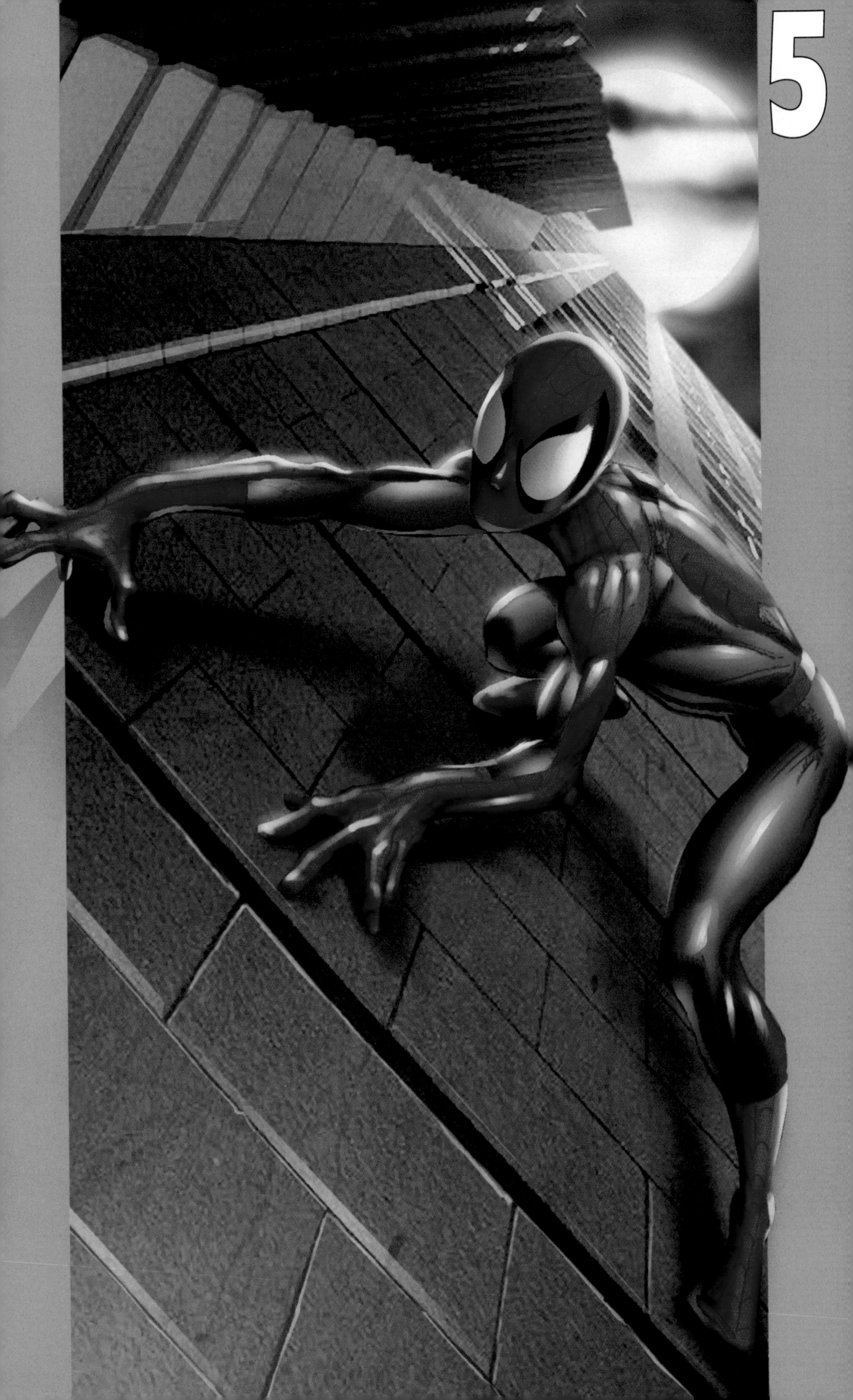

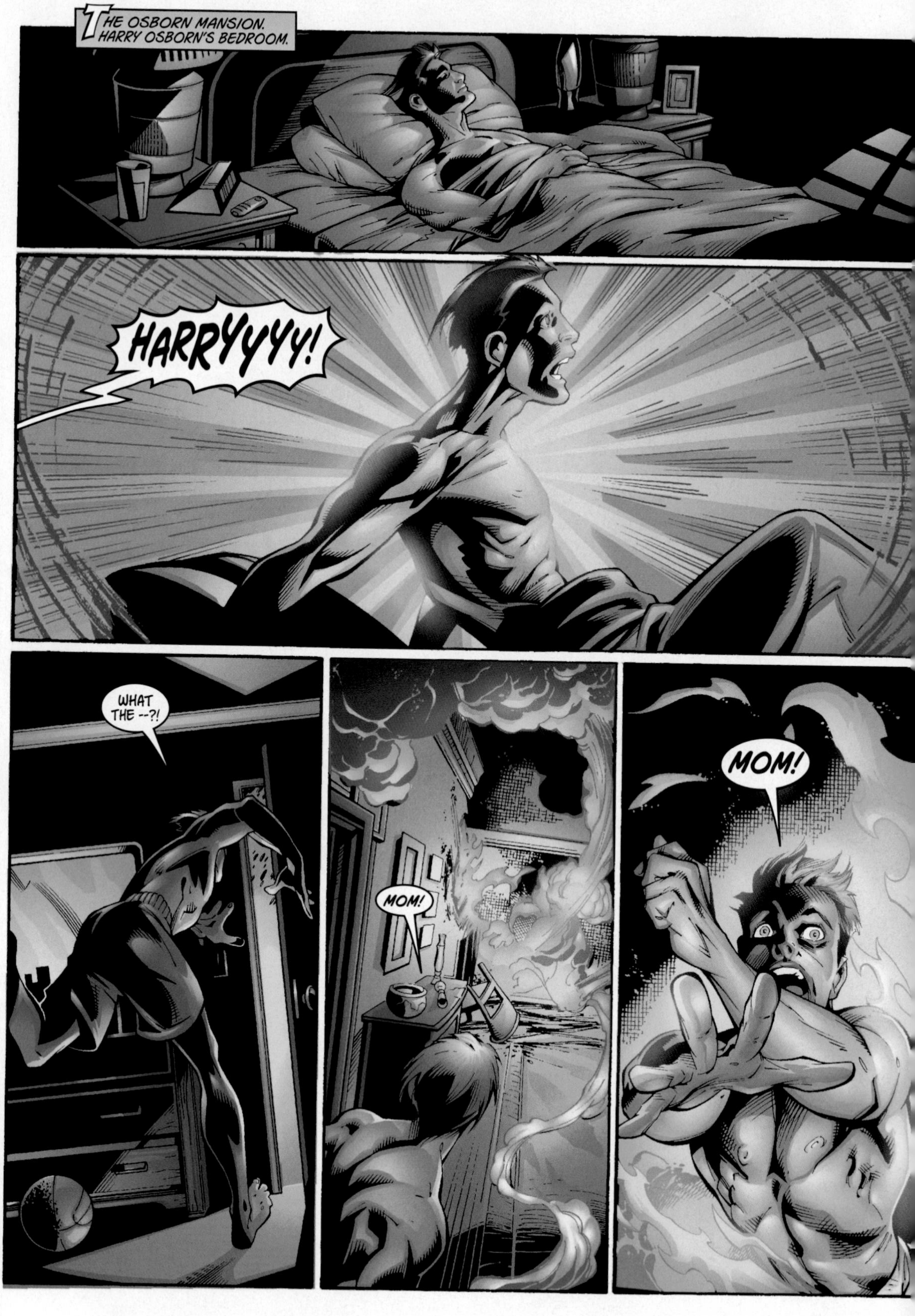
THE OSBORN MANSION. HARRY OSBORN'S BEDROOM.
HARRYYYY!
WHAT THE --?!
MOM!
MOM!

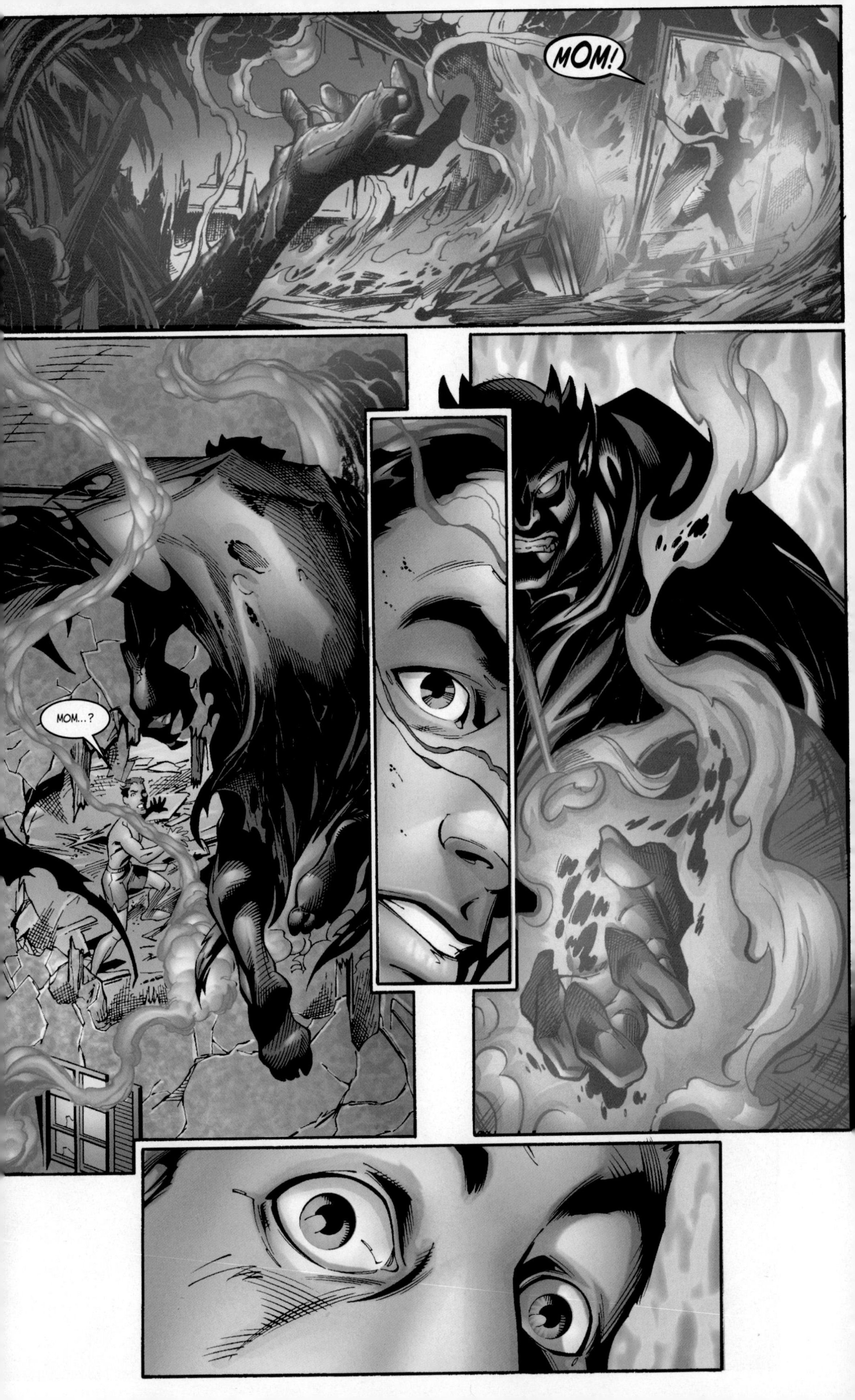
MOM!
MOM...?

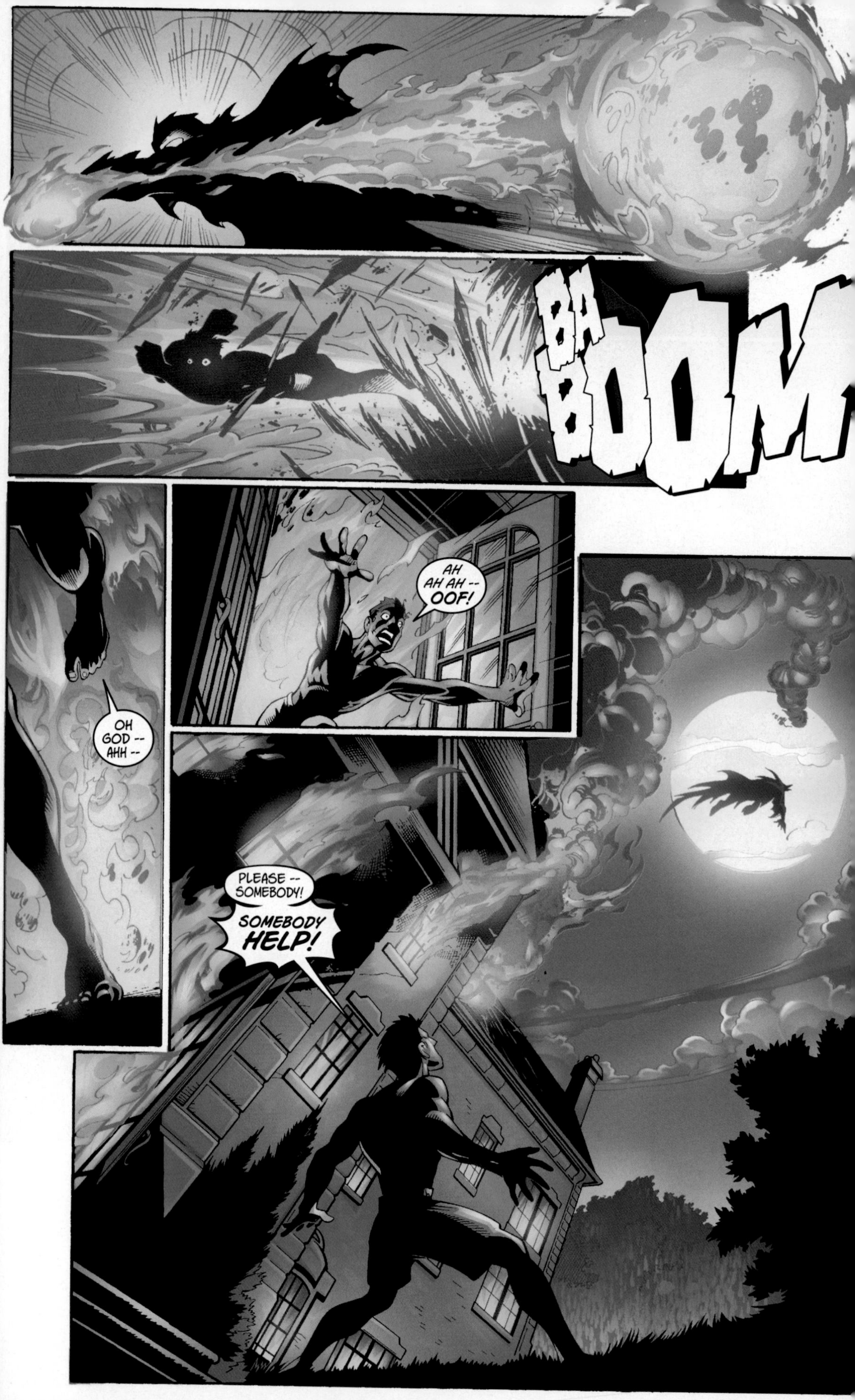
BA BOOM
OH GOD -- AHH --
AH AH AH -- OOF!
PLEASE -- SOMEBODY!
SOMEBODY HELP!

YES, WE -- WE HEARD A NOISE IN THE BACK.

AND TO BE HONEST, WE BOTH THOUGHT IT WAS PETER.

BECAUSE PETER USES THE BACK ENTRANCE MOST OF THE TIME.

BUT BEN CALLED OUT TO HIM -- AND HE DIDN'T ANSWER.

AND RIGHT THEN -- I DON'T KNOW WHY -- BUT RIGHT THEN I KNEW SOMETHING WAS WRONG.

I KNEW THAT SOMEONE WAS IN OUR HOUSE. I COULD -- I COULD JUST TELL FROM THE KIND OF SILENCE.

BOTH OF YOU WERE IN THE LIVING ROOM?

YES.

AND I THINK BEN KNEW SOMETHING WAS WRONG TOO, BECAUSE HE GOT UP FIRST.

HE GOT UP AND HE CALLED OUT TO PETER AGAIN.

THERE WAS NOTHING FOR A SECOND -- THEN WE HEARD A PAN DROP.

BEN LOOKED AT ME AND SAID HE THOUGHT A SQUIRREL GOT IN THE HOUSE.

AND I SAID I NEVER HEARD OF THAT HAPPENING IN QUEENS.

THEN I LOOKED IN THE DOORWAY OF THE KITCHEN -- AND THERE HE WAS.

"HE -- HE WAS STANDING THERE IN THE DOORWAY -- HE WAS SHAKING -- AND HE ASKED US WHERE WE KEPT OUR MONEY.

"BEN TOLD HIM WE DIDN'T HAVE ANY. AND WE DIDN'T. NOTHING."

AND THE GUY JUST GOT REAL AGITATED AND SCREAMED:

"GIVE ME ALL YOUR MONEY!"

AND BEN -- HE -- HE JUST HE --

"I GUESS IT WAS JUST THE TENSION OF THE SITUATION -- THE RIDICULOUSNESS -- I DON'T KNOW -- THE WAY THINGS HAVE BEEN GOING LATELY.

"BUT -- BEN HE -- HE KIND OF CHUCKLED AND SAID: YOU PROBABLY HAVE MORE MONEY THAN WE DO."

AND THE -- THE CHUCKLE KIND OF --

-- I DON'T KNOW --

-- IT REALLY MADE HIM MAD.

AND THAT WAS IT.

HE JUST RAN OUT THE WAY HE CAME AND --

WHAT HAPPENED NEXT, MA'AM?

OH, NO.

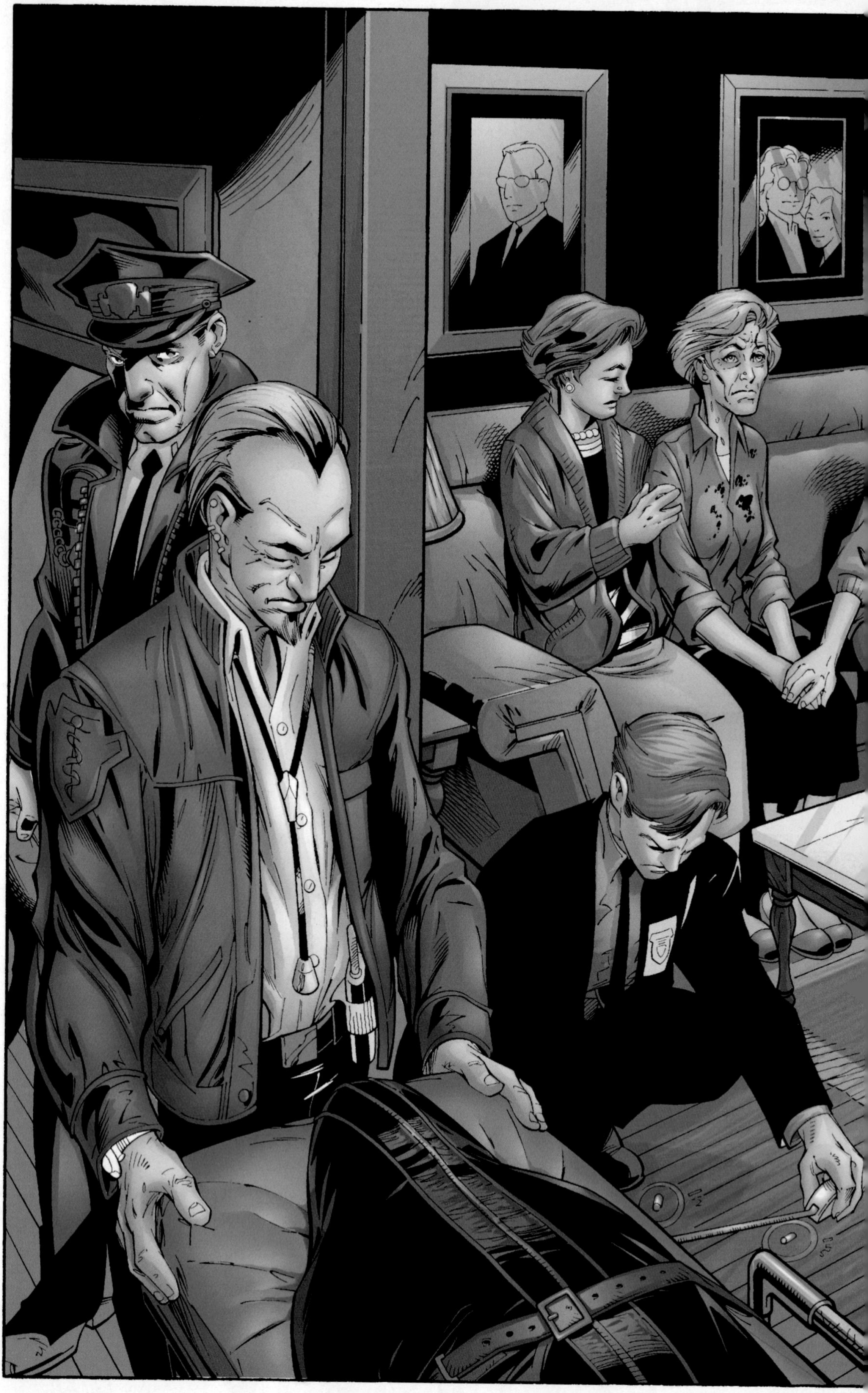

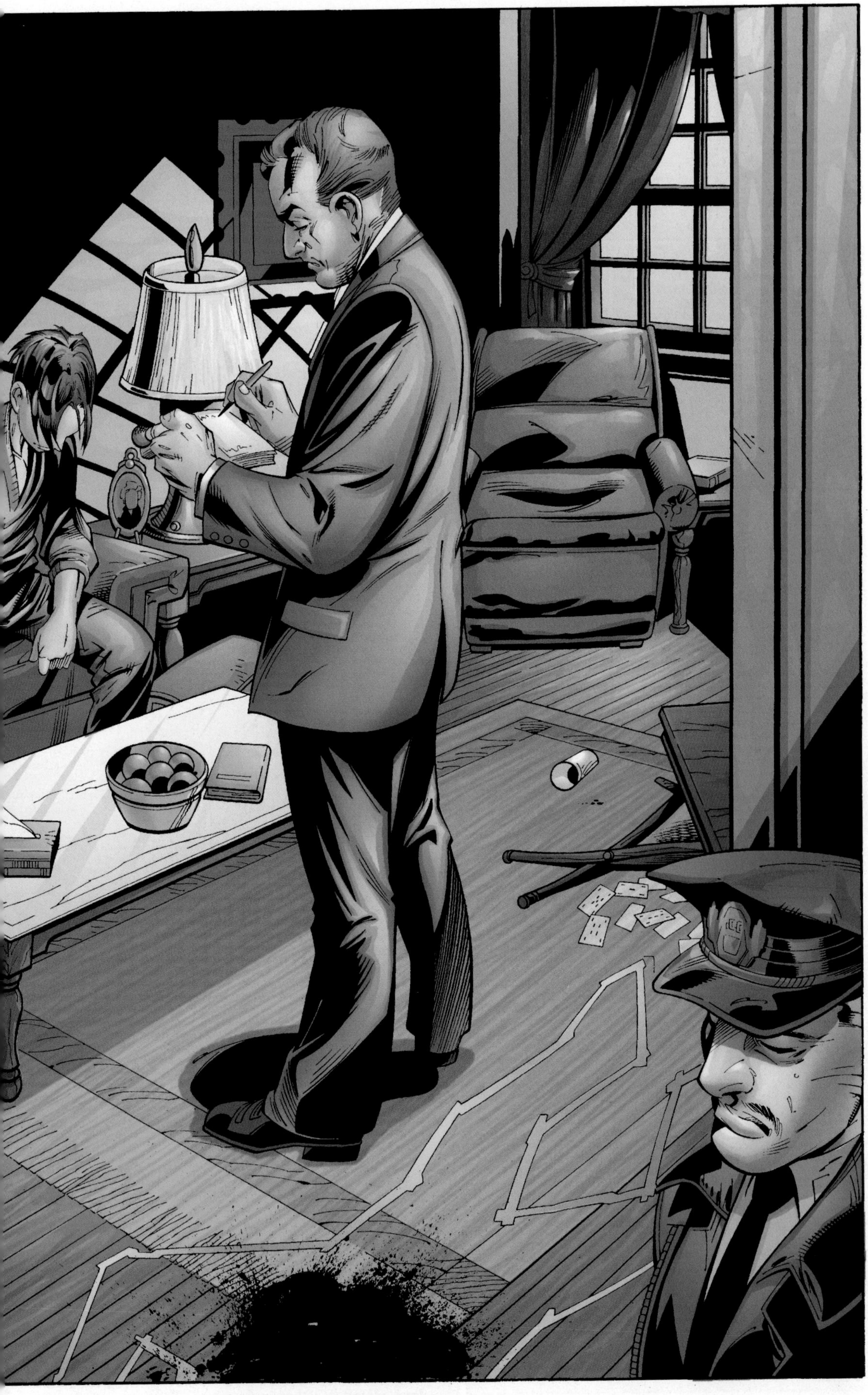

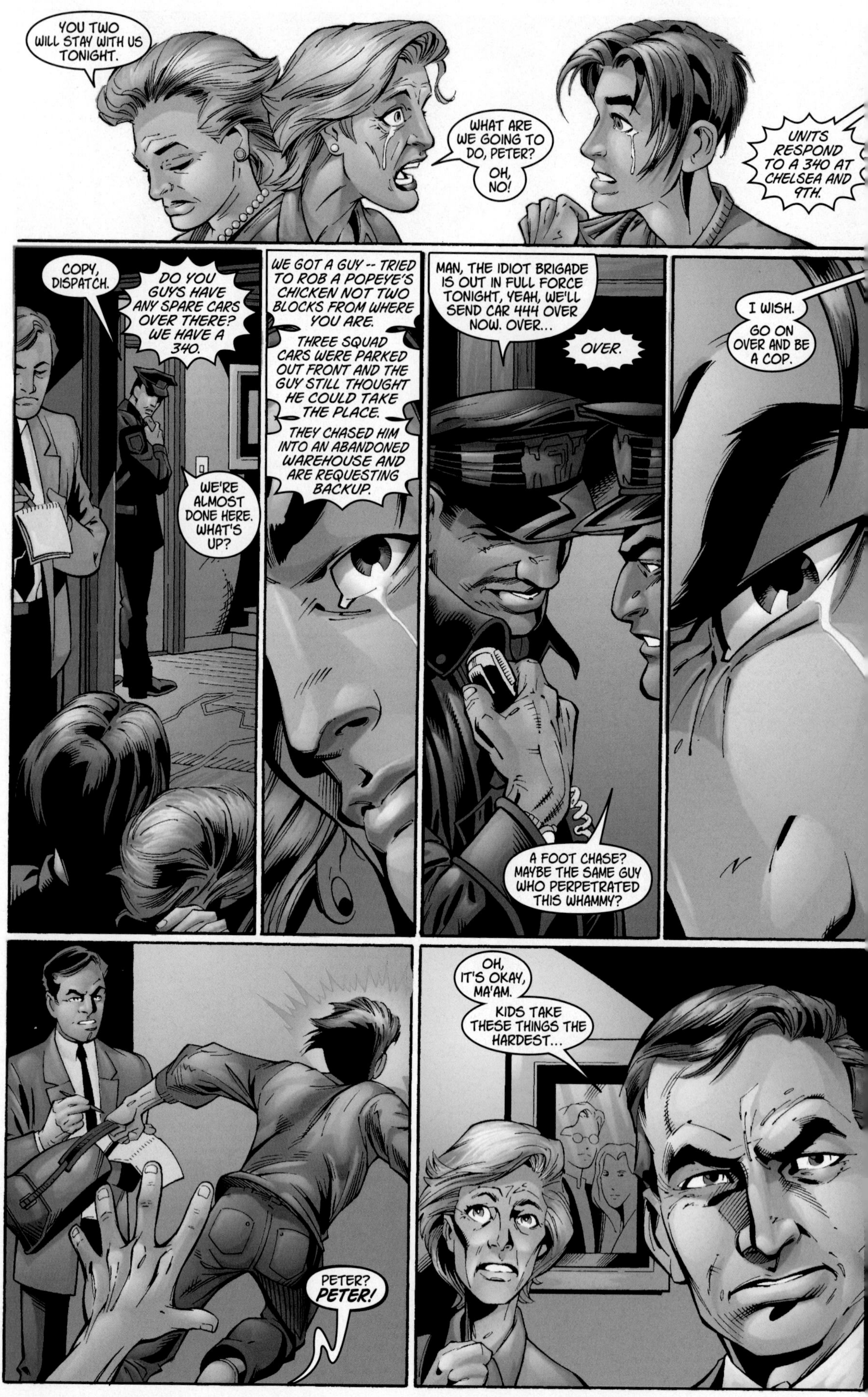
YOU TWO WILL STAY WITH US TONIGHT.
WHAT ARE WE GOING TO DO, PETER?
OH, NO!
UNITS RESPOND TO A 340 AT CHELSEA AND 9TH.
COPY, DISPATCH.
DO YOU GUYS HAVE ANY SPARE CARS OVER THERE? WE HAVE A 340.
WE'RE ALMOST DONE HERE. WHAT'S UP?
WE GOT A GUY -- TRIED TO ROB A POPEYE'S CHICKEN NOT TWO BLOCKS FROM WHERE YOU ARE.
THREE SQUAD CARS WERE PARKED OUT FRONT AND THE GUY STILL THOUGHT HE COULD TAKE THE PLACE.
THEY CHASED HIM INTO AN ABANDONED WAREHOUSE AND ARE REQUESTING BACKUP.
MAN, THE IDIOT BRIGADE IS OUT IN FULL FORCE TONIGHT, YEAH, WE'LL SEND CAR 444 OVER NOW. OVER...
OVER.
A FOOT CHASE? MAYBE THE SAME GUY WHO PERPETRATED THIS WHAMMY?
I WISH.
GO ON OVER AND BE A COP.
PETER? PETER!
OH, IT'S OKAY, MA'AM.
KIDS TAKE THESE THINGS THE HARDEST...

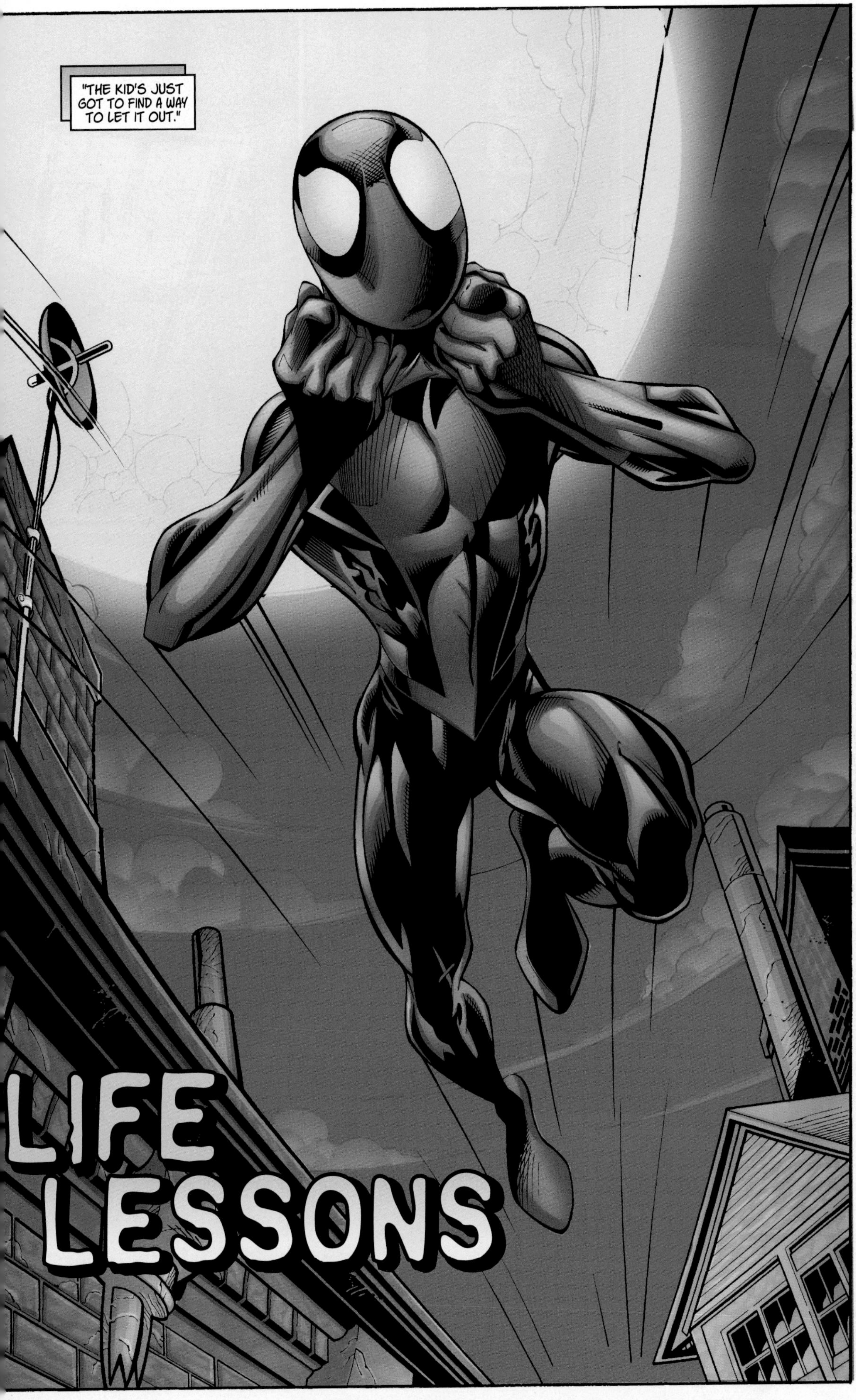
"THE KID'S JUST GOT TO FIND A WAY TO LET IT OUT."
LIFE LESSONS

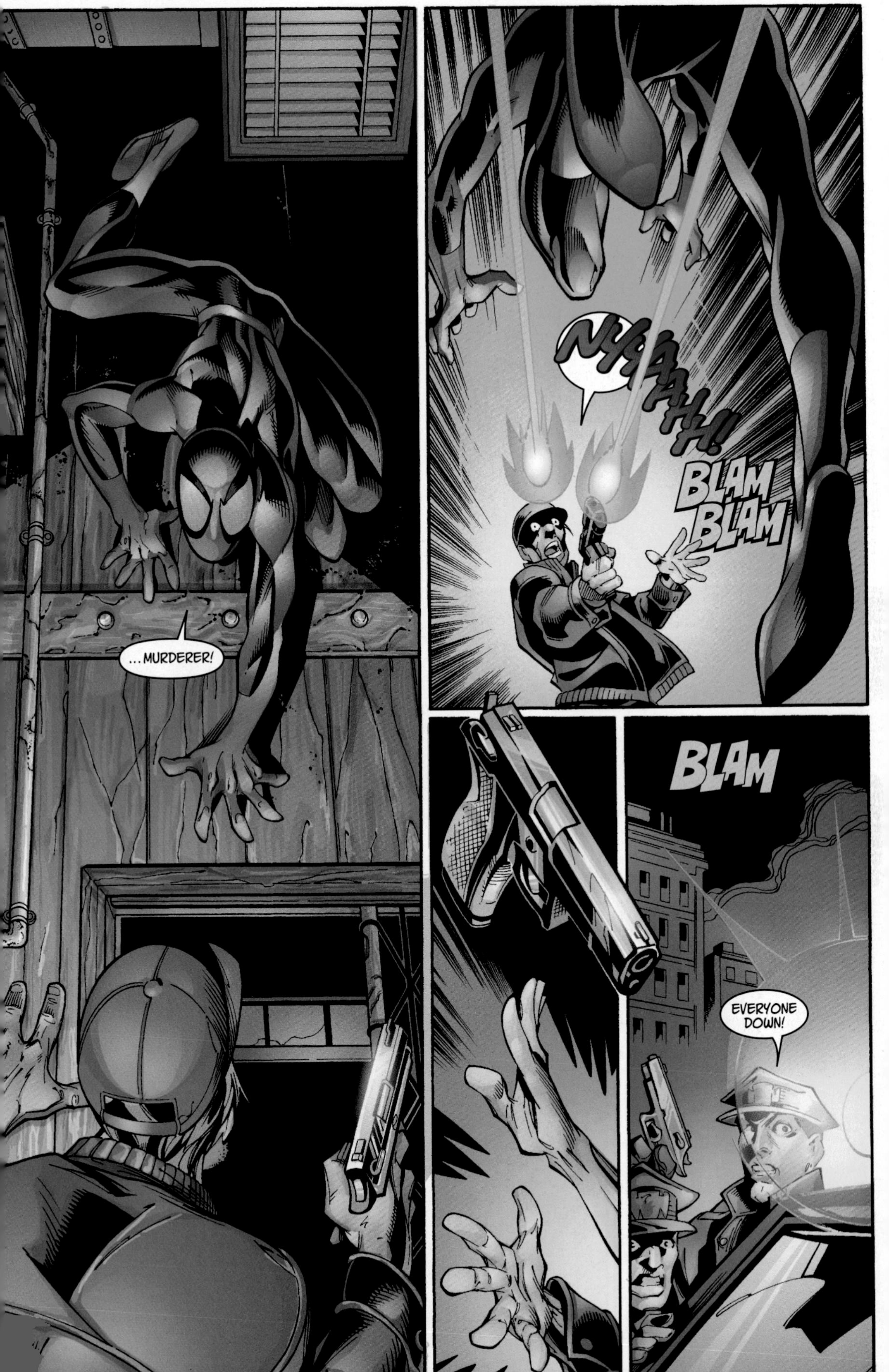

...MURDERER!
NYAAAHH!
BLAM BLAM
BLAM
EVERYONE DOWN!

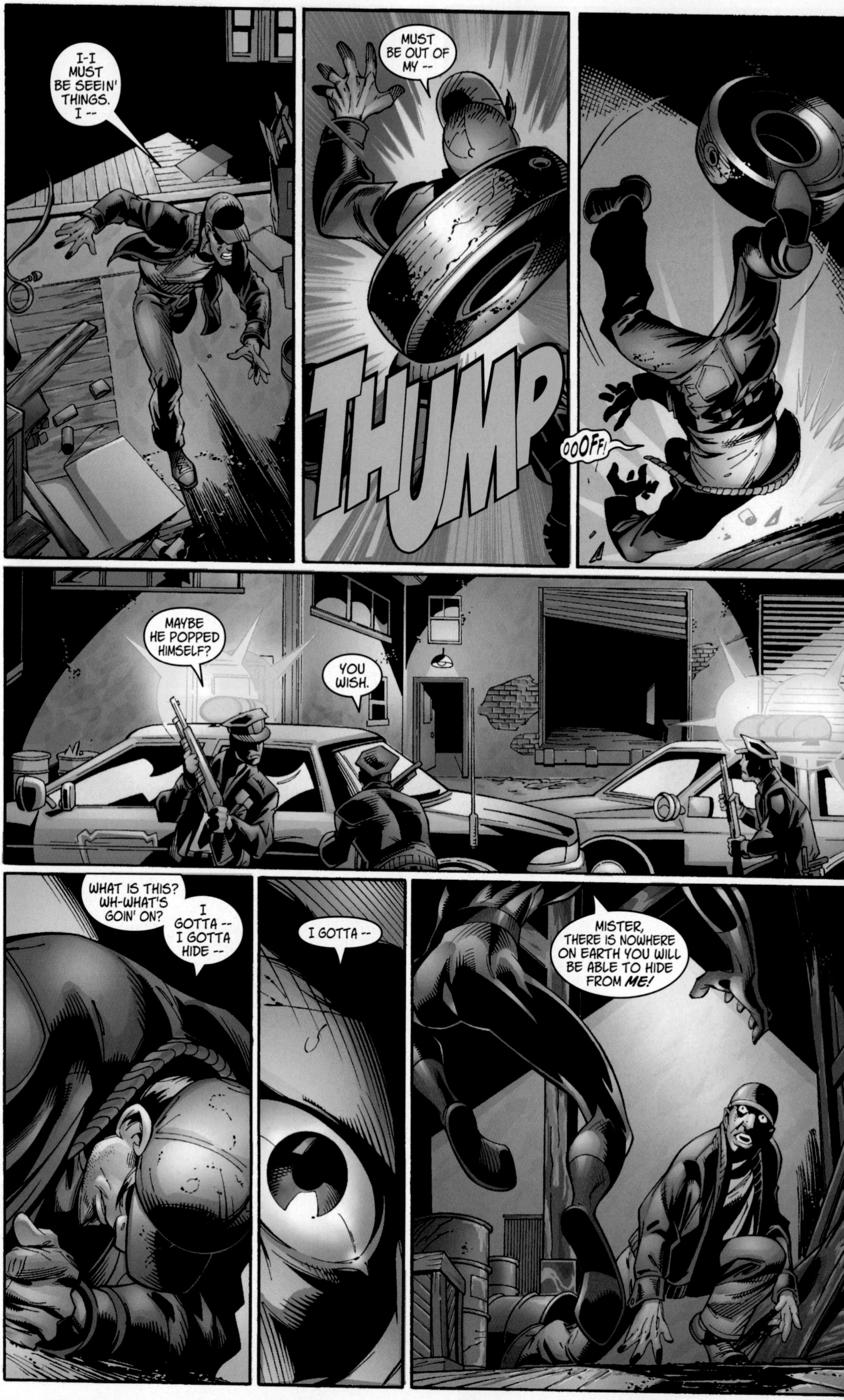

I-I MUST BE SEEIN' THINGS. I --
MUST BE OUT OF MY --
THUMP
OOOFF!
MAYBE HE POPPED HIMSELF?
YOU WISH.
WHAT IS THIS? WH-WHAT'S GOIN' ON?
I GOTTA -- I GOTTA HIDE --
I GOTTA --
MISTER, THERE IS NOWHERE ON EARTH YOU WILL BE ABLE TO HIDE FROM *ME!*

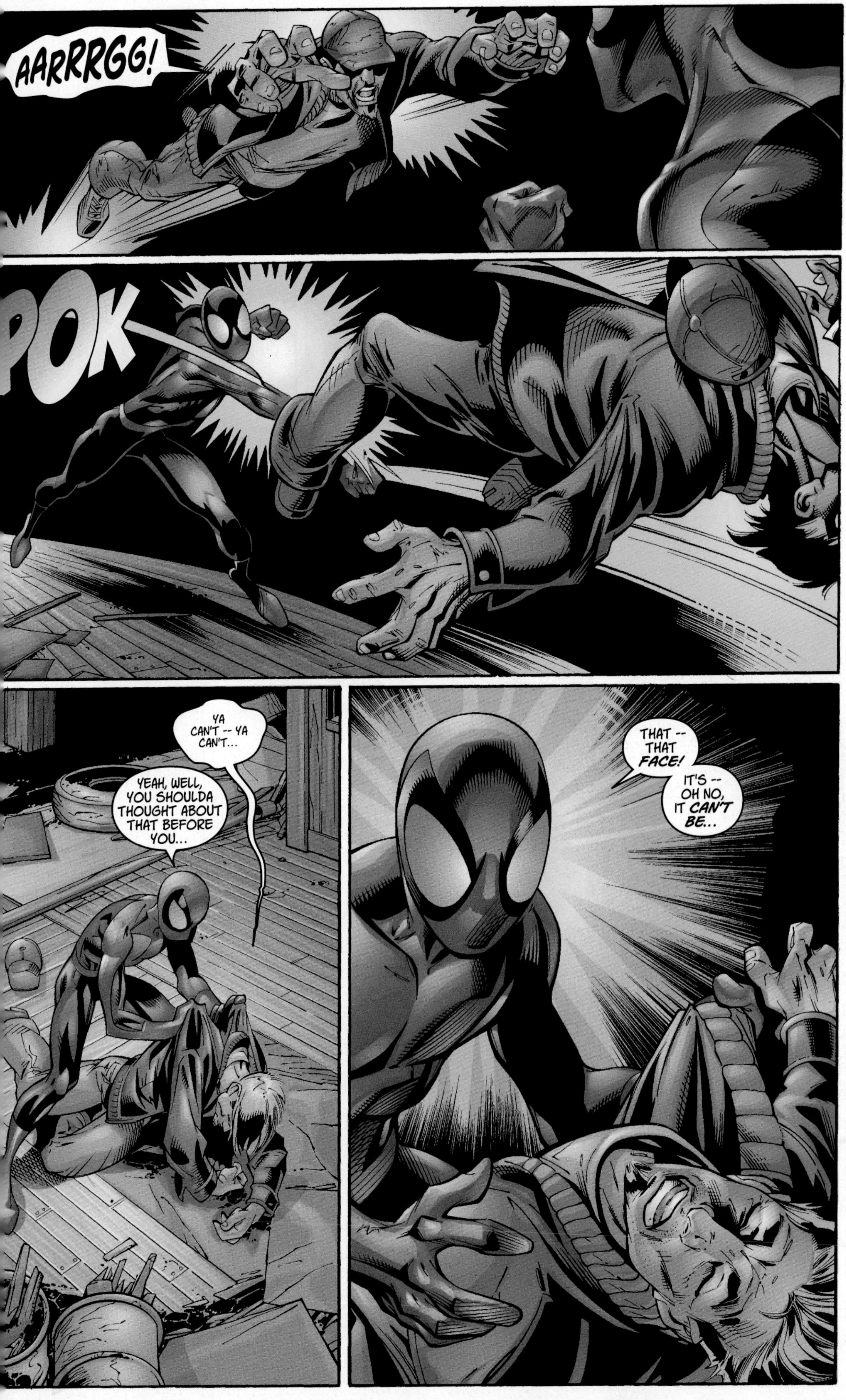
AARRRGG!
POK
YA CAN'T -- YA CAN'T...
YEAH, WELL, YOU SHOULDA THOUGHT ABOUT THAT BEFORE YOU...
THAT -- THAT FACE!
IT'S -- OH NO, IT CAN'T BE...

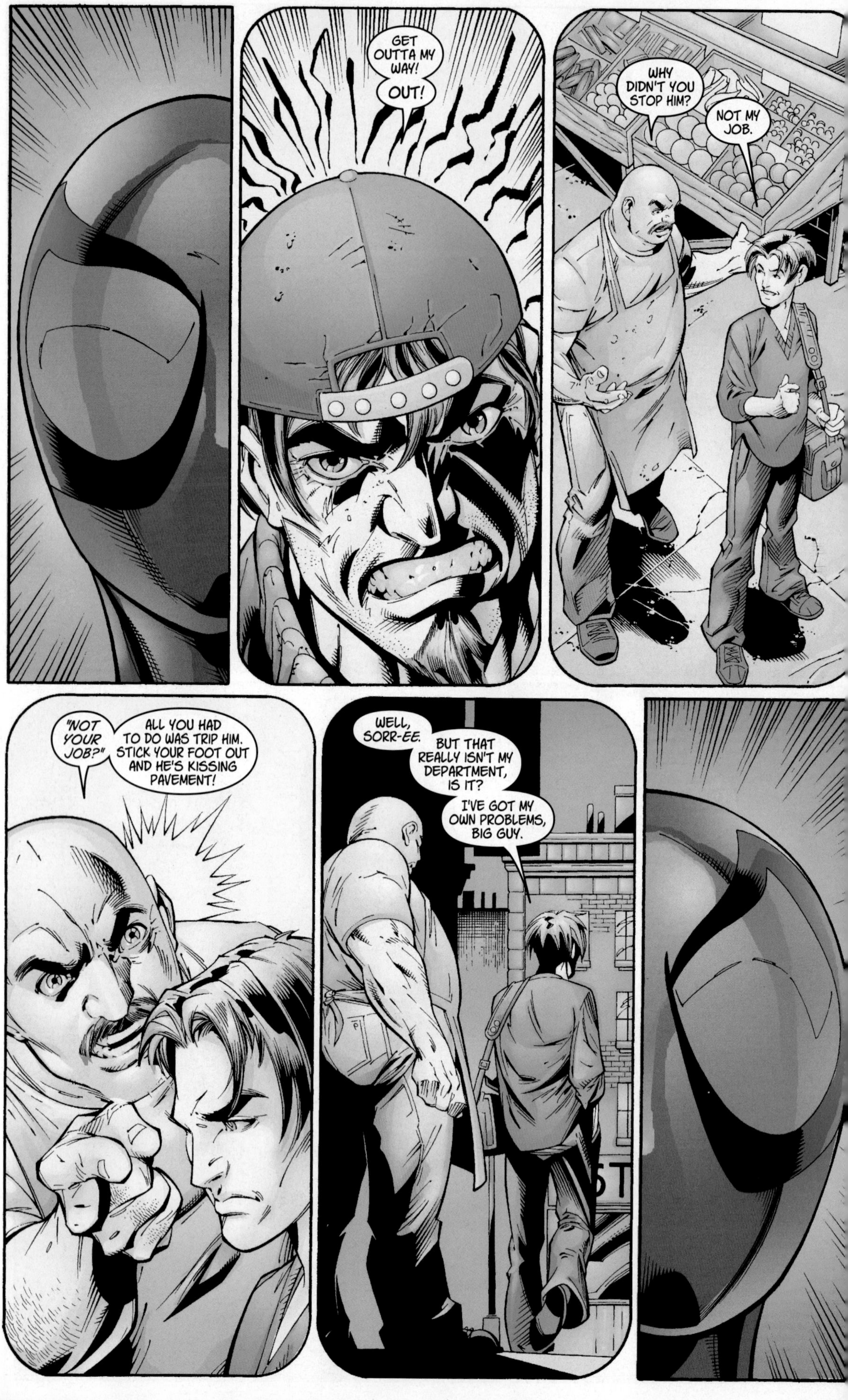
GET OUTTA MY WAY!
OUT!
WHY DIDN'T YOU STOP HIM?
NOT MY JOB.
"NOT YOUR JOB?"
ALL YOU HAD TO DO WAS TRIP HIM. STICK YOUR FOOT OUT AND HE'S KISSING PAVEMENT!
WELL, SORR-EE.
BUT THAT REALLY ISN'T MY DEPARTMENT, IS IT?
I'VE GOT MY OWN PROBLEMS, BIG GUY.

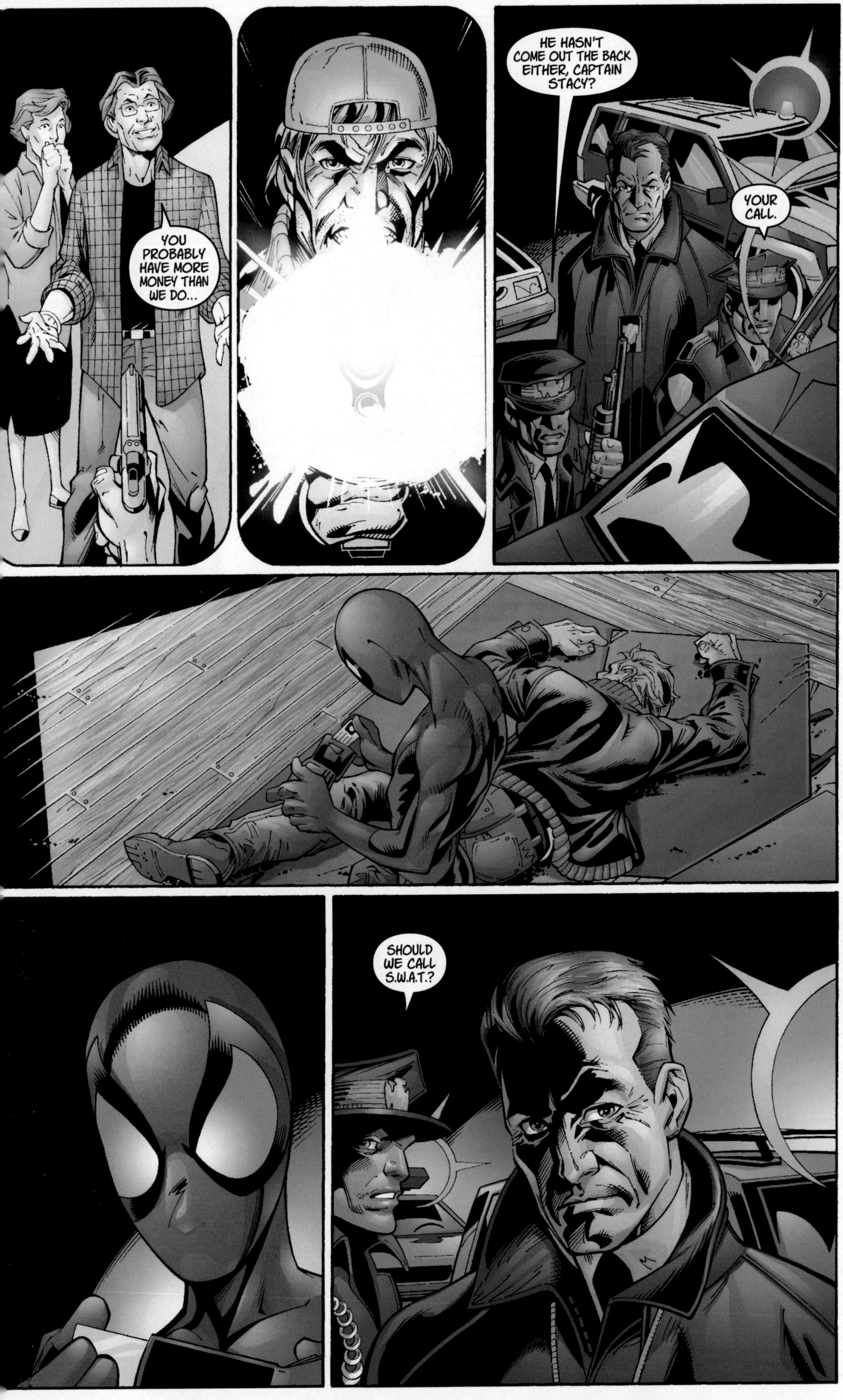
YOU PROBABLY HAVE MORE MONEY THAN WE DO...
HE HASN'T COME OUT THE BACK EITHER, CAPTAIN STACY?
YOUR CALL.
SHOULD WE CALL S.W.A.T.?

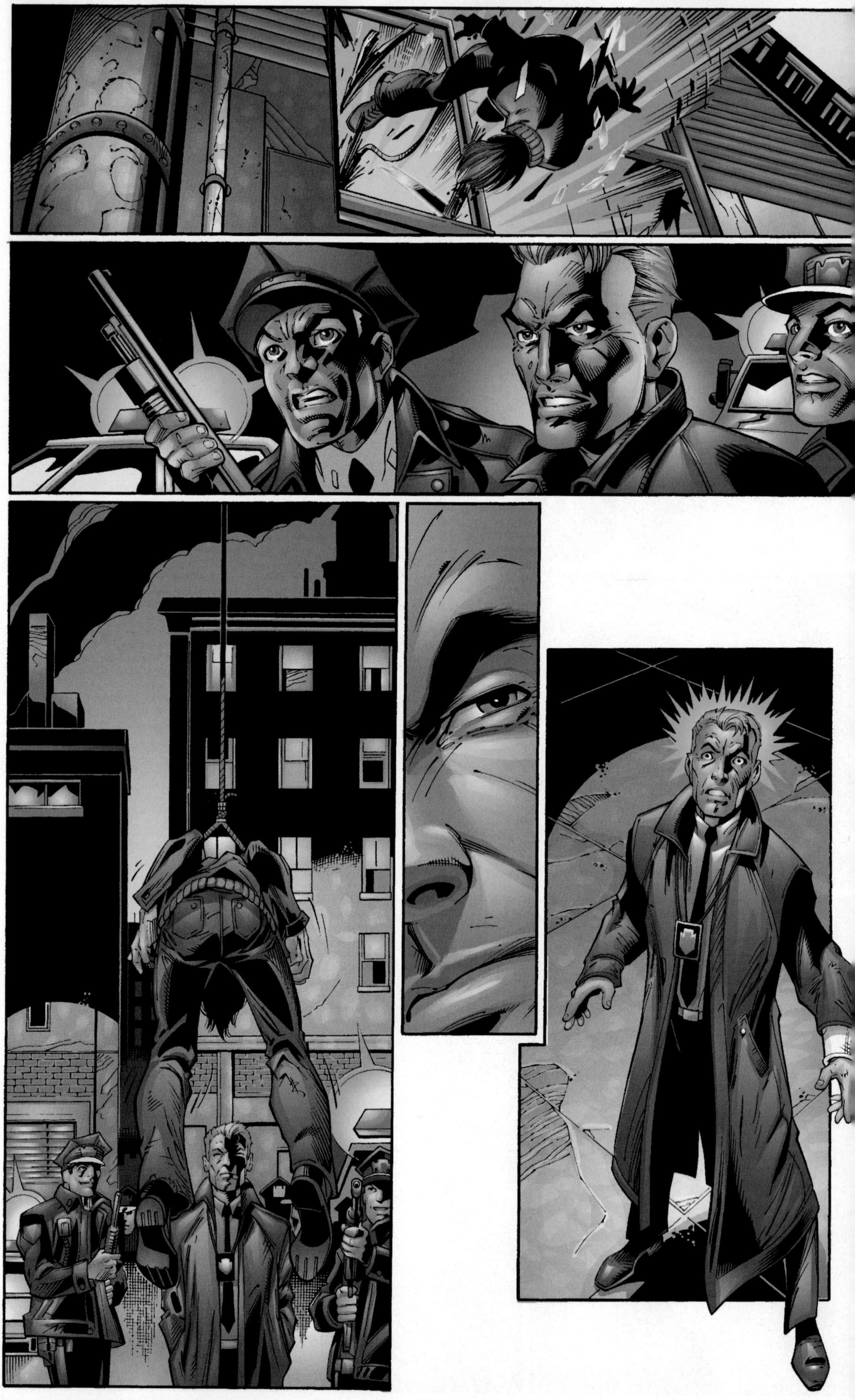

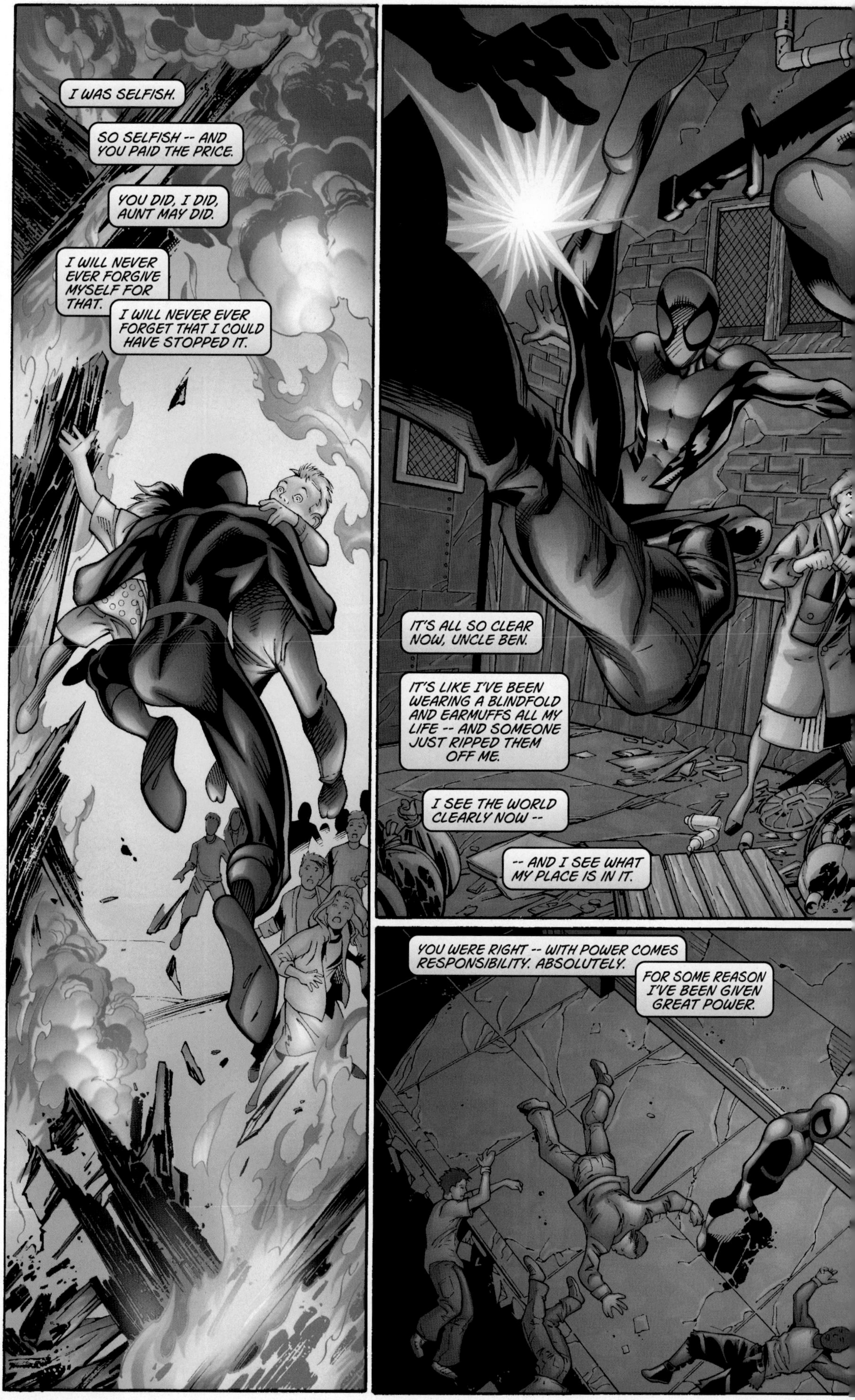
I WAS SELFISH.
SO SELFISH -- AND YOU PAID THE PRICE.
YOU DID, I DID, AUNT MAY DID.
I WILL NEVER EVER FORGIVE MYSELF FOR THAT.
I WILL NEVER EVER FORGET THAT I COULD HAVE STOPPED IT.
IT'S ALL SO CLEAR NOW, UNCLE BEN.
IT'S LIKE I'VE BEEN WEARING A BLINDFOLD AND EARMUFFS ALL MY LIFE -- AND SOMEONE JUST RIPPED THEM OFF ME.
I SEE THE WORLD CLEARLY NOW --
-- AND I SEE WHAT MY PLACE IS IN IT.
YOU WERE RIGHT -- WITH POWER COMES RESPONSIBILITY. ABSOLUTELY.
FOR SOME REASON I'VE BEEN GIVEN GREAT POWER.

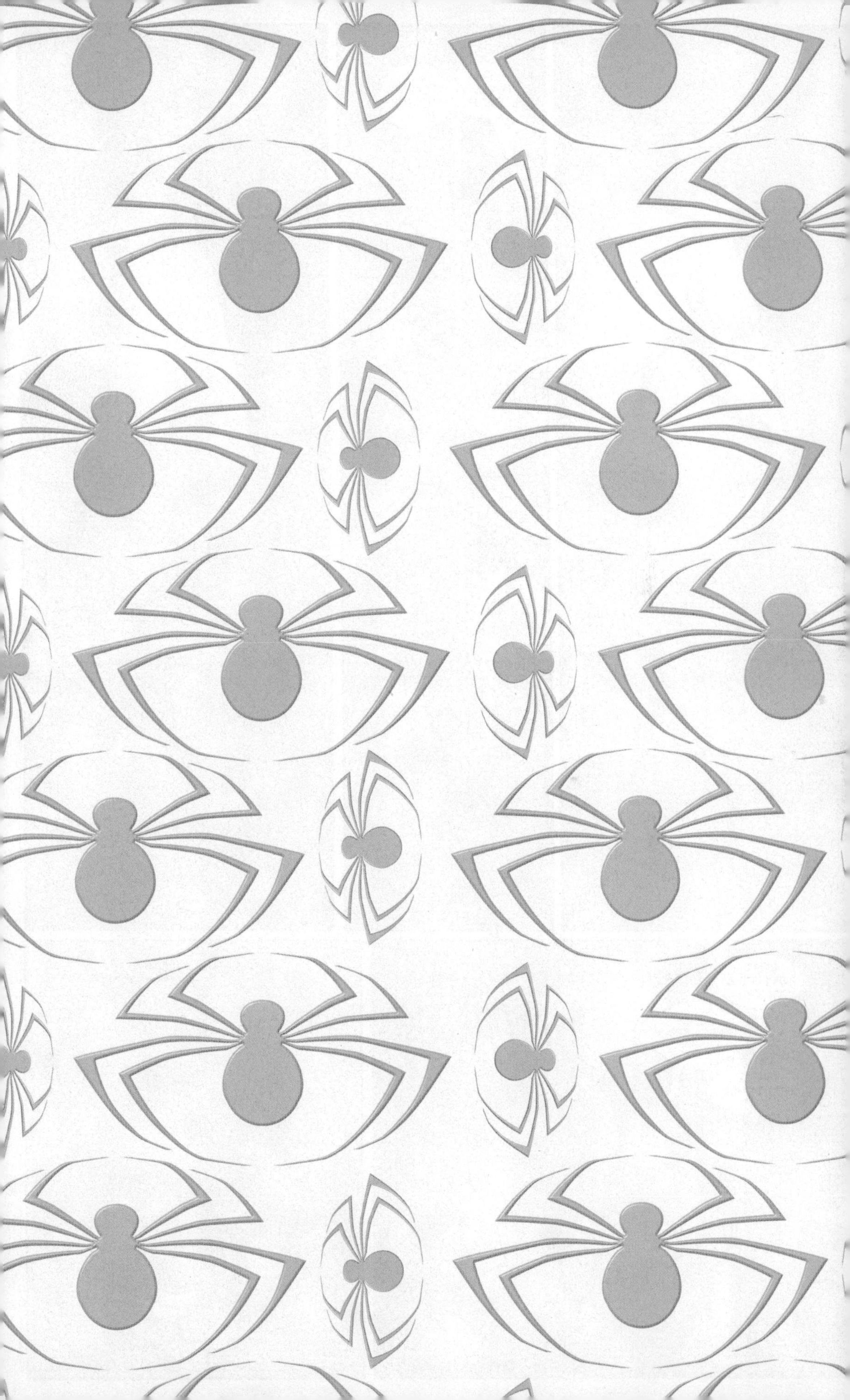

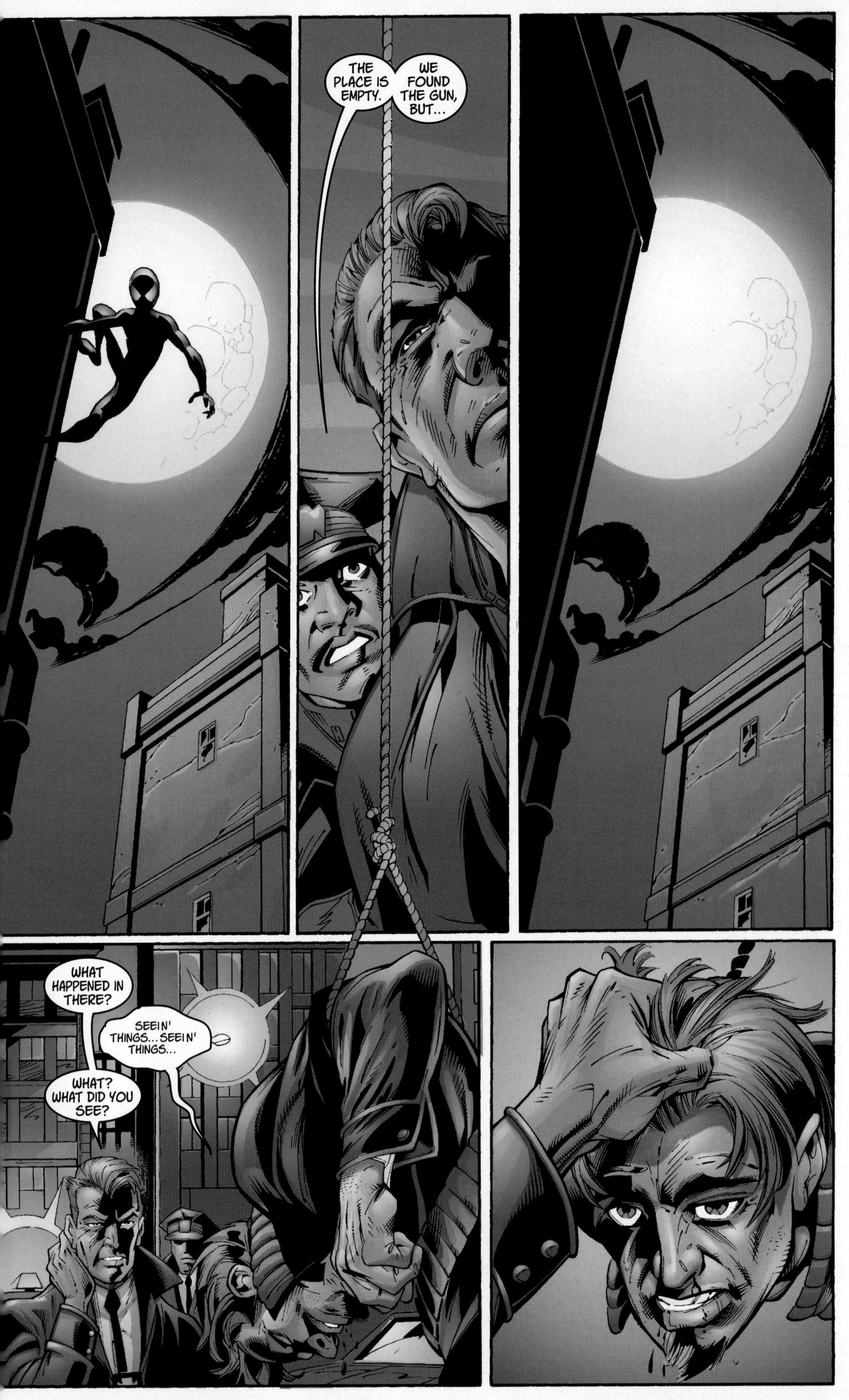
THE PLACE IS EMPTY.
WE FOUND THE GUN, BUT...
WHAT HAPPENED IN THERE?
SEEIN' THINGS... SEEIN' THINGS...
WHAT? WHAT DID YOU SEE?

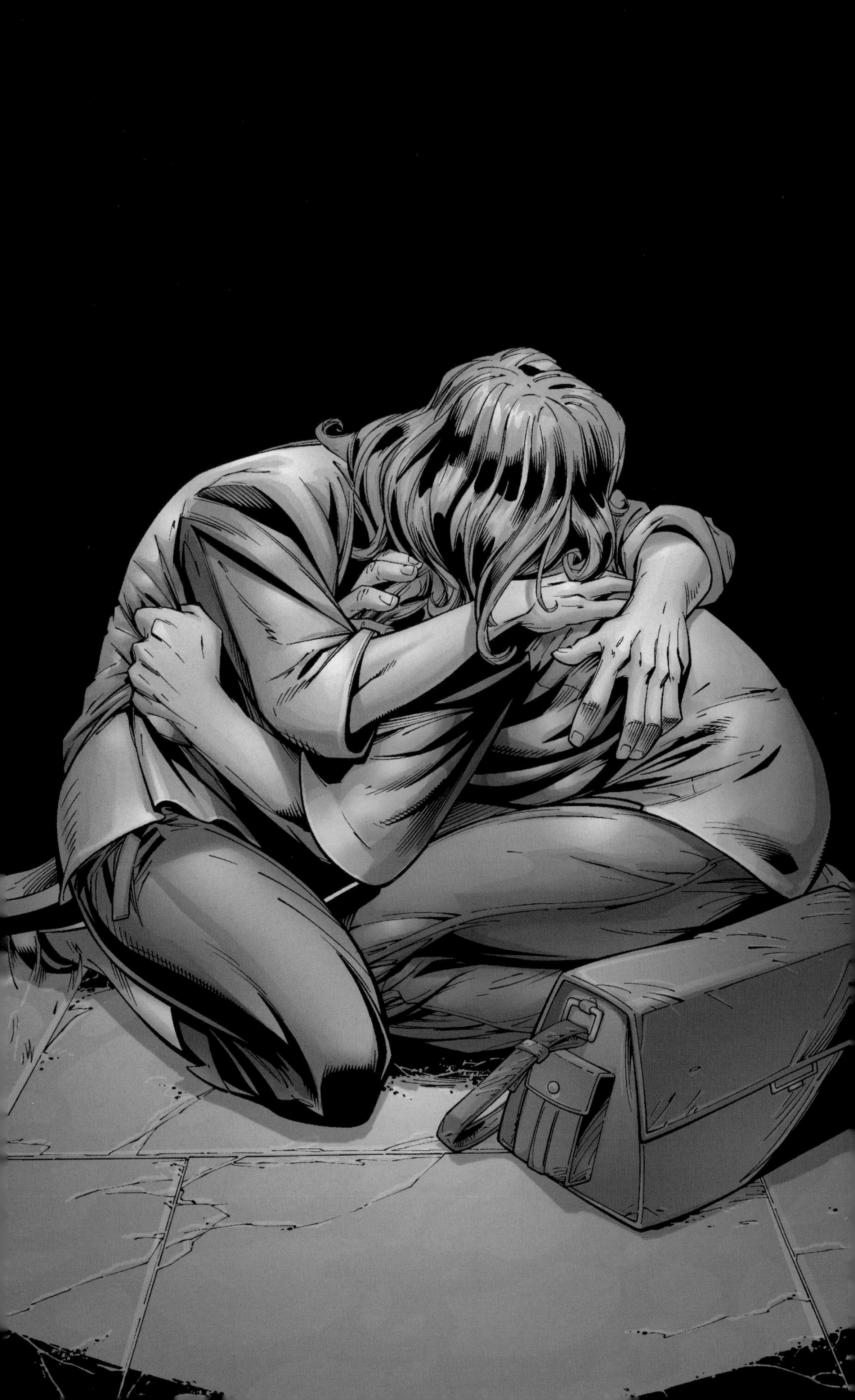

6

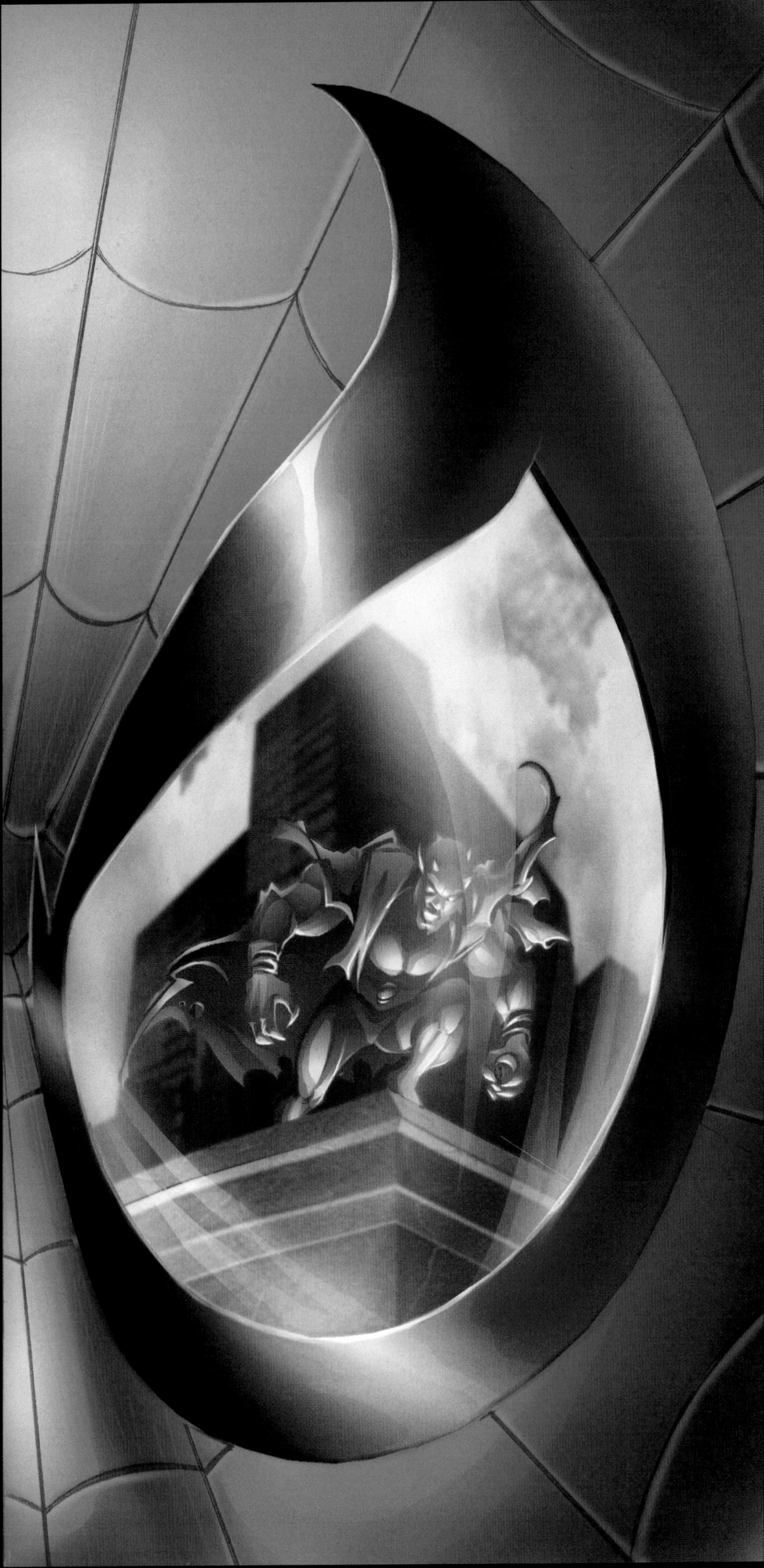

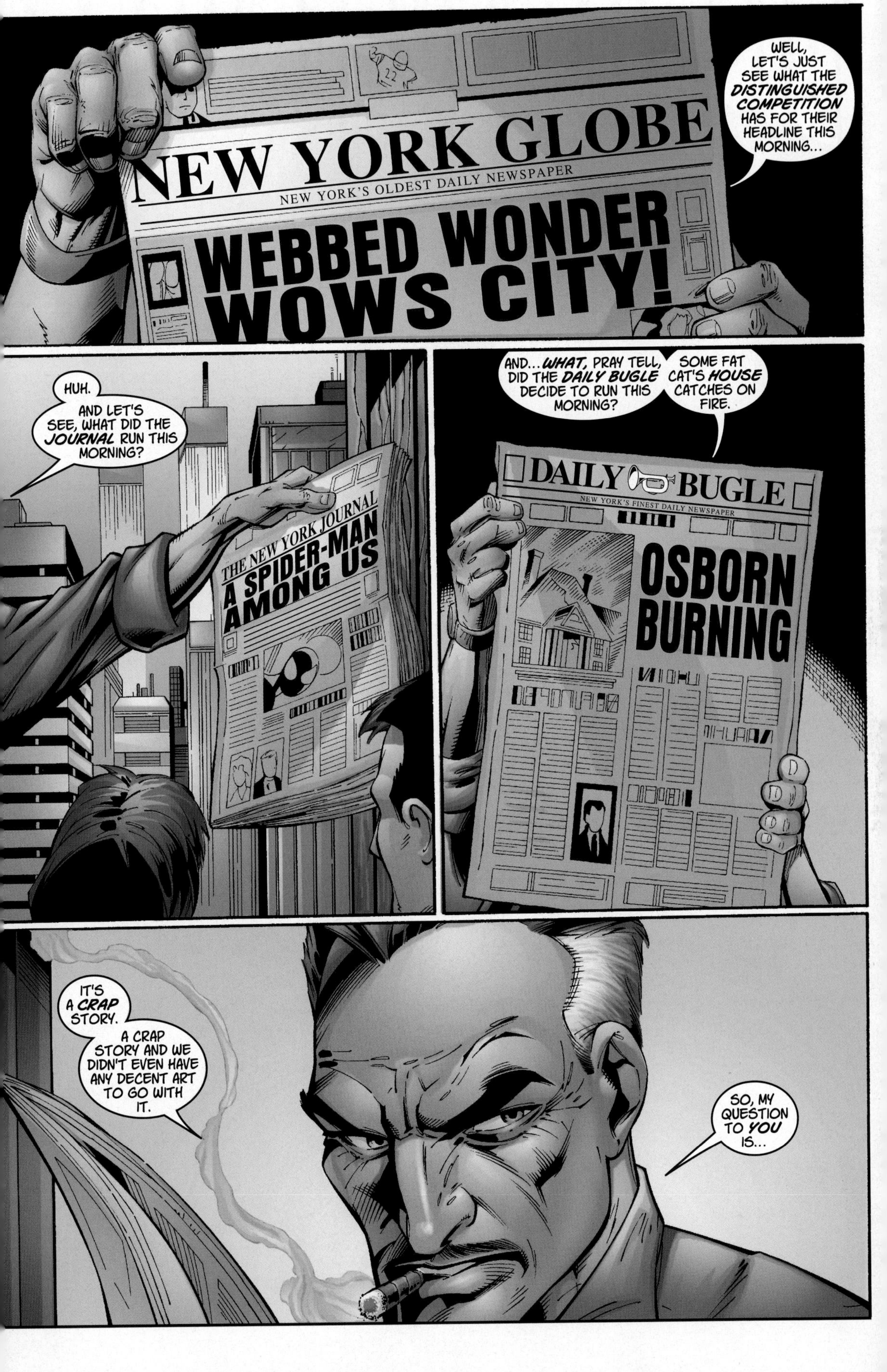
WELL, LET'S JUST SEE WHAT THE DISTINGUISHED COMPETITION HAS FOR THEIR HEADLINE THIS MORNING...
NEW YORK GLOBE
NEW YORK'S OLDEST DAILY NEWSPAPER
WEBBED WONDER WOWS CITY!
HUH.
AND LET'S SEE, WHAT DID THE JOURNAL RUN THIS MORNING?
THE NEW YORK JOURNAL
A SPIDER-MAN AMONG US
AND... WHAT, PRAY TELL, DID THE DAILY BUGLE DECIDE TO RUN THIS MORNING?
SOME FAT CAT'S HOUSE CATCHES ON FIRE.
DAILY BUGLE
NEW YORK'S FINEST DAILY NEWSPAPER
OSBORN BURNING
IT'S A CRAP STORY.
A CRAP STORY AND WE DIDN'T EVEN HAVE ANY DECENT ART TO GO WITH IT.
SO, MY QUESTION TO YOU IS...

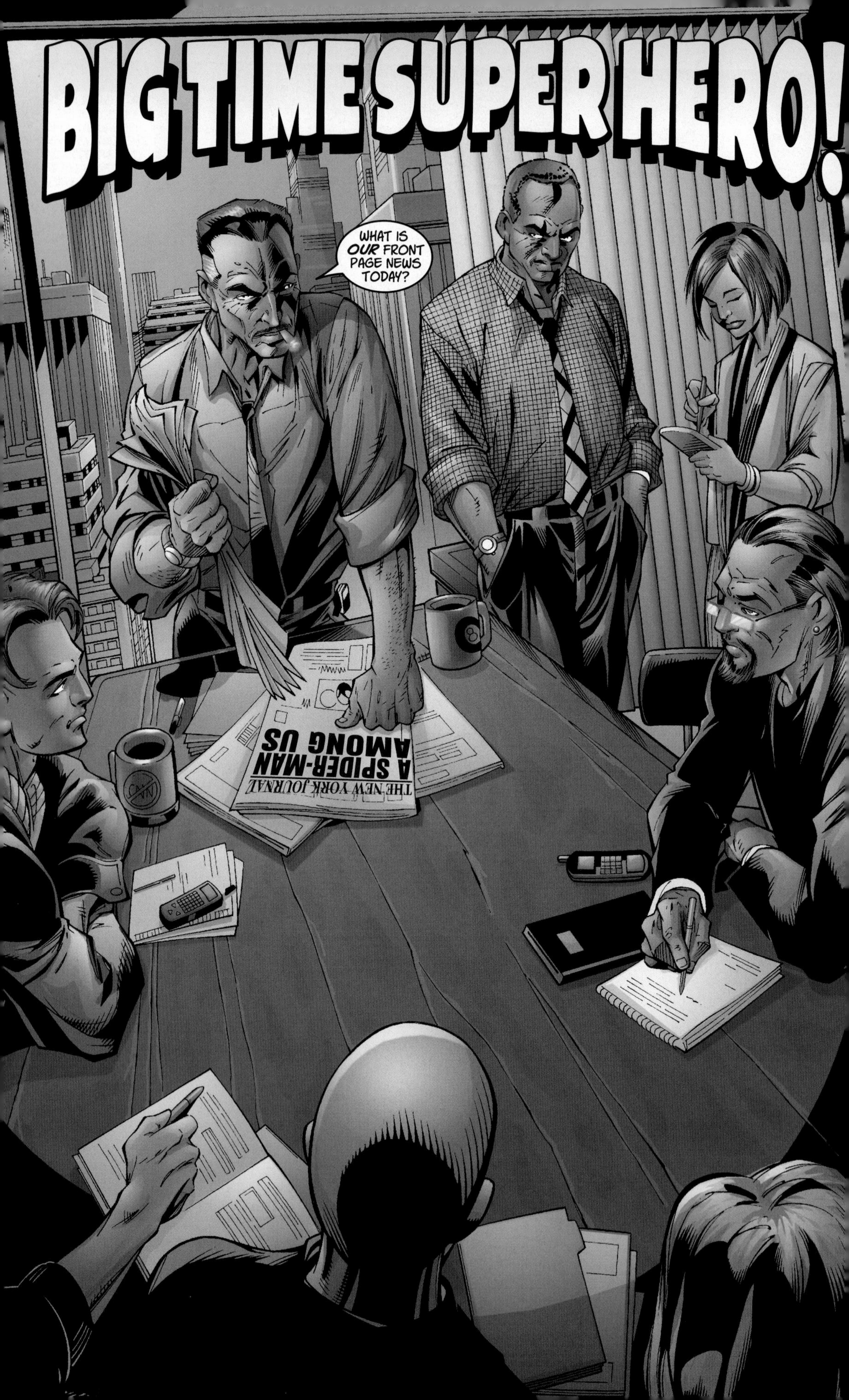

BIG TIME SUPER HERO!
WHAT IS OUR FRONT PAGE NEWS TODAY?
THE NEW YORK JOURNAL
A SPIDER-MAN AMONG US

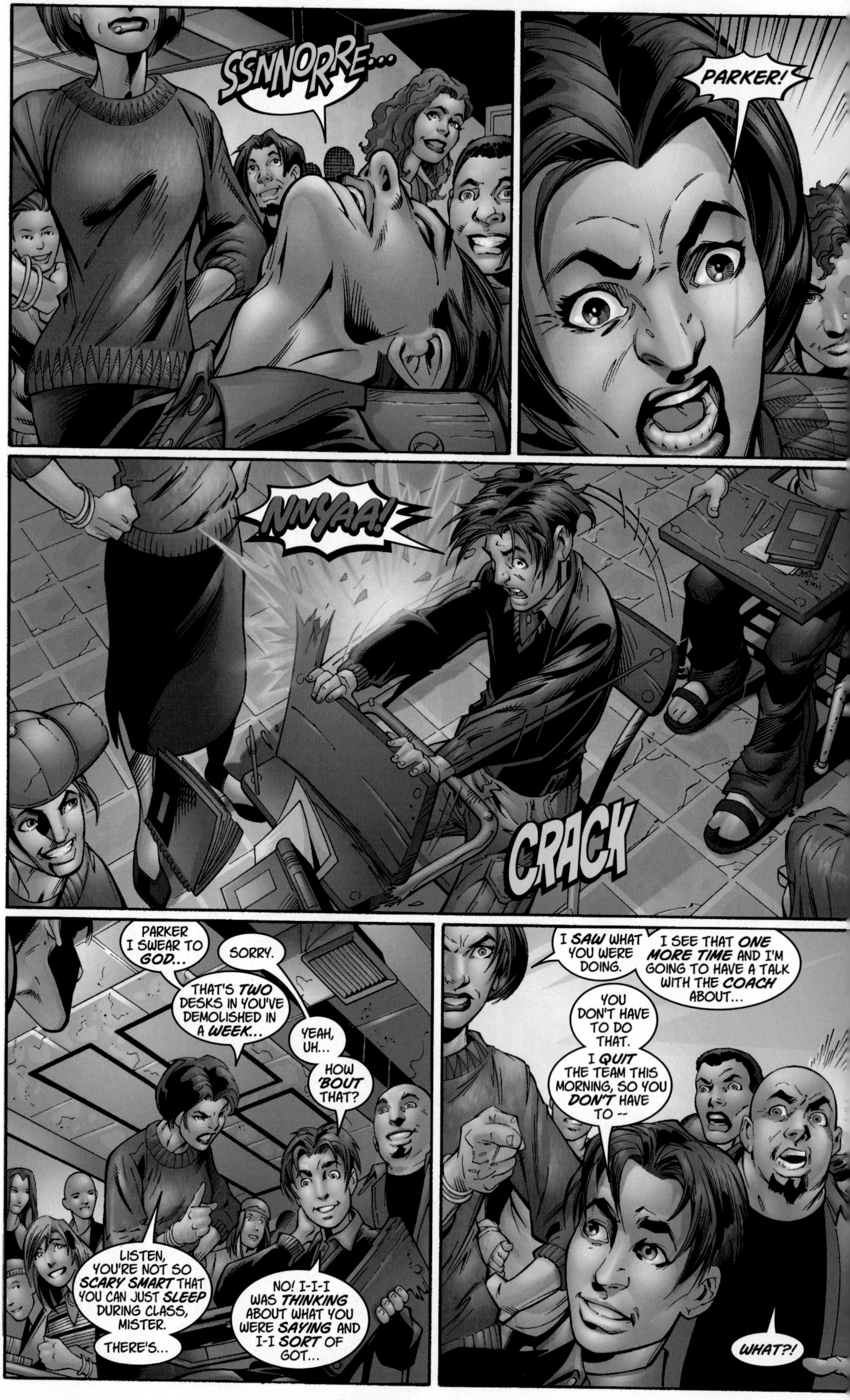
SSNNORRE...
PARKER!
NNYAA!
CRACK
PARKER I SWEAR TO GOD...
SORRY.
THAT'S TWO DESKS IN YOU'VE DEMOLISHED IN A WEEK...
YEAH, UH...
HOW 'BOUT THAT?
LISTEN, YOU'RE NOT SO SCARY SMART THAT YOU CAN JUST SLEEP DURING CLASS, MISTER.
THERE'S...
NO! I-I-I WAS THINKING ABOUT WHAT YOU WERE SAYING AND I-I SORT OF GOT...
I SAW WHAT YOU WERE DOING.
I SEE THAT ONE MORE TIME AND I'M GOING TO HAVE A TALK WITH THE COACH ABOUT...
YOU DON'T HAVE TO DO THAT.
I QUIT THE TEAM THIS MORNING, SO YOU DON'T HAVE TO --
WHAT?!

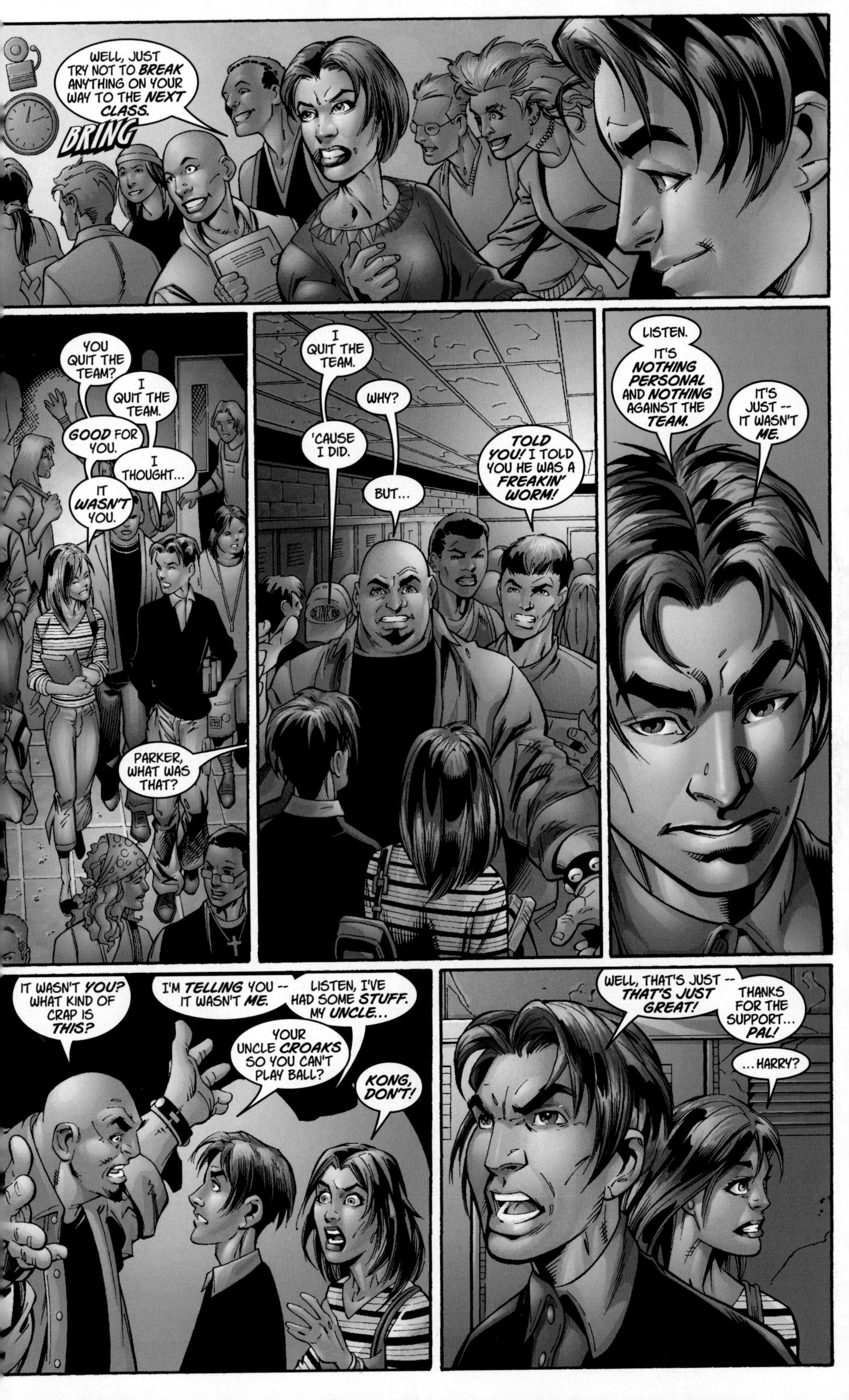

WELL, JUST TRY NOT TO BREAK ANYTHING ON YOUR WAY TO THE NEXT CLASS.
BRING
YOU QUIT THE TEAM?
I QUIT THE TEAM.
GOOD FOR YOU.
I THOUGHT...
IT WASN'T YOU.
PARKER, WHAT WAS THAT?
I QUIT THE TEAM.
WHY?
'CAUSE I DID.
BUT...
TOLD YOU! I TOLD YOU HE WAS A FREAKIN' WORM!
LISTEN. IT'S NOTHING PERSONAL AND NOTHING AGAINST THE TEAM.
IT'S JUST -- IT WASN'T ME.
IT WASN'T YOU? WHAT KIND OF CRAP IS THIS?
I'M TELLING YOU -- IT WASN'T ME.
LISTEN, I'VE HAD SOME STUFF. MY UNCLE...
YOUR UNCLE CROAKS SO YOU CAN'T PLAY BALL?
KONG, DON'T!
WELL, THAT'S JUST -- THAT'S JUST GREAT!
THANKS FOR THE SUPPORT... PAL!
...HARRY?

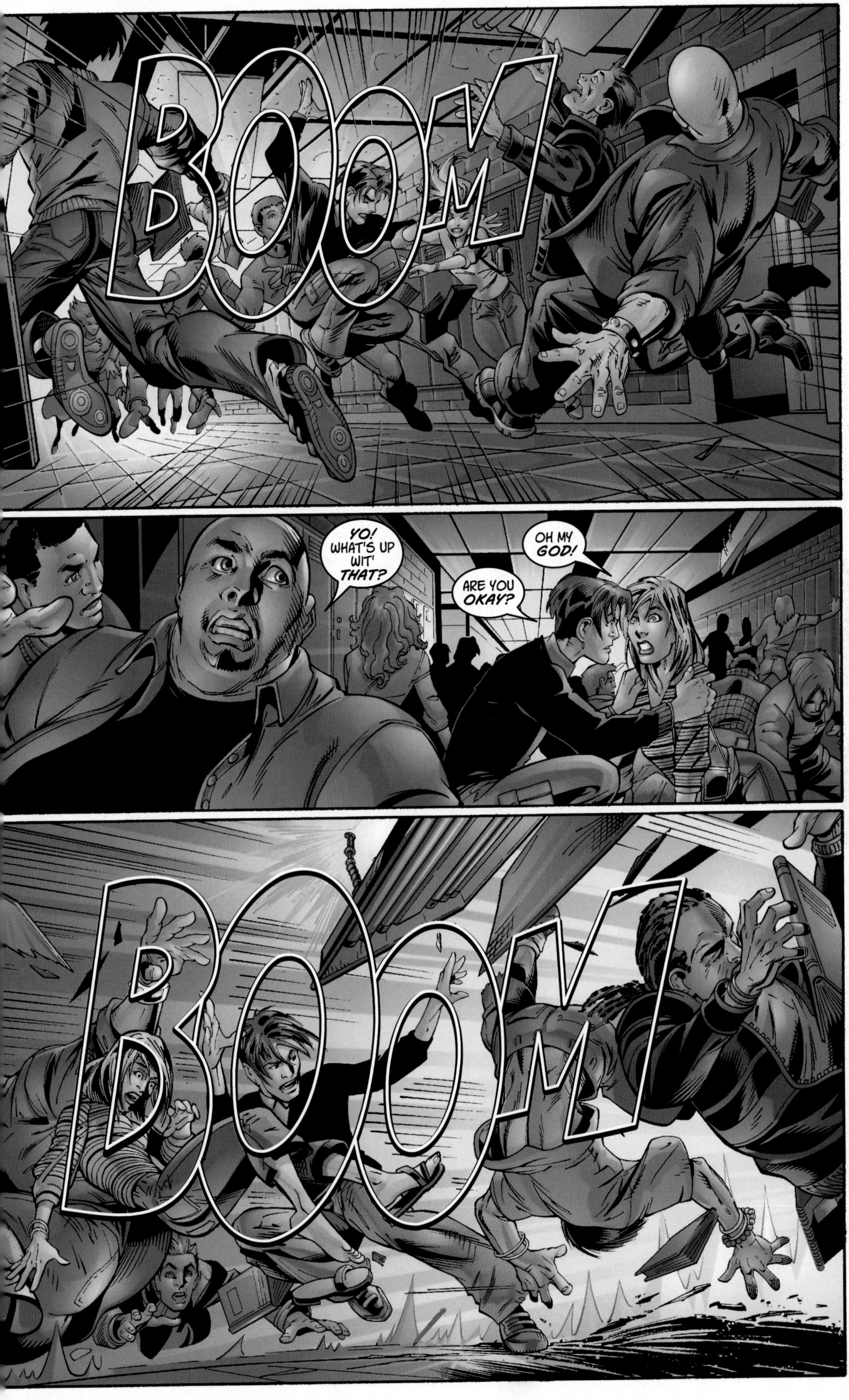
BOOM
YO! WHAT'S UP WIT' THAT?
OH MY GOD!
ARE YOU OKAY?
BOOM

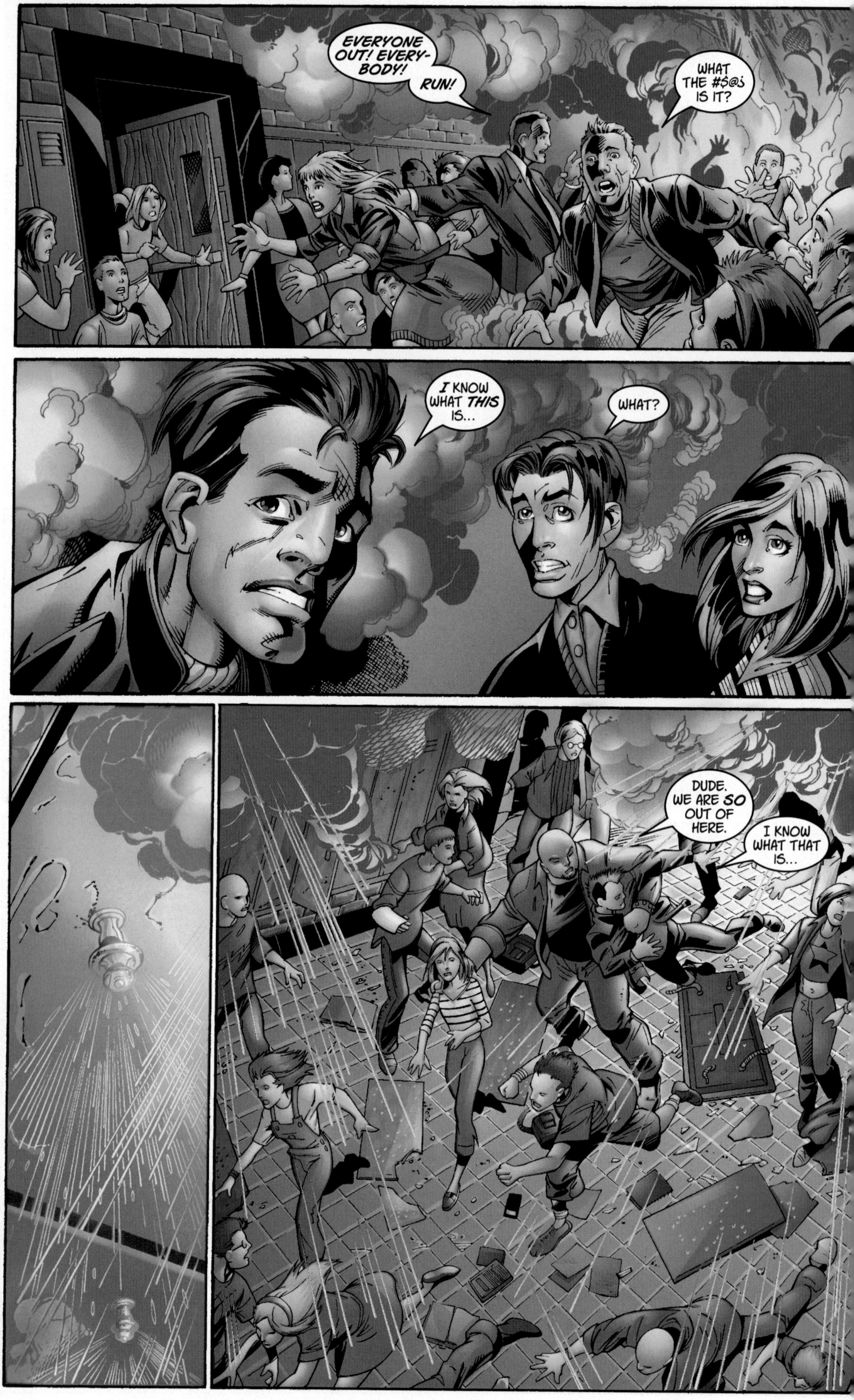
EVERYONE OUT! EVERY-BODY!
RUN!
WHAT THE #$@¿ IS IT?
I KNOW WHAT THIS IS...
WHAT?
DUDE. WE ARE SO OUT OF HERE.
I KNOW WHAT THAT IS...

HEAD'S UP!

BIG TIME *SUPER HERO* COMIN' THROUGH!

DUDE! SERIOUSLY -- IF HE *BLEW UP* OUR SCHOOL...

...HE IS *TOTALLY MY HERO.*

WHOA...

MAN, I'M GOING TO *HAVE* TO WORK OUT *ANOTHER* SYSTEM FOR EMERGENCIES.

DUDE. WE ARE **SO** OUT OF HERE.

I KNOW WHAT THAT IS...

IT'S TIME TO HOP INTO ACTION.

IT'S TIME FOR...

WAIT...

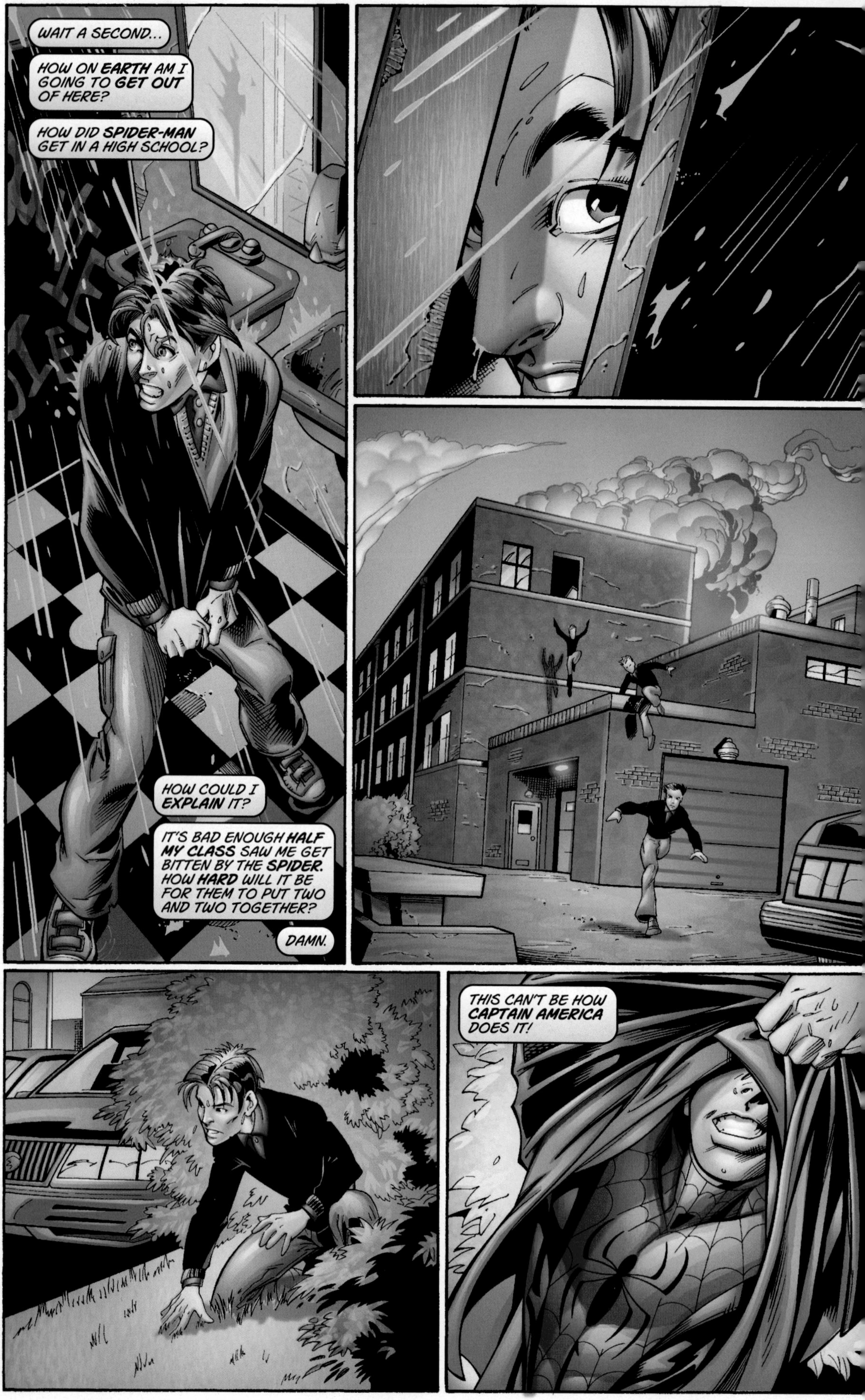
WAIT A SECOND...
HOW ON EARTH AM I GOING TO GET OUT OF HERE?
HOW DID SPIDER-MAN GET IN A HIGH SCHOOL?
HOW COULD I EXPLAIN IT?
IT'S BAD ENOUGH HALF MY CLASS SAW ME GET BITTEN BY THE SPIDER. HOW HARD WILL IT BE FOR THEM TO PUT TWO AND TWO TOGETHER?
DAMN.
THIS CAN'T BE HOW CAPTAIN AMERICA DOES IT!

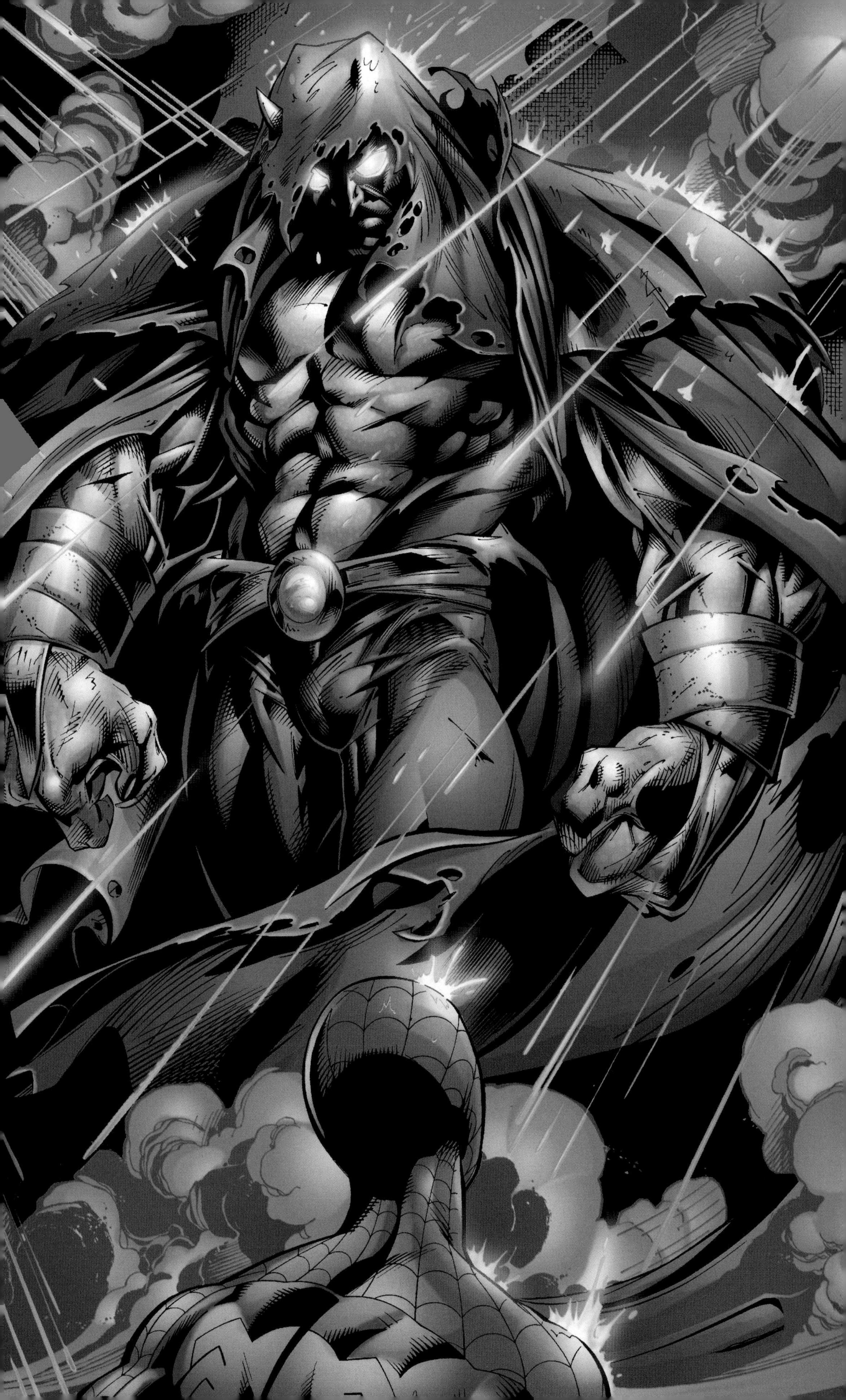

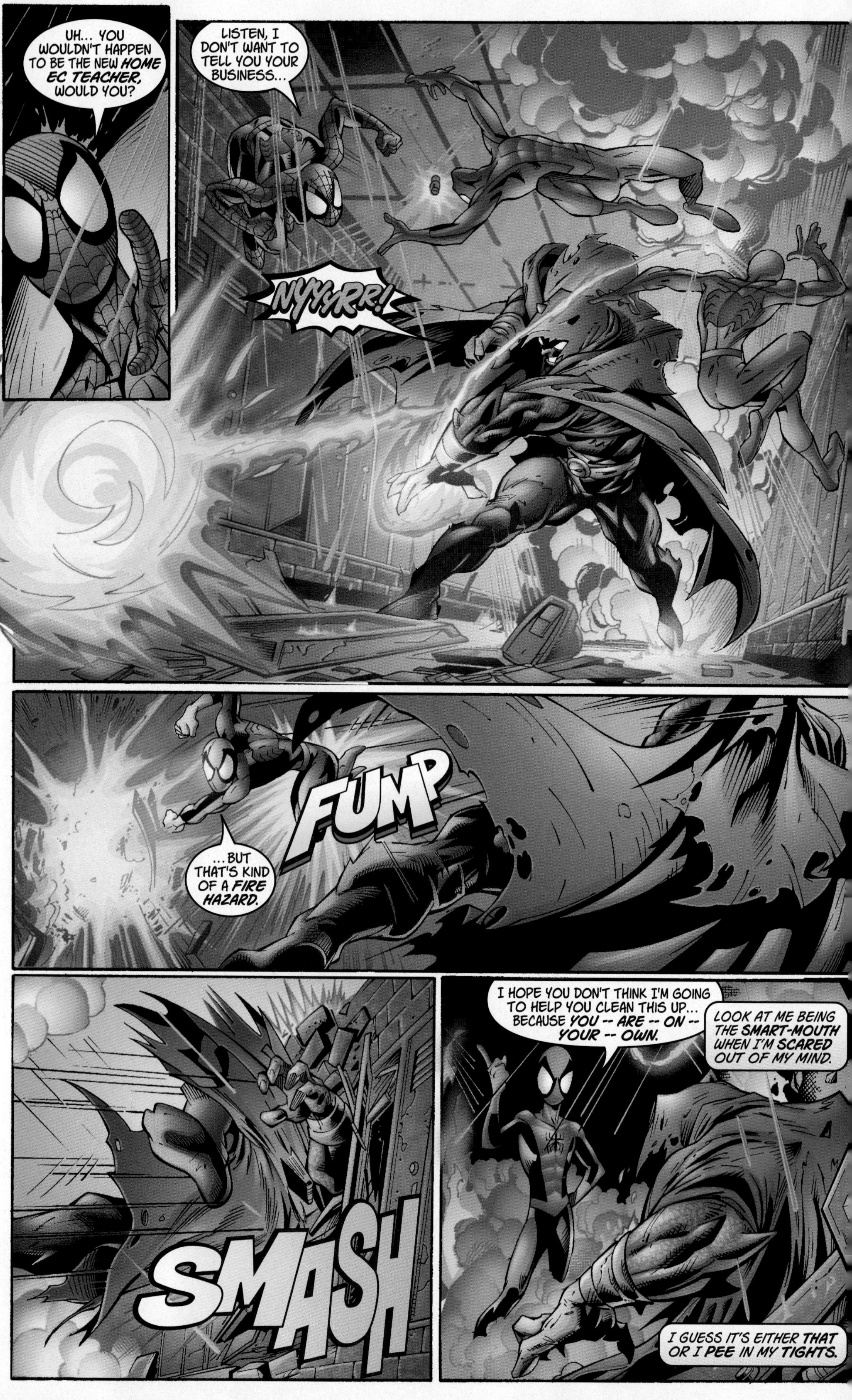
UH... YOU WOULDN'T HAPPEN TO BE THE NEW *HOME EC TEACHER,* WOULD YOU?
LISTEN, I DON'T WANT TO TELL YOU YOUR BUSINESS...
NYYYRR!
FUMP
...BUT THAT'S KIND OF A *FIRE HAZARD.*
SMASH
I HOPE YOU DON'T THINK I'M GOING TO HELP YOU CLEAN THIS UP... BECAUSE *YOU -- ARE -- ON -- YOUR -- OWN.*
LOOK AT ME BEING THE **SMART-MOUTH** WHEN I'M **SCARED** OUT OF MY MIND.
I GUESS IT'S EITHER **THAT** OR I **PEE** IN MY **TIGHTS.**

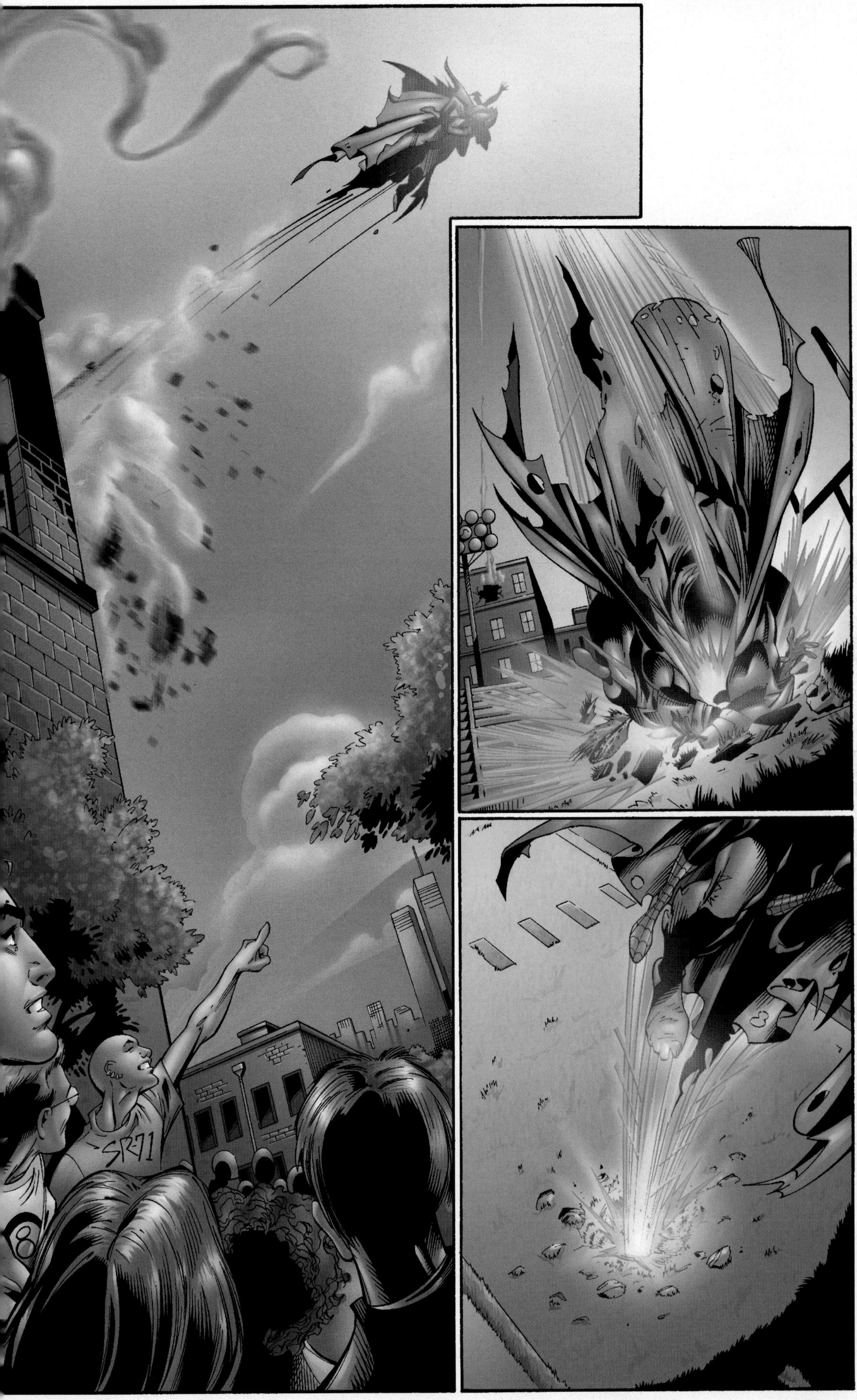
SR-71

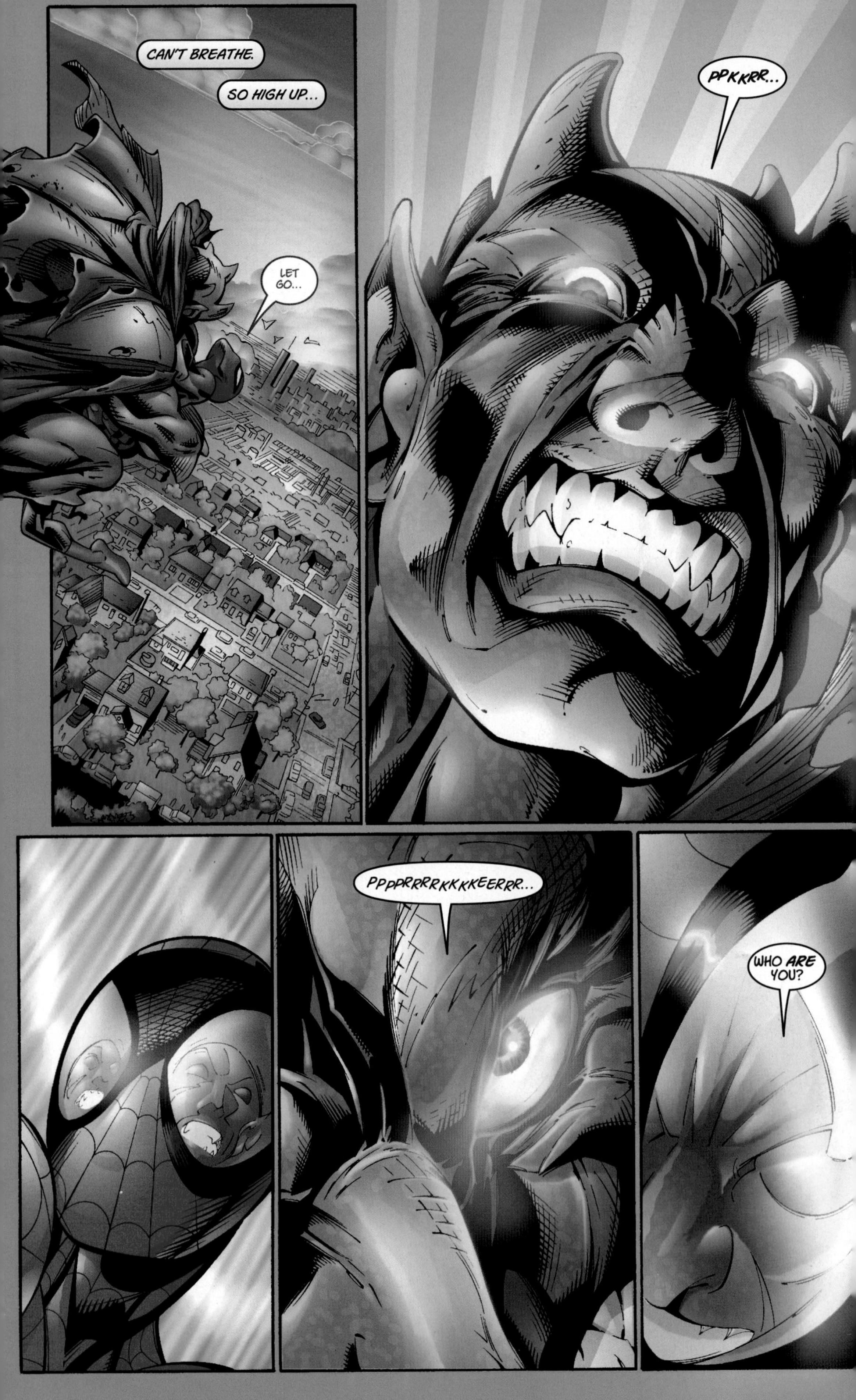

CAN'T BREATHE.
SO HIGH UP...
LET GO...
PPKKRR...
PPPPRRRRKKKKEERRR...
WHO ARE YOU?

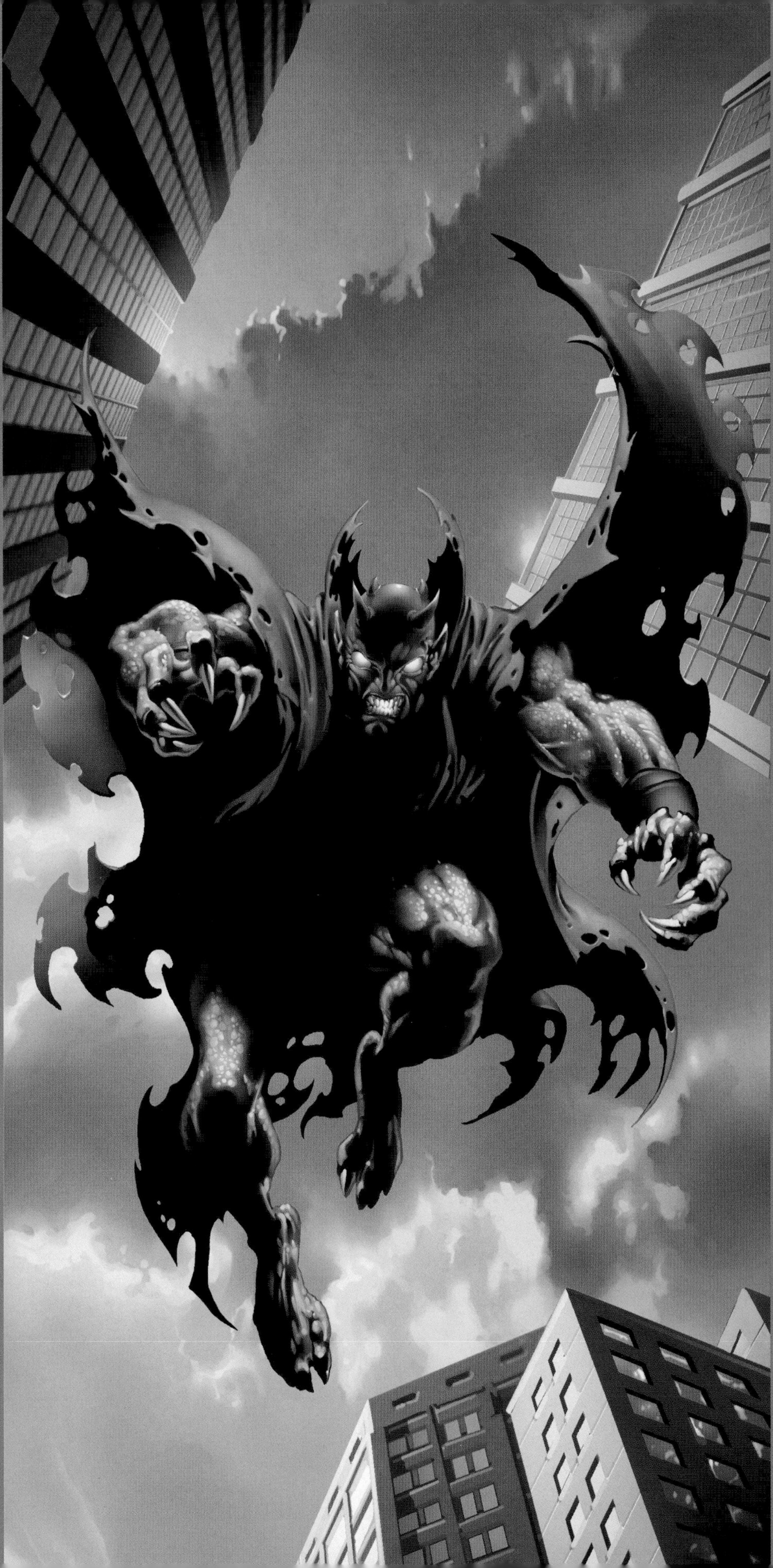

7

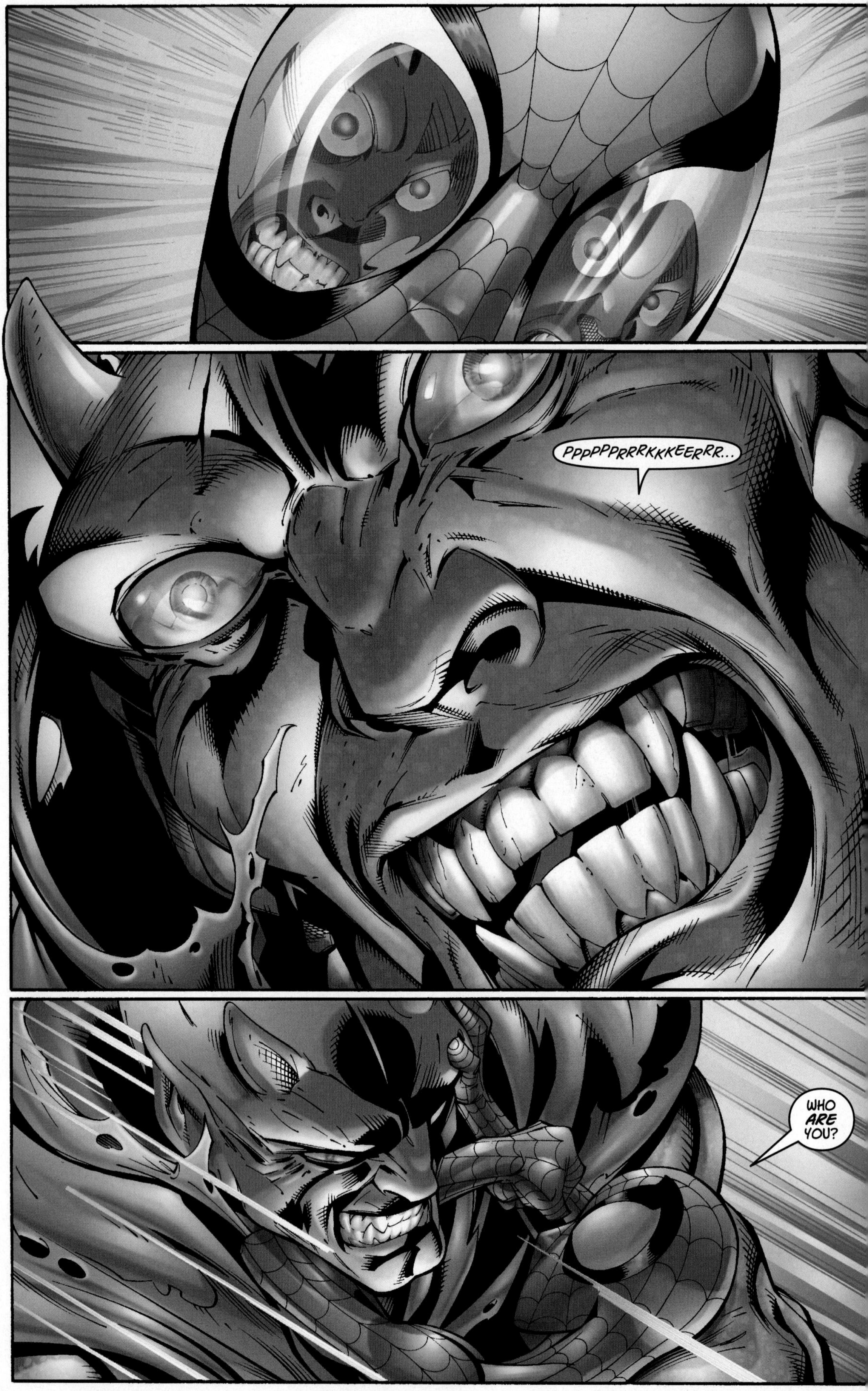
PPPPPPRRRKKKEERRR...
WHO ARE YOU?

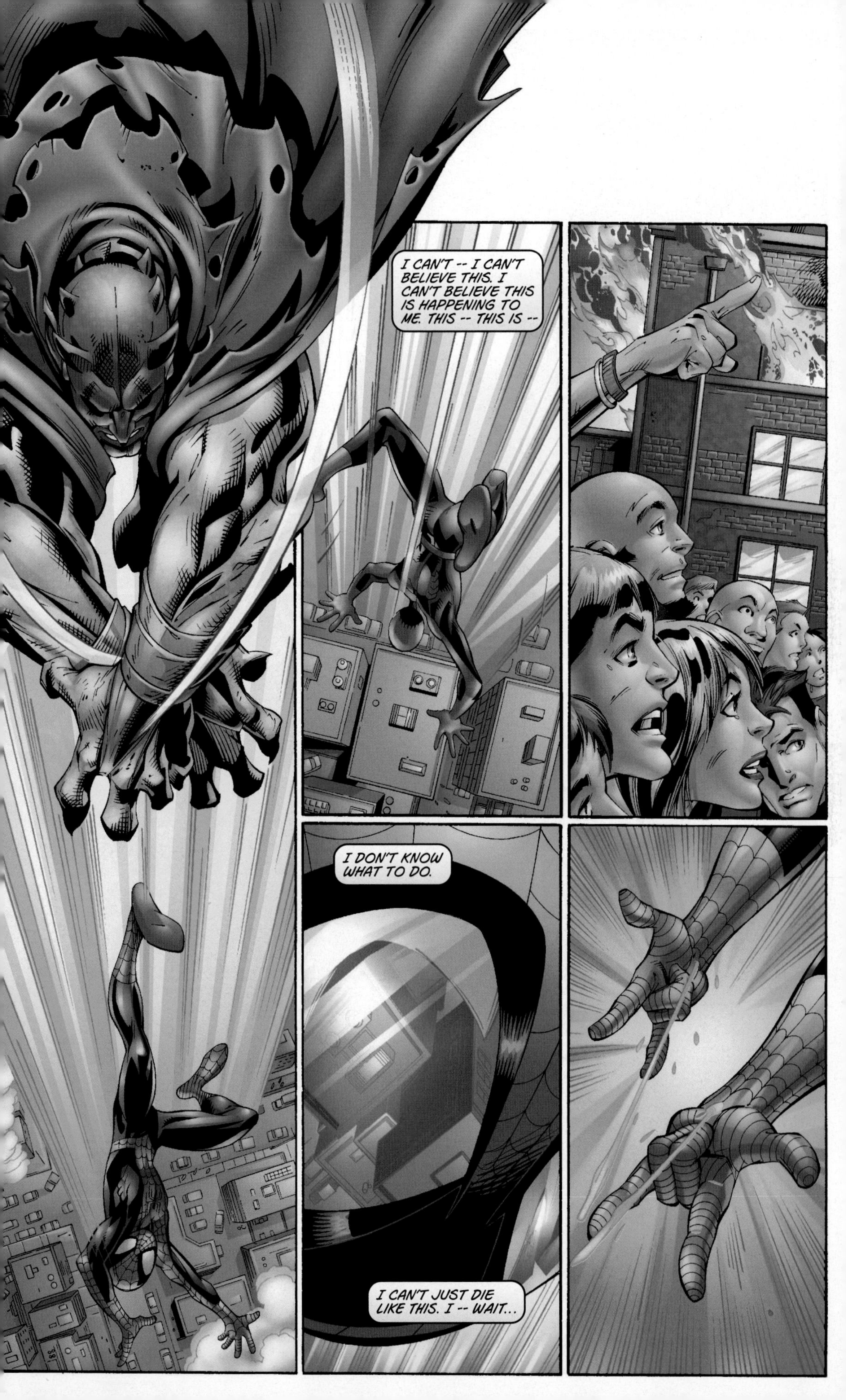
I CAN'T -- I CAN'T BELIEVE THIS. I CAN'T BELIEVE THIS IS HAPPENING TO ME. THIS -- THIS IS --
I DON'T KNOW WHAT TO DO.
I CAN'T JUST DIE LIKE THIS. I -- WAIT...

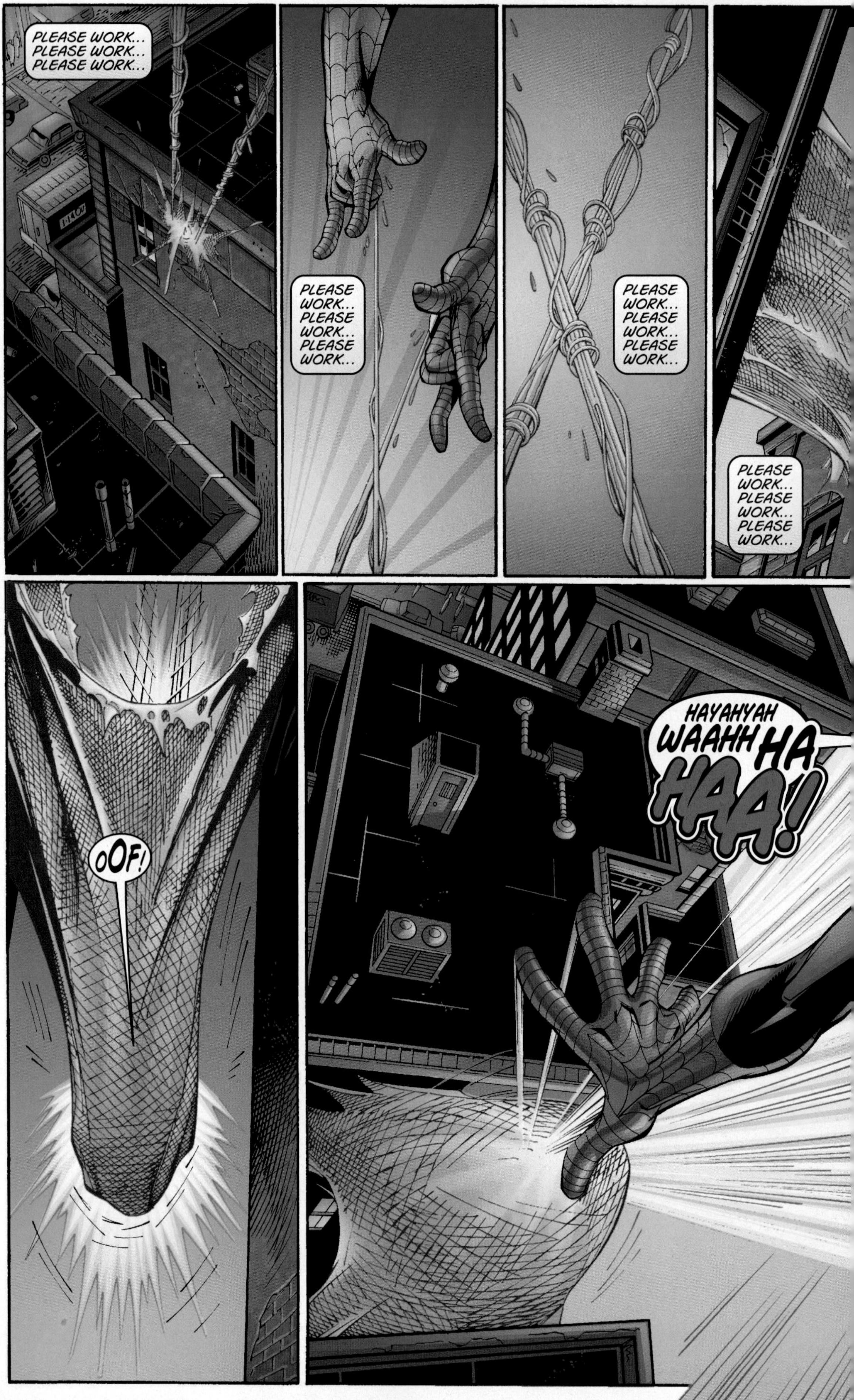
PLEASE WORK... PLEASE WORK... PLEASE WORK...
PLEASE WORK... PLEASE WORK... PLEASE WORK...
PLEASE WORK... PLEASE WORK... PLEASE WORK...
PLEASE WORK... PLEASE WORK... PLEASE WORK...
OOF!
HAYAHYAH WAAHH HA HAA!

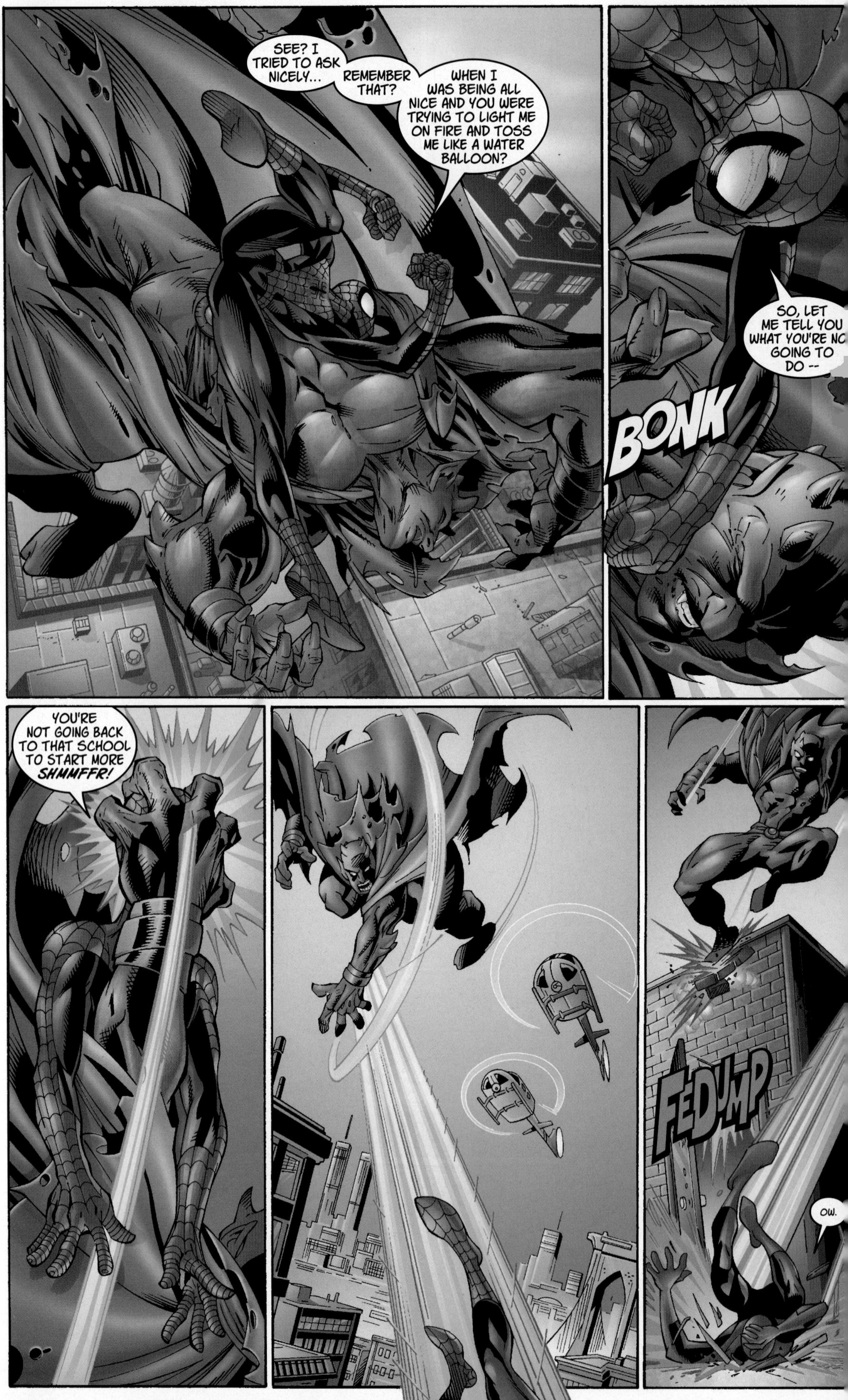
SEE? I TRIED TO ASK NICELY...
REMEMBER THAT?
WHEN I WAS BEING ALL NICE AND YOU WERE TRYING TO LIGHT ME ON FIRE AND TOSS ME LIKE A WATER BALLOON?
SO, LET ME TELL YOU WHAT YOU'RE NO GOING TO DO --
BONK
YOU'RE NOT GOING BACK TO THAT SCHOOL TO START MORE SHMMFFR!
FEDUMP
OW.

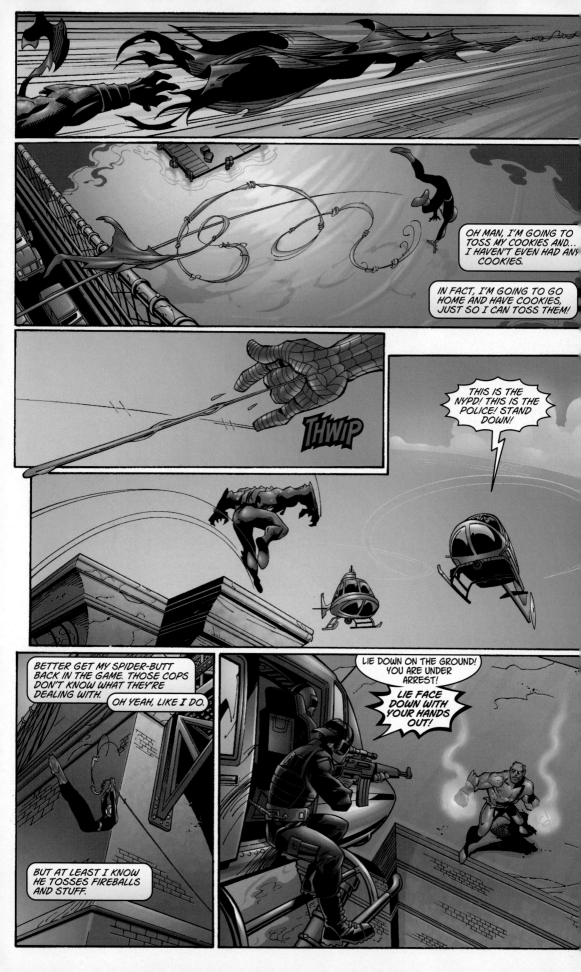

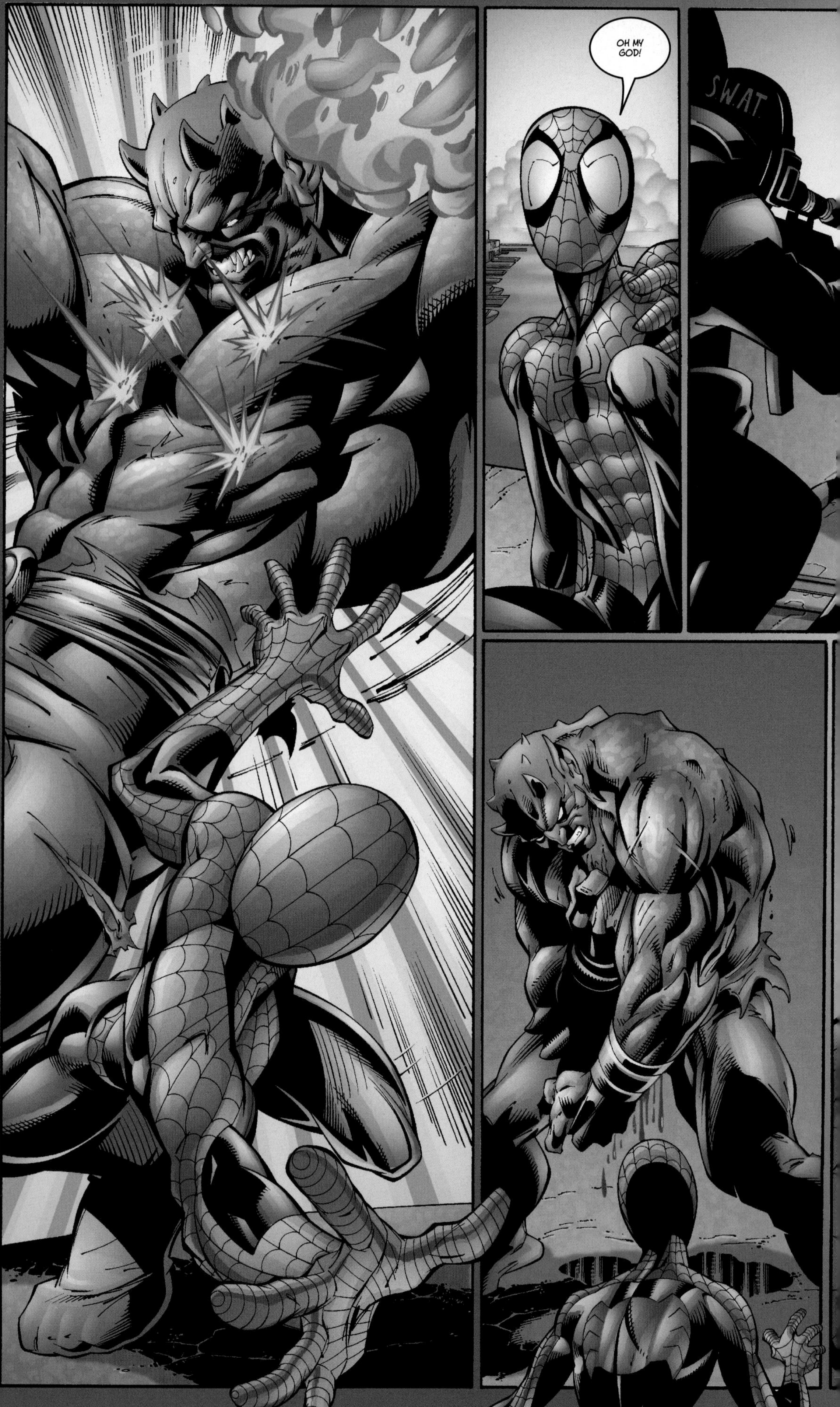
OH MY GOD!
S.W.A.T.

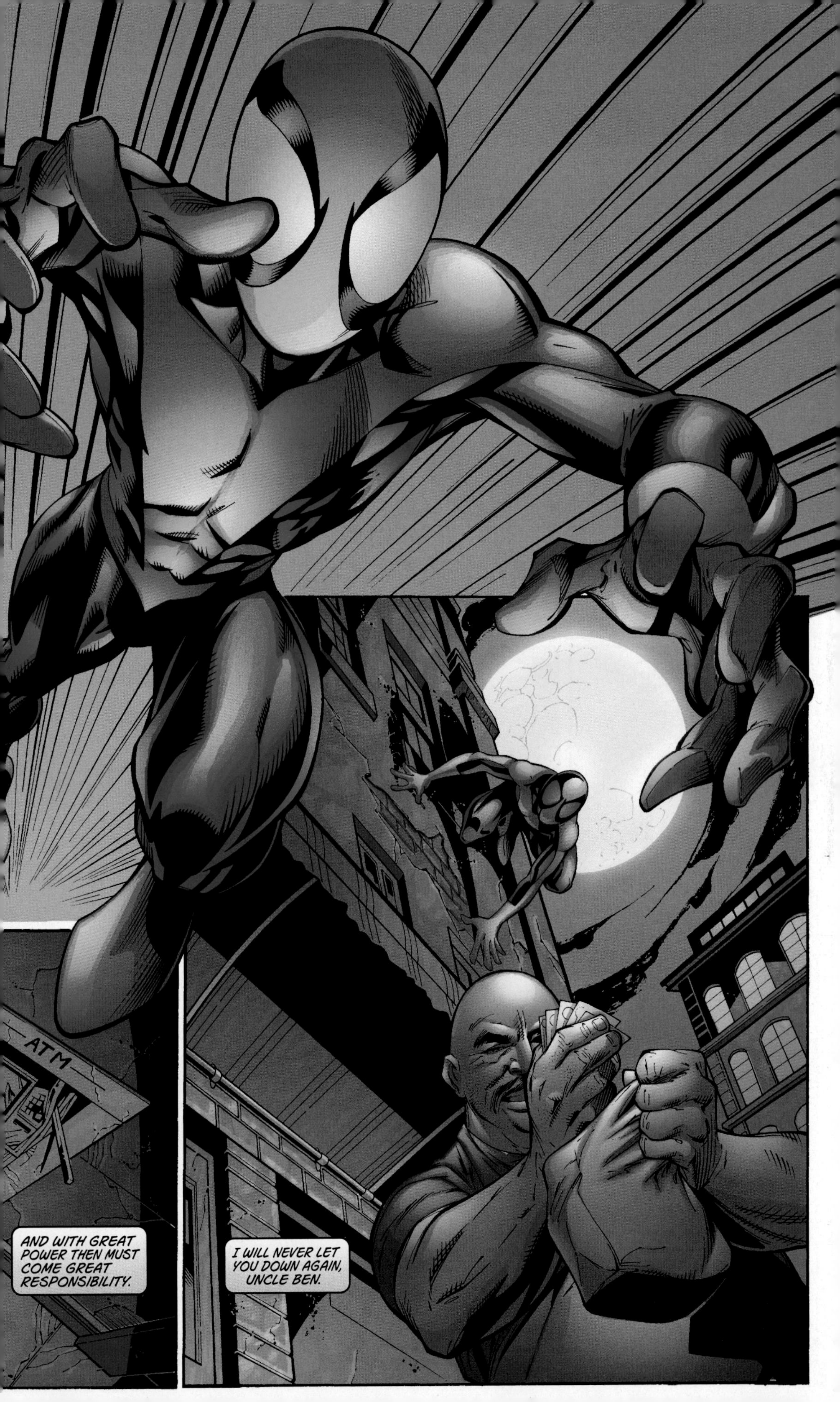
ATM
AND WITH GREAT POWER THEN MUST COME GREAT RESPONSIBILITY.
I WILL NEVER LET YOU DOWN AGAIN, UNCLE BEN.

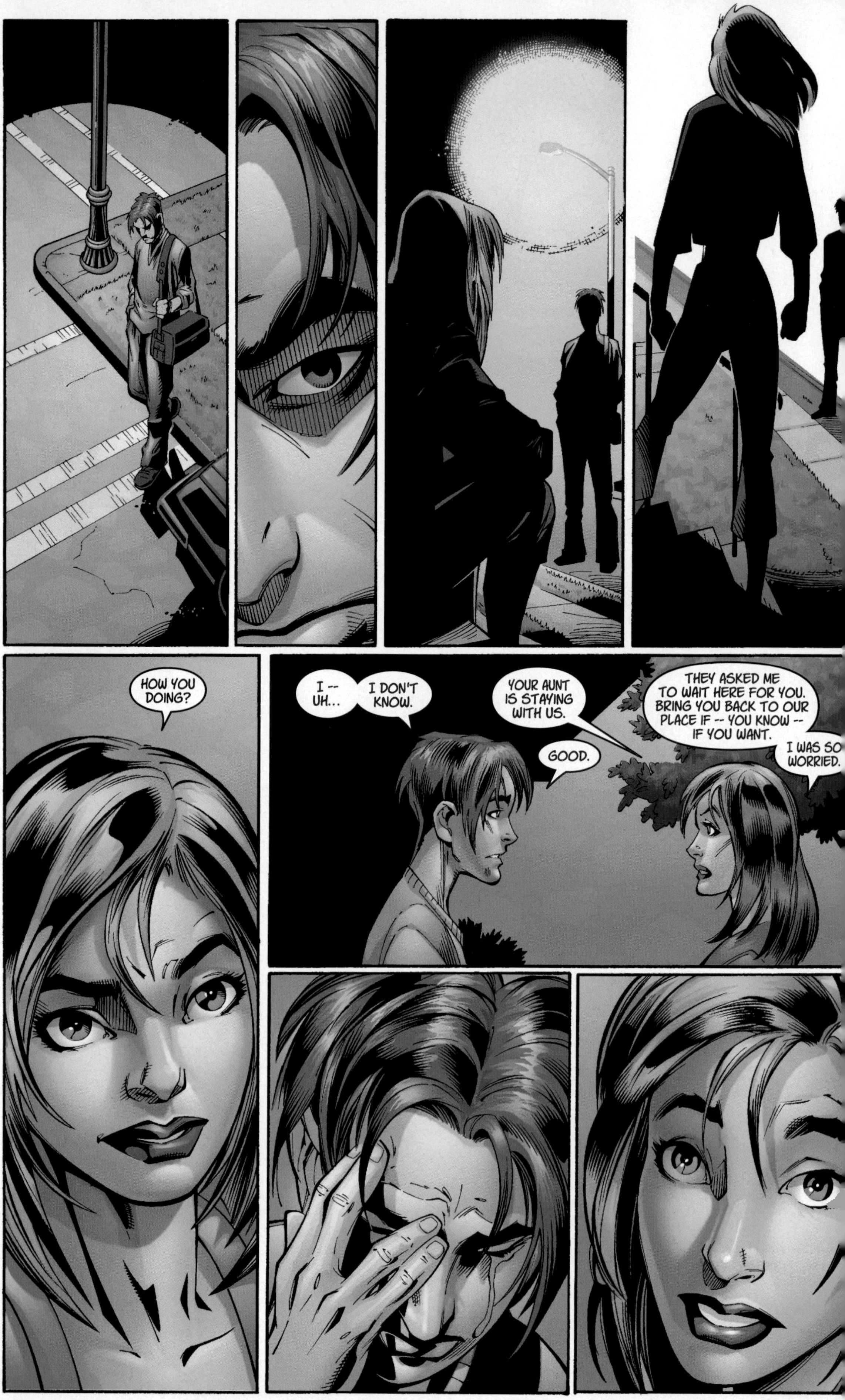
HOW YOU DOING?
I -- UH...
I DON'T KNOW.
YOUR AUNT IS STAYING WITH US.
GOOD.
THEY ASKED ME TO WAIT HERE FOR YOU. BRING YOU BACK TO OUR PLACE IF -- YOU KNOW -- IF YOU WANT.
I WAS SO WORRIED.

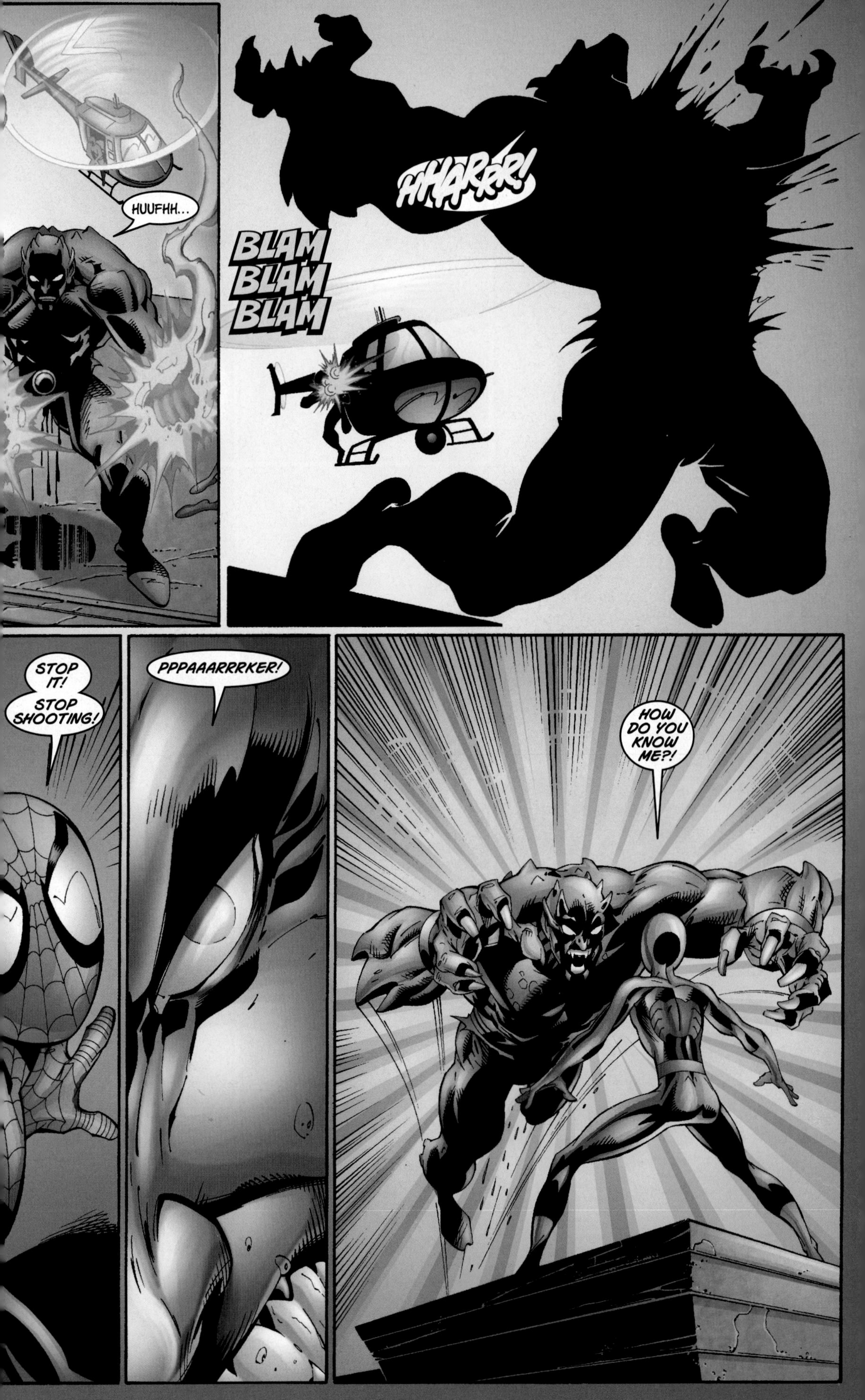
HUUFHH...
HHARRR!
BLAM
BLAM
BLAM
STOP IT! STOP SHOOTING!
PPPAAARRRKER!
HOW DO YOU KNOW ME?!

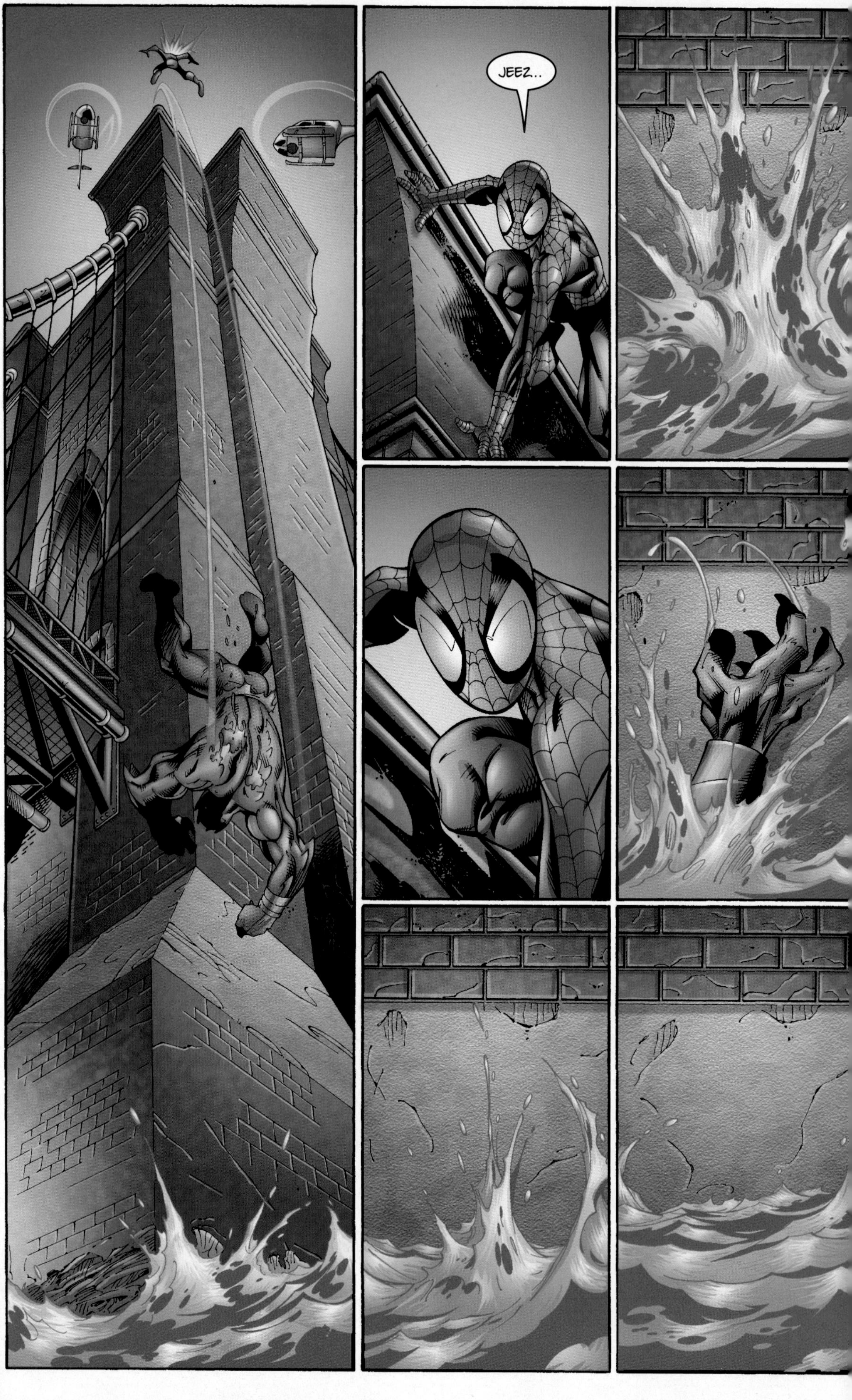
JEEZ...

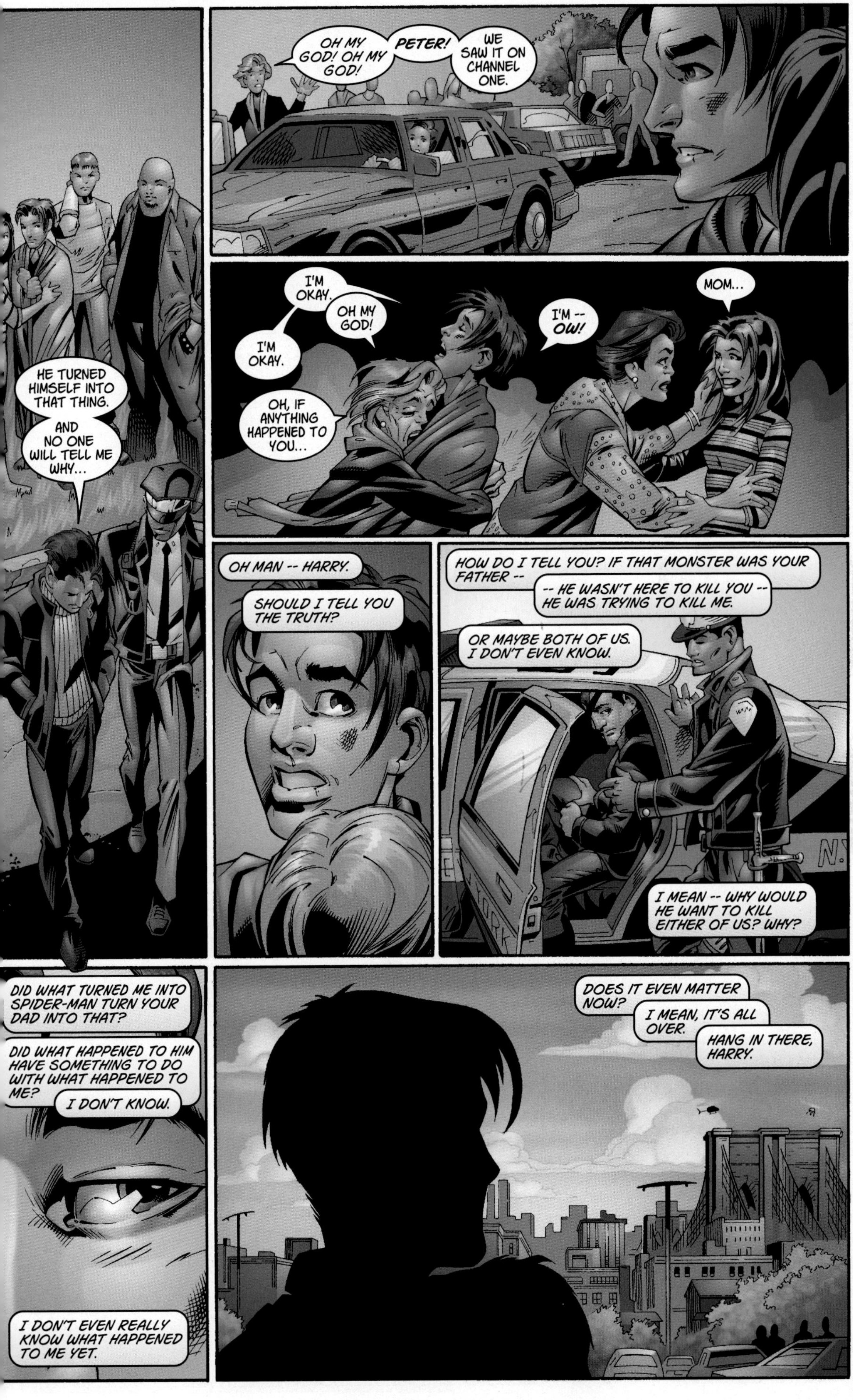
OH MY GOD! OH MY GOD!
PETER!
WE SAW IT ON CHANNEL ONE.
HE TURNED HIMSELF INTO THAT THING.
AND NO ONE WILL TELL ME WHY...
I'M OKAY.
OH MY GOD!
I'M OKAY.
OH, IF ANYTHING HAPPENED TO YOU...
I'M -- OW!
MOM...
OH MAN -- HARRY.
SHOULD I TELL YOU THE TRUTH?
HOW DO I TELL YOU? IF THAT MONSTER WAS YOUR FATHER --
-- HE WASN'T HERE TO KILL YOU -- HE WAS TRYING TO KILL ME.
OR MAYBE BOTH OF US. I DON'T EVEN KNOW.
I MEAN -- WHY WOULD HE WANT TO KILL EITHER OF US? WHY?
DID WHAT TURNED ME INTO SPIDER-MAN TURN YOUR DAD INTO THAT?
DID WHAT HAPPENED TO HIM HAVE SOMETHING TO DO WITH WHAT HAPPENED TO ME?
I DON'T KNOW.
I DON'T EVEN REALLY KNOW WHAT HAPPENED TO ME YET.
DOES IT EVEN MATTER NOW?
I MEAN, IT'S ALL OVER.
HANG IN THERE, HARRY.

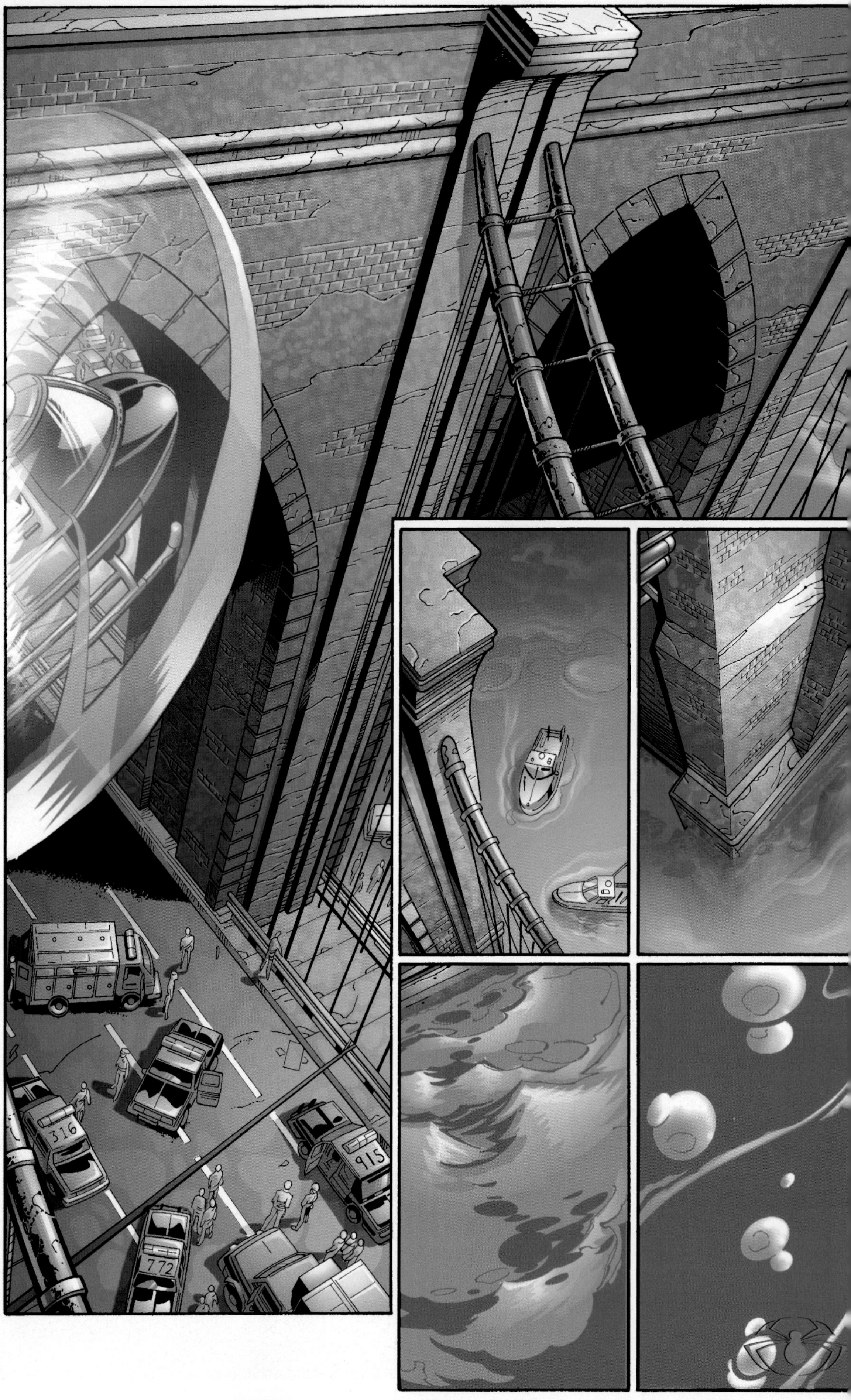
316
915
772

PETER PARKER

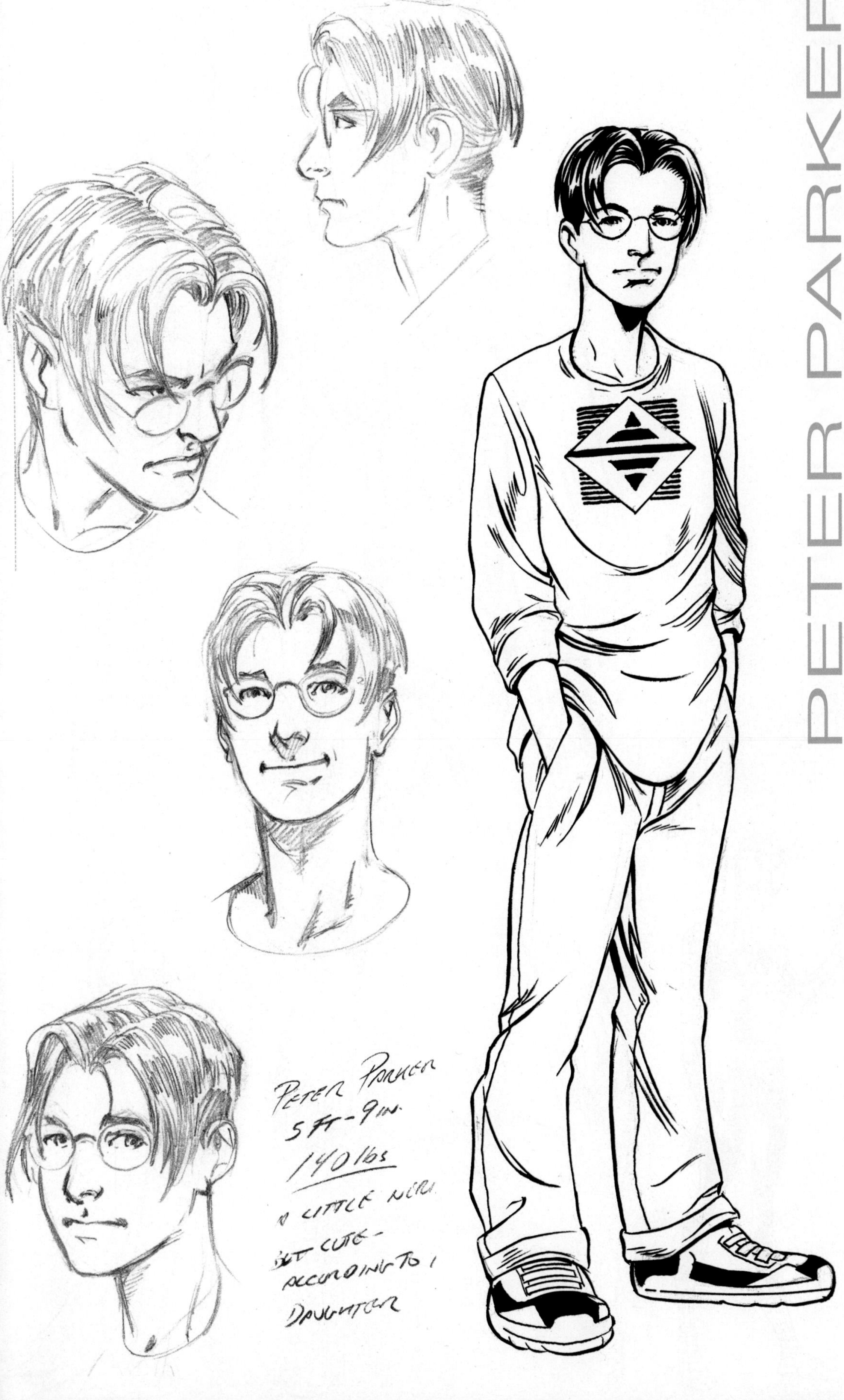
PETER PARKER
5 FT - 9 IN.
140 lbs
A LITTLE NERD
BUT CUTE -
ACCORDING TO 1
DAUGHTER

SPIDER-MAN

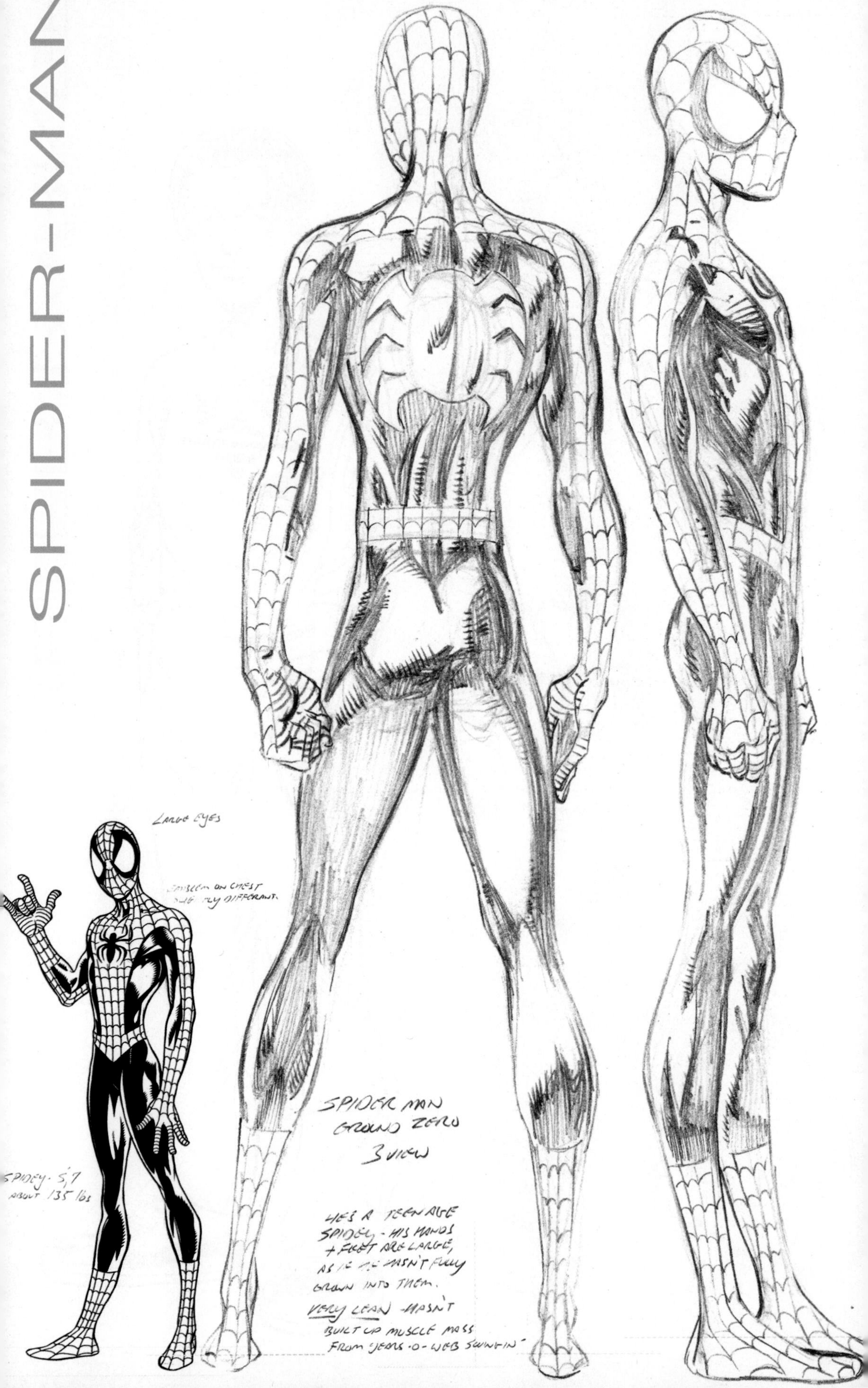

LARGE EYES

EMBLEM ON CHEST A LIL'LY DIFFERENT.

SPIDEY- 5'7
ABOUT 135 lbs

SPIDER MAN
GROUND ZERO
3 VIEW

YES A TEENAGE
SPIDEY - HIS HANDS
+ FEET ARE LARGE,
AS IF HE HASN'T FULLY
GROWN INTO THEM.

VERY LEAN HASN'T
BUILT UP MUSCLE MASS
FROM YEARS -O- WEB SWINGIN'

MARY JANE

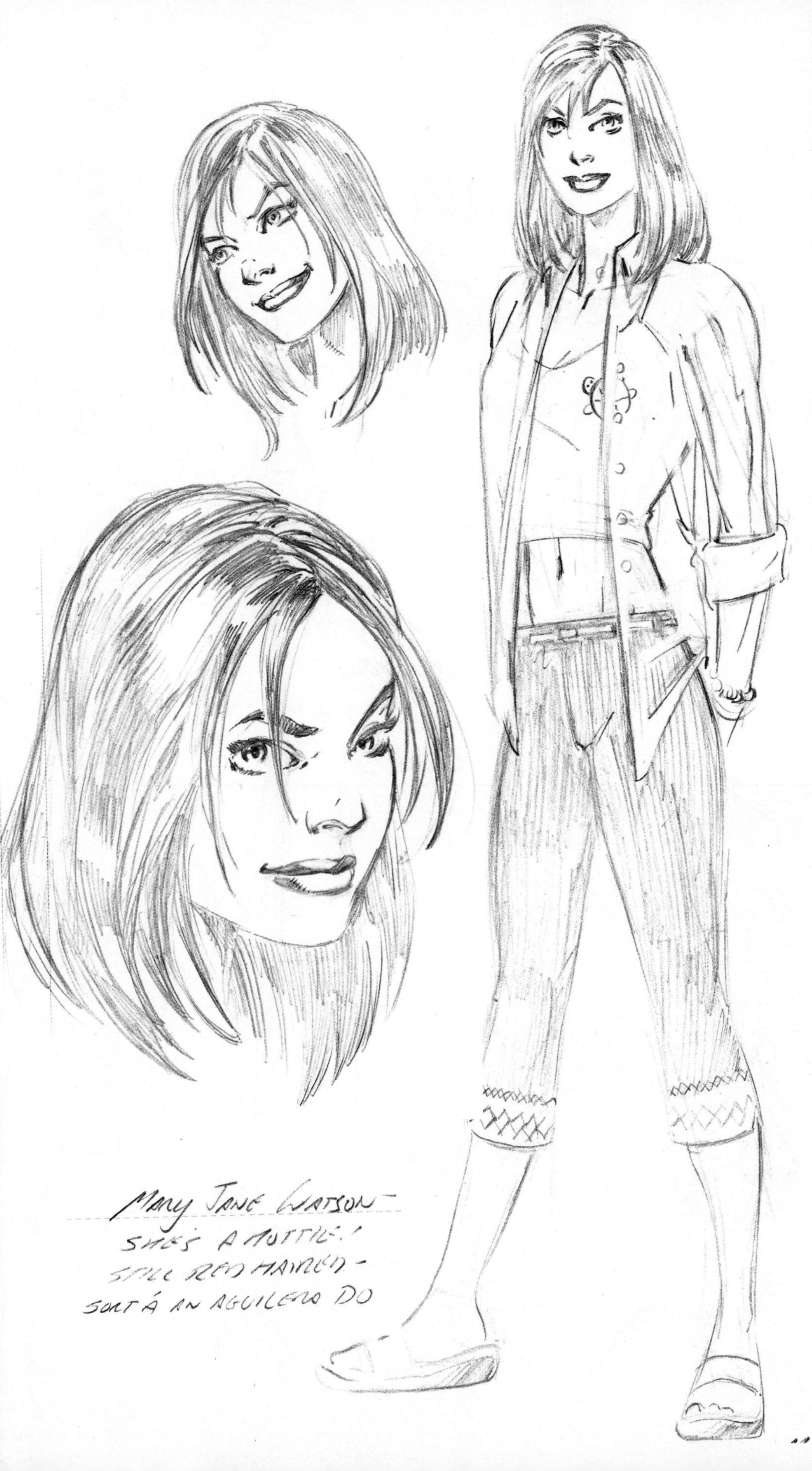

Mary Jane Watson –
SHE'S A HOTTIE!
STILL RED HAIRED –
SORT A AN AGUILERA DO

AUNT MAY

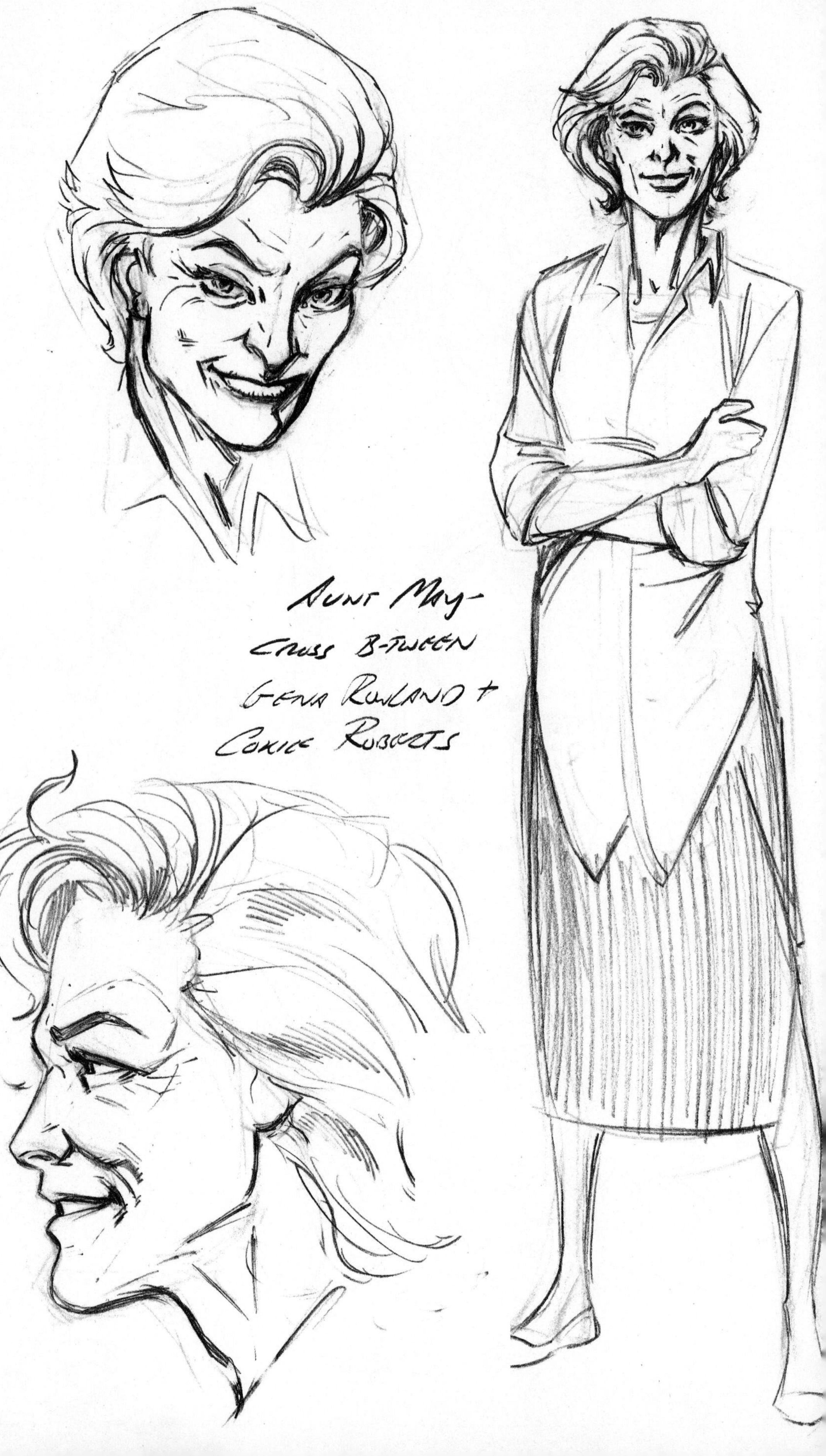
AUNT MAY-
CROSS B-TWEEN
GENA ROWLAND +
COKIE ROBERTS

UNCLE BEN

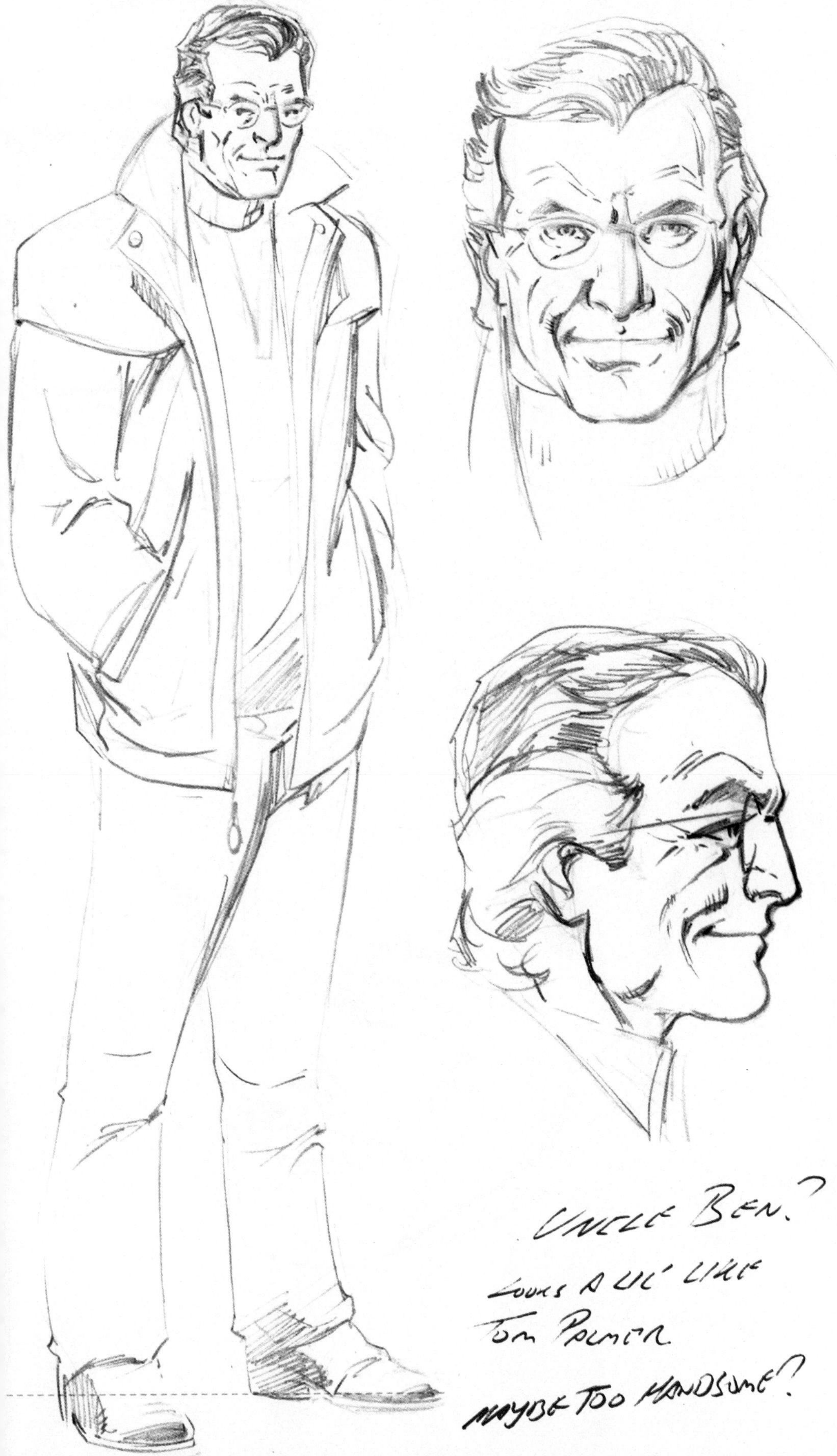
UNCLE BEN?
LOOKS A LIL' LIKE
TOM PALMER
MAYBE TOO HANDSOME?

NORMAN OSBORN

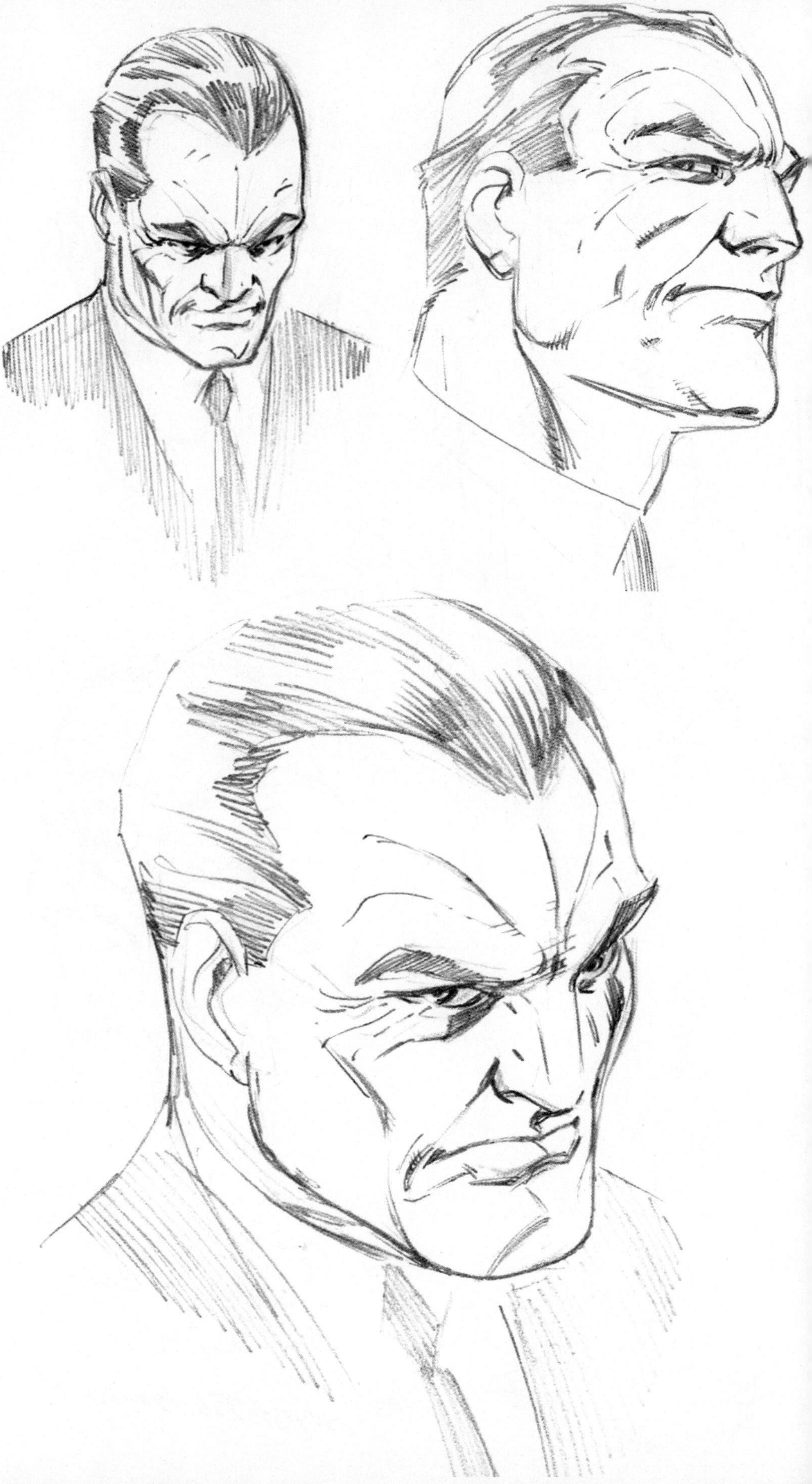

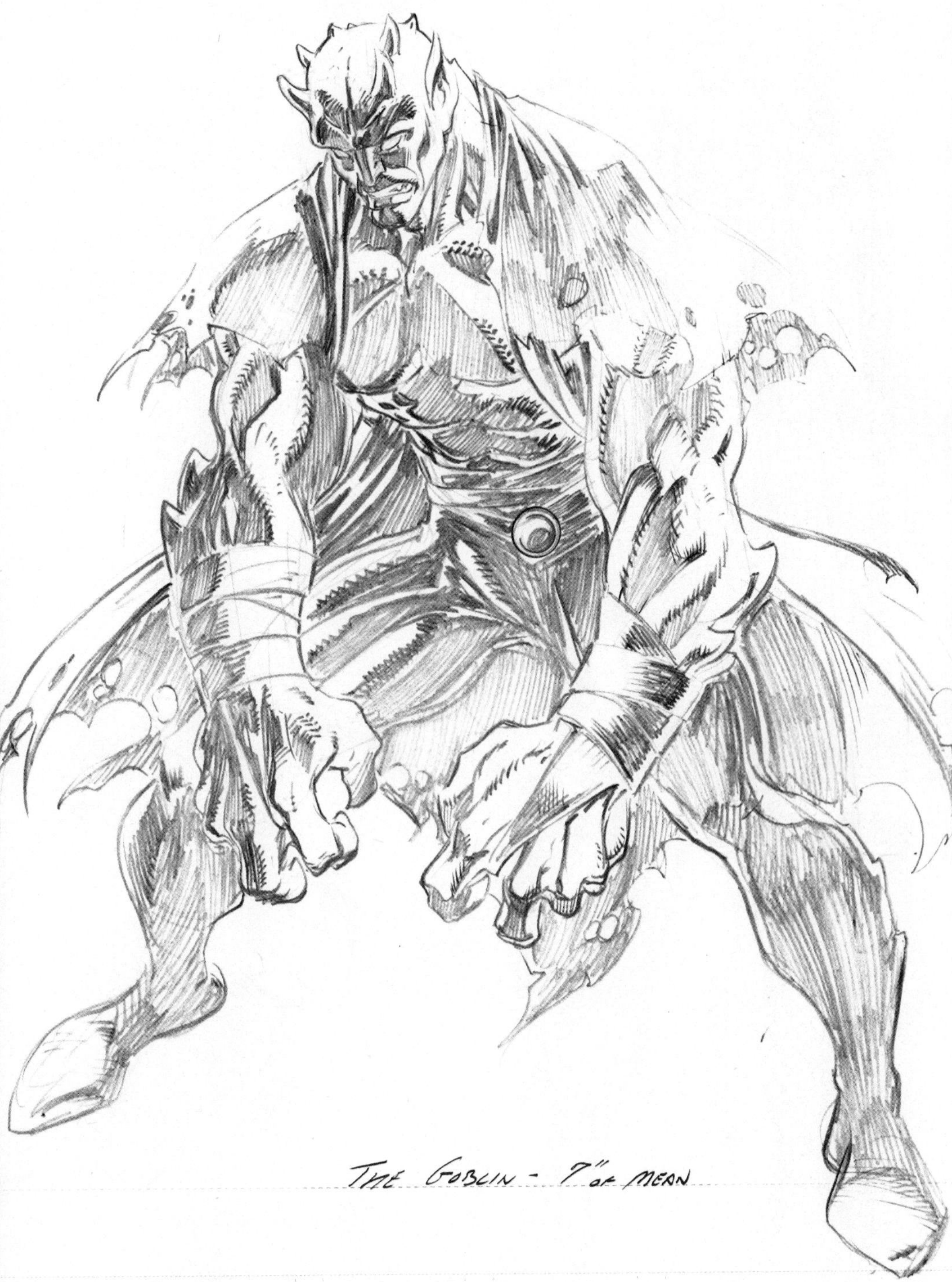
THE GOBLIN - 7" OF MEAN

HARRY OSBORN

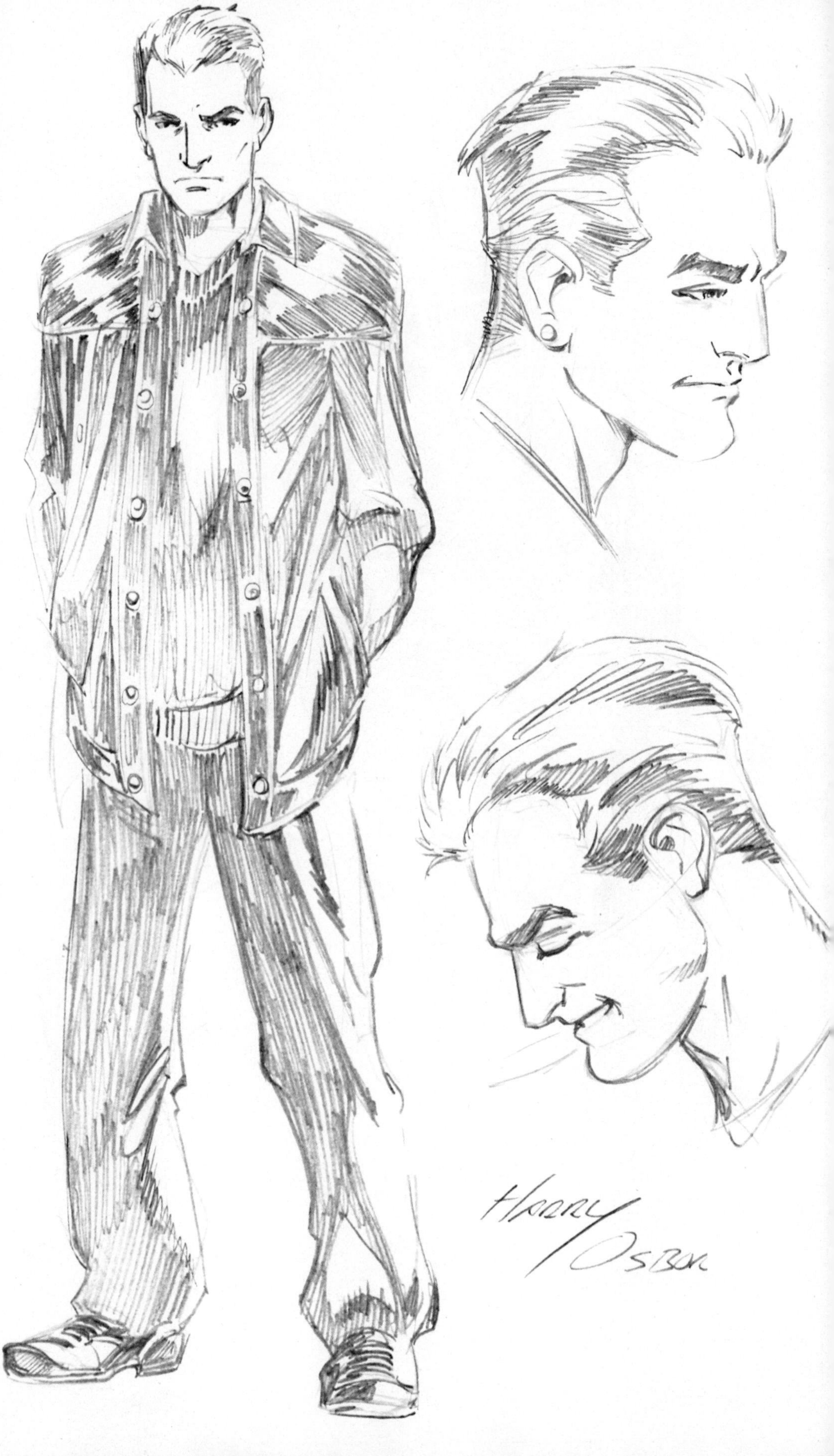
HARRY

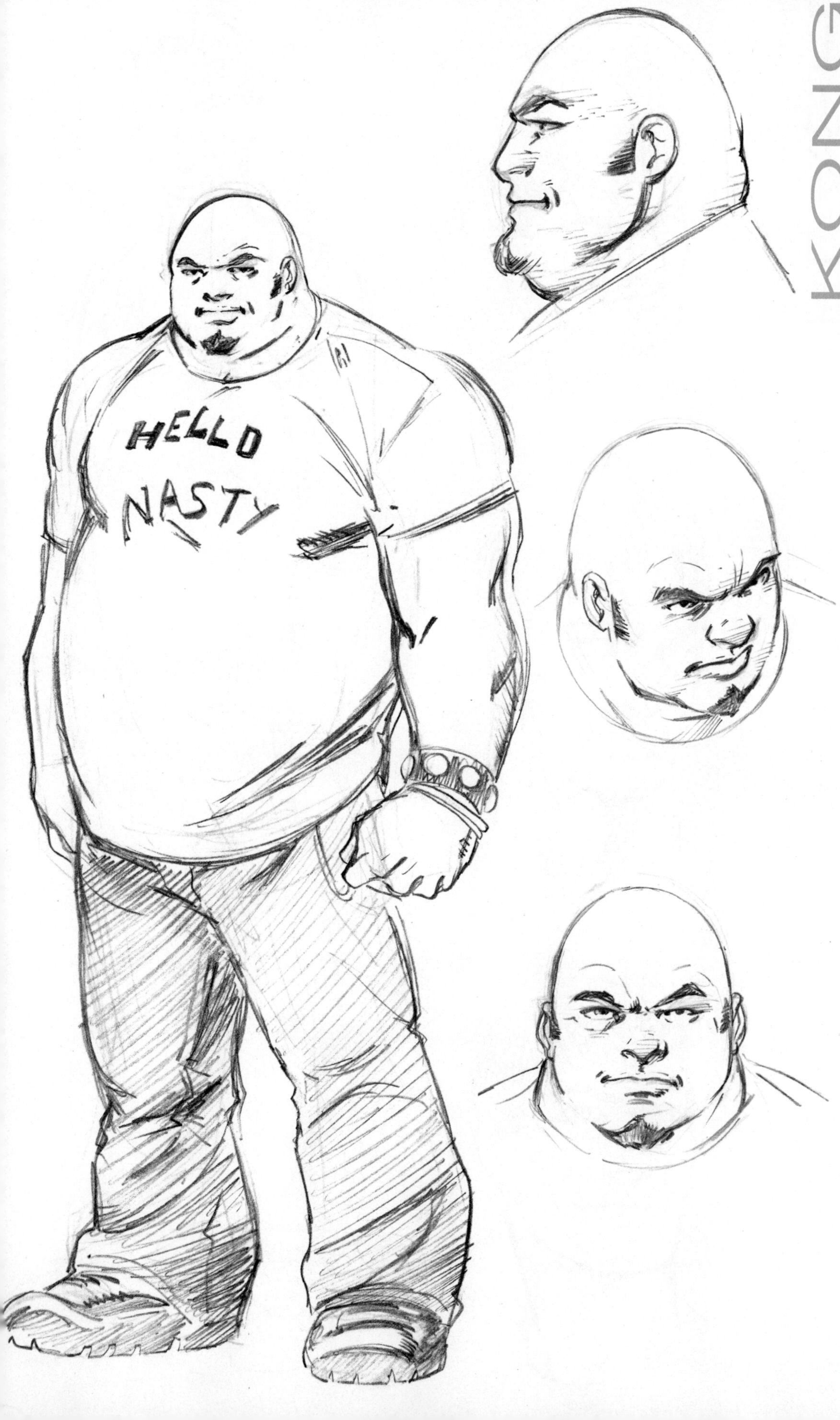
HELLO
NASTY

KONG

FLASH

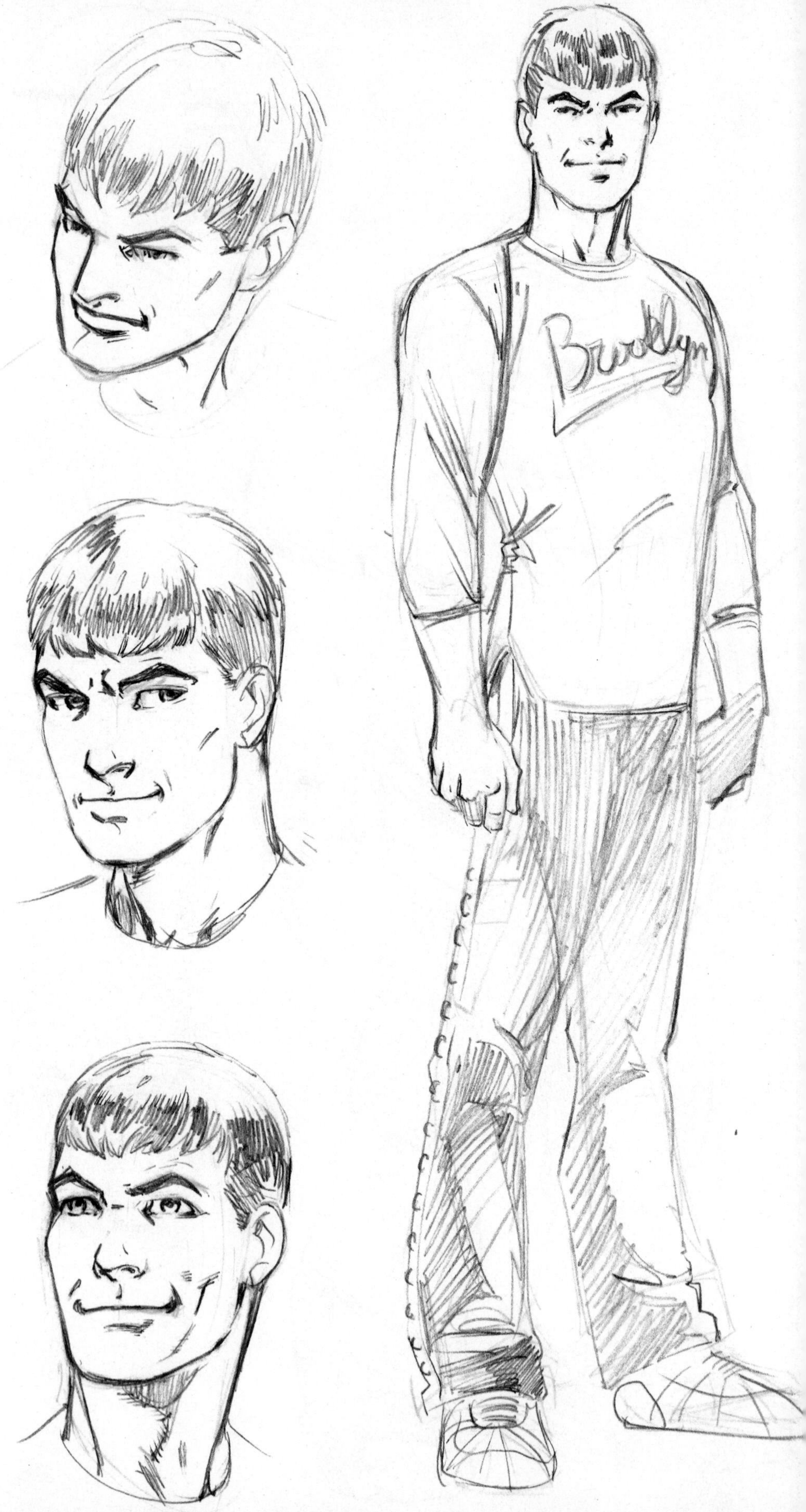
Brooklyn